The cover photo: Business photo created by jannoon028
www.freepik.es
Cover design by Cristina Valeria G. from Freelancer.com
Graphic design by Kris Nielson Design - www.krisdesign.ca

The comments and opinions expressed in this calendar are precisely
that; "opinions" and opinions are never right or wrong, they are simply
"opinions." It is not the intention of the author to coerce, force, or
influence anyone other than to move them closer towards God. Further,
it is not the intention of the author to solicit funds or donations (however, donations to this Ministry are appreciated, although tax receipts
are unavailable). Suggested book reading/posters etc., are just that,
"a suggestion." With a few exceptions, the author of this publication
does not know the authors of the books that he is recommending.

If this devotional is a blessing to you, and if you have comments or
suggestions, please get in touch with the author at:
info@newstartministries.ca

**www.newstartministries.ca**

# Acknowledgments

Thank you, Graeme Henderson, for your terrific editing. You are amazing, and I could not have completed this project without your wise input (for the second time)!

Graeme is a full-time missionary with YWAM (Youth with a Mission) and, as with all "YWAMers," needs prayer and financial support (they work as volunteers). You can reach out to Graeme, support him and learn about his ministry and plans at:
modernday.org/field-workers/graeme-henderson
or email him directly at: graemephenderson@gmail.com.

Thank you, Kris Nielsen, for your usual great design and all the "extras" you do for me. You're the best! (design@krisdesign.ca)

Thank you, Cristina Valeria G. from www.freelancer.com, for your terrific cover design! I highly recommend you!

I am very grateful to my good friend Dr. Selwyn Stevens of Jubilee Resources, who has been a constant source of information for years. In my opinion, Dr. Stevens is the world's leading expert on cults, apostasy, and apologetics. He also happens to be a really good guy who doesn't mind sharing his material, which I have used throughout this publication. He has written close to 100 books, and you can download much of his material from his website for free. Selwyn is also a complete "Facebook addict" and posts some excellent stuff seven days a week! "Follow him," and you will learn lots! Thanks, buddy! You're a blessing...   https://jubileeresources.org

# Who is "Doc"?

Stuart R. Watkins, Ph.D was born and raised in Calgary, Alberta. He worked for two winters in the hotel industry and spent three summers working as a cowboy, trail guiding in beautiful Banff National Park in the majestic Canadian Rockies. He graduated in 1981 with a Bachelor of Business Administration and began his career in entrepreneurship at the age of 23, owning and operating several successful businesses.

Returning to post-secondary education 22 years later, he completed a Bachelor of Theology, a Master's and then a Doctorate of Apostolic Leadership (Practical Ministry) and finally a Ph.D. in Ministerial Studies (Economics). His passion has always been to help people, whether teaching biblical economics and Christian business principles or offering excellence training for marketplace ministries and businesses. An entrepreneur for 40+ years, he owns an investment company, a publishing company and serves as a financial, operational and strategic planning consultant to churches, charities and non-profit organizations. He teaches internationally and bi-annually hosts conferences in Rwanda in conjunction with his work there with Compassion Canada. He is the author of: *"Biblical Economics 101: Living Under God's Financial Blessing"* (2nd printing – Nov. 2020); *"Life is a Test - A Daily Devotional Volume I"* (Jan. 2022); *"Life is a Test - A Daily Devotional Volume 2"* (Dec. 2022)

Dr. Watkins is a licensed minister of the Gospel with Eagle World-Wide Ministries in Hamilton, Ontario and commissioned by the Global Spheres Centre in Corinth, Texas as a Business Apostle, a Deliverance Minister, and a Christian Author. He is a member of the Global Council of Nations, the Canadian and International Coalition of Apostolic Leaders, the International Society of Deliverance Ministers, and the Calgary Christian Connect Group.

At home in Alberta, he enjoys music, fine dining, skiing, fitness, gardening, and collecting western art and antiques. Somehow, he manages to read one to two books a week! He is a Life Member and past President (5 terms) of the Trail Riders of the Canadian Rockies. For further information about his teaching classes and consulting, contact him at: info@newstartministries.ca

Written by Fred Schuman, Renewal Counselling, Calgary, AB.

# What's up with "Doc"?

I worked at a Christian summer camp in Alberta several years ago. It is customary for everyone (including staff) to be given a "nickname." Mine was "Doc" (because of my education), and they gave me no choice in the matter; the name stuck. I seldom use my first name anymore because people often do not spell it correctly and tend to shorten it (which I do not like), so "Doc" is easy to remember, pretty hard to misspell and gets rid of the formality of "Dr. Watkins."

# Doc's Book Club?

An expression says that "every man has one vice." I have one; books! Out of my vast library (would you believe I have nine bookcases? - six of which are eight feet tall), I have read over 2000 non-fiction Christian books and researched/written over 130 papers. As much as I believe that the Word of God (the Bible) is the final Word on issues and should not be "interpreted" (just read it!), reading from good authors can educate and confirm the Word. I have made recommendations periodically throughout this book, and with a few exceptions, I do not personally know the authors, but I know their credentials and reputations.

I use the New King James Version, and for explaining issues and ease of understanding, I like the New International Version, which I often quote in this book. I enjoy reading The Living Bible as a good comparison, and the Message and Passion versions are fun too! If you are a beginner, I suggest the Living Bible for starters. Read (in this order) Ephesians, James, Romans, 1 and 2 Corinthians, Colossians, Hebrews, then John, Luke, Mark, and Matthew. Next, finish the rest of the New Testament (you can leave the Book of Revelation for a while yet), and then start at the beginning of the Old Testament. Find a gospel preaching, faith teaching, and spirit-filled church, and go as you do this!

# Notes:

When I finished writing Volume 1 of this two-part series, I actually had written 13.5 months. After reviewing the book, I realized that some days were "a bit weak" (Holy Spirit wrote the good ones - about 80% - I wrote the others!), so I decided to take those days out and replace them with the extras that I had written. I thought that this project would end, but God had other plans. He told me to keep writing, and I said, "I can't do this!" He replied, "I know; you type, and I'll write." Therefore, what you are about to read is 80% Him and not me! The rest is history. Please enjoy and reflect on His Words. I have typed these challenging thoughts, tests and ideas as much for myself as for any of you; trust me, I have!

I am a Canadian citizen living in sunny southern Alberta. We Canadians spell a few words differently than many other countries, using British spelling practices. Examples include "colour," "favourite," "blest," "cheque," and "centre." Out of respect for my Canadian heritage, I am retaining my Canadian culture in the writing style and the spelling of some words.

This devotional will undoubtedly stimulate some thoughts and questions in your mind (at least, I hope so). Please feel free to email me with any questions you may have, and I will do my utmost to answer them; before you ask, there is no charge (you already bought the book!) Feedback is always important too. Please connect with me through my website. Thank you!

If you have not already, you will see that I always refer to Holy Spirit as "Holy Spirit;" I never refer to Him as "the Holy Spirit." That is because Holy Spirit is not a "thing" or an "it"; Holy Spirit is a person - part of the Trinity of God (Father, Son, Holy Spirit). I do not believe that referring to Holy Spirit as "the" fits the person of God that Holy Spirit exemplifies.

I refuse to capitalize the name satan. I know that that is grammatically incorrect, but satan doesn't deserve the honour, and besides, it's my book. He has done everything he can to stop its publication, so this is my revenge on him.

One of the things I've learned about book publishing is that selling books is all about marketing, and the best form of marketing is word of mouth which comes from reviews and endorsements. If you enjoy this devotional, I would very much appreciate it if you could go to Amazon, Indigo, or Barnes & Noble and write a review. If you desire, an endorsement emailed to me would be greatly appreciated. A review on "Goodreads" is appreciated as well.

In some instances, I may have repeated myself in this devotional. The theme yes, but the wording, no, as I have used different examples and scriptures to make the point. Why repeat them? Because some things are just too important and need to be heard again, and again, and again... Learning the bible is a life-long, revelational journey.

On the 15th of each month, I will introduce you to God's month. Why am I teaching God's calendar? I taught in Volume One that the universe is one great big cycle. Biblically, months are critical. The ancient Jews recognized that every month was a new prophetic season. Every month has its own meaning, and the purpose is to move forward in God's plan. Therefore, understanding the month helps you stay in touch with God. We can receive God's blessings by aligning ourselves with His cycle (calendar/timing). Is it wrong not to honour God's months? No, but you can miss out on His blessings because you're out of His timing.

Each month I will refer to a stone/mineral that aligns itself with the tribe for that month and also a constellation in the sky. My editor was concerned that these subjects might be mistaken for "new age" or astrology and suggested that I explain the difference.

According to the Canadian Oxford dictionary, astrology *"is the study of the movements and relative positions of celestial bodies interpreted as an influence on human affairs."* This is part of the New Age phenomenon, where the skies, the moon and the stars influence human behaviour. Nothing could be further from the truth! Conversely, astronomy *"is the study of the universe and its contents beyond the bounds of the earth's atmosphere."* When God created the heavens, one purpose of the sun, moon and stars was to serve as signs to mark time - the seasons, days and years. He gave us this in His calendar in Genesis 1:14. The stars even sing to God! (Job 37:8) Use this site to download God's calendar to your computer calendar. www.heb.cal.com (and it is free!)

Please look at my website; there are many "free things" like blogs, bible studies, sermons, videos, book suggestions, etc.

Enjoy this devotional! May God shield you from all works of the enemy as you read, study, and grow towards Him (Eph. 6:10-18).

**"Doc"**

**"Have I now become your enemy by telling you the truth?"**
(Gal. 4:16 NIV)

# Dedication

I dedicate this book to my two closest friends, Larry Dayment and Bill Corry.

Larry owns one of the best and biggest cattle ranches in Southern Alberta. Our backgrounds are entirely different, and we have nothing in common from an agricultural perspective! However, Larry and I can sit at the kitchen table with a bottle of good scotch and solve all the world's problems in a matter of a few hours; if folks would just listen to us! Larry, you are the most patient man and one of the most intelligent and educated men I've ever met. You have always been there for me, especially in my desperate times. Thank you.

Bill, like Larry, you were always there for me as well when I needed you, and you know what and when I mean. I doubt I would be alive today if it had not been for you. You are a "pastor's pastor" and have ministered to me so many times that I've lost count. You are a "gentleman and a scholar." Thank you, and bless you, sir.

I also want to dedicate this book and acknowledge Dr. Robert Heidler, who has taught me more than anyone I have ever met. Robert, you are the finest teacher in the body of Christ today, and my whole life has changed because of you and your ministry. Thank you.

## It is Time to Advance.

No matter how you look at life, there's a time when you need to pull up your socks and move forward to advance yourself in the Kingdom of God. No better time than the first of the year! Review the year and note how far you've come in the last year. God is always speaking to you about your destiny; hopefully, you've been making notes throughout the past year about the next steps. If you have not, start this year! Set aside time each week when you spend at least an hour or so with Him. Talk to Him, listen to Him, and journal.

January is an excellent month to fast and listen to the Lord for what He may want to do with your life in this next year. Break free from the things that have kept you captive and in bondage in the last year, and like Lot's wife, do not look back! (see Gen. 19) Make a list of the "bad stuff" - your sinful behaviour and situations you handled poorly and take a stand. Draw a line in the sand and commit to making changes and improvements in your life. The past is over; leave it there; forgive yourself and move on.

**Doc's Book Club:** Read *"Redeeming the Time; Get Your Life Back on Track with the God of Second Opportunities"* by Dr. Chuck D. Pierce.

*Life* is a test... What is God saying to you for this new year?

## What is Trust?

According to Merriam-Webster, it is *"assured reliance on the character, ability, strength, or truth of someone or something."* One of the most complex and challenging parts of being a Christian is learning to trust God. It goes hand-in-hand with the word "thankfulness," and the truth is that trust and thankfulness together will get you safely through the day. If you are focussed on trusting God, then you're not focused on fussing about all the details of life and worrying about things that probably aren't going to happen anyway. Thankfulness keeps you from whining and complaining. My experience in life is that the more a person has an indignant attitude, the more they complain. How do we do this - be thankful and trust God? It's a tall order.

The solution is to keep your eyes focused on Him, an exercise in faith. It is a decision and a free choice you must make hundreds of times a day. The good news is that the more you do it, the easier it becomes. Thought patterns of trust become engrained into the psyche of your brain. It can become second nature to you to trust God in everything, but trust and gratitude do take practice. In time it becomes second nature for you to fall into a state of trust and faithfulness rather than your old habits of fear, worry and ungratefulness.

*"But I trust in you, Lord; I say, 'You are my God.'"* (Ps. 31:14)

*"So then, just as you received Christ Jesus as Lord, continue to live your lives in him, rooted and built up in him, strengthened in the faith as you were taught, and overflowing with thankfulness.* (Col. 2:6-7)

*"Cast all your anxiety on him because he cares for you."*
(1 Peter 5:7)

*"Trust in the Lord with all your heart and lean not on your own under standing."* (Prov. 3:5)

 is a test... Can you trust God?

## How Valuable Are You? (Part 1 of 3)

You are everything to God! Why wouldn't you be? He created you. Perhaps one of our most significant problems in life is that we do not realize how incredibly valuable we are in the eyes of God. We need to focus more on how God sees us than how we see ourselves. If we don't, we can go through life making many avoidable mistakes relating to our identities. We are like a person who is the legal owner of a vast fortune that sells it off for something less than its actual worth: alcohol, Illicit sex, drugs, lust for things etc. Maybe it's pride, prestige and fame in the entertainment industry or a particular high office in the church. However, nothing compares to the value of our God-ordained and God-centered inheritance, which we receive in exchange for our sins.

God wants to move in His power in our lives. He wants us to be more successful, healthier, and more of a blessing to others while learning more about Him and ourselves. We are to learn how to be soldiers in a battle that has been forced upon us (i.e., the war with satan, which we win if we fight!) as we enter the training camp of the greatest teacher and helper that ever lived - Holy Spirit. What's the obstacle? Our desire to be independent ("I can do it!") instead of dependent upon Him.

*Life* is a test... Are you independent from Him or dependent on Him?

## How Valuable Are You? (Part 2 of 3)

In the Garden of Eden, satan said to Eve, *"...you will be like God, knowing good and evil...."* (Gen. 3:5). Who would not want that? What was the real root of the lie? The promise of independence. Once you know good and evil, you have a choice to make, and you can choose either, and that "ability to choose" is called "independence."

The Greeks were the first to exercise their choice thinking that the solution to life's problems was knowledge and science. This explosion of science has not solved humanity's most fundamental issues like injustice, war, poverty, and disease; the world is in a bigger mess than ever before (who will forget 2020 and 2021!) Man has tried various religions and established rules and systems of worship so complex that there is no need for God. Just obey their rules! They are all the same if you study Judaism, Islam, Buddhism, Hinduism, etc. It's all about something you must do to get from some deity. Christianity is not a religion but a relationship based upon grace. All you need to do is confess, surrender, and then receive. Another way that man seeks independence from God is by attempting to get rich with material possessions and control. It is all about pride and power. "I can do it; I am a self-made man!" Right...

"Worldly people" basically consist of all those who have decided to be independent and not submit themselves to the authority of God's appointed King - the Lord Jesus Christ. It takes much more strength to humble and submit yourself to Jesus Christ than taking pride in yourself and becoming a self-made man.

*Life* is a test... Are you self-made or God-made?

## How Valuable Are You? (Part 3 of 3)

To become followers of Jesus, we must make sure that our sins are forgiven by true repentance and faith. Secondly, we must pronounce the sentence of death over our rebellious and independent egos. Jesus said this quite well in Luke 14:33: *"In the same way, those of you who do not give up everything you have cannot be my disciples."*

The bottom line? We must give it all up, folks - family, friends, money, career, prestige, honour - all of life. It's not our life anyway; it's His to do with as He pleases since He created us. We are not owners of anything; we are stewards of His possessions (He owns everything Ps. 50:10). We are stewards of our bodies, which He created (temples of Holy Spirit 1 Cor. 6:19). Every breath that you take is because of Him. Once we genuinely renounce all these worldly things, God may choose to return any of these things that fit the purpose He has and the plans for our lives. *"For I know the plans I have for you,"* declares the Lord, *"plans to prosper you and not to harm you, plans to give you hope and a future."* (Jer. 29:11) Our dependence then is solely on God.

Sometimes it may take a crisis, even a disaster, to bring us to a place where we fully realize that we need God. As the expression goes, "there are no atheists in a foxhole." In Acts 27:20, Paul says that all hope had been given up. Was this the purpose of Paul's trials? To bring him to a place where he had no hope left? Now, Paul would have nothing to hope for except God Himself. That was when he proved that God is all-sufficient because God brings us to a place of total reliance and dependence upon Him to demonstrate that He is truly dependable.

*Life* is a test... Have you surrendered? It is a daily event.

## In the Doldrums?

If we allow "the doldrums" to get us down, life can be mundane, but it doesn't have to be. Too many people fall into the same old, same old trap. They have the same job (which they dislike) and lifestyle - nothing new or exciting. Or they could be trapped in addictions without knowing it (including video games, addictive sports/hobbies, constantly checking their phone etc.). Inside, many people are longing for something new, different, challenging, and adventuresome…

However, life is often what we make of it, and it does not have to be anything like the previous paragraph. Every day can be an adventure if we take the time to listen to His voice and follow Him. Life is not dull with God, even through the hard times; he is there with care, comfort and ideas to overcome every obstacle. The good times are there, too, for He desires to activate us in our Giftings, and our Gifts are always something we like to do and are good at. Praying and obeying leads to a life of Holy excitement and fullness of our own desires and His too! Life with God is never dull!

You have a big part in this; pray and obey, and the mundane days will grow fewer and fewer and give way to life being one big adventure!

*"Success is no accident. It is hard work, perseverance, learning, studying, sacrifice and most of all, love of what you are doing or learning to do."* Pele

*Life* is a test… Is your life an adventure?

## Call On His Name!

The way God made the human mind is that it can switch from one thought to the next in about .25 of a second. It really is an incredible machine that He made. This ability also leads to the fact that satan can instantly have fiery attacks on your mind. He will do everything and anything that he can to pull you out of alignment with God's peace and take you down a road of discouragement, anger, offence - you name it. In short, we are constantly engaged in massive warfare, spiritually speaking. The devil dislikes your closeness to God and sends demons to destroy that intimacy. What should we do in response?

In the thick of the battle, quietly call out His Name ("Jesus") and ask Him to help you. As soon as you do that, the struggle is no longer yours but rather His, and your role is to trust Him to fight it for you. As I have mentioned in Volume 1 of *"Life is a Test,"* our greatest failure as Christians is that we do not know the unlimited power at our disposal by using the Name of Jesus. At the end of time, it is very accurate that *"at the Name of Jesus every knee should bow, in heaven and on earth and under the earth, and every tongue acknowledge that Jesus Christ is Lord, to the glory of God the Father."* (Phil 2:10-11) People who use "Jesus" or "Jesus Christ" insensitively and as a shoddy swear word will fall in terror on the day they meet Jesus. However, those that know Jesus and have drawn closer to Him trusting Him and His Name, will be filled with glory, joy and everlasting life.

*Life* is a test... Have you called on His Name in your time of need? Try it next time you need Him!

## Life is a Challenge.

Although the world defines a person by status, wealth or accomplishments, God's Kingdom does not work that way. Since God is no respecter of persons (Acts 10:34 - which means that He treats everybody equally), it makes no difference who you are and what you have done. For us to enter into the Kingdom of Heaven, we must all go through our own trials and tribulations (Acts 14:22).

None of us enjoy trials, and often we can be shaken by them. But it is part of life. *"No one should be shaken by these afflictions; for you, yourselves know that we are appointed to this"* (1 Thess. 3:3, NKJV). Amid our trials, God is with us, giving us the grace needed for Him to do a mighty work in and through our lives. Some experience minor afflictions, others mediocre; for others still, they are significant. Jesus said of Paul in Acts 9:16, *"I will show him how much he must suffer for My Name."* Just as God did with Paul, so He will do with you and I; we will be transformed into the likeness of Jesus, a testimony to our faith. The furnace of life is what makes us stronger...

1 Cor. 15:58 says, *"Therefore, my beloved brethren, be steadfast, immovable, always abounding in the work of the Lord, knowing that your labour is not in vain in the Lord."* (NKJV) Sometimes we want something so badly in life, and when we get it, it loses its lustre. We need to be doing what the Lord is telling us to do. People will ask, "why is this happening to me?!" Here is why: Rom. 5:3 says, *"Not only so, but we also glory in our sufferings, because we know that suffering produces perseverance."* Psalm 112:6 says, *"Surely the righteous will never be shaken; they will be remembered forever."*

 is a test... The next time you have a trial can you remember to stop and ask God what it is all about and ask Him how to get through it?

## The Root of Societies Problems.

When God brought humans into the world, He laid the foundation for the world: *"And God blest them, and God said unto them, Be fruitful, and multiply, and replenish the earth, and subdue it: and have dominion over the fish of the sea, and over the fowl of the air, and over every living thing that moveth upon the earth."* (Gen: 1:28 KJV) God intended for man to be unified and go forth and multiply, doing this together as a team. We call it the Holy sacrament of marriage. What went wrong?

I believe it started with taking prayer out of the schools. Without the covering of consistent prayer, sexual promiscuity increased, which is one of the critical things that has led to an increase in divorce. A crisis was created for all, especially men, as fatherlessness increased. At the heart of this are a hundred other dysfunctions society suffers from today because men, for the most part, are not what they should be… Men have lost their identity, and society is paying the price. God's foundation was for both parents to raise their children together as a team. Children need their mothers, especially up until about the age of 12, and after that, they need a man in their life, regardless of whether they are a boy or a girl, to champion them into adulthood. The solution? It's the same solution for all the world's problems…

Get back to the foundation of the world, which is the Word of God, the Bible. The world has no answers to its problems and never will. Men need organizations like Promise Keepers, as well as consistent men's bible studies and mentoring. Correct this and watch all the "ills of our society" disappear. Simple stuff…

*Life* is a test… Men, who is mentoring you? Whom are you mentoring?

## Life is Simple.

*"Now all has been heard; here is the conclusion of the matter: Fear God and keep his commandments, for this is the duty of all mankind. For God will bring every deed into judgment, including every hidden thing, whether it is good or evil."* (Ecc. 12:13–14)

The more I study the Bible, the more I realize how simple life is; it's not any more complicated than this:

**1. Fear God.** Fearing God is to hate sin. (Proverb 8:13), and it is also the beginning of wisdom (Ps 111:10). So, hate your sin, not others, because their sin is between them and God. Just hate yours. Looking after yourself and your life with God is a full-time job, so you focus on that, and it will keep you busy for your entire life.

**2. Keep His commandments.** The Bible is filled with them. Read Deuteronomy, Psalms, Proverbs, Ephesians, Romans, and James - you get the point. Why does God have so many rules? He establishes them for our protection. For example, the sacrament of Holy Matrimony and having a monogamous relationship with the person you're married to of the opposite sex is there for several reasons. One is to protect you physically from disease, and as I have explained before, intercourse is a union of two spirits, known as a soul tie. If you have sexual soul ties with others beyond your spouse, your life will be filled with negative issues.

When your body dies, you will be brought into judgment by God. All the unseen things in secret in your life will be seen and known. The places where you have repented and asked Jesus to forgive and cleanse will be forgiven (Heb. 12:24). Those who have never accepted Jesus as their Lord and saviour and are living in complete rebellion will also be judged accordingly. That type of fear in the Lord should make anyone and everyone progressively move towards making Jesus the Lord of their lives and living out their lives with and for Him. It's not rocket science, folks!

*Life* is a test... Is the Christian walk complicated or simple to you?

*Life is a test...*

## Have You Ever Thought About This?

Have you ever sat down and thought for a moment about what Jesus did for you and I? God became flesh and dwelt among us (John 1:140). He taught, healed, cast out demons and prayed. His goal was to transform His people from reliance on the Mosaic Law to a new freedom of His shed blood on the cross. That, of course, meant that He had to go to that cross.

He stood on trial largely quiet and let Himself be falsely accused of His own free will (He could have called 12 Legions of angels down and defeated his enemies - Matt. 26:53). Then He chose the most challenging path and received 37 lashes. Interestingly, the scientific/medical field has determined that there are 37 categories of human disease. Coincidence?? 1 Peter 2:24 says, *"who Himself bore our sins in His own body on the tree, that we, having died to sins, might live for righteousness - by whose stripes (aka lashes) you were healed."* He hung on a cross, naked, nails in His hands and feet, bleeding, mocked, despised by men and then His body died of asphyxiation. He did all of that for you.

When you asked Him into your heart, He gave you His Name, His Word, His authority, His eternal life, His mind, and His Spirit. There is not a thing in this world that He would not do for you.

**Doc's Book Club:** Watch the movie, *"**The Passion of the Christ**"* produced & directed by Mel Gibson. Note: there is a sequel in production.

*Life* is a test... This is what He did for you; what have you done for Him?

## Praise and Worship.

It seems that many contemporary churches these days have not grasped what praise and worship are and the difference between them. "Worship" is not singing some songs on Sunday, sometimes with feigned forced smiley expressions. Further, worship is not entertainment or theatrics. Nor is worship the same as praise.

We praise God (thank Him) with our soul (mind, will and emotions) and our spirits as a willful act of giving glory to Him. This opens the door for His presence to be with us. Then once this door opens, we begin to worship, and that is when we enjoy a genuinely spiritual union with Him and Jesus.

Worshipping God is the holiest activity a person can do in life. However, it can only happen when our souls are under control and submission to our spirits together, working in harmony. Sometimes this union can be just resting in Him with complete silence as the love of Jesus pours over us. It's about Him, not us.

Again, it is the "control thing," us surrendering and letting Him in as we sit back and quietly rest in His love. Spend some daily time just with Him...

"Love is my foundation,
Obedience is my strength,
Praise is my weapon,
Worship is my warfare!"

Worship will get you through some of the roughest times in your life, because it shifts your focus from the problem to the problem solver.

*Life* is a test... Can you rest with Him?

## 10 Things to do When God Seems to be Saying "No." (Part 1 of 2)

It is something that happens to every Christian. We pray and pray, and nothing seems to happen. We get confused because we think "no" is not an answer. "No" is a very valid answer. So, what do you do with that no?

**1.** Trust Him. He knows the future, and you don't. Spending all your time figuring out His next move is like trying to manipulate God. Let Him do His highest good.

**2.** Trust His heart. Like any parent loves their child, He loves you more than you ever know.

**3.** Trust His Word. Do you know God intimately? You need to read His Word over and over again. You need to understand how fair and loving He was in the bible and how He cared for His people. He cares the same for you.

**4.** Trust His grace. Sometimes He says no because He wants us to see the sufficiency of His grace.

**5.** Trust His call on your long-term goals. Every day He is separating "the wheat from the chaff" in your life. He is conforming you to the image of His Son (read Rom. 8:29). Because you cannot see the future, it just might be that it's not "no," but instead, it's "not now."

*Life* is a test... If God answered "no" to something you've been asking, how do you respond?

## 10 Things to do When God Seems to be Saying "No." (Part 2 of 2)

**6.** Check your prayer life. God is looking for "constant contact." Even the little things in life, like asking Him to help you find a parking spot. Better yet, exercise faith and thank Him in advance for the parking spot!

**7.** Did you complete the last assignment that He gave you? Perhaps you're not moving forward because you didn't do what He asked you to do last time. If you are not sure, ask Him.

**8.** Reflect on the past and think about the number of times He got you out of a jam and opened doors for you etc. In other words, check His record. He knows what He's doing.

**9.** Check your "sin level." Where sin is prevalent and where we have asked selfishly for something, you cannot expect God to give us a yes response.

**10.** Remember that God's timing is perfect, and ours isn't. Often ours is based upon impatience, lust or fear.

*Life* is a test... How is your "constant contact" with Him?

# January  15

One thing I wanted to do with this devotional was to emphasize the Hebrew calendar, the calendar that God gave His people. Though most of the world follows the Gregorian calendar, it is worth considering taking the Hebrew calendar into account as well. After all, it is how God originally designed the yearly calendar to look. Here's the first month:

## The Month of Sh'vat (Jan/Feb - Part 1 of 2)

**Alphabet:** The letter is "TZADIK" – which symbolizes the "righteous one."

**Tribe:** Asher; - pleasure, happiness, delicious, fatness;

**Characteristics:**
- This month, righteousness becomes your foundation.
- This month is about getting back on track.
- This is the month to develop the plan for sustaining the generations of your family.
- This month, shout, "my blessings are on the way!"

**Constellation:** Aquarius (the water carrier) - your roots awaken to the water of life.

**Colour/Stone:** Light olive green or yellow/citrine quartz

**Scripture:** Ps. 17. Acknowledge that everything you need will be added to you as you seek first the Kingdom of God and Jesus' righteousness.

Asher was the eighth son of Jacob through Leah's maidservant Zilpah. There were lots of good prophecies spoken over him by Moses. Asher's farm had very fertile soil with plentiful crops, and he exported to other tribes. Consequently, his tribe was very prosperous. Since the tribe was strong, it was used as the rearguard to protect the rest of the tribes. Asher was blest with every potential for every earthly blessing, including mineral resources.

However, Asher took the wrong path in life! He was a bit of a coward and hesitant to go into battle. He did not drive out the Canaanites but allowed them to live among his tribe and at the time of the Judges, and he didn't fight! Deborah rebuked Dan and Asher for not fighting (Jud. 5:17). However, he listened to Deborah and repented. In Judges 6-7, an army was needed, and Asher responded! 1 Chron. 12:36-38 says that the second-largest Army came from Asher.

## The Month of Sh'vat (Jan/Feb - Part 2 of 2)

However, Asher messed up again! He joined the northern tribes and rebelled against Judah and worshiped idols. Hezekiah asked the northern tribes to repent and rejoin Judah. Asher is one of the few tribes in 2 Chron. 30:11 that did. The result? Asher was not a lost tribe like most of the northern tribes were.

Asher was there for the Messiah to come! In Luke 2:36, we read about Anna, and she was from the tribe of Asher. She was a prophetess, an elderly widow who devoutly worshiped God with regular fasting and praying. She was also one of the first people to recognize, in faith, the baby Jesus as God's promised Messiah.

**Understanding the tribe of Asher and how to pray to be in alignment with God this month.**

This month, prosperity is an issue. Pray for the economy. It is a month that has a theme about oil. Pray for oil-dependent economies worldwide (like the Province of Alberta, where I live - we have the second-largest oil reserves in the world after Saudi Arabia). Pray for God to take you beyond "milk" and into God's substance. Repent for any mistakes you've made in managing your money. Repent for not tithing and making offerings (if that is the case). Remember that "repent" means to confess your sin and the second part of the word means to change. So, start changing.

In January, you need to re-program your body for healthier eating if you go through a fasting process. God will show you how to eat differently when you complete your fast.

- God is calling us to choose the tree of life.
- Righteousness is your foundation.
- Taste and see that God is good!
- Change your mind, and you will prosper!
- Don't let self-pity and condemnation control you.

*Life* is a test... Do you notice in the story of Asher how many times he repented and got back on track? Something that we all need to do.

## Are You a Pest?

If you are, then you are in good company!

Paul is generally regarded as one of the most influential people in the bible. He founded several Christian communities in Asia Minor (modern Turkey) and Europe from the mid-30s to the mid-50s AD and is mainly responsible for establishing what we know as the Christian Church. He started life as a Pharisee and participated in the persecution of the early disciples of Jesus and the Jews. In the Book of Acts, chapter 9, Paul travelled on the road from Jerusalem to Damascus to arrest Jews when the risen Christ appeared to him in a great bright light. He was struck blind, but after three days, his sight was restored by Ananias through his ministry in Damascus, and Paul began to preach that Jesus of Nazareth was the Jewish Messiah and the Son of God (Acts 9:20–21). Approximately half of the Book of Acts deals with Paul's life and works. Fourteen of the 27 books in the New Testament have traditionally been attributed to Paul's writing.

Paul was arrested and put on trial, and here is the opening "pitch" by the prosecution: *"For we have found this man a perfect pest (a real plague), an agitator and source of disturbance to all the Jews throughout the world, and a ringleader of the (heretical, division-producing) sect of the Nazarenes."* (Acts. 24: 5 AMP) My point? Here is a man who essentially built the church, wrote about half of the New Testament, and changed the world, yet his enemies regarded him as a "pest." So, if you're doing what Paul did, keep doing it; if you're not doing what he did, then start being a "pest."

*Life* is a test... Are you a pest? Is the devil scared when you get out of bed in the morning?

# The Church Needs to Grow Up!

As a whole body, the church is supposed to be discontent with carnal ways and immaturity. The Bible says that as we grow in Christ, we are to put away childish things and grow up spiritually. In other words, be more like Jesus. *"When I was a child, I spoke as a child, I understood as a child, I thought as a child; but when I became a man, I put away childish things."* (1 Cor. 13:11 NKJV)

Back in 1981, when I was first saved, there was a significant difference between the church and the secular world. The church had a lower divorce rate, lower abuse rate, and higher rate of healthy people, both financially and physically. However, today sociologists and pollsters will tell you that the numbers are pretty much the same across the board. Why? We have all the answers, so what's the problem? The problem is that our churches are not teaching what they should be, and the people are not applying the Word of God in their lives.

I attended a seminar last year, and one of the panel speakers (an apostle/pastor who leads a vast church) said that, in his opinion, 80% of the churches should be closed. It was intended as a joke, we all laughed, but his point was made. The churches are not preaching "fire and brimstone," salvation, sin, Holy Spirit, Gifts. etc. Not only that, but what we are hearing from many pulpits today is the "feel-good power of positive thinking" messages and, in some cases, blatant apostasy. The solution? Preach the true WORD from the Bible, forget about political correctness and making people feel good. Jesus didn't, so why shouldn't we be like Him? WWJD?? We should all be living and preaching the uncompromised Word of God. Nothing more nothing less.

*Life* is a test... How do you feel about the scripture in the first paragraph? Are you putting away childish behaviour?

## How Did the Apostles Die?

The Bible only mentions the deaths of two apostles; James, who was put to death by Herod Agrippa I and Judas Iscariot, who committed suicide. The deaths of the other ten apostles are known by tradition or the writings of early Christian historians: Simon, surnamed Peter - crucified upside down; Andrew - crucified upside down on an X-shaped cross; Phillip - crucified; Bartholomew - skinned alive and beheaded; Matthew - burned-to-death; Thomas - impaled by a spear; James (the Lesser) - stoned and clubbed-to-death; Simon (the Canaanite) - axed-to-death; Jude (Thaddeus) - axed to death.

Why would these men put themselves in a position against the status quo of society, against the ruling Romans, to the point of losing their own lives? Simply because, regardless of the circumstances that they were in, they refused to deny that Jesus was the King of Kings and Lord of Lords. They knew who Saul was, a Pharisee and persecutor of Jews, and then they knew of his miraculous transformation on the road to Damascus. The Disciples were persecuted, and the only reason they put up with that is that they had spent time with Jesus, even though they did not understand who and what He was until after He died and rose from the grave. It is estimated that over 200 people die every day around the world for the simple reason that they believe that Jesus is Lord. Thousands die every year just in Nigeria alone.

**Doc's Book Club:** Read *"The Book of Martyrs"* by John Foxe.

*Life* is a test... Are you willing to be persecuted for your belief in Jesus? Pray for those who are if you are not persecuted regularly.

## What's Missing in our Churches?
## Simply, the Fruit of the Spirit. (Part 1 of 4)

The phrase "fruit of the spirit" comes from Galatians 5:22-23: *"But the fruit of the Spirit is love, joy, peace, forbearance, kindness, goodness, faithfulness, gentleness, and self-control. Against such things there is no law."*

It is derived from the Greek language and means "fruit," simple enough. It can also be translated as offspring, deed, action, or result. Today we might use the word "fruit" in a phrase such as the "fruit of our labour" to communicate the results of our effort. - something to show for our work, in a paycheque, a finished project etc. In this scripture, the development, or the work of the Spirit in a believer's life, is love, joy, peace, patience, kindness, goodness, gentleness, and self-control.

Paul contrasted the acts of the flesh in the three verses prior, Galatians 5:19-21: *"sexual immorality, impurity and debauchery; idolatry and witchcraft; hatred, discord, jealousy, fits of rage, selfish ambition, dissensions, factions and envy; drunkenness, orgies, and the like"* to the good fruit of the Spirit.

*Life* is a test... Can you keep the fruit in you all the time? No one can. Keep reading tomorrow as I expand this further.

## Spiritual Fruit. (Part 2 of 4)

There is a difference between Spiritual Gifts and Spiritual Fruit. Gifts are precisely that; a gift that God gives believers, and they are Spiritual Gifts, not loans with conditions for they are irrevocable (Rom. 11:29). Even if we don't use them or misuse them, we still have them. In volume 1 of *"Life is a Test,"* I wrote about this subject. You can also download a poster that lists 30 Spiritual Gifts from my website, with scriptures for each. The nine Spiritual Fruits are more like characters of behaviour. Love is, of course, listed first, which is then part of the other eight which are different ways in which love manifests itself:

**Joy** is love rejoicing.
**Peace** is love resting.
**Long-suffering (aka patience)** is love forbearing.
**Kindness** is love serving others.
**Goodness** is love seeking the best for others.
**Faithfulness** is love keeping its promises.
**Gentleness** is love ministering to the hurt and pain of others.
**Self-control** is love in control.

These Fruits are listed in Galatians 5:22-23, and the seven stages of growth of these Fruits are listed in 2 Peter 1:5-9: *"For this very reason, make every effort to add to your faith goodness; and to goodness, knowledge; and to knowledge, self-control; and to self-control, perseverance; and to perseverance, godliness; and to godliness, mutual affection; and to mutual affection, love. For if you possess these qualities in increasing measure, they will keep you from being ineffective and unproductive in your knowledge of our Lord Jesus Christ. But whoever does not have them is nearsighted and blind, forgetting that they have been cleansed from their past."*

*Life* is a test... The Fruits of the Spirit are integral to our daily walk. Try posting a list of the Fruits of the Spirit on your bathroom mirror or somewhere you can stop and read through them each day.

## Spiritual Fruit. (Part 3 of 4)

### 1. Go to the Source of the Fruit.

Developing the Fruit of the Spirit comes from a relationship with the Lord. We can struggle in our flesh to discipline ourselves, keep our peace, remain faithful, live joyfully, respond in love and more. However, it seldom works. We are just not good enough to live on our own. We need Holy Spirit, and by spending time and developing a relationship with Him, appreciating how much He loves us, and understanding who He is and whom He wants to be in us, we begin to yield to Jesus and then it becomes as natural as walking down the street. It's that "constant contact" concept of allowing Him in us all the time.

### 2. Blockages? Remove them.

With "constant contact," the shortcomings of our lives become apparent. The Lord will bring to your mind areas that need His healing; the junk in our lives; unforgiveness, sins, addictions, places where He told us to do something, and we missed it. Jesus asks us to extend forgiveness to everyone, including ourselves (Matt. 6:14-15).

3. Before I go any further, there is a vital clarification I wish to make. As I said yesterday, there is a difference between Spiritual Gifts and spiritual fruit. Remember this, offended people, and people with sin in their lives may still experience miracles, Words of knowledge, strong preaching, and may even administer healing. But these are Gifts of the Spirit, not fruits. We will be judged according to our fruit, not our Spiritual Gifting. A gift is given, and fruit is cultivated.

*Life* is a test... Instead of trying in the flesh to keep the fruit in you, have you tried pursuing "constant contact?"

## Spiritual Fruit. (Part 4 of 4)

### 4. Put Your Fruit on the Tree - You!

We cannot claim to have fruit in our lives until we're willing to put it on display - let your light shine! For example, if we need to exhibit patience, we don't have patience until we show the fruit of patience. It won't happen until we surrender all and let Him put that patience in us. Just as fruit on a tree starts small and grows, the fruit of the Spirit must evolve, too. When we develop our relationships with the Lord and remove blockages, we create a healthy spiritual environment that encourages growth. Folks, this takes time - a lifetime! Just keep moving forward with it.

### 5. It's All About Jesus and Holy Spirit, not you.

*"'For in him we live and move and have our being.' As some of your poets have said, 'We are his offspring.'"* (Acts 17:28, KJV) Our goal is to be more like Jesus every day and grow towards Christ. His presence in our lives becomes all-encompassing. His thoughts, His will, His manners, and behaviours become ours. Say this out loud, "it is not about me; it's about Jesus!" When we need the fruit of the Spirit, it is there because Jesus is there. If not, then stop and ask Him for it. (and sometimes you may want to ask Him to hurray! LOL)

*Life* is a test... Memorize the fruits and then keep them in the forefront of your mind.

# The Fruit of the
# SPIRIT

There is a difference between Spiritual Gifts and Spiritual Fruit. Gifts are precisely that; a gift that God gives believers, and they are exactly that, Gifts, not loans with conditions for they are irrevocable (Rom. 11:29). Even if we don't use them or misuse them, we still have them. (The "Gifts of the Spirit" Poster is available as part of this poster series.)

There are 9 Spiritual Fruits that are more like characters of behaviour. Love is listed first, which is then part of the other eight, which are different ways in which love manifests itself.

- Joy is love rejoicing.
- Peace is love resting.
- Long-suffering is love forbearing.
- Kindness is love serving others.
- Goodness is love seeking the best for others.
- Faithfulness is love keeping its promises.
- Gentleness is love ministering to the hurt and pain of others.
- Self-control is love in control.

The "Fruit" Poster is part of the Christian Manifesto Poster series. Produced in Calgary, Alberta, Canada, by New Start Ministries Ltd. These posters are available for sale from: www.newstartministries.ca COPYRIGHT 2022.

"The Fruit of the Spirit" Poster can be downloaded and printed in any size for $7.95 CAD.

# From Prostitute to Pillar of Faith.

I always tell my children that they are filled with potential. We all must learn to make every day count and not miss the presented faith opportunities. If we do not choose to follow the Lord by serving others, our most significant potential will never be realized.

In the Book of Joshua, chapter 2, we read about Rahab, a prostitute who, by her occupation, had not made good "life choices." However, when she saw that the two spies Joshua had sent to the City of Jericho were "the children of God," she suddenly changed her tune and realized that she needed to get "right with God." Her past sins became irrelevant when she chose a future with these men, asking them to protect her family later if she protected them. By aligning with God's covenant plan at the risk of her life, she was selected to be part of Jesus' life and live by faith. You can read about it in the book of Joshua, chapter 2.

Hebrews 11 is known as the chapter about faith. It starts in verse one with a description of what faith is (*"the substance of things hoped for the evidence of things not seen"*) and then goes on to describe all the "heroes of faith" in the bible. Guess who is in verse 31? Rahab!

*"By faith the prostitute Rahab, because she welcomed the spies, was not killed with those who were disobedient."* (Heb. 11:31)

*Life* is a test... To realize our full potential in life, we must live in Jesus. Are you doing that?

For the first nine months of this year, I will discuss the nine Fruits of the Spirit.

## The first Fruit of the Spirit - Love (Part 1 of 6)

Jesus spoke a great deal about love. What exactly does the word love mean? There are three kinds of love: Eros, Philos and Agape.

Eros love is physical/emotional love. Western culture calls it "romance." From the Greek word "erotas" and it was not always viewed in a positive light by the Greeks as it cannot be maintained and tends to wear off (aka "the honeymoon is over"). Relationships built exclusively on Eros don't last, but still, it is an important part. *"The husband should fulfill his wife's sexual needs, and the wife should fulfill her husband's needs."* (1 Cor. 7:3)

Philos in today's terms, means "brotherly love." It involves showing loyalty, giving sacrifice, showing appreciation and is a more "noble form" (aka "strong friendship") of love not equating to sex. It can be between friends, family, and spouses. This love is a "give and take" relationship needed as a foundation for marriage but is not unconditional. *"And Jonathan made a covenant with David because he loved him as himself."* (1 Sam. 18:3)

Agape Love is selfless, sacrificial, and "turns the other cheek"; it is unconditional and is the highest form of love in the Bible, the kind that God shows us. *"This is how God showed his love among us: He sent his one and only Son into the world that we might live through him. This is love: not that we loved God, but that he loved us and sent his Son as an atoning sacrifice for our sins."* (1 John 4:9-10) Jesus replied: *"Love the Lord your God with all your heart and with all your soul and with all your mind."* (Matt 22:37) Agape love can be the hardest to give, as it truly is a giving of yourself, much beyond what most of us are comfortable with. Jesus said that we must love giving this kind of love quite a challenging command!

*Life* is a test... How hard is it for you to give (love) unconditionally?

## The first Fruit of the Spirit - Love (Part 2 of 6)

Did you know that God loves you? God is saying to us, "look, there is nothing more than you can do to make Me love you more than I already do! Conversely, there is nothing that you can do to make Me love you any less." * Why does He feel that way? He loves for no other reason than simply "because." You are His creation, and He is good at what He does. That is His nature; He's good, very good. After all, He made you, didn't He?

His whole purpose, being, and nature is love and to love. That means you were always loved, are always loved, and will be forever always loved. That's because He never changes, and therefore His love never changes. So, get used to it - He loves you!

*"And so we know and rely on the love God has for us. God is love. Whoever lives in love lives in God, and God in them."* (1 John 4:16)

His love does not increase as you "get better" because He already loves you at 100% of His capacity. Even if you have no plans to walk with Him and have no plans to live your life for Him, He still loves you 100%. Why? Because that is simply who He is. He loves all the way, every way, all the time. He doesn't change - *"I the Lord do not change"* (Mal. 3:6), but we can change. Change what? Our ability to receive His love. He wants us to grow more like Him. Who and what is He? Love; nothing more and nothing less...

*"And surely I am with you always, to the very end of the age."* (Matt. 28:20) Why? Because He loves you! He really does!

*Life* is a test... Do you understand how much He loves you?

* Obviously my paraphrase of what God is saying to us.

## Power Points about Love: (Part 3 of 6)

There are a lot of practical examples I can give to show what love is and how to live it well. Here are a few of the points I believe are most key to showing love in the big ways as well as the small ways:

- Begin by asking God to fill your heart with love this day.
- Pray for the desire to see others as God sees them.
- To express our love to God, we must learn how to love one another without walking in envy or strife. We must have love that endures and covers with silence. We must intentionally learn how to treat one another, avoid offence, and seek God for wisdom and direction in every area of our lives.
- When we become rooted and grounded in God's love, His power is released in our lives. That's when we can say to our mountains, *"Be thou removed."* (Mark 11: 23-24 KJV)
- Prayer connects us to God and establishes our love relationship with Him; as a result, compassion is developed within us.
- When Jesus' compassion moves you, you will see Him.
- The love of God says, "What can I do for you?" It constantly gives.
- The more time we spend developing a relationship with God, the less time we'll spend operating in fear.
- Spending time with God needs to be our number one priority to live in love because God is love.
- The devil understands how lethal faith is to his plans. So, to stop our faith, he attacks our love with the weapon of anger. If he can distract us, he can short-circuit our faith.
- We cannot live in harmony if we are full of ourselves.... full of pride.

*Life* is a test... Which of these points connects with you most? Are you challenged by any?

## Power Points about Love: (Part 4 of 6)

I hope yesterday proved helpful for you. We'll spend one more day going into it! To carry on from yesterday talking about love, here are more points and one-liners I've learned over the years about love and how to love well:

- Every time we reach out to take revenge or gossip, we sow seeds that hurt ourselves. Then, because love is not in operation, faith is hindered.
- Patience doesn't mean putting up with something. Instead, it means "constancy; continuance." If you apply patience to your faith, it means you are constantly believing in the Word of God.
- When we speak without restraint, pride, not love, is the motivation.
- To be like Him, we must allow our character to be stretched and moulded into His image.
- If you have trouble with past offences, take them to God.
- Unforgiveness hinders our faith and is the most significant blockage to the blessings of God. It hinders our prayers.
- Don't tell God how much you love Him if you are unwilling to change, and love is the evidence of change.
- With His love as the motivating factor behind all we do, nothing will be impossible for us.
- Do not defend your sin.
- Our ability to love others is directly related to the condition of our hearts.
- Pray that the love of God will be unlocked and poured out on your everyday life. His love let loose on earth through you is an exhilarating experience. Seek God for His love and seek to be a vessel of that love.
- All we get when we live to please ourselves is a selfish, self-absorbed heart. Living to please God and love others will take us out of the enemy world of self and into new heights with God.
- We are to continually fill ourselves with His truth for us, combat lies, and stay in His Word.
- Your hurts can make you bitter or better.
- When you do something to bless someone, you are doing it for Jesus.

*Life* is a test... Are you challenged by any of these points?

## Love in Conclusion: (Part 5 of 6)

**Finally:**

**1.** Offer your life to God completely.
**2.** Turn away from the world's philosophies.
**3.** Be changed by filling your mind with God's plan.
**4.** Humble yourself before God.
**5.** Accept yourself and accept others as part of God's plan.
**6.** Use your Gifts and do not compare yourself with others.
**7.** Love and honour others.
**8.** Be joyful and put your hope in God.
**9.** Bless those who wrong you. Don't stoop to cursing them.
**10.** Live in harmony with one another.

Love is not a feeling; it is an overwhelming passion to help, bless, deliver, comfort, strengthen, and give joy to others, just as Jesus always does. If we are not seeking God and fellowshipping with Him, we will not deliver the very things only God's Spirit knows - another person's needs. We are commanded in scripture to submit to one another (Eph. 5:21), which means considering someone else.

*Life* is a test... Remember to allow God to work; everything doesn't have to be solved today.

## Love in the Word (Part 6 of 6)

To conclude this 6 day series on Love, here are several scriptures for you to "chew on" that talk about love. Some are exhortations, others are perspectives. We must love, friends. Take time to consider each scripture thoroughly.

*"A new command I give you: Love one another. As I have loved you, so you must love one another. By this everyone will know that you are my disciples, if you love one another."* (John 13: 34-35)

*"We know that we have passed from death to life, because we love each other. Anyone who does not love remains in death."* (1 John 3:14)

*"And be kind to one another, tenderhearted, forgiving one another, even as God for Christ's sake hath forgiven you."* (Eph. 4:32)

*"But anyone who hates a brother or sister is in the darkness and walks around in the darkness. They do not know where they are going, because the darkness has blinded them."* (1 John 2:11)

*"Dear friends, let us love one another, for love comes from God. Everyone who loves has been born of God and knows God. Whoever does not love does not know God, because God is love. This is how God showed his love among us: He sent his one and only Son into the world that we might live through him. This is love: not that we loved God, but that he loved us and sent his Son as an atoning sacrifice for our sins. Dear friends, since God so loved us, we also ought to love one another. No one has ever seen God; but if we love one another, God lives in us and his love is made complete in us."* (1 John 4:7-12)

Rom. 5:5 says that *"the love of God is shed abroad in our hearts."* (KJV)

Rom. 8:28 says that *"all things work together for good to them that love God."* (KJV)

*Life* is a test... God's love is the key to all of life.

## Notch it Up a Bit.

We are called to praise and worship God through how we live and through a church we are faithful to. We must remember, though, that we are not called to simply "praise." There is much more to it than that! It's warfare. Anything that becomes "warfare" essentially means making degrees and proclamations into the heavenly realms. Example: "I praise you, Lord, that you overpower the darkness in the heavenly realms. I praise you that your angels are defeating the enemies of this world and in the supernatural world." Next, take the prayers you are praying about and the needs of others and turn them into aggressive intercessory warfare prayers. Speak words that agree with the bible. In other words, degree God's Word back to Him!

Let the songs you sing be much more than just a church ritual. Let them be tied into songs of deliverance, like singing Psalms 92 and 101. This should all be done with a strong element of faith - *"it calls into being things that were not."* (Rom. 4:17) Of course, while you are doing all of this, make sure that you have on the whole armour of God (Eph. 6). We need to understand that we are warriors, and that no foe can come against us, but further, don't just be defensive but offensive! Kick the devil's butt!

When I prayer walk at night around my neighbourhood, I am doing all the above, and I destroy demonic forces built during the witching hour (midnight to 3:00 am) by witches, warlocks, and demonic forces. Any Christian that does this needs to know their authority.

 is a test... Remember to praise and then worship.

*Life* is a test...

# God is on a Building Project!

God often refers to the church as His house. In Eph. 2:20 it says, *"You, too, are built upon the foundation laid by the apostles and prophets, the cornerstone being Christ Jesus himself."* (GNB) 1 Peter 2:5 says, *"You also, like living stones, are being built into a spiritual house."*

God is in the middle of the most incredible restoration building project in history. He is not building a church building but a house which is us. We are the building materials. We are the living stones put together with Jesus as the cement. This begins with the foundation of the Spiritual Gifts: the Apostle, Prophet, Teacher, Pastor, and Evangelist. They work together with a common purpose, utilizing all the rest of the Gifts (30 of them - see the poster on the next page) to equip every believer to do the work of Jesus.

Why does God want His church to be restored? To host His glory! His glory was kept in the Ark of the Covenant and the temple in the Old Testament. But since we are the temple, He wants Himself to be inside of us instead of a physical building. 1 Cor. 3:16 says, *"Don't you know that you yourselves are God's temple and that God's Spirit dwells in your midst?"*

God is restoring the church to His plan, and the result will be a great end-time harvest.

*Life* is a test... Are you taking into account that you are a "church" for Holy Spirit in your day-to-day living?

# What **Spiritual Gifts** has God given you?

1. **Administration** - The Gift of Administration is the exceptional power that God gives to Christians to clearly understand the immediate and long-range goals of a particular unit of the Body of Christ and devise and execute effective plans to accomplish those goals. (Luke 14:28-30 • Acts 6:1-7 • Acts 27:11 • 1 Corinthians 12:28 • Titus 1:5)

2. **Apostle** - The Gift of Apostle is the exceptional power that God gives to Christians to assume and exercise divinely imparted authority to establish the foundational government of an assigned sphere of ministry within the Church by setting things in order. (Luke 6:12-13 • 1 Corinthians 12:28 • Ephesians 2:20 • Ephesians 4:11-13)

3. **Celibacy** - The Gift of Celibacy is the exceptional power that God gives to Christians to remain single and enjoy it, to be unmarried and not suffer undue sexual temptations. (Matthew 19:10-12 • 1 Corinthians 7:7-8)

4. **Craftsman** - The Gift of Craftsman is the exceptional power that God gives to Christians to design and craft items based on an inherent skill given by God to create objects to glorify God. (Exodus 28:3 • Exodus 28:28 • Exodus 35:10 • Exodus 35:35 • Exodus 38:4)

5. **Deliverance** - The Gift of Deliverance is the exceptional power that God gives to Christians to cast out demons and evil spirits. (Acts 8:5-8; 16:16-18 • Matthew 12:22-22 • Luke 10:12-20)

6. **Discerning of Spirits** - The Gift of Discerning of spirits is the exceptional power that God gives to Christians to know whether certain behaviour purported to be of God is really divine, human or satanic. (Matthew 16:21-23 • Acts 5:1-11 • Acts 16:16-18 • 1 Corinthians 12:10 • 1 John 4:1-6)

7. **Evangelist** - The Gift of Evangelist is the exceptional power that God gives to Christians to share the gospel with non-believers in such a way that they become Jesus' disciples and responsible members of the Body of Christ. (Acts 8:5-6 • Acts 8:26-40 • Acts 14:21 • Ephesians 4:11-13 • 2 Timothy 4:5)

8. **Exhortation** - The Gift of Exhortation is the exceptional power that God gives to Christians to minister words of comfort, consolation, encouragement and counsel to other members of the Body in such a way that they feel helped and healed. (Acts 14:22 • Romans 12:8 • 1 Timothy 4:13 • Hebrews 10:25)

9. **Faith** - The Gift of Faith is the exceptional power that God gives to Christians to discern with extraordinary confidence the will and purposes of God for His work. (Acts 11:22-24 • Acts 27:21-25 • Romans 4:18-21 • 1 Corinthians 12:9 • Hebrews 11)

10. **Giving** - The Gift of Giving is the exceptional power that God gives to Christians to contribute their material resources to the work of the Lord liberally and cheerfully, above and beyond the tithes and offerings expected of all believers. (Mark 12:41-44 • Romans12:8 • 2 Corinthians 8:1-7 • 2 Corinthians 9:2-8)

11. **Healing** - The Gift of Healing is the exceptional power that God gives to Christians to serve as human intermediaries through whom it pleases God to cure illness and restore health apart from the use of natural means. (Acts 3:1-10 • Acts 5:12-16 • Acts 9:32-35 • Acts 28:7-10 • 1 Corinthians 12:9, 28)

12. **Helps** - The Gift of Helps is the exceptional power that God gives to Christians to invest the talents they have in the life and ministry of other members of the Body, thus enabling those others to increase the effectiveness of their own spiritual gifts. (Mark 15:40-41 • Luke 8:2-3 • Acts 9:36 • Romans 16:1-2 • 1 Corinthians 12:28)

13. **Hospitality** - The Gift of Hospitality is the exceptional power that God gives to Christians to provide an open house and a warm welcome to those in need of food and lodging. (Acts 16:14-15 • Romans 12:9-13 • Romans 16:23 • Hebrews 13:1-2 • 1 Peter 4:9)

14. **Intercession** - The Gift of Intercession is the exceptional power that God gives to Christians to pray for extended periods and see frequent and specific answers to their prayers, to a degree much greater than that which is expected of the average Christian. (Colossians 1:9-12 • Colossians 4:12-13 • Acts 12:12 • James 5:16-18 • Luke 22:41-44 • 1 Timothy 2:1-2)

15. **Interpretation** - The Gift of Interpretation is the exceptional power that God gives Christians to make known the message of another person who speaks in tongues. (1 Corinthians 12:10, 30 • 1 Corinthians 14:13 • 1 Corinthians 14:26-28)

16. **Knowledge** - The Gift of Knowledge is the exceptional power that God gives to Christians to discover, accumulate, analyze, and clarify information and ideas pertinent to the Body's well-being. (Acts 5:1-11 • 1 Corinthians 2:14 • 1 Corinthians 12:8 • 2 Corinthians 11:6 • Colossians 2:2-3)

17. **Leadership** - The Gift of Leadership is the exceptional power that God gives to Christians to set goals in God's purpose for the future and communicate these goals to others so that they voluntarily and harmoniously work together to accomplish those goals for the glory of God. (Luke 9:51 • Acts 15:7-11 • Romans 12:8 • 1 Timothy 5:17 • Hebrews 13:17)

18. **Mercy** - The Gift of Mercy is the exceptional power that God gives to Christians to feel genuine empathy and compassion for individuals, both Christian and non-Christian, who suffer distressing physical, mental or emotional problems and to translate that compassion into cheerfully-done deeds which reflect Christ's love and alleviate the suffering. (Matthew 20:29-34 • Romans 12:8 • Mark 9:41 • Luke 10:33-35 • Acts 11:28-30 • Acts 16:33-34)

19. **Miracles** - The Gift of Miracles is the exceptional power that God gives to Christians to serve as human intermediaries through whom it pleases God to perform powerful acts that observers perceive to have altered the ordinary course of nature. (Acts 9:36-42 • Acts 19:11-20 • Romans 15:18-19 • Acts 20:7-12 • 1 Corinthians 12:10, 28 • 2 Corinthians 12:12)

20. **Missionary** - The Gift of Missionary is the exceptional power that God gives to Christians to minister whatever other spiritual gifts they have in a second culture. (Acts 8:4 • Acts 13:2-3 • Acts 22:21 • Romans 10:15 • 1 Corinthians 9:19-23 • Ephesians 2:6-8)

21. **Musician** - The Gift of Musician is the exceptional power that God gives to Christians to play an instrument skilfully and/or create musical compositions and/or communicate by song, music that inspires others and offers praise and worship to God. (1 Chronicles 15:16-27 • 1 Chronicles 16:42 • Deuteronomy 31:19 • Deuteronomy 32:34)

22. **Pastor** - The Gift of Pastor is the exceptional power that God gives to Christians to assume long-term personal responsibility for the spiritual welfare of a group of believers. (John 10:1-18 • Ephesians 4:11-13 • 1 Timothy 3:1-7 • 1 Peter 5:1-3)

23. **Poverty** - The Gift of Voluntary Poverty is the exceptional power that God gives to Christians to renounce material comfort and luxury and adopt a personal lifestyle equivalent to those living at the poverty level in a given society to serve God more effectively. (1 Corinthians 13:1-3 • 2 Corinthians 6:10 • 2 Corinthians 8:9 • Acts 2:44-45)

24. **Preaching/Speaking** - The Gift of Preaching/Speaking is the exceptional power that God gives to Christians to minister by speaking publicly (or through writing) the Word of God to instigate teaching, revelation, evangelism, and knowledge. (1 Peter 4:11)

25. **Prophecy** - The Gift of Prophecy is the exceptional power that God gives to Christians to speak in a language they have never learned and/or to receive and communicate an immediate message of God to His people through a divinely anointed utterance. (Luke 7:26 • Acts 15:32 • Acts 21:9-11 • Romans 12:6 • 1Corinthians 12:10, 28 • Ephesians 4:11-13)

26. **Service** - The Gift of Service is the exceptional power that God gives to Christians to identify the unmet needs involved in a task related to God's work and make use of available resources to meet those needs and help accomplish the desired results. (Acts 6:1-7 • Romans 12:7 • Galatians 6:2, 10 • 2 Timothy 1:16-18 • Titus 3:14)

27. **Teaching** - The Gift of Teaching is the exceptional power that God gives to Christians to communicate information relevant to the health and ministry of the Body and its members in such a way that others will learn and learn well. (Acts 18:24-28 • Acts 20:20-21 • 1 Corinthians 12:28 • Ephesians 4:11-13)

28. **Tongues** - The Gift of Tongues is the exceptional power that God gives to Christians to speak in a language they have never learned and/or to receive and communicate an immediate message of God to His people through a divinely anointed utterance in a language they never learned. (Mark 16:17 • Acts 2:1-13 • Acts 10:44-46 • Acts 19:1-7 • 1 Corinthians 12:10, 28 • 1 Corinthians 14:13-19)

29. **Wisdom** - The Gift of Wisdom is the exceptional power that God gives to Christians to know the mind of the Holy Spirit in such a way as to receive insight into how given knowledge may best be applied to specific needs arising in the Body of Christ. (Acts 6:3, 10 • 1 Corinthians 2:1-13 • 1 Corinthians 12:8 • James 1:5-6 • 2 Peter 3:15-16)

30. **Worship Leader** - The Gift of Leading worship is the exceptional power that God gives to Christians to accurately discern the heart of God for a particular public worship service, to draw others into an intimate experience with God during the worship time and to allow the Holy Spirit to change directions. (1 Samuel16:23 • 1 Chronicles 9:33 • 2 Chronicles 5:12-14)

## Spiritual Gift Classifcations within the Five-Fold Ministry

| **Apostle** | **Prophet** | **Evangelist** | **Teacher** | **Pastor** |
|---|---|---|---|---|
| Apostle | Prophecy | Evangelist | Teacher | Pastor |
| Leadership | Discernment | Faith | Wisdom | Adminstration |
| Giving | Exhortation | Miracles | Knowledge | Hospitality |
| Celibacy | Intercessor | Healing | Mercy | Service & Help |
| | Tongues & Interpretations | Missionary | Preaching | Worship Leader |
| | Musician | Deliverance | | Poverty (voluntary) |
| | | | | Craftsman |

"The Spiritual Gifts" Poster can be downloaded and printed in any size for $7.95 CAD.

www.newstartministries.ca

*is a test...*

## Yes, You *Can* Do It, but...

One of the biggestt sections in any bookstore these days is the "how-to section." There are life instructions about every conceivable topic. Our society teaches us that we are to be "successful, happy, wealthy..." and that you can set your mind to anything you want to do; with hard work and discipline - "you can do it!" Well, yes, but let's look at it another way. Firstly, there is nothing wrong with many of those concepts, as our Father God wants those things for us. Wouldn't any parent? However, that is not the point; the issue is how we will get from "A to B." Undoubtedly, "success" works for some people; we see it every day! However, it seems to miss about 95% of the population, even though it is available to everyone. God has a more accessible and better plan...

You are far better off to set your mind to what His mind is for you to do. You can have your thoughts, dreams, and vision, but you can only take it so far. (BTW, you can call them "your" dreams if you wish, but who do you think planted them there?) Man's wisdom, apart from God is quite frankly flawed. If we depend on His wisdom and guidance, we will walk much more peacefully and with less work and stress than any path we can dream of. The Father always has a good plan for us, and all we must do is be determined to be in His will instead of our own.

*"The blessing of the Lord makes one rich, And He **adds no sorrow with it**."* (Prov.10:22)
*"Those who think they know something do not yet know as they ought to know."* (1 Cor. 8:2)
*"Instead, you ought to say, 'If it is the Lord's will, we will live and do this or that.'"* (James 4:5)

*Life* is a test... You can be successful (with lots of work,) but with God it's a much easier. Which do you think is a better choice?

# February

# 3

## Two Worlds, Two Choices.

The world's way of pursuing riches is grasping and hoarding; "He who gets the most toys wins the game." Right... Isn't that what Hollywood people do when they make it rich in the entertainment industry? It's about seeing how many beautiful homes you can own, cars you can drive, and airplanes you can fly. "Stuff" can give you happiness for a short time, but it never gives you that deep inner peace and joy that only comes from the divine presence of Jesus.

*"The blessing of the Lord makes one rich, And He adds no sorrow with it."* (Prov. 10:22 NKJV)

There is no sin in obtaining riches if you know what they are for (building the Kingdom of God - Deut. 8:18). You receive riches, peace, eternal life etc. by letting go, turning your life over to Him, returning what is His (tithing), and then giving. Give yourself to Him and your money; the more you do, the more He fills you with inexpressible, heavenly joy, peace, healing, and finances.

Remember in the mornings to worship Him in the beauty of silence and because of His Holiness. Yes, He wants your pocketbook, but that's not just what He wants. It is a test of your heart (Matt. 6:21), but more importantly, He wants you and then you will be blest going in and blest going out. (Deut. 28:6)

*Life* is a test... Which world are you in?

# The Christian Life
# COMMANDMENTS

1. Be humble. (I Peter 5: 6-7)
1. Be humble. (I Peter 5: 6-7)
2. Live by faith. (Romans 1:17)
3. Give to the poor. (Proverbs 19:17)
4. Listen more, and talk less. (James 1:19)
5. Be kind to unkind people. (Ephesians 4:32)
6. Know when to keep quiet. (Proverbs 15: 1-2)
7. Confess your mistakes and sins. (I John 1:19)
8. Life is not fair; get used to it. (Ephesians 9:11)
9. Strive for excellence, not perfection. (Titus 3:8)
10. Be on time. Don't make excuses. (Philippians 2:4)
11. Don't worry about anything. Trust God. (Matthew 6:25-27)
12. Stop blaming others for your circumstances. (Romans 2:1)
13. Bless someone when they cut you off in line. (Luke 16:27)
14. Cultivate good manners, including table manners. (Titus 3:2)
15. Love God and your neighbours as yourself. (Mark 12:30-31)
16. Tithe 10% of your gross income to your church. (Malachi 3:10)
17. Change your circumstances with positive confessions. (Matthew 12:37)
18. Exercise and take care of your temple of the Holy Spirit every day. (3 John 1:2)
19. Return what you borrow in better shape than when you borrowed it. (2 Kings 6:5)
20. Take time daily to be alone with God, and learn to hear His voice. (John 10:27-28)
21. Learn from the past. Plan for the future, and live in the present. (Deuteronomy 4:9)
22. Do something nice anonymously. God knows about it; no one else has to. (Matthew 6:4)
23. When you travel, learn everything about the country you are going to. (2 Timothy 2:15)
24. The entire world can change if people would humble, pray, seek and turn to God. (II Chronicles 7:14)
25. Meditate on the Word daily. "This Book of the Law shall not depart from your mouth, but you shall meditate on it day and night, so that you may be careful to do according to all that is written in it. For then you will make your way prosperous, and then you will have good success." (Joshua 1:8 ESV)

The "Life Commandments" Poster is part of the Christian Manifesto Poster series. Produced in Calgary, Alberta, Canada, by New Start Ministries Ltd. These posters are available for sale from: www.newstartministries.ca   COPYRIGHT 2022

"The Christian Life Commandments" Poster can be downloaded and printed in any size for $7.95 CAD.

www.newstartministries.ca

# Why Worry?

Matt. 6:25-34 says, *"Therefore I tell you, do not worry about your life, what you will eat or drink; or about your body, what you will wear. Is not life more than food, and the body more than clothes? Look at the birds of the air; they do not sow or reap or store away in barns, and yet your heavenly Father feeds them. Are you not much more valuable than they? Can any one of you by worrying, add a single hour to your life?"*

Many voices are battling each other with you for control of your mind in our world, especially when you sit in silence. We tend to run around in circles trying to think things through independently and obey the various voices directing our lives. The result is brokenness and a fragmented, frustrating way of life.

How do we filter these voices and hear God? Start to worship and ask Holy Spirit to give you discernment and to filter out "the other voices;" which may be commitments, jobs, burdens, finances, or simply technology! Our minds can only think of one thing at a time so, therefore, just spend that time thinking about Jesus. Jesus squelches the voices of the demons that are trying to influence you. Walk closely with God listening for His directives in enjoying His companionship. Focus on Him instead of yourself and all the other junk running around in your head, and that stuff will soon dissipate.

*"When he has brought out all his own, he goes on ahead of them, and his sheep follow him because they know his voice."* (John 10:4)

*Life* is a test... Are you practicing just listening to Him?

# February

**5**

## A Homework Project!

Read starting from the Book of Acts right through to Revelation and look for the phases, "in Christ," "in Him," or "in Whom." When you find them, say to yourself, "That's me!" Sounds bold and brash? Yes, it sounds like it is, but "not so, when you know so."

There is nothing brash about it; it is simply the truth. The greatest single thing that Christians need to know and understand in their hearts is to know who and what they are in Christ Jesus. We must begin to see ourselves according to how God sees us and how the Word is laid up for us in the scriptures. See yourself making firm, concrete decisions about life and operating in love and discipline and power and self-control instead of considering all the problems you and the world have. The world is caught up with the five human senses, which does nothing but lock them into a natural realm existence. We are to be in this world but not part of it (John 17:16).

*Life* is a test... If now's not a good time to read through Acts to Revelation, when is?

*Life is a test...*

# The Roller Coaster of Life.

We often hear that life is a roller coaster, filled with ups and downs (especially our emotions)... but does it have to be??

When the Bible says to be in this world but not a part of it, * it means that we don't have to do things the way everybody else does. The world seems to live by its emotions, but the Bible does not tell us to live that way. When your feelings tend to be like a roller coaster ride, stop and simply let truth prevail. What truth? The only truth in this world is the truth of what Jesus said: *"I am the way and the truth and the life"* (John 14:6), and no one else has ever said that, and no one ever will. Stand firm on the foundation of God's Word and refuse to allow discouragement or disappointment to plunge you into darkness so that you jump into the proverbial roller coaster car and go for a spin. Stay in the light, and He will be there to help you establish peace and strength in your heart.

We must learn to trust God and allow Him to show us the way and give us the means to solve complex problems. That's not going to happen if we're on the roller coaster! So, the key is to quiet our thoughts and emotions and be still. Refuse to allow fear and discontentment to derail your life. Live in peace with yourself and with your neighbour.

*"Be still, and know that I am God..."* (Ps. 46:10)

*"Pursue peace with all people, and holiness, without which no one will see the Lord."* (Heb. 12;14 NKJV)

*Life* is a test.... How do you handle stress when it comes?

* My paraphrase from 1 John 2:15

## "Conclusion" Prayers.

*"The Lord bless you and keep you; the Lord make His face shine on you and be gracious to you; the Lord turn His face toward you and give you peace."* This prayer is called, "The Prayer of Moses," from Num. 6:24-26. in which God told Moses how to teach Arron to bless the Israelites. (Note: I pray this prayer over my three children every night - and have for 26+ years).

At a conference that I attended, I spoke with one of the keynote speakers and later, we had some correspondence back and forth about her book. In one of her emails, she concluded the email with the following prayer:

*"May the Lord bring fresh hope to your heart today. May He make a way where there seems to be no way. May our Heavenly Father protect you in the places you feel most vulnerable. And may He establish you in His love, His peace, and His purpose today and every day."* What a wonderful blessing this was to me!

Some takeaways from these prayers:

**1.** "Hope" is an "earnest expectation" of what God will do. Heb. 11:1.
**2.** "Make a way," as in, praying that He makes a way.
**3.** Although not a direct quote, the reference "protect you." The scriptures on this are many: Ps. 91: 1-16, Ps 23: 1-6, Ps. 32:7, Deut. 31:6, Ps 138:7, 1 John 5:18.
**4.** "Love and purpose" is Jesus' "middle name!" 1 John 4:7-12, 16; John 3:16, Jer. 29:11, Matt. 28:18-20, Rom. 8:28, Prov. 16:4.

*Life* is a test... Pray these over your family, everyday.

# What Dad Used to Say.

Remember when you were a child and your parents would say some things to you like: *"clean up your room, sit up straight at the table, hold your knife and fork properly,"* etc. etc. and you hated those comments? For those that have become parents, you now find yourself saying precisely the same thing to your children! One of my Dad's favourite expressions he used to say to me, especially when I was going through a difficult time, was, "It will build your character." I used to get so angry when he said that! I didn't care to have my character built! As an adult, now I can see his point and find myself saying the same thing to my children!

The truth about Christianity is that it does not necessarily build your character (although it will); instead, it reveals your personality. Christianity breaks you down into who you are and what you are trying to accomplish in life. We usually think that our lives are "all about me." Isn't that what a two-year-old says and maintains? Me! Me! Me! I want! I want! I want! Give me! Give me! Give me! Tragically so many people in this world never change from that. They live their lives for themselves, what they want, and what they can create and have.

Being a Christian is about turning life over to God and allowing Him to "break me, mould me, make me" into a new creation with a new heart and new life. That process reveals who we are and the truth about whom we are now after the born-again experience. Therefore, as we go through "the fiery furnace of life;" it reveals our character, and that will continue for the rest of our lives.

*Life* is a test... Who is "running your ship?" You or Him? Read the story about the Potter and the potter's wheel in Jeremiah chapter 18.

# Thankfulness

It can be a difficult concept to be thanking God when things go wrong, yet that is what His Word tells us to do. Why? Well, there is an element of mystery with this idea. God is saying, "you give thanks to me, regardless of your feelings, and I will give you joy regardless of your circumstances and the situation(s) that you are dealing with." * Really? Yes. It makes no sense, does it? Why would we even consider giving anyone, including God, thanks for the pain we are going through?? Rather irrational. It seems complex and, well, just a plain dumb idea. Or is it? We are not giving Him thanks for the problem per se; we are giving Him thanks for whatever purpose in what we are going through. He knows what is best for us. Perhaps it is a punishment to get our attention; maybe it is a test (remember, Life is a Test!) or a way to teach us something. The bottom line is that it is a spiritual act of obedience to thank Him and trust Him. Those who obey Him are invariably blest whether the pain continues or not.

Why does God ask this of us? Because it opens our hearts to His presence and our minds to His thoughts. *"'For My thoughts are not your thoughts, neither are your ways my ways,' declares the Lord. 'As the heavens are higher than the earth, so are my ways higher than your ways and my thoughts than your thoughts.'"* (Is. 55:8-9) Circumstances may not change, but like turning on a light switch, bringing His presence into the situation enables us to worship, praise, give thanks, and be open to hearing Him. It also helps to reduce the pain and frustrations of whatever we are going through. *"Give thanks in all circumstances; for this is God's will for you in Christ Jesus."* (1 Thess. 5:18)

*Life* is a test... Can you give Him thanks in **all** circumstances?

* (my paraphrase)

## Get WISE Counsel.

Yes, the Bible says that we should get wise counsel (Prov. 1:5), and the key here is the word "wise." We must be cautious in choosing from whom we're going to ask for help. Not everybody you meet is a sounding board, and sometimes that includes our family and friends. They can be our biggest enemies (Matt 10:36). Some Christians have tainted souls with unhealed hurts, wounds, and pains of the past, and they filter life through those previous experiences. The wisdom they have to offer, all with well and good intentions, comes not from a place of healing, peace and reconciliation but rather from a gut of bitterness and resentment. "Well, that happened to me once..." And then they go on to tell you about their sad tale, which has led to bitterness and grief.

Always remember that God's wisdom is pure, filled with peace and reasonable. God will never ask you to do more than you can do. We must all learn to discern the difference between our wisdom, the words of other wounded people, and God's wisdom. When making an important decision in life, or even an everyday decision like buying something at a store, stop for a moment and see whether you feel a sense of peace in your gut.

*"Who is wise and understanding among you? Let them show it by their good life, by deeds done in the humility that comes from wisdom. But if you harbour bitter envy and selfish ambition in your hearts, do not boast about it or deny the truth. Such "wisdom" does not come down from heaven but is earthly, unspiritual, demonic. Where you have envy and selfish ambition, you find disorder and every evil practice. But the wisdom that comes from heaven is first of all pure; then peace-loving, considerate, submissive, full of mercy and good fruit, impartial and sincere." (James 3:13-17)*

*Life* is a test... When you make a decision, do you feel at peace?

# Never Complain.

Never complain. It tends to drag us down and put us into a position of depression and anger, not to mention the fact that it opens the door to failure. Remember the words we speak go into the atmosphere and the heavenly realms. Since our battles are not in the natural world but with principalities, powers, and evil forces in the heavenly realms (read Eph. 6), what happens is our words can be grabbed by demons whose job it is to hinder the progress of any destiny that you were trying to achieve. The Bible is quite clear on this one as it says that *"life and death are in the power of the tongue."* (Prov. 18:21) It is better to be silent than allow complaining words to be spoken. Further, the Bible says that we should do everything with a willing spirit and a happy heart.

So, what to do? Stop, sit down, pray, and put everything into His hands. *"Come on to me all the more heavily laden and I will refresh you."* (Matt. 11:28) Frankly, all our problems are not our problems. They are His problems, and they aren't problems for Him! God did not make us to shoulder heavy burdens. It's not our job. The more of Him in our lives, the more He can spare us from suffering the enemy's plans to inflict pain upon us.

*Life* is a test... Is your speech more often positive or negative?

## Frustration

Refuse to allow frustration to be the driving force in your life. Yes, we can all feel justified when someone causes us grief or irritation, but these are pathways for resentment to build. We think of an act of entitlement rising in our hearts, even so much as to go into revenge. However, all that emotional junk and baggage will not change anything. An old expression says that bitterness towards others is like mixing a batch of poison for that person, but then you drink it instead of them. All those negative emotions will only block your way to spiritual wisdom. The key is to live in peace and forgiveness. Not easy, but Jesus never said life was easy. He did say, though that He would be there for us whenever we asked.

Instead of having these emotions boil up inside you, and you stress out, bring your dissatisfaction, pain, and hurt to the altar and leave it there with God. He knows about your problems, He knows how to deal with them, and there are so many things that you do not understand in life, but He does. Drop all your negative junk at His feet because it's His problem, not yours, and for Him, it's not a problem.

*"Cast all your anxiety on him because he cares for you."* (1 Peter 5:7)

*Life* is a test... Do you let negative emotions boil over or can you keep your peace?

# The Pick and Choose "Church." (Part 1 of 2)

The 21st-century church has fallen prey to satan's traps of twisted doctrine and various false teachings that Christians (including pastors) have been foolish enough to believe.

**1.** "God is love" Translation: "Any kind of 'love' is OK." Often "love" means hormones working overtime. "If it feels good, do it" (I wrote about love on January 25).

**2.** "Don't get hung up with doctrine and specifics." Translation: "I only believe what suits me." People pick what they want out of the Bible, life, and the world, creating a pot-puri of beliefs and then worship that. It is called idolatry.

**3.** "I believe much of the Bible stuff, but I also believe in reincarnation, karma, meditation etc." Translation: "I believe what gives me peace and whatever I feel like." I piecemeal my religion and believe what I want; whatever gives me some comfort.

**4.** "I believe in evolution. Religion is false." Translation: "I worship Mother Earth." In other words, they worship creation but not the creator. (When I lived in Banff, we used to call them "tree huggers.")

**5.** "My church accepts everyone." Translation: "We do what we want." Jesus accepted everyone, but He chastised the religious people and did not accept anyone's sin. He told the woman caught in adultery to go and "sin no more." (John 8:11)

**6.** "The Bible is not relevant in today's modern society. It's just a collection of Old Testament stories." If people have studied the Word of God, they would know that this statement is entirely false. The Bible has stood the test of time; it is sharper than a two-edged sword (Heb. 4:12), and "all Scripture is God-breathed" (2 Tim.3:16). *"Prophecy never had its origin in the human will, but prophets, though human, spoke from God as the Holy Spirit carried them along."* (2 Peter 1:21) If true, the Bible should be the most important and treasured document ever created. 1817 prophecies in the Bible have come to pass.

*is a test...*

# The Pick and Choose "Church." (Part 2 of 2)

**7.** "A loving God would never send anyone to hell." Translation: "I can live whatever life I want because if God loves me like He says He does, He will not send me to hell." God does not send anyone to hell other than satan, according to the Book of Revelation, because hell was made for him. When our bodies die, our souls go to the "H place" or the other "h place," which is of our own free will. God has told us to choose where we want to go, so He doesn't "send" anyone anywhere! *"This day I call the heavens and the earth as witnesses against you that I have set before you life and death, blessings and curses. Now choose life, so that you and your children may live"* (Deut. 30:19). *"For God so loved the world that He gave His one and only Son, that whoever believes in Him shall not perish but have eternal life."* (John 3:16)

**8.** "God gave us sex. I can use it the way I want." Translation: promiscuity reigns! Firstly, God kept sex between a married man and a married woman to protect them from disease and to procreate. Secondly, people do not understand that intercourse is the joining of two spirits and two souls. Yes, sex manifests itself physically, but it is a spiritual event. Any sexual activity outside of marriage makes for wrong soul ties.

**9.** "It's my money; I earned it. I'll spend it on myself and from time to time, I might give some to the church." It amazes me how people will spend exorbitant money in restaurants and leave a 20% tip but can't give God 10%. Go figure... No, it is not your money because nothing in this world is yours. God owns everything and allows you to steward it for a period of time (Ps. 50:10).

We can't just believe what we want or follow a fatalist attitude that everything happens for a reason. No, we believe the Word of God, or we don't. The consequences you will experience when your body dies.

*Life* is a test... Life is a choice and death is by default. Which is it for you?

**www.newstartministries.ca**

## The Month of Adar (Feb/Mar - Part 1 of 2)

**Appointed Times:** The feast of Esther is on the 13th day; Purim is on the 14th day.

**Alphabet:** The letter is "KUF" - removing the masquerade, entering the joy of the Lord.

**Tribe:** Naphtali - "Naphtali" means to struggle and prevail; a time of celebration that your curse is overturned.

**Characteristics:**

- Your identity should be reflected this month, spiritually as well as physically.
- This is a month to deliver yourself of worry through breaking curses.
- Stop the fear in yourself, and guard yourself against idolatry.
- This is the month to develop spiritual war strategies so that demonic decrees sent against you can be broken.
- This is the month that the roots of depression and despair can be broken through into faith.

**Constellation:** Pisces (the fishes) - You have an identity in the invisible world.

**Colour/Stone:** Purple/Amethyst

**Scripture:** *"Yet who knows whether you have come to the Kingdom for such a time as this?"* (Es. 4:14)

Naphtali is the story of redemption! When Naphtali joined in the idolatry of the northern tribes, they put themselves under a curse and ended up in captivity. When the remnants of the tribe turned back to God, they broke the curse, and the door to their future opened. They leaped forward into a destiny that was far beyond anything they could have imagined! When they turned to God, God exalted them! Naphtali was despised, and Nazareth, a town in their land, was the lowest of the low. It's interesting that it became Jesus's hometown where He based His ministry.

In Revelation 7, we find the last mention of Naphtali in the Bible, where 12,000 from the tribe will be sealed with "the seal of the living God," which means the best is yet to come for Naphtali!

## The Month of Adar (Feb/Mar - Part 1 of 2)

Adar is the time of Purim when the curse is overturned (read about it in the Book of Esther). Purim is a time to celebrate that the enemy tried to destroy Israel, but he was defeated! Israel had an enemy that always wanted to kill them; a frequent one was the Amalekites. They attacked Israel coming out of Egypt, plundered them in Gideon's day and attacked Ziklag taking David's family as captives. God instructed Saul to destroy the Amalekites, but Saul disobeyed. In Esther's day, Haman, a descendant of the Amalekites, came and tried to eliminate all Jews! They always came to steal, kill and destroy. Purim is a time to overcome the evil forces in your life.

**Understanding the tribe of Naphtali and how to pray to be in alignment with God this month.**

In the month of Adar, if you feel that you are under a curse and nothing seems to be going right for you, then Adar is the month to break the curse. You can break a curse any month if you turn to God and repent, but in Adar, there is a special anointing. Draw near to God this month, break off every curse, and prepare to leap into your future. Adar is a month to learn your identity and become whom God created you to be. If you've made mistakes, Adar is the anointed month for you to repent best and get back on track.

**Doc's Book Club:** Read *"They Shall Expel Demons"* and *"Blessing or Curse,"* both books written by Derek Prince.

*Life* is a test... Is your schedule in line with God's?

# Who Was (Is) This Man Called Jesus?

Good question. Such a good question that Jesus asked it to His disciples. The Pharisees had said that He was a teacher; some said He was a prophet. Some thought that He was John the Baptist, and some thought He was Elijah raised from the dead. Only the Apostle Peter received revelation knowledge and knew the truth. Where did he get that from? Holy Spirit.

Jesus replied to Peter, *"But what about you?" He asked. "Who do you say I am?" Simon Peter answered, 'You are the Messiah, the Son of the living God.' Jesus replied, 'Blessed are you, Simon son of Jonah, for this was not revealed to you by flesh and blood, but by my Father in heaven. And I tell you that you are Peter, and on this rock, I will build my church, and the gates of Hades will not overcome it. I will give you the keys of the kingdom of heaven; whatever you bind on earth will be bound in heaven, and whatever you loose on earth will be loosed in heaven.'"* (Matt. 16: 15-19)

We cry out to Jesus when we want to be born again. We cry out to Him in a moment of fear or need. Remember that Jesus said He would send "a comforter" known as Holy Spirit. He lives inside of you if you know Jesus, and you can call on Him anytime, 24/7. Read John 14:16 and John 16:7-15.

*Life* is a test... Who is Jesus to you?

## The Ekklesia.

How do we define the church? The English word "church" descends from an Old English word "cirice," akin to an Old High German word, "kirihha." Both words derive from the Greek "kuriakos," the term "Lord." When they wrote the books of the New Testament, the apostles could have used kuriakos, but it appears only twice in the Bible: in 1 Cor. 11:20 (the Lord's supper) and Rev. 1:10 (the Lord's Day). Neither usage contains any reference to "church." Instead, the apostles used the word "Ekklesia" over 100 times. Bible dictionaries, and lexicons, agree that "Ekklesia" means "called out" and generally implies a governmental assembly of people. Essentially the Ekklesia in the New Testament is a group of people who have been called out of the world to form a government, which essentially is what the Kingdom of God is; a form of government. Jesus said that on this rock, He would build His Ekklesia. What is our part?

**1. Bless:** Bless, don't blast. Speak peace to every house you enter. *"When you enter a house, first say, 'peace to this house.'"* (Luke 10:5)
**2. Fellowship:** Befriend, don't avoid. Listen for felt needs. *"Stay there, eating and drinking whatever they give you... Do not move around from house to house."* (Luke 10:7)
**3. Minister:** Heal, don't judge. Pray for the felt need. *"Heal the sick who are there"* (Luke 10:9a)
**4. Proclaim:** Declare that the Kingdom of God, with all its goodness, peace and joy, has come to this place. *"The Kingdom of God has come to you."* (Luke 10:9b)

*Life* is a test... Are you doing your part in the Ekklesia?

# Be the Church!

Lots of people are dedicated to church attendance. That is a good thing; Jesus did that. Therefore, we should too. The question is, what are you doing while you are there?

"Church" is not a building, a place we go to, or a weekly or biweekly event. As I mentioned yesterday, the word "church" is derived from the Greek word "Ekklesia," a governing body of people. The traditional church has been a building where a "congregation" meets to hopefully get filled with something that benefits them and gives them a place to socialize and perhaps give some of their time in "good works." Not anymore...

The Ekklesia are to be warriors! We will never change the world by just going to church. We will only change the world by being the church! Occasionally, I am asked by a non-believer, "well, if there is a God, why are people starving in Africa." My standard "pat answer" is, "because you are not doing anything about it."

God gave us this earth and everything in it and told us to take dominion over it and set up guidelines to rule. Then His Son came and gave us our job description: *"go out into the world and make disciples of all men."* (Matt. 28:19) The world's problems would go away in less than a year if all 8 billion of us knew Jesus and lived our lives for Him. Simple stuff...

*Life* is a test... Are you "in" church on Sundays or "in the church" all week long?

# The Second Fruit of the Spirit - Joy
## (Part 1 of 7)

Part of our walk with the Lord is to have joy down in our hearts. God loves it when we have joy, and the devil hates it. I have written in the past about religious spirits, and one of the ways to recognize one is to see how much joy a person has in their life. A religious spirit will always oppose joy and laughter. Religion wants you to be mournful, sullen and feel guilty. I remember growing up in a Church that was all about obeying the rules on Sunday. No laughing, no raising your hands in worship, no shouting for joy, but instead kneeling in submissiveness and praying sorrowful repentant prayers. However, that is not what God's Word says:

- Deut. 28:47 says that *"a curse will come upon you if you do not serve the Lord joyfully."*

- Ps. 5; 11 says, *"But let all who take refuge in you be glad; let them ever sing for joy."*

- 1 Chron. 16: 8-10 says, *"Give praise to the Lord, proclaim His Name; make known among the nations what He has done. Sing to Him, sing praise to Him; tell of all His wonderful acts. Glory in His Holy Name; let the hearts of those who seek the Lord rejoice."*

- 1 Chron. 16: 23- 25 says, *"Sing to the Lord, all the earth; proclaim His salvation day after day. Declare His glory among the nations, His marvellous deeds among all peoples. For great is the Lord and most worthy of praise; He is to be feared above all gods."* Verse 34-35 says, *"Give thanks to the Lord, for He is good; His love endures forever. Cry out, 'Save us, God our Savior; gather us and deliver us from the nations, that we may give thanks to Your Holy Name, and glory in Your praise."*

*Life* is a test... Is Sunday a time of joyful praise or a solemn, sulky, silent time?

## The Second Fruit of the Spirit - Joy
### (Part 2 of 7)

- Ps. 126: 2 *"Our mouths were filled with laughter, our tongues with songs of joy"*

- Job 8: 21 *"He will yet fill your mouth with laughter and your lips with shouts of joy."*

- Phil 4: 4 *"Rejoice in the Lord always. I will say it again: Rejoice!"*

God exhorts and commands us to be filled with joy and joy under all circumstances. Therefore, it is a commandment and to be joyless would be contradictory to how we are told to live. Proverbs 17:22 says that if you have joy in your life, it will make you healthy! *"A cheerful heart is good medicine."* Yes, God indeed wants us blest financially, in our health, and in relationships, but there is also a reason for that. God wants us so blest, overwhelmed and overflowing with blessing, grace, and goodness that other people look at us and say, "what's that guy got? Whatever it is, I want that too!"

It is at this point that people get confused. They think that happiness and joy are things that just happen to them, but our joy of the Lord is not based on outside circumstances. Our society thinks that if things are going well, they will be happy, and if they're not, they should complain and be unhappy. Their worldview would say that they have a right to do that! However, that is not what the Bible says. God commands us to rejoice and says it's a sin to whine and complain. If God commands you to rejoice, then you have a choice about whether you will do that or not. Some people live in such a state of proverbial unhappiness that it becomes a habit, and they live their whole lives that way. Everyone on this planet has both negative and positive experiences; bad times and good times, victories, and failures, but we all have a choice as to what we will focus on, the good or bad.

*Life* is a test... Do you ride the emotional rollercoaster of life's ups and downs, or are you grounded in God's joy?

**www.newstartministries.ca**

# The Second Fruit of the Spirit - Joy
## (Part 3 of 7)

Again, we see in life that our thoughts determine the outcomes of life. Simply, thoughts become words, words become actions (after we've spoken the words), actions become habits, habits become our character, and our character leads and determines our life. Thoughts then are the starting point so fill your mind with thoughts of joy. James said in chapter one of his book: *"Consider it pure joy, my brothers and sisters, whenever you face trials of many kinds because you know that the testing of your faith produces perseverance. Let perseverance finish its work so that you may be mature and complete, not lacking anything."* (James 1: 2-4) We are not to live a life of self-pity, struggle with depression, murmur or complain because we miss the blessings that God has planned for us if we do. As with everything in life, it's a choice.

There are things that God says in His Word that if we are to do, He will give us joy:

**1.** We can be a giver! Why is it better to give than to receive? (Acts 20:35) Because it gives you joy! (The word "give" appears 1433 times in the NIV translation).

**2.** Choose to remember the good things in life. That describes Phil. 4:8.8 *"Finally, brethren, whatever things are true, whatever things are noble, whatever things are just, whatever things are pure, whatever things are lovely, whatever things are of good report if there is any virtue and if there is anything praiseworthy - meditate on these things."* (NKJV) If you start meditating on these things, you can't help but get joyful!

*Life* is a test... Do you see joy as a gift from God?

## The Second Fruit of the Spirit - Joy
### (Part 4 of 7)

Continuing from yesterday about inherit joy:

**3.** Be thankful! 1 Thess. 5:18 says, *"In everything give thanks: for this is the will of God in Christ Jesus concerning you."* Ps. 107: says, *"O give thanks unto the LORD, for He is good: for His mercy endureth forever."* Eph. 5:20 says, *"Giving thanks always for all things unto God and the Father in the Name of our Lord Jesus Christ."* (all from KJV)

**4.** You do deserve a break today, so take a day off! It's called the Sabbath or Shabbat. It is God's first commandment in the Bible, and we are to celebrate God, worship Him and take a day of rest.

Is. 58:13-13 says, *"If you keep your feet from breaking the Sabbath and from doing as you please on my holy day if you call the Sabbath a delight and the Lord's holy day honourable, and if you honour it by not going your own way and not doing as you please or speaking idle words, then you will find your joy in the Lord."*

Even the unsaved will be blest if they keep the Sabbath. *"And foreigners who bind themselves to the Lord to minister to Him, to love the name of the Lord, and to be His servants, all who keep the Sabbath without desecrating it and who hold fast to My covenant - these I will bring to My holy mountain and give them joy in My house of prayer."*

*Life* is a test... Are you honouring the Sabbath?

# The Second Fruit of the Spirit - Joy
### (Part 5 of 7)

We're in big trouble if we do not have a scriptural basis for all we discuss relating to faith! As we continue to talk about joy, consider other parts of the Bible have similar themes.

**5.** Forgiveness is a great way to eliminate burdens and guilt and have joy in your heart. Get rid of your junk, forgive and move on, and you'll have joy in your heart.

**6.** Cares of the world. *"Humble yourselves, therefore, under God's mighty hand, that he may lift you up in due time. Cast all your anxiety on Him because He cares for you."* (1 Peter 5: 7-8)

**7.** Command yourself to be joyful, right from the inner parts of your soul. If David could do it, you can! Here, in the Psalms David commands his soul to "toe the line!" *"Bless the Lord, O my soul; And all that is within me, bless His holy name! Bless the Lord, O my soul, And forget not all His benefits: Who forgives all your iniquities, Who heals all your diseases, Who redeems your life from destruction, Who crowns you with lovingkindness and tender mercies, Who satisfies your mouth with good things, So that your youth is renewed like the eagle's."* (Ps. 103:1-6 NKJV)

**8.** Just humble yourself to God and let His river of joy flow in you.

*Life* is a test... I read Ps. 103 every day. Try reading it every day for a week and see what impact it has on you.

## The Second Fruit of the Spirit - Joy
### (Part 6 of 7)

We must not let joy just be an inward thing. Express your joy! God tells us to shout for joy, so do that and let it all hang out! You can choose the next time you go shopping to smile and let the joy of the Lord come out of you, or you could be grumpy and rude to everyone you see; the choice is yours. None of us are dependent on circumstances for joy, but you can see the joy in all your situations and remember to praise Him in all things. Further, there's even more of a reason to shout for joy when God does bless you!

Be thankful for the people in your life, your family, and your friends and be grateful for the victories in your life. A thankful heart acknowledges His blessings.

If your heart is so hardened from negative thinking and perhaps even tragedies and disappointments, well, there is a time to grieve, and then there's a time to move on. A hard reality may be for some but a reality that must be realized is that sitting on the pity pot for too long is selfishness. The world doesn't stop needing help and God doesn't stop wanting to use you. The solution of how to move forward? Repent, and let God plant His joy in your heart so that you live a life overwhelming in His joy. Yes, this can be difficult and much work, but God never said life would be easy. What He did say was that we will be victorious in everything that we do if we submit ourselves to Him.

*Life* is a test... How is your joy level today?

## The Second Fruit of the Spirit - Joy
### (Part 7 of 7)

A synonym for the word joy is gladness. Merriam-Webster defines the word "gladness" as: *"experiencing pleasure, joy, or delight: made happy; marked by, expressive of, or caused by happiness; full of brightness and cheerfulness."*

Since this is a fruit, the source of our gladness is not circumstances, conditions of our lives, or other people. Psalms 4:7 says, *"You have put gladness in my heart."* (NKJV) Therefore the source of gladness is God. When we get overburdened with life's circumstances and issues, we have to look deep into our hearts to find gladness; if He put it there, then it's there. The Apostle Paul said he chose contentment and gladness despite all his trials, including being shipwrecked, beaten, persecuted, and imprisoned. Rather than get depressed over the challenges, he chose gladness. *"That is why, for Christ's sake, I delight in weaknesses, in insults, in hardships, in persecutions, in difficulties. For when I am weak, then I am strong."* 2 Cor. 12:10 The next time you're having a bad day, remind yourself of Paul's life. James said to *"count it all joy."* (James 1:2)

Psalm 37:4 is how King David responded with his own gladness. *"Delight yourself in the Lord, and He will give you the desires of your heart."* Our challenge in life, then, is to put all the other worrisome thoughts of life out of our minds and focus on Jesus, and then that gladness in our heart will begin to rise.

*Life* is a test...Can you focus on gladness/joy when times are tough?

## He Is Not Condemning you!

*"Therefore, there is now no condemnation for those who are in Christ Jesus, because through Christ Jesus the law of the Spirit who gives life has set you free from the law of sin and death."* (Rom.8:1-2)

*"Jesus straightened up and asked her, 'Woman, where are they? Has no one condemned you?' 'No one, sir,' she said. 'Then neither do I condemn you,' Jesus declared. 'Go now and leave your life of sin.'* (John 8:10-11)

When you were born again, you had a new birthright, and that right is a life free of condemnation. Jesus died on the cross to set you free. Therefore, you don't need to take all your sins and mistakes onto your lap. He said you're free!

To stay that way, walking down a road of freedom and joy, we must keep ourselves completely fixed on Jesus. Rather than be a sheep walking the course of the world with all its attractions which can eventually lead to a path of destruction and then finally eternity in hell, be a sheep of the Father, listening for His voice and direction. He will tell you that you are loved, forgiven, and no longer condemned.

*"My sheep listen to my voice; I know them, and they follow me."* (John 10:27)

*Life* is a test... Are you a worldly sheep or a Godly sheep?

# The Power of Your Words.

Did you know that your words have power? To be more specific, it's God's Words that we should speak out and back to Him. Why? Because God is moved by the Words that we speak, especially when we speak Words that He first spoke. Look at Jeremiah chapter 1. It says, *"I am on watch to carry out My Word."* God is telling Jeremiah that God is watching to fulfill it quickly when His Word is declared. Further, it says in Is. 55:11, *"So shall My Word be that goes forth from My mouth; It shall not return to Me void, But it shall accomplish what I please, And it shall prosper in the thing for which I sent it."*

It is essential that we guard our mouths and not voice any kind of unbelief. We should not murmur and complain. Instead, be careful that we declare what God has already said. In other words, claim His promises! Satan will tell you one thing, and you need to be quick to say, "no, that's not going to happen, devil, because that is not what the Lord says." Then quote scripture and tell satan in certain terms that the Lord has said over a given situation.

As you speak God's Word into your atmosphere, you will establish God's will on the earth. That is why close to the beginning of the Lord's prayer we see, "**Thy Kingdom come thy will be done on earth as it is in heaven.**" (Matt 6:10 KJV)

*Life* is a test... Are you speaking God's Words or yours?

## Grace (Part 1 of 3)

God either loves all of us, or He loves none of us. He is not biased, racist, prejudiced, and He has no respect for individual people over others; He respects us all. *"Then Peter opened his mouth, and said, Of a truth, I perceive that God is no respecter of persons."* (Acts 10:34 KJV) God's amazing grace can and will make you a new person because His grace is more significant than all your sins.

God's grace has no limits or bounds because it is beyond the understanding of mankind. Grace will set you free from the cruelty and domination by others. Some people are prisoners to other people's foolish opinions, their unreachable demands, and their dominating and manipulation of your life. You can be set free of that. Quit trying to please the tyrants that are trying to control you. Who is anyone to speak ill of you? You are God's child!

Take charge of your life, or someone else will. Regardless of what you do or don't do, you're going to be blamed and criticized for something by someone else. As that old expression goes, "You can't please all the people all the time," so don't even bother trying. Forget about what other people say. You are a child of the living God. Instead, go on and enjoy your life and make the decisions you and God have made together, and if you do, it will be a remarkable, amazing God-filled, happy and prosperous life. What other people say or think about you doesn't matter. Grow some thick skin, for their words are "water off a duck's back!" All that matters is that you are aligned with God and doing His will. Forget the rest of it…

*Life* is a test… Deep down, do you really care what others think??

## Grace (Part 2 of 3)

Some people are caught in the performance trap. They try to earn other people's approval by what they do or do not do. Forget about them. You matter to God, and that is all that matters. The bottom line is that you can be a people pleaser or a pleaser of the Father. The question is, which one of these will you choose? *"Am I now trying to win the approval of human beings or God? Or am I trying to please people? If I were still trying to please people, I would not be a servant of Christ."* (Gal. 1:10) Giving grace towards others, as God gives it to you, will set you free to forgive others, and then you are free to allow others to be who they are even when they are different from you.

Grace is more significant than legalism. Legalism is satan's theology, the definition of which is to keep man-made religious rules to obtain righteousness with God. You can't live under grace and law at the same time. If you can be saved by what you do, Christ died in vain. You are not held by what you do, but by whom you know - Jesus Christ, the Son of the living God.

Grace loves the unlovable. Grace is showing mercy to the merciless. Grace is offering good to those who are bad. Grace forgives the unforgivable. Does this describe you, or can you only love those people who love you? 1 John 4: 8 says, *"Whoever does not love does not know God, because God is love."*

*"A new command I give you: Love one another. As I have loved you, so you must love one another."* (John 13:34)

*Life* is a test... Are you more in the business of pleasing people or pleasing God?

## Grace (Part 3 of 3)

Granting forgiveness without a change in conduct makes the grace of God an accomplice to evil. People sin repeatedly and claim they are covered by grace. We can't go through life continually sinning, doing whatever we want, going to church on Sunday and polishing our halos, confessing our sin, and then going back and doing it all over again. It's not only being dumb but also an insult to the cross. Do you remember what Jesus said when He called out the woman in adultery? He forgave her and said, *"go and sin no more."* (John 8:11) Jesus administered forgiveness, but He expected her to change. That is what the word repent means; "change." *"But where sin increased, grace increased all the more."* (Rom. 5:20)

If you believe that Jesus Christ is the son of God, and the cross is the basis of forgiveness, that Holy Spirit inspired the Word of God and that you have confessed your sins and asked Jesus Christ into your life, then you are saved by grace. If someone else has done that, they are saved by grace too; therefore, we have no right or authority to judge them and speak ill of them.

*"For if, by the trespass of the one man, death reigned through that one man, how much more will those who receive God's abundant provision of grace and the gift of righteousness reign in life through the one man, Jesus Christ!"* (Rom. 5:17)

*"For sin shall no longer be your master, because you are not under the law, but under grace."* (Rom. 6:14)

*Life* is a test... Are you making excuses for your sin, or owning your mistakes and trying to change?

*Life* is a test...

# Christianity is a Covenant Relationship.
## (Part 1 of 4)

Christians are in covenant with God, so what does the word "covenant" mean? It comes from the Hebrew word "Berith," the root of which means "to cut." In the time of the Bible, covenants were very, very personal, significant and binding. If you gave someone your absolute assurance that you would do something or commit to a specific action, then you would make what was called a blood covenant, which was pledging your life. The process involved killing an animal - a calf or sometimes a bird - and then cutting the body in half. They would place each half of the animal on the ground, and then both "parties to the contract" would walk between the halves of the dead-blooded animal. As they did that, both people were pledging themselves in the covenant. The pledge said, "if I fail to keep this covenant, may the thing that has happened to this animal happen to me!" A blood covenant was considered a grave matter and not rescindable. It was "a done deal." Usually, it was a life-long commitment to watch out for each other, protect each other, and provide for each other. It was not a matter to be taken lightly by either contracting party.

Why blood? This miracle fluid that runs through our bodies is the basic foundation of our operation. It is the "river of life" which, if it fails, the entire body fails. God decreed that blood was sacred and not to be consumed as it is life itself. (Deut. 12:23)

**Doc's Book Club:** Read *"A Divine Revelation of the Powerful Blood of Jesus: Healing for Your Spirit, Soul, and Body"* by Mary K. Baxter.

*Life* is a test... In volume 1, I devoted a few days to writing about the power of blood in the Bible. Have you studied the power and significance of blood in the Bible?

# Christianity is a Covenant Relationship.
## (Part 2 of 4)

This same solemn blood covenant between two people is the same kind of commitment that God made with Abraham and his offspring. That includes you and I! Why? Gal. 3:29 says, *"If you belong to Christ, then you are Abraham's seed, and heirs according to the promise."* As Christians, we are adopted and born-again into the family of Abraham, which means we receive all the benefits from the original covenant God made with him. What was the covenant? *"So the Lord said to him, "Bring me a heifer, a goat and a ram, each three years old, along with a dove and a young pigeon. When the sun had set, and darkness had fallen, a smoking firepot with a blazing torch appeared and passed between the pieces. On that day, the Lord made a covenant with Abram and said, 'To your descendants I give this land, from the Wadi of Egypt to the great river, the Euphrates.'"* (Gen. 15 9-10; 17-18 edited for space)

In a nutshell, God said, "may I cease to exist if I fail to keep this covenant!" That was the first covenant, and many more of them can be found through the Bible. God is in a covenant relationship with you! The Bible is a covenant book, God's plan is a covenant plan, and His blessings are covenant too. When a person comes to know Jesus as their Lord and Saviour, they enter into a covenant relationship with the God of the universe! Of course, this comes with conditions for us, and we must understand what makes the covenant.

*Life* is a test... Have you thought about the strength of the Covenant that God has with you?

# Christianity is a Covenant Relationship.
## (Part 3 of 4)

Just as you gave your word and turned your life over to God, He gives you His Word and is absolutely committed to you. This means that you literally laid down your life for your covenant partner which is what Jesus did for you! He gave His life for you, and God asks for nothing more and nothing less when you are born-again. Romans 8:32 says, *"He who did not spare his own Son, but gave him up for us all - how will he not also, along with him, graciously give us all things?"*

Translated in no uncertain terms is if you walk with God in covenant, there is no blessing that He will withhold from you. What the conditions are for us is that we must be absolutely committed to Him as covenant "goes both ways." We can't live our own life and then when we get in trouble, cry out to God and ask Him to fix the mess. Covenant partners make a pledge and commitment to each other and put the interests of the other party ahead and above their own. Then from this mutual blood-borne commitment, every covenant blessing from God flows! Therefore, we can say and know how much Jesus loves us; enough to become a sacrificial lamb on the cross and shed His blood for us.

*Life* is a test... When you decree God's Word, there is power in phrases like *"in the Name of Jesus; by the blood of the lamb."* Use it!

# Christianity is a Covenant Relationship.
## (Part 4 of 4)

So what's in it for us? The list is endless, and I don't have enough space. However, here's a summary:

**1.** Entrance into the Kingdom of God, which is a form of government.
**2.** Authority in that government gives you power over satan and all his demons.
**3.** Your spirit (now regenerated) and soul (mind, will and emotions) never die, so "you" will live forever. However, your body dies, and when that day comes, you will be granted entrance into paradise known as "heaven."

Psalm 103 has a good list of the rest of the covenant benefits:

**4.** Upon your conversion to Christ, which is your part of the covenant deal, He immediately washes your sins with His blood and forgives you.
**5.** He heals all your diseases.
**6.** He redeems your life from destruction and keeps you safe.
**7.** He crowns you with loving-kindness and compassion.
**8.** He satisfies your desires with good things.
**9.** Your youth is renewed like the Eagles.

It sounds like a real deal to me! Therefore, you have no fear of death if you are in the covenant.

*"For to me, to live is Christ and to die is gain."* (Phil. 1:21-23)

*"Jesus said to her, "I am the resurrection and the life. The one who believes in me will live, even though they die, and whoever lives by believing in me will never die."* (John 11:25-26)

*Life* is a test... Can you think of a better contract than this one?

# THE BLESSING

In the **NAME** of **JESUS,** I bless you with the **PROMISES** of **GOD,** which are **YES** and **AMEN.** I pray the **HOLY SPIRIT** will make you **HEALTHY** and **STRONG** in **BODY, MIND** and **SPIRIT** and move you in **FAITH** and **EXPECTANCY.**

May **GOD'S ANGELS** be with you to **PROTECT** and **KEEP YOU.**

**GOD BLESS YOU WITH:**

- **ABILITY, ABUNDANCE,** and an assurance of **HIS LOVE** and **GRACE**
- **CLEAR DIRECTION** and a **CONTROLLED** and **DISCIPLINED LIFE**
- **COURAGE** and **CREATIVITY**
- **SPIRITUAL PERCEPTION** of **HIS TRUTH**
- **GREAT FAITH, HIS FAVOUR** and **MAN'S**
- **GOOD HEALTH** and a **GOOD (AND GODLY) SPOUSE**
- **HANDS** to **BLESS OTHERS**
- **HAPPINESS, FULFILLMENT, CONTENTMENT, HOPE,** and a **GOOD OUTLOOK ON LIFE**
- **A LISTENING EAR, LONG LIFE** and an **OBEDIENT HEART TO THE SPIRIT OF GOD**
- **HIS PEACE, PLEASANT SPEECH,** and a **PLEASANT PERSONALITY**
- **PROMOTION, PROTECTION, PROVISION, SAFETY** and **STRENGTH**
- **FINANCIAL SUCCESS**
- **TRUST AND WISDOM**

**AND MAY GOD BLESS YOU WITH:**

Goodness and mercy following you all the days of your life, that you might dwell in the house of the Lord forever.

The Lord bless you and keep you.
The Lord makes His face shine upon you and be gracious to you.
The Lord turns His face towards you and gives you peace.

I bless you in the Name of the Father, the Son, and the Holy Spirit. **AMEN.**

**The Blessings that you receive when you make that covenant with Jesus!**

"The Blessing" Poster can be downloaded and printed in any size for $7.95 CAD

**www.newstartministries.ca**

# Firstfruits

God promised that if we honour Him by giving Him the firstfruits, the best of our harvest (what we earn), He will keep us and bless us. It's important to understand that the tithe comes first, 1/10 of everything you earn, which He owns, and then a firstfruits love offering of whatever is your best. It doesn't have to be something of large size just something that's meaningful. It is most interesting that the firstfruit is the thing that "puts you over the edge" beyond the tithe and brings in such a massive blessing.

What makes firstfruits so significant? It shows God how much we are honouring Him. Essentially what we are saying is, "Lord, I'm giving to you my first, my best, and by doing so, putting you first in my life!" It says we are to *"Honour the Lord with your wealth, with the firstfruits of all of your crops; then your barns will be filled to overflowing, and vats will brim over with new wine."* (Prov. 3:9-10) *"Seek first His Kingdom and all His righteousness, and all these things shall be added to you."* (Matt. 6:33 NKJV)

Firstfruits are one of the foundational principles of the Kingdom of God. Some people assume that the concept of firstfruits is just in the Old Testament, but it is not; it is all throughout the Bible. In Paul's letter to the Corinthians, we see that Jesus is the "firstfruit" of a new creation. (1 Cor. 15:20) Then, in his letter to the Romans, he says, *"For if the firstfruit is holy, the lump is also holy..."* (Rom. 11:16 NKJV). We go through life with mundane things consuming our time; then, we figure out how to fit God into our lives. We have this all backwards - we need to give God the first of everything we do, including our time and our money.

*Life* is a test... Are you honouring God with firstfruits?

## Tomorrow and tomorrow and tomorrow*

" I don't know what tomorrow holds, but I do know who holds tomorrow." I'm not sure where this quote came from, but a friend sent it to me one day, and I liked it (if anyone knows where this quote originates, please let me know; thanks). None of us know what tomorrow holds, so why would anyone seek fortune-tellers and read horoscopes? (or "horror scopes," as I call them!) The experts who study financial markets cannot predict the stock market, but some make a lot of money selling their advice. Go figure... There is, however, someone that does know about tomorrow in very great detail. Holy Spirit! As a Christian, you have the right and the ability to sit down with God and have a chat anytime you want. Furthermore, there is no way that we can know the future, so why would we spend our time figuring it out and fussing about it?

What's the bottom line? Trust... Yes, it is hard to trust God; it probably is one of the most complex parts of being a Christian. Why? Because we want to be in control all the time, and the root of that is pride, which is the root of all sin. It's a vicious circle! The answer? Give it up! Turn it over to Him, and then go and have a good night's sleep. *"Trust in the Lord with all your heart and lean not on your understanding; in all your ways submit to Him, and He will make your paths straight."* (Prov. 3:5-6) *"Come to me, all you who are weary and burdened, and I will give you rest. Take my yoke upon you and learn from me, for I am gentle and humble in heart, and you will find rest for your souls. For my yoke is easy and my burden is light."* (Matt. 11:28-30)

*L*ife is a test...  Are you worrying about tomorrow or living one day at a time and trusting Him?

\* Macbeth, act 5, scene 5

# Be Careful of Judging.

When we judge others, we run the risk of exposing our sin. If you point out another person's sin, be careful that God does not reveal your own! The bible says, *"Whoever would foster love covers over an offence."* (Prov. 17:9)

Case in point: Elijah got off track. He ran from Jezebel and was depressed and suicidal. This is the same mighty man of God that slew the prophets of Baal and called down fire from heaven. We can see a good life from reading and studying Elijah until he prayed against Israel. *"God did not reject his people, whom he foreknew. Don't you know what Scripture says in the passage about Elijah - how he appealed to God against Israel."* (Rom. 11:2) My point?

When a prophet/intercessor starts praying "against" anyone, they are no longer praying the will of God. We pray "for" people, not "against" them. If we pray "against," then we open the door to manipulation and control, which the bible says is like witchcraft. We are to pray "for" people in such a way that if they do not respond, then we pray for God to remove them as an impediment. For example, rather than pray "against" a political leader who is sinning which is against the Word of God, pray for them to see the light of God and for God to remove them. We have no right to pray against them as a person, or anyone else for that matter. Judging is not our job. Holy Spirit's job is to convict, God's job is to forgive, and our job is not to judge but to love.

*Life* is a test... Are you praying for or against others?

## Check These Out!

I thought that I would do something a bit different today.

Every so often I run across websites that I find are quite significant in terms of how God is moving worldwide. Have a look at these under a sub-menu called "Websites Worth Watching" on my website. Also, while you're at it, check out the videos under "Videos Worth Watching." Enjoy...

1. https://www.allpeoplefree.com
2. https://www.sentinelgroup.org
3. https://www.hoperadio.net

*Life* is a test... It's my birthday today, and to celebrate it, there is no test today!

## A Question to ask God, every day.

We need to view each day as an adventure! God, what do you have planned for me today? What will You reveal to me about your world, yourself, and me? Perhaps instead of religiously (pun intended) letting your day timer run your life, be attentive to what He says. He can be trusted. You can confide in Him as He is your guide and counsellor. Share your dreams with Him, which empowers Him to bring them to pass. Remember that prayer is just having a conversation with Him, with you doing most of the listening.

A life lived in "constant contact" with Him will never be dull! It won't be predictable, either! Each day, you can expect Him to surprise you with something, and it may not always be what you want, but it will be what is best for you - maybe being late for something saved your life.

Case in point: after the twin Trade Centre Towers in New York City came down in 2001, testimonies surfaced weeks later from many Christians who were unexpectedly delayed getting to their jobs in the towers that day. God spoke to one lady who was a block away from entering her office in one of the Towers, and God told her to turn around and run the opposite way. Good thing that she was in constant contact! Rather than getting frustrated when you are delayed, accept it as the grace of God. Perhaps being late for a meeting protected you from a car accident!

Before you even get out of bed tomorrow, ask God about the day He has planned for you!

*Life* is a test... Who is going to plan your tomorrow? You or Him?

## The Five-fold Ministry.

God is in the process of rebuilding His Ekklesia. Ephesians 2:20 states that the church's foundation *"shall be built upon the foundation of first, apostles and then prophets."* Apostles are burning to see people work together and yearn for unity. An Apostle always sees the bigger picture and what's everyone to work together.
An Apostle is very visionary – he makes declarations about people and speaks with authority.

A Prophet's sole purpose in life is to ask, "how can I hear God more clearly?" He seeks God through dreams and visions and wants to know God's heart and purpose. Next, Teachers who love truth and the Word have a hunger for education and meaning; "what is God trying to teach me?" Fundamental in thought, Teachers have firm foundations for themselves, and a breach of that is serious, a loss of honour! A Pastor has a genuine concern for others; "empathy and compassion" is his "middle name." He wants to know how others are doing and wants to help them. The role of the Pastor is to comfort the sheep. The Evangelist has a burning passion for those who do not know Jesus and loses sleep over it! He is always looking for an opportunity to witness.

In many cases around us, we see a sad reality: Churches that could be growing are stagnant or shrinking. One of the reasons for this is that churches aren't helping people step into their callings and Gifts, which would enable them to have the capacity to take care of more people. God wants churches to grow, and He wants Spiritual Gifts to flourish in the church as it expands so it can multiply in size!

*Life* is a test... What Gifts do the people in charge at your church have?

## The Blessing Realm.

Did you know that you were the apple of Father's eye? What does every dad want to do? Spoil his kids; Jehovah is no exception.

Imagine yourself walking in abundant blessings every day. God is a blessing God and wants you to overcome and be blest beyond measure. Jesus said, *"Repent, for the Kingdom of Heaven has come near."* (Matt. 3:2) Why repent? So that He can bless you! Yes, you can have it all now; your body does not need to die first. The Kingdom of Heaven is a spiritual realm place, and its foundation is love. (i.e., *"For God so loved the world that He..."* John 3:16). It is a place of God's presence that you can experience anytime you wish.

God's plan and His heart's desire that we live in and connect to this realm while we are still here on earth. That is why Jesus prayed back to Father, *"Your Kingdom come, Your will be done, on earth as it is in heaven."* (Matt. 6:10)

Before Adam fell, mankind lived in the fulness of the blessing. Jesus came back as the second Adam (1 Cor. 15:45) to get us "back on track." Jesus declared that we were to be blest with every spiritual blessing in the heavenly realms, with everything we would need about life (Eph. 1:3; 2 Peter 1:2-4).

Get close to the spiritual realm through praise and worship and then sit back and wait for the blessings to come.

**Doc's Book Club:** Read *"The Blessing"* by Kenneth Copeland.

*Life* is a test... Can you walk in the blessing every day? YES!

*Life* is a test...

## The Month of Nisan* (Mar/Ap) - Part 1 of 3)

**Appointed Times:** Passover, Unleavened Bread and Firstfruits.
**Alphabet:** The letter is "HEI," which signifies a sort of violent praise. To the Jews, the letter Hei pictured the wind blowing through a lattice over a window. Prophetically this means a window with the wind of God blowing down into you every year.
**Tribe:** Judah; means praise; a month of thanking God for deliverance.
**Characteristics:**
- Repentance, redemption, and the beginning of miracles.
- This is a month for you to watch your speech and a time to put your best foot forward.
- Passover means miracles, redemption and repentance from a cold season.
- Jesus died on Passover, and He became the Passover lamb and rose on the day of firstfruits.
- It is a beginning month and also the month of the Exodus (read about it in the Book of Exodus).
- Nisan is a month to align your life to receive an abundant harvest.
- Praising God is an act of warfare, so expect warfare this month.
- Celebrate the Passover Lamb (Jesus), a time when heaven and earth connect.
**Constellation:** Aires the Ram (Lamb)
**Colour/Stone:** Blue Topaz
**Scripture:** The Book of John

Initially, the Hebrew year started in the month of Tishri. However, when God initiated Passover, He put Israel into a yearly redemption cycle and commanded that Nissan now be the first month. The first commandment was given to the newly born nation when they prepared to leave Egypt. *"This month, the month of Nissan, shall be for you, the first of the months."* (Ex. 12:2) (Note: The Head of the Year- aka New Years - is celebrated in the fall during Tabernacles).

"Nisan" has nothing to do with a car!

## The Month of Nisan (Mar/Ap - Part 2 of 3)

Through watching the stars and the moon's position, the Israelites could tell time, the seasons, and the months. This is not "astrology." It is "astronomy," and God called us to watch the heavens. This month is associated with the constellation of Aries, the ram (i.e., lamb), which is very appropriate for Passover. The heavens are declaring God's glory! God created the stars in heaven as markers in the sky (Gen 1:14).

Nissan is the month to declare, "Spring has come!" * It's a month for harvest, miracles, and a time to enter the Passover celebration. It's a month that sets the course for your future. Come before God in praise and let the wind of God open a portal of blessing over you.

Passover is a turning point; it's a time for the church to come out of concealment and rise in power! Repent of anything that you have put your trust in that is not of God. Declare that the blood of Jesus, our Passover lamb, releases a fresh anointing for healing and miracles in the church. God is ready to lead His church out of Egypt (any bondage you and the church are in). God says, *"Let my people go... to worship Me."* (Ex. 8.1)

This is the month of redemption, so you would want to be sure to ask God to tell you His redemptive plan for your life; He has a plan for you! (Jer. 29:11) Redemption means a price was paid for you, which unlocks every prison door that held you captive.

The story of the original Passover and the Exodus of the Jews from bondage in Egypt can be found in Ex. 12. Passover was a foretelling or prequel to the true Passover Lamb, the Lamb of God that takes away the sin of the world, Jesus who died on a cross for us (John 1:29).

* It is definitely not spring here in Alberta and many other parts of North America and Europe! However, it is spring in Israel.

*Life* is a test...

## The Month of Nisan (Mar/Ap - Part 3 of 3)

Nissan is the month of the beginning of miracles. God has called some of you to operate in miracles, which are part of your gifting and destiny. We are all called to lay hands on others and pray for healing and deliverance. Speaking our thankfulness to God for our deliverance is crucial during this month.

If you make negative confessions during Nisan, you will have trouble the rest of the year. Negative confessions will take seed in you instead of positive confessions grabbing the wind and changing your spiritual atmosphere and blessings. I have repeatedly written about the subject of watching your words!

Nisan is a month of financial importance - especially among those who are in leadership/governing positions. Nisan is the controller month. A business enterprise or institution controller is the chief accounting officer who can guide or manage economic activities and performance. Our nation's tax system is linked to this month which is no coincidence. Tithing and honouring God with offerings and firstfruits opens the door for supernatural payment of debt.

**Understanding the tribe of Nisan and how to pray to be in alignment with God this month.**

Pray and ask the Lord to give you strategies to be rightly aligned in these times. If you submit to the Lord and are in the right place at the right time, your life will align with God's purposes and plans. Those who do not celebrate Passover fail to remember where they have come from and thank God for bringing them out of the bondage of sin. Thank God for how He continues to deliver us.

*Life* is a test... Have you ever celebrated Passover? Unlike modern Easter celebrations, it's totally biblical. Study the origins of Easter and then compare it to Passover.

## Life is Difficult; get used to it.

Life is not easy for anyone. Avoiding pain and challenging times does not work because it catches up with us. It seldom works anyway. Jesus said that we would face problems, so what is the solution?

Don't pray that life gets easier, but rather pray for the strength and wisdom to get through the tough times. Don't pray for fewer problems; pray for more skills. Don't pray for fewer challenges; they are what make you grow.

As you journey through life with God, gain confidence that as you grow with Him, the two of you, as a team, can handle anything! This wisdom comprises three parts, promises in the Bible (of which there are 8,810), your relationship with God, and then there is your wisdom and experiences in life from the past hopefully, past experiences and mistakes you've learned from! If not, you are destined to repeat them, which is OK; sometimes, we need to go through the same things more than once.

Look back on life and see how Jesus was walking with you hand and hand and helped you through difficult times. You might think, "yes, but that was then...." Well, God is the same yesterday, today and tomorrow (Heb. 13:8), which is the basis for your confidence (in Him, not you!) In His presence, you live and move and have your being (Acts 17:28).

*Life* is a test... What are you praying for? An easier life or God's will?

# What Are You Thinking About?

What occupies your mind, most of the time, becomes your God. Perhaps the thing on your mind is worry. If you routinely begin to worry and you create a habit of it, it may become a stronghold in your mind created by fear and sin. Over time these strongholds can become idols in our lives.

Or perhaps what you think about is sports. There is nothing wrong with sports as physical activity or entertainment until it becomes all-encompassing in your life - an obsession if you like. Then a harmless, even beneficial activity becomes your God. I have met people throughout my life who are completely infatuated with their sports team, their hobby, or the sporting activity they are engaged in. Some people can't function without a daily trip to the gym or must ride their bike for 10 km. Health is essential, but not when it takes precedence over faith. Any interest can become the centre of a person's life. Jesus said that He wants to be the centre.

God is not a killjoy Father! He wants us to be blest, happy, healthy - prosperous in every way. He asks us a question; Do you want all of this through your methodology or mine? Submit to Me, resist the devil, (James 4:7), live my way, and I will give you the desires of your heart (Prov. 37:4) Life is a battle, and I will train you as a warrior, protect you from satan, and give you your marching orders as a soldier in my army" (Matt 28:19). Rehearsing your troubles and turning activities into obsessions is putting other things in your life first, instead of Me.*

*"You shall have no other gods before me."* (Ex. 20:3-5)

*Life* is a test... What's on your mind? Are you obsessed with anything?

*My paraphrase of God speaking.

## The Third Fruit of the Spirit - Peace
### (Part 1 of 5)

*"The tongue also is a fire, a world of evil among the parts of the body. It corrupts the whole body, sets the whole course of one's life on fire, and is itself set on fire by hell."* (James 3:6) What causes the majority of life's problems? Our mouths...

It is responsible for division, strife, arguments, divorces, entire wars; the list goes on. What does the Word of God tell us to do? At the first sign of strife, be a peacemaker. *"Blessed are the peacemakers, for they will be called children of God."* (Matt 5:9) Considering that Jesus said that we had to come to Him like little children (Matt. 18:3), I guess the best way to be a child is to be a peacemaker.

The ideal way to handle strife is to counteract it in one of two ways. First, with love; then, if you're not getting anywhere, simply walk away until everybody cools down. Use your faith, smile, and be like water on a fire. Praising God for all things in life tends to defuse the situation. Pray for good things to happen to others.

Here is a prayer for you: "Lord, help me to set a guard over my mouth and keep watch over the door of my lips" (Ps. 141:3). Please help me keep my spiritual antenna up to discern the beginnings of strife and therefore be on guard so that I do not fall into the trap of participation in the enemy's plan. Give me the strength and wisdom in guidance to be a peacemaker in every situation."

*"Praise God in all things."* (1 Thess. 5:18)

*Life* is a test... Are you a peacemaker or a warmonger?

# The Third Fruit of the Spirit - Peace
## (Part 2 of 5)

What is peace? How do we define it? Many would say it is the absence of strife or difficulty. I would argue that that doesn't necessarily paint the full picture. If you are too tired to fight, that does not give you peace. Peace is not absolute tranquility, the removal of risk and responsibility, nor the total security or absence of problems and tension. People think that if they can just get more money, a better job, or accomplish some task in life, they will have happiness and peace. But it never works out that way. As long as you're alive, there will be problems; battles to fight, victories to win, and some to lose.

The only thing we can do is what Jesus told us to do in Matt. 16:24: *"Then Jesus said to His disciples, 'Whoever wants to be my disciple must deny themselves and take up their cross and follow me.'"*

In other words, pick up the task that He has called you to do, which is the start of life itself. There are mountains to climb and giants in your life to defeat. You have responsibilities to do and principles to conquer. Why? You are a warrior; you were born into the battle zone of life and the army of God. Too many people will say, "well, I am not a warrior; I'm just an old sinner, saved by grace..." Well, you were an old sinner, and you were saved by grace, but now you're born again into the army of God! Christ did not die for you to crawl your way to heaven wearily! Read Rom. 3: 22-27.

*Life* is a test... Are you stuck in the "old sinner mentality?" Then get unstuck!

## The Third Fruit of the Spirit - Peace
### (Part 3 of 5)

Some people say Christianity is a crutch or a reprieve from reality. No! The Christian faith of the Bible is a set of blueprints to show you how to engage life's challenges. It's a call to war to learn, grow and conquer, not a call to be a crutch or a call to death. Christianity is not escapism. It's engagement. Christianity is converting adversity into opportunity. It takes back what satan has taken and returns it to its rightful owner. You! Christianity is about giving and forgiveness. It's about fighting the good fight of faith without giving up until victory is won. Christianity is about resisting the devil so that he can flee from you. Christianity knows that nothing is impossible without Christ. Christianity is about counting it all joy. Christianity is about victory and peace which is ours through faith in Jesus Christ. Phil. 4:7 says, *"And the peace of God, which transcends all understanding, will guard your hearts and your minds in Christ Jesus."* How? Why?

You can be happier in the combat zone of life than you can in the comfort zone because comfort does not bring peace. You can be more comfortable in the lion's den with Daniel than you can be living like a wealthy king. You can be more comfortable in the fiery furnace of life when the fourth person standing next to you is Jesus Christ than the coward standing outside saying no to Him. There can be more peace in the battle than sitting on the sidelines. The only catch is simply letting go of your agenda and heading into battle with Jesus at your side. There is peace in all your battles and even in death. Death? Yes, because it says in John 11:25, *"I am the resurrection and the life. The one who believes in me will live, even though they die."* (John 11:25)

Remember that your last breath here is your first breath in heaven, and it's better there than here.

*Life* is a test.... Is being a Christian for you like having a crutch, or is it a way of life?

# The Third Fruit of the Spirit - Peace
## (Part 4 of 5)

Yes, Jesus is indeed the Prince of Peace, (Is. 9:6) but he did not come to give us peace. Jesus knew that there would never be complete peace. He said in Matt 10:34, *"Do not suppose that I have come to bring peace to the earth. I did not come to bring peace, but a sword."*

What Jesus meant in saying this was that a sword divides, and Jesus Christ is the divider of everything on earth. He divides weeds from tares, sheep from goats, light from the darkness. He tells us to choose the broad or narrow way and speak truth. Each day you can be separated either into being a disciple of Jesus Christ or a slave to satan. Paul said in Romans 5:1, *"Therefore, since we have been justified through faith, we have peace with God through our Lord Jesus Christ,"* This is not possible without total surrender to Him. Therefore, it is only for the people that choose Jesus to be the Lord of their lives. There is no peace for the wicked. Look at what Isaiah 57:21 says, *"'But the wicked are like the tossing sea, which cannot rest, whose waves cast up mire and mud. There is no peace,' says my God, '"for the wicked.'"*

*Life* is a test... Are you giving your day to be a disciple of Christ or a slave to satan?

# The Third Fruit of the Spirit - Peace
## (Part 5 of 5)

Peace is a gift from God, and He gives it only to those who kneel to His son Jesus Christ and confess Him as Lord of their life. Peace is the opposite of hatred. So, what's the answer? God, of course.

Where is peace found? It is never mentioned in the Bible as a goal of life. Instead, peace is the consequence of something; the fruit of the Spirit is peace. Peace is the fruit of reconciliation. In every man, there is a conscience. Nothing marks a person more without peace than guilt. It will follow you wherever you go until you confess it to God and get your life turned around. *"Peace I leave with you; my peace I give you. I do not give to you as the world gives. Do not let your hearts be troubled, and do not be afraid."* (John 14:27)

We are to be the peacemakers, and we are to change the world and not allow the world to change us. Peacemaking is proactive; a decision to do something instead of talking about it. People say, "well, I just can't forget." Well, yes, you can, you just don't want to. To make peace, confess all sin before God, take responsibility for your life decision, seek righteousness and honesty, and all things and peace will come. Don't forget, *"Blessed are the peacemakers, for they will be called children of God."* (Matt.5:9)

*Life* is a test... Do you have a reputation as a peacemaker?

## You have an Invitation! (Part 1 of 3)

*"For my thoughts are not your thoughts, neither are your ways my ways," declares the Lord. "As the heavens are higher than the earth, so are my ways higher than your ways and my thoughts than your thoughts."* (Is. 55:8-9)

Some people are intimidated by this scripture and regard it as a "limiting passage." They think that because they don't think like God, they can't possibly communicate with Him or get to a high spiritual place and rest with Him. No, it's an invitation! How can that be? Simple; 1 Cor. 2:16 says, *"The mind of Christ is something all believers have, as the Apostle Paul said, and those who have the mind of Christ are able to discern spiritual things that the natural man (or the unbeliever) cannot understand or see."* John 12:40 says, *"He (aka satan) has blinded their eyes and hardened their hearts, so they can neither see with their eyes, nor understand with their hearts, nor turn - and I would heal them."* There would be a lot more healings in this world if people were not blinded to God by satan.

If you are born again and filled with Holy Spirit, then you automatically have access to the mind of Christ (Rom. 5:1-2; Acts 2:38). Through Holy Spirit, God has made us to be *"partakers of the divine nature"* (2 Peter 1:4) so that we can have all things that pertain to life and godliness through the knowledge of Himself.

*Life* is a test... Read the first chapter of 2 Peter.

## You have an Invitation! (Part 2 of 3)

The mind of Christ changes the way we think to understand and communicate with God Himself. We gain new desires and qualities, like compassion (Matt. 9:36), humility (Phil. 2:5), and other Fruits of the Spirit (Gal. 5:22-23). God gives us a new vision, new dreams, and a new purpose in life aligned with His (Luke 19:10), and we can see the reality before us that this world is temporary and messed up! The gospel's good news is that we are meant for an eternal world, so we do not love this world we presently are in. It is temporal, and it will end the day your body dies, then you will be with Jesus and out of here!

*"Do not love the world or anything in the world. If anyone loves the world, love for the Father is not in them. For everything in the world-the lust of the flesh, the eyes, and the pride of life - comes not from the Father but from the world. The world and its desires pass away, but whoever does the will of God lives forever."* (1 John 2:15-17)

How do we get this mind of Christ? Like everything else, through faith in Jesus Christ (John 1:12; John 3:16; 1 John 5:12). We receive a glorified existence:

*"To them, God has chosen to make known among the Gentiles the glorious riches of this mystery, which is Christ in you, the hope of glory."* (Col. 1:27)

*"Through him, we have also obtained access by faith into this grace in which we stand, and we rejoice in the hope of the glory of God."* (Rom. 5:2)

*Life* is a test... Is your mind growing into being more Christ-like?

## You have an Invitation! (Part 3 of 3)

This process of having the mind of Christ is not difficult to do. It is an open invitation to anyone who repents, confesses their sin, and asks Jesus into their life. However, that does not mean the "old you" goes away. We still give in to the lure of sin and can still be hindered by false doctrines (Gal. 5:7-12) and a spirit of religion. Likewise, we can choose to use our new life in unhealthy ways (Gal. 5:13-15). That is why we are to listen to what Paul said in Rom.12:2: *"I appeal to you, therefore, brothers, by the mercies of God, to present your bodies as a living sacrifice, holy and acceptable to God, which is your spiritual worship. Do not be conformed to this world, but be transformed by the renewal of your mind, that by testing you may discern what the will of God is, what is good and acceptable and perfect."*

Our minds need to be consistently renewed, rejecting the mind of the flesh, and accepting and being transformed into the mind of Christ. All who have the mind of Christ, those who belong to Him, will be sanctified (which means set apart) and changed into a new person that Holy Spirit leads.

*Nevertheless, God's solid foundation stands firm, sealed with this inscription: "The Lord knows those who are his, and, Everyone who confesses the name of the Lord must turn away from wickedness."* (2 Tim. 2:19) The process does not happen overnight; it takes a lifetime. *"....being confident of this, that he who began a good work in you will carry it on to completion until the day of Christ Jesus."* (Phil 1:6)

*ife* is a test... Have you accepted Jesus' open invitation to become more like Him every day?

# How Are You Responding to "Boiling Water?"

The same boiling water makes an egg hard and a potato soft.

The world changed considerably between 1900 and 1914 due to the industrial revolution. The world was then plunged into its first World War. Massive advancements followed this in technology, another World War, the cold war, computers, the internet, cell phones and then a significant change with the advance of terrorism worldwide, especially since 2001. Now we find ourselves in another world change starting with Covid 19 in 2020. *"The only constant in life is change"* - Heraclitus.

The question is, how are you responding to all of this? Satan knows that Jesus is on His way soon, so that's why we're seeing the world fall apart because satan knows that his time is limited (Rev. 12:12) and that he has lost (read the Book of Revelation - we win!) Why is he panicking and putting so much pressure, pain, destruction, and tribulation into the world? The best analogy I have come up with is this: when Hitler knew that he would lose the war, he instructed his armies to retreat and destroy everything in their path. What was the point of that if he knew he had lost? Because that's the way he thought, and I don't think there's any question that he was controlled by satan. Now we have a world filled with "boiling water."

How are you coping with the world's turmoil? Our only focus should be to concentrate on the Word of God. Here are three scriptures to help you with that: 2 Cor. 2:16-18; Deut. 31:6; Jos. 1:9. Check them out!

*Life* is a test... Are you a hard egg or a soft potato in this world of boiling water?

# The Seven Mountains. (Part 1 of 2)

(I have made reference in this book to the Seven Mountains of Cultural Influence. My editor has suggested that I need to explain this in greater detail. So Ed, here you go... What follows is my understanding as was taught to me by my mentor and spiritual father Peter Wagner. If anything is missing or incorrect, then would someone please correct me? Many thanks.)

Years ago, Loren Cunningham, the founder of YWAM (Youth with a Mission) and Bill Bright, the founder of Campus Crusade for Christ, had lunch together and discovered that God had both given them a similar download - showing them what has become known as the *"Seven Mountains of Cultural Influence:"* business, government, media, arts and entertainment, education, family, and the church. This concept was further prayed about and consequently taught by Lance Wallnau and Johnny Enlow. Peter heard it from Johnny, and he taught it to me at Glory of Zion in Texas. Although nonbelievers will refer to it as a movement which I disagree with, it gained popularity with the publication of Lance Wallnau and Bill Johnson's *"Invading Babylon: The 7 Mountain Mandate"* in 2013.

Followers claim that the Biblical base for this concept is derived from Revelation 17: 9 which reads, *"And here is the mind which hath wisdom. The seven heads are seven mountains."* (KJV) The detractors and the ones that condemn the "movement" or idea, think that the church believes that their mission to take over the world and is justified by Isaiah 2:2 *"Now it shall come to pass in the latter days that the mountain of the Lord's house shall be established on the top of the mountains."*

Well, not really. The church is not trying to take over the world or control every element of it, it is trying to influence it for the sole purpose of making disciples of all me. (Matt 28:19). That is our mission. As Peter said, "Christians do not have to be in charge of everything. It is just that the people who are in charge need to make decisions that reflect Biblical principles For example, if a Mormon where to be in high influence in the mountain of family that would be a good thing." (from my notes taken in Peter's class)

*Life is a test...*

## The Seven Mountains. (Part 2 of 2)

Each of us is spiritually gifted in different God-ordained areas. The question is, how are we using those Gifts to influence the Seven Mountains for Christ? What are we doing to become "change agents" to solve the world's problems? You can start at home in your own family, church and community. We need the desire and the faith to do it. Change your belief system, your finances, and how you spend your time in your life. Does it match God's plans? When you vote, do you vote for candidates that will make solid Biblical decisions?

**RELIGION:** With a plethora of categorized religions worldwide, it's the Church's responsibility to reach the lost with the love and Gospel of Jesus Christ and expand the Kingdom in ministerial efforts, nationally and internationally.

**FAMILY:** God is calling fathers and mothers (both spiritual and biological) to bring order to the chaos that the enemy has unleashed against families.

**EDUCATION:** A re-introducing of Biblical truth and Bible-centric values is the key to the renewal and restoration of the failing education system.

**GOVERNMENT:** We must see a shift in this arena to preserve the Christian heritage that Canada and many other countries were founded. The goal is to put righteous political leaders that will positively affect all aspects of government.

**ARTS/ENTERTAINMENT:** The arts and entertainment industries wield significant influence. The body of Christ needs powerful, righteous men and women unafraid to take their God-given talent into the arts and entertainment arenas.

**BUSINESS:** We believe it is the Lord's will to make His people prosperous and that He desires His Church to use its wealth to finance the work of Kingdom expansion. Simply put, prosperity with a purpose.

**MEDIA:** We believe it is the Lord's will to have the truth spoken and transmitted through the world.

We believe that the church is the foundation of the seven mountains, for Jesus said that *"upon this rock I will build my church; and the gates of hell shall not prevail against it."* (Matt. 16:18 KJV). Further God instructed Adam to *"have dominion"* (Gen. 1:26) and Jesus was the *"second Adam"* (1 Cor, 15:45) for the sake of continuance of that decree.

*Life* is a test... Which mountain do you see yourself influencing?

# It's None of Your Business!

To close this month and ride on the coattails of the last two days, I thought this was an excellent place to put this message. Do not concern yourself with what other people are doing. It's none of your business. They have free will to choose their course of action whether you agree with them. You are not judge or jury of them or anyone else except yourself. It is enough for us to pay attention to our behaviours and ensure that we walk in the light of Jesus regardless of what is happening around us. You focus on yourself; that's a full-time job.

God made you in His image; He loves you, cares for you, and is available to communicate with you 24/7. If we concern ourselves too much with others, we fall into the trap of judge mentalism.

*"...and to make it your ambition to lead a quiet life: You should mind your own business and work with your hands, just as we told you, so that your daily life may win the respect of outsiders and so that you will not be dependent on anybody."* (1 Thess. 4:11-12) *"Besides, they get into the habit of being idle and going about from house to house. And not only do they become idlers but also busybodies who talk nonsense, saying things they ought not to."* (I Tim. 5:13)

*"Who are you to judge someone else's servant? To their own master, servants stand or fall. And they will stand, for the Lord can make them stand."* (Rom. 14:4) *"So then, each of us will give an account of ourselves to God. "* (Rom. 14:12)

*Life* is a test... How are you doing at your full-time job of looking after yourself? (and minding your own business?)

*Life is a test...*

## The News Media.

We must be careful of the voices we are listening to. News media and social media seek to tell us all a story from a perspective and give us a set of answers that fits their prerogative. Whether you sit on one side of a particular political issue or the other, it's clear that the disunity that is spread even among Christians because of the finger-pointing, name-calling, and blame-shifting is extremely damaging. There are issues that should raise our eyebrows as Christians, no matter which side we lean towards! Be aware of what your "side" is saying and how they act. We show what we believe by how we act. Ensure it lines up with scripture! Case in Point: How can you vote for a candidate that supports abortion?

I would go so far even to say be careful where higher education comes from. Education without love or a sense of morality can do severe harm, whether it's from a Christian establishment or not. Many of the educated elite I've met that don't know God have hearts of stone. We must pray that these people turn to God, and He will fix their hearts. *"I will give them an undivided heart and put a new spirit in them; I will remove from them their heart of stone and give them a heart of flesh. Then they will follow My decrees and be careful to keep my laws. They will be my people, and I will be their God."* (Ez. 11:19-20)

We must not find all our answers in our governments either. I know that in Canada, we had quite a lot of disruption and governmental inconsistency with the handling of COVID-19, which I know frustrated many people - myself included! Whether we agree with the direction the nation is headed or not, we as a nation must hold our governments accountable if/when they lie and pray for them. Whether you believe our nation today looks like Germany in 1931 (a civil liberties lawyer friend told me this), or you're optimistic, we must be praying for our leaders and hold them accountable for what they say they'll do. Who is keeping them accountable?

*Life* is a test... Do you like where the country is going? If not, take action! Pray, send letters. Jesus never protested; He prayed.

## Are You Teachable? (Part 1 of 2)

If you are unteachable, God will take notice. You will never have to worry about God teaching you anything because He won't bother you.

*"Whoever loves instruction loves knowledge, But he who hates correction is stupid."* (Prov. 12:1)

*"The way of fools seems right to them, but the wise listen to advice."* (Prov. 12:15)

*"A wise son heeds his father's instruction, but a mocker does not respond to rebukes."* (Prov. 13:1)

If you are unteachable, then there is no correction in your life, and if there is no correction, then there is no direction (or you go the wrong direction). Think about what a navigator does in an airplane. He makes course corrections! No correction and you get the wrong direction! Without God's law, you have no vision and *"Where there is no vision, the people perish"* (Prov. 29:18), and there is no blessing.

Therefore, we must thank God in all things. We must thank Him for the teaching that is taking place, even if, at the time, that seems to be an impossible thing to do. Ask Him! "Lord, what are you trying to teach me in this _____ (experience, problem, pain crisis etc.)? When I reflect on my own life, I would say that my single personal success factor has been my ability to learn. I have had as many failures and made as many mistakes as the next guy (probably more), but I never quit, and I was(am) always teachable.

*Life* is a test... Does pride keep you unteachable?

## Are You Teachable? (Part 2 of 2)

How does Holy Spirit correct? Through Himself, through the Word of God and others.

If you are born again, Holy Spirit lives inside of you. When we stop, wait, seek Him, and listen, He will give us answers. However, it's up to us to decide whether we will receive those answers (aka wisdom) and thus be "teachable." Think about it. Only a fool would have a connection to someone (Holy Spirit) who can give them all the answers to anything but then sit back and not receive it and not learn from it.

No book in the world will give you more wisdom and revelation than the Holy Bible. It was inspired by Holy Spirit and written by men, a concept I had never really understood until I started writing books. If you had told me five years ago that I would be an author, I would've said you were smoking some powerful stuff! You are reading this book ONLY because of Holy Spirit's inspiration! Holy Spirit's inspired the Bible and continues to inspire you and me if we take the time to stop, listen and study the Word (Jos. 1:8).

Don't be inactive though while waiting for Holy Spirit to lead; get counsel from other wise Christian people too: *"Let the wise listen and add to their learning, and let the discerning get guidance."* (Prov. 1:5) *"The way of fools seems right to them, but the wise listen to advice."* (Prov. 12:15) *"Plans fail for lack of counsel, but with many advisers, they succeed."* (Prov. 15:22) However, make sure that you ask God to bring WISE people into your life that will not lead you astray.

*Life* is a test... Are you allowing yourself to be corrected?

# Don't Make Comparisons.

Recently, I have become a Harry Connick Jr. fan. He has class and professionalism, and I like his songs and musical arrangements. He is also a devout Roman Catholic. One of my favourite songs that he has recorded is "I Love You Just the Way You Are," which reminds me of how Jesus sees us...

Do you know what is remarkable about God? We don't have to try to be someone we are not. Like this song, God loves you "just the way you are!" Why wouldn't He? He created you; you are the apple of His eye even before the world was formed (Eph.1:4). He decided who and what you were to be and therefore loaded you with the necessary Spiritual Gifts and natural talents and called you *"for such a time like this"* (Es. 4:14) to be doing His will. Your job? To discover the hidden mysteries of your life - who you are - and then get to work living your life and fulfilling your call.

The worst thing that you can do is compare yourself to others. Why? You are you, and there is no one on this planet of 8 billion people who even resembles you. Making a comparison of you to others is an insult to God. Reject comparisons and the junk that goes with it - insecurity, jealousy, frustration. Embrace who God made you be, discover more about "you," and move forward with Him in blessing.

*"For we dare not class ourselves or compare ourselves with those who commend themselves. But they, measuring themselves by themselves, and comparing themselves among themselves, are not wise."* (2 Cor. 10:12)

*Life* is a test... Are you making comparisons between yourself and others?

# God Inhabits Our Praises!

When we go into our prayer closet, it seems that we can sometimes turn our prayers into a lamenting and begging time. "Oh God, why is this happening to me?" Or "Oh God, what do I do about_____? I don't want _____ to happen and I do want _____ to happen!"

Sound familiar? If you are not doing any or all the above now, you probably did at one time! Try this... *"Praise the Lord. Praise the Lord, Oh my soul. I will praise the Lord all my life; I will sing praise to my God as long as I live."* (Ps. 145: 1-2)

We are supposed to do this when we pray to God and talk with Him. God says that He *"inhabits the praises of His people."* (Ps. 22: 3 KJV) That being the case, it would make logical sense that the best way to do that is to forget the "bawling and squalling" technique and try the praise approach since He says that that is where He lives (inhabits).

You can try different types of praise. The "canned approach" is to list things you were thankful for and go for it! This is a measured and disciplined approach which is fine. God loves it! Then sometimes, just let the joy of the Lord, being in His presence, flow out of you. Joy and thankfulness in your heart leaves plenty of room for God. That's when the mysteries of your life and of the Bible are revealed. Answers come forth, and the blessings flow from the throne room of His heart into your heart. Then revelation knowledge comes!

*Life* is a test... How many ways can you think of to praise God?

## Why We Need to Worship.

*"For you, this whole vision is nothing but words sealed in a scroll. And if you give the scroll to someone who can read, and say, "Read this, please," they will answer, "I can't; it is sealed." Or if you give the scroll to someone who cannot read, and say, "Read this, please," they will answer, "I don't know how to read." The Lord says: "These people come near to me with their mouth and honour me with their lips,   but their hearts are far from me. Their worship of me is based on merely human rules they have been taught."* (Is. 29:11-13)

The vision and destiny for your life are written down in a document and sealed in the heavenly realms. Wouldn't you like to know what it says? How do we get it to open? Here's the answer: it's through worship. That's why the prophetic gifts can become activated in a church service. Worship unlocks the scrolls in the heavenly realms and brings forth the Word to the prophets. In Revelation 19:10, a man whom John encounters says, *"Worship God! For the testimony of Jesus is the spirit of prophecy!"* My point?

True worship unlocks the scrolls and gives us God's vision and heart for our future in the heavenly realms. True worship is not just honouring God with music through our lips, and mouths and instruments, but mainly from the inner depths of our hearts. Do you want to know God's plans for you? (Jer. 29:11) Get into your prayer room, shut off the noise of life, and just worship Him. Do this repeatedly; fast for a day or two as well. Continue, and your scrolls will be opened. Soon after that, revelation Words will flow.

*Life* is a test.... Would you like to know what God has planned for your life? Worship...

*Life is a test...*

## Clothed with God's Glory.

Adam and Eve were clothed with the glory of God. Allow me to explain. The human being is the only creature not clothed in the natural from the outside. Birds have feathers; mammals have fur, even reptiles have very thick skin. The crown of glory from God covered and protected Adam and Eve from the inside out, and that glory completely covered them. When they sinned, the light of God went out, and they discovered that they were naked. They had only seen each other in the glory of God, but now with no glory, they felt ashamed.

Deut. 30:6 says, *"The Lord your God will circumcise your hearts and the hearts of your descendants, so that you may love Him with all your heart and with all your soul, and live."* This means that God will cut away from your heart sin. In Gal. 2:20, it says that when we accepted Jesus as Lord, we *"were crucified with Christ and I no longer live, but Christ lives in me. The life I now live in the body, I live by faith in the Son of God, who loved me and gave himself for me."* The Word of God kills that old self, and then that coat of glory comes upon you in the spiritual realm.

You have been born again, your heart has had the sin cut out of it, and now you must decide to stay that way or fall back into your old ways. Choose to walk according to the fact that you have been clothed in the glory of God as Adam and Eve were! For God has clothed you as He did with Adam and Eve. Deut. 30:15-16 says, *"See, I set before you today life and prosperity, death, and destruction. For I command you today to love the Lord your God, to walk in obedience to him, and to keep his commands, decrees, and laws; then you will live and increase, and the Lord your God will bless you in the land you are entering to possess."* My point? "Life is a Test;" the test here is to see which one you will choose. God or the world.

*Life* is a test... What will you choose this day?

# God's Judgement Upon a Country
## (Part 1 of 4)

It's easy today to look around and think the world is a mess. We can find causes, but most of the time, it's hard to pinpoint exactly where things went sideways. I propose that how we got into this mess is because we fell away from God's Word. We can correct the situation by dedicating ourselves to the Word of God, repenting and following His laws.

**1.** The first commandment God gave a man and a woman in Genesis 1:28 was to have children ("bear fruit and multiply"). However, we now have a decreased population rate between economical fear, various sexual identity movements, and abortion. This brings trouble for the present and the future. When a nation's birth rate declines, the average age of that nation gets higher. Then, there are not enough young people working in the economy, paying taxes to support social security etc.

**2.** God gives a nation the leader it deserves.

We have certainly seen that in Canada in the last six years. I have written about "sheep and goat nations," and with many of the anti-God policies implemented by the government in Canada, we are now a goat nation. This is a form of judgment. How? God often gives a country a leader that reflects its people's sin and rebellious nature. The people of Israel desired to have a King, which God did not want. He gave in, and the people had nothing but one problem after the next. You can read about it in 1 Sam., 1 Kings and 2 Kings. Canada has always been a leader in the world for liberal policies that are anti-God, so we are getting exactly what we voted for.

# God's Judgement Upon a Country
## (Part 2 of 4)

**3.** This, of course, leads to a divided nation. Canada is no longer one nation under God as it was founded, but in my opinion, a large land-mass made up of five different countries or cultures. For example, most of Alberta is conservative as is British Columbia until you get to the Fraser Valley, where most of the population resides. Then suddenly, you get farther left and anti-God policies. I usually travel to the Fraser Valley once or twice a year, and honestly, I feel like I've gone to another country. Jesus said that *"a house divided against itself could not stand."* (Mark 3:5) When I was a kid, there was no such thing as protesting, and now it is regarded as a sanctified right of every Canadian even though it's nowhere in the Constitution or the Canadian Bill of Rights. When we see an increase in crimes within our cities, with people killing each other within their communities, protesters, and riots, it's just evidence of another form of judgment by God.

**4.** They become pleasure-seeking more than responsible citizens. Most of our young generation these days are focused on their rights without considering their responsibilities. In the book of Ezekiel, chapter 16, we see what happens when people disobey God. Verse 50 says, *"They were haughty and did detestable things before me. Therefore I did away with them, as you have seen."* We live in a "turned away from God generation" filled with self-centeredness, narcissism, a lack of morality, and the worst of it is that no one thinks any of this is wrong. Is. 5:20-21 says, *"Woe to those who call evil good and good evil, who put darkness for light and light for darkness, who put bitter for sweet and sweet for bitter. Woe to those who are wise in their own eyes And clever in their own sight."*

I don't mean these things to spread further unease or condemnation. I say them to raise conviction. Are we living these ways? Are we letting our family live these ways freely? We must be sensitive to the Spirit and His leading.

# God's Judgement Upon a Country
## (Part 3 of 4)

**5.** The nation has false prophets. Who is largely to blame? The answer may surprise you, but it's the church. It doesn't teach sin, and some have gone down the road of complete apostasy (which I taught in Volume 1 of *"Life is a Test,"* September 2-5). During the days of Jeremiah, false prophets prophesied that Jerusalem would have peace and safety even though they were about to be sacked by Babylon (Jer. 23:16-17). At that time, the false prophets outnumbered the true prophets, and we are seeing history repeat itself today. The Christian church sits idly by while the false liberal anti-God rhetoric makes headway in our country. Look how much change we've seen in the last two years: Churches are locked down, pastors are thrown in prison, over 60 churches burned to the ground, and no one can counsel anyone dealing with transgender issues, even if the person wants counselling! Meanwhile, pastors preach "feel good" messages, which may or may not have anything to do with the Word of God.

**6.** Innocent blood is shed.  Whether it be crime, riots, or abortion, God hates the shedding of innocent blood (Prov. 6:17). It defiles the land as we saw when Cain killed his brother (the land cried out - Gen. 4:10), and the whole country is defiled according to Numbers 35:30-34 when innocent blood is shed. Destruction will come to any nation unless there is massive repentance and laws change.

*Life* is a test...  Study Jer. 23 and Num. 35

*L*ife *is a test...*

# God's Judgement Upon a Country
## (Part 4 of 4)

**7.** The innocent and vulnerable become prey. God does not like bullies and the people that prey on the less fortunate. Whether it be people in poverty, victims of sex trafficking, illegal immigrants, victims of scams and crimes...the list goes on. No matter how we "slice and dice this," God's judgement is upon any nation that does not use His laws as its foundation. Canada, the USA, the UK, France, Germany, and many other first-world countries are now entirely polarized. Man cannot solve his problems. The solution?

*"...Return to the Lord your God, for He is gracious and compassionate, slow to anger and abounding in love, and he relents from sending calamity."* (Joel 2:13)

*"Return, Israel, to the Lord your God. Your sins have been your downfall!"* (Hosea 14:1)

*"Therefore tell the people: This is what the Lord Almighty says: 'Return to me,' declares the Lord Almighty, 'and I will return to you,' says the Lord Almighty."* (Zech. 1:3)

*"If you return to the Almighty, you will be restored: If you remove wickedness far from your tent."* (Job 22:23)

*"Let us examine our ways and test them, and let us return to the Lord."* (Lam. 3:40)

*L*ife is a test... Can you see the solution? It's in the Bible!

## This Too Shall Pass...

Let's face reality; life is not easy for anyone. Seemingly for some more than others, but life is about struggles, pain, failures - and *"Life is a Test."* (so I heard one time...) However, life goes so much better with Jesus in it!

There are seasons and cycles in life and times when we have a "low point." People hurt us, and we fall victim to trials, false accusations, rejection - the list goes on. Like Joseph, we are betrayed by family and thrown into the prison of heartache and pain.

These low points can, we allow it, turn your prison cell of pain into a cubicle of God's love. As always, turn to God; turn to one the one that can be there for you, take your pain away and set you free, the one who *"heals the brokenhearted"* (Ps. 147:3). Remember, Jesus holds the key to every door (Matt.19:19; Rev. 1:18), which includes the door to your healing. Jesus suffered pain and the darkness of separation from God, which means we don't have to. As any good father would, God wants to reveal His deepest love in your pain to give us the joyous victory we can have. He can use catastrophe to launch you into your most glorious triumph. Remember the story of Joseph? He went from prison to managing a master home, went back into prison and then, in 24 hours, went from the prison to the palace (see Gen. 37-50). Remember Joseph the next time you're at a "low point," this too shall pass. His strength will become yours, and His mercy will heal your whole wounded soul. You will rise again.

*"The Spirit of the Sovereign Lord is on me, because the Lord has anointed me to proclaim good news to the poor. He has sent me to bind up the brokenhearted, to proclaim freedom for the captives and release from darkness for the prisoners, to proclaim the year of the Lord's favor and the day of vengeance of our God to comfort all who mourn, and provide for those who grieve in Zion - to bestow on them a crown of beauty instead of ashes, the oil of joy instead of mourning, and a garment of praise instead of a spirit of despair."* (Is. 61: 1-3)

*Life* is a test... Have you studied the life of Joseph?

## Faith is the Way of Life. (Part 1 of 2)

For whom? Us! All those that have made Jesus the Lord of their lives. Why? Because the *"just shall live by faith"* (Heb. 10:38). What does "just" mean? According to the Canadian Oxford Dictionary, "just" means *"acting or done in accordance with what is morally right or fair."* A synonym would be "righteous," which means *"following religious or moral laws."* Therefore, for those that follow the laws of God, they are the "just."

Therefore, by our faith in God, all that we have in this life - spirit, soul and body - is in the Kingdom of God. Jesus said that the *"Kingdom of God is within you"* (Luke 20:21), and the way we access the Kingdom is through faith. Why and how? Well, when you were born again and baptized into the body of Christ, created in His image, you were given access by faith, genuine Bible faith - not wishing. Faith brings whatever is needed or wanted - *"the Lord is my shepherd I shall not want"* (Ps. 23) - out of the unseen world and causes it to manifest in the seen world. That is how God made the world, right from the start in Genesis chapter 1 when He *"spoke."*

Man's method is 180° in the opposite direction, for he seeks to be successful and prosperous through hard work by the sweat of his brow (Gen. 3:19). Notice that Proverbs 10:22 says, *"The blessing of the Lord makes one rich, And He adds no sorrow with it."* We are to live by faith and die by faith. It's the way of life. Living and dying is part of it - your body, not your spirit and soul. We are not to be afraid of death because we have already died. How? When you were born again, you died unto yourself, and that's the only dying you are ever going to do (John 3:3-7). When your body quits working, you will have the last breath on earth, immediately followed by your next breath in paradise, * where Jesus has a mansion for you designed to your liking waiting for you (John 14: 2-6).

*Life* is a test... Are you afraid of death? If so, why?

* I say that figuratively because I don't think spirits and souls actually breathe!

## Faith is the Way of Life. (Part 2 of 2)

Some people will say, "well, you never know when your number is up, and there is nothing you can do about it." The Bible says we will *"die at an appointed time."* Quoting verses like Heb. 9:27, *"Just as people are destined to die once, and after that to face judgment,"* to back it up. Well, yes and no. In Hebrews 9:26, it says that Jesus put away death; *"But he has appeared once for all at the culmination of the ages to do away with sin by the sacrifice of Himself."* In Prov. 3:1-2, it says, *"My son, do not forget my law, But let your heart keep my commands; For the length of days and long life And peace they will add to you."* That means you can add to the time of appointed death and take away from it. *"The wages of sin are death."* (Rom. 6:23) Sin will take you earlier than your appointed time. Nothing could be done to shorten or add to it if it was a set day. We die before the appointed time because of the abuse that we do to our bodies, the negative words we hear or speak about ourselves, the overeating, the poor diet, the lack of exercise etc. We die before time because of poor decisions, bad timing, not listening and being in constant contact with God. This leaves us open to being in the wrong place at the wrong time.

Deuteronomy 29:9 says, *"Therefore keep the words of this covenant, and do them, that you may prosper in all that you do."* Prospering then is not dying any sooner than you're supposed to. Although Paul indeed said, *"For to me, to live is Christ, and to die is gain"* (Phil 1:21), it does not mean we are to go prematurely. Why not get there soon? It is heaven, after all. Because God wants you here to work out your flesh issues and mostly to witness to others as we are all to be labourers in the end-time harvest. You can't do that if you are "there" instead of "here."

*Life* is a test...Are you keeping sin out to live a longer life?

# The Month of Iyar (Ap/May - Part 1 of 2)

**Alphabet:** The Letter is "VAV." It is a picture of a connecting pin. It means linking or connection. If you move correctly in Iyar, the rest of the year connects appropriately.

**Tribe:** Issachar; the month to understand the mysteries of God.

**Characteristics:** - Natural healing will manifest, dealing with processing thoughts, dealing with the soul's conscience, and receiving spiritual advice. *"I am God your healer."* (Ex. 15:26)

- This month is linked with light, which signifies increased revelation. Light is the opposite of darkness. This is the month you need to light up with His glory.

**Constellation:** Taurus (the bull). To the Hebrews, the bull was the symbol of strength. This constellation reminds you to find your place to increase your strength. We should be moving from strength to strength.

**Colour/Stone:** Royal Blue/Lapis

**Scripture:** Is. 60

This is the month that the Israelites transitioned from Egypt to Sinai. When they were blocked, they murmured and complained and complained about not having water, demonstrating a lack of trust and faith in God, who delivered them from Egypt (how soon they forgot!) As we transition this month from redemption at Passover to provision at Pentecost, it is a time to align with God; otherwise, you will be out of alignment for the rest of the year. It is also an excellent time to spring-clean the junk in your life!

When we rely upon the Lord, He is faithful to be there for us and lead us through the "hills and valleys of life." This month, there is an anointing for looking and observing to find a place of self-improvement so your strengths can manifest and increase. This month, choose to trust God and be determined to keep moving toward the goal. God says if you listen to Me, I will heal you, so ask God and keep asking. Israel did not pass all the tests, but it still made it. It is called grace! Believe God's promises, get moving, and don't murmur!

# The Month of Iyar (Ap/May - Part 2 of 2)

**Understanding the tribe of Iyar and how to pray and be in alignment with God this month.**

The month of Iyar is associated with your conscience, linked with your thought processes and emotions. The conscience is the overlaying window or "eye" between your spirit and soul. Therefore, this is the month God wants you to cleanse your conscience. If your conscience is not clean, a mesh will form that hinders the wind of His Spirit. Therefore, during the month of Iyar, you need to deal with your soul - your mind, will and emotions.

**1. God wants to reveal His mysteries to us** (Deut. 29:29; 1 Cor.4:1). Why does He have mysteries?

- To hide the truth from the devil. (1 Cor. 2:7-8)
- Our minds are too limited. (i.e., try to explain the Trinity to someone who has never heard it before!)
- To keep us looking in the Word for the answers (it keeps us hungry for Him).

**2. What mysteries?**

 - His whole plan for our salvation (Eph. 6:19).
 - Jesus coming to earth as a man (1 Titus 3:16).
 - Union of Jews and Gentiles in one body (Eph. 3).
 - Gentiles sharing in Israel's blessings (Eph. 3:6).
 - Our resurrection with immortal bodies (Cor. 15).
 - Israel's complete and final restoration (Rom.11:25).
 - That Jesus will rule everything (Eph.1:9 -10).
 - The union of man and woman in marriage (Eph. 5:31-32).
 - Jesus living in you through the Spirit (Col. 1:27).

*Life* is a test...Are you cleaning out your junk?

**www.newstartministries.ca**

# Deception; satan's Greatest Talent.

*"And even if our gospel is veiled, it is veiled to those who are perishing. The god of this age has blinded the minds of unbelievers so that they cannot see the light of the gospel that displays the glory of Christ, who is the image of God."* (2 Cor. 4:3-4)

*"He has blinded their eyes and hardened their hearts, so they can neither see with their eyes, nor understand with their hearts, nor turn - and I would heal them."* (John 12:40)

Deceived people don't know they are deceived, people. Think about this: if a person was a member of a cult and knew they were, would they stay in it? Satan has limited powers, but one that he does have and is exceptionally good at, is deception. The Canadian Oxford dictionary defines it as *"the act or an instance of deceiving; the process of being deceived. A thing that deceives; a trick or sham."* Synonyms include the words *"delusion"* and *"false."*

Most people who get into deception about life do so because they don't know the Bible - meaning they don't know what God says about the issues of life. If we examine the last two years concerning the Covid pandemic, we see not only a huge fear of sickness emerging but a huge fear of death. Why? Because most people don't know what awaits them after death. They are biblically illiterate, which is why we all need the objective standard of the Holy Bible in our beliefs, values and lifestyles.

**Doc's Book Club:** Read *"Deceived; Who Me?"* by Craig Hill.

*Life* is a test...   Is there anything in your life you may be deceived about?

is a test...

## Gossip

The Bible teaches us to live at peace with all men (Rom. 12:18). Well, there is no peace if people gossip. If we look at the root of this sin, it is based on jealousy and insecurity. We want to make others look bad, to boast ourselves up, and make ourselves look better in the eyes of others. Gossip can also be used to vent anger. No matter, it is a sin by no other name.

Additionally, gossip can be used against you. There are people out there, including Christians, that will seek to take advantage of you in every way they can. As I have said before, the most significant enemy can be the people you live with (Matt 10:36).

The Book of James talks about the damage that a person's tongue can do: *"When we put bits into the mouths of horses to make them obey us, we can turn the whole animal. Or take ships as an example. Although they are so large and are driven by strong winds, they are steered by a very small rudder wherever the pilot wants to go. Likewise, the tongue is a small part of the body, but it makes great boasts. Consider what a great forest is set on fire by a small spark. The tongue also is a fire, a world of evil among the parts of the body. It corrupts the whole body, sets the whole course of one's life on fire, and is itself set on fire by hell."* (James 3:3-7) For additional reading on the subject, check out: Prov. 16:28, Eph. 4:29, Lev. 19:16, and 1 Tim. 5:13.

There is not much that I can add to these scriptures. It's simple; we must stop doing it. Keep a lookout for others who have wagging tongues. They will probably come against you if you remind them of their gossiping. Instead, forgive them.

*Life* is a test...Remember this: *"A gentle answer turns away wrath."* (Prov. 15:1)

# "Be Still, and Know that I am God."
## (Ps. 46:10)

**Be Still:**
- stop talking
- turn off your phone!
- stop commenting
- listen
- stop arguing
- stop questioning and complaining
- stop the strife

**And Know:**
- stop doubting; it is a form of atheism
- have faith
- not your opinion but His

**That I am God:**
- God is Almighty
- God is in control
- God is love
- God is King
- God is your hope, rock and fortress
- God is an ever-present help in times of trouble
- God is your Father
- God is your Shepard
- God will lead, nourish, protect, and restore you.

*Life* is a test... What part did you miss?

# The Fourth Fruit of the Spirit - Patience
## (Part 1 of 4)

Sometimes the English Bible will use more than one word in its translation. Such is the case with the word "patience," translated from the Greek language which uses two different words. The Greek word "Hupomonē" means "a remaining under," as when a person bears up under a burden. It is when we are "steadfast;" when life is complicated. The other Greek word is "Makrothumia," which has two meanings; "long" and "temper." In Gal. 5:22, "patience" literally means having a "long temper," In other words, keeping your cool when you are being tried. The KJV translates it as "longsuffering." A patient person can endure much pain and suffering without complaining. Don't we all wish! A patient person keeps his cool when others may not be. He takes a "chill pill" and waits for the Lord to move in the situation that he is in. Like all the rest of the Fruits of the Spirit, we have it in us. We just must remember to use it!

How do you have patience? Although it takes guts and perseverance, it essentially comes from a position of power. Anyone can get angry; anyone can take revenge; those two skills do not need a lot of practice or intelligence. Let your emotions go, and it will happen automatically! Patience is essentially the ability to have restraint and maintain clear level-headed careful thinking. It takes a strong person to do that, whereas losing our patience is a sign of weakness. We exercise compassion when we have patience for someone who's getting on our nerves, we exercise hope for someone when we see that they need deliverance and if we look in the mirror, we can even have patience for ourselves!

What's the secret to having patience? It's the same secret that is the common denominator with all nine Fruits of the Spirit. Let go and turn it over to God. Then Holy Spirit works through us, making us more Christ-like with every trial and tribulation. In other words, as my dad would say, "it builds your character." (I know you just love this topic, don't you? Hey, I write this stuff for me too!)

**_Life_ is a test...**

# The Fourth Fruit of the Spirit - Patience
## (Part 2 of 4)

2 Thess. 3:5 says, *"And the Lord direct your hearts into the love of God, and into the patient waiting for Christ."* (KJV) So there you have it; a prayer that the Lord will direct your hearts into patience. I wrote about grace on March 1st, 2nd, and 3rd. Those two words, "grace" and "patience," are tied together. In a nutshell, patience takes a "chill pill," and grace turns the other way from people or the difficulties of life that come against us.

God is patient with us, and He has buckets of grace for each of us too. Rom. 2:4 says that God's patience leads to our repentance. Rom. 9:22 points out that only God's patience prevents Him from destroying us. Peter speaks of the patience of God in 1 Peter 3:20, pointing out that God had patience with the evil people of Noah's day, and delayed judgment if possible (see Genesis 6). Jonah had no patience for the people of Nineveh, but God did (Read the Book of Jonah).

What is the opposite of patience? Wanting revenge, irritation, losing your cool - anything that does not include peace. God does not want us to live in a state of being unhappy and irritable but one of peace (John 14:27). He wants all these negative emotions replaced with hope and praise. *"Why, my soul, are you downcast? Why so disturbed within me? Put your hope in God, for I will yet praise Him, my Savior and my God."* (Ps. 42:5)

God is patient, and His Spirit lives in us. We can if we tap into it with "constant contact" and become patient ourselves. When we do that, we leave room for Holy Spirit to work in our relationships and ourselves. Again, it's the same old story of trust in God.

*"Be still before the Lord...and wait patiently for him; do not fret when people succeed in their ways,...when they carry out their wicked schemes."* (Ps. 37:7)

## The Fourth Fruit of the Spirit - Patience
### (Part 3 of 4)

After Ephesians and Acts, James is probably my favourite book because it teaches more about life than any other book of the Bible. *"Be patient, then, brothers and sisters, until the Lord's coming. See how the farmer waits for the land to yield its valuable crop, patiently waiting for the autumn and spring rains. You too, be patient and stand firm, because the Lord's coming is near. Don't grumble against one another, brothers and sisters, or you will be judged. The Judge is standing at the door! Brothers and sisters, as an example of patience in the face of suffering, take the prophets who spoke in the name of the Lord. As you know, we count as blessed those who have persevered. You have heard of Job's perseverance and have seen what the Lord finally brought about. The Lord is full of compassion and mercy."* (James 5:7-11)

*"Wait for the Lord;...be strong and take heart...and wait for the Lord."* (Ps. 27:14)

*"The Lord will fight for you; you need only to be still."* (Ex.14:14)

The worst part about losing your patience is that you're making a terrible representation of Jesus. How was your light shining when you were ripping into the employee at the fast-food drive-through for not putting ketchup with your takeout order? To keep your patience, remember the pain of having to apologize later…

My favourite prayer is, "Lord, give me patience, but hurry!" All kidding aside, we need to remember something; *"God can do far more than we could ever ask for or imagine."* (Eph. 3:20 NIRV) We get impatient with others and with God when He doesn't answer our prayers or do things the way we think they should be done.

*Life* is a test... I hate to ask, but how are you doing with patience?

*Life* *is a test...* 

# The Fourth Fruit of the Spirit - Patience
## (Part 4 of 4)

Oh yes, patience. I tried it once; I didn't like it. Perhaps it is one of the side-effects of being self-employed all my life. I want everything completed by Tuesday of next week!

The problem with patience (i.e., not having enough of it) is that we succumb to our restlessness and fall into the trap of "making things happen." It's all about instant gratification instead of waiting on the Lord and getting His very best for us. When things go well with our plans, we say it was a "blessing of the Lord" when sometimes it is the fruit of fear. Our fear is that God may not come through when we expect Him to. It should reveal the truth in our hearts and our ulterior motives, and if we humble ourselves, it should direct us to more intimacy with God so that we don't make the same mistake again.

When we know God and are intimate with Him and He with us, we know He wants to bless us in every way. If we walk by faith, we can anticipate His gifts and blessings while at the same time we're willing to wait for them. Moses waited 40 years; Abraham waited for 25, but along the way, he messed up and listened to the cries of his wife and Ishmael was born (via Abram's maid Hagar), which is another whole story (read Gen. 16).

Patience does not develop overnight; you need patience to build tolerance. God's power and goodness are crucial to the development of patience. Col. 1:11 tells us that we are strengthened by Him to "great endurance and patience," Our patience is further developed and strengthened by resting in God's perfect will and timing.

*Life* is a test... I am a "work in progress" when it comes to patience. How about you?

# What the Bible is Not.

If you are looking for a quick fix or perhaps a boost to your self-esteem, reading the Bible would not be my first choice. It is a book (or, more accurately, a group of 66 books) that will "wreck" you more than anything I can think of.

For example, try reading the Book of Romans on a day when your ego is all puffed up. It will "put you in your place" when the light goes on. We realize how hopelessly arrogant, selfish and foolish we are to think that we are the centre of our universe and that our sense of well-being and happiness is, more than anything else, God's job.

Our society rates "success" as the ultimate pinnacle of life. "Freedom 55" for those that have "worked hard" and "made it;" self-interest is a "virtue" and an excellent tool to use to guide our lives. I recently met a lady my age, who claims to be a Christian but never prays, reads the Word, seldom attends church and is desperate to remarry after becoming a widow. ("I know that God will provide me with another man.") I hesitate to read into things too much but I sensed a person who lives their life for them and has no little clue what a personal relationship with Jesus is about.

In Romans, we discover that this infatuation with self is, in essence, evil. These thoughts and ideas completely contradict who God is and what our relationship with Him is supposed to be. GOD is the point, not us! He gets the worship and glory, not us and our desires, accomplishments, etc.

Our evil demands (which is what they are) - that sense that our well-being will be honoured by Him, deserves punishment. He declares us guilty of our selfishness and separated unto Him by sin. Our ONLY saving grace is to turn from our wicked, self-centered ways and make Jesus the front, center and very essence of our being.

*Life* is a test... Who is the centre of your universe? You or Him?

## Maturing; another word for pain.

Growing up is hard to do. Another word for it is "sacrifice," - which is another word for "marriage," but that's another story for another day...

The reality of life is that we do not grow when life is easy and fun; instead, we grow in difficult times. No one can escape this, and rather than fight it, a better course of action is to face the difficult times, for they are part of the process of becoming more Christ-like. Alternatively, we can make the mistake of choosing to run from the hard times, but that will hinder our growth in the long term.

With different cycles and obstacles of life, we can become more compassionate and assertive as we grow in faith. We will fall more in love with Jesus! I know this is not what you want to hear but this is a choice, pain for growth. Both Peter and Paul learned obedience to Jesus from the things that they suffered. If this were not the case, then we'd be all grown up by the time we were 12! As we enter a pathway of maturity in Christ, there will be hardships. Look at what the apostle Paul said in Acts 14:22: *"...strengthening the disciples and encouraging them to remain true to the faith. 'We must go through many hardships to enter the kingdom of God,' they said."* Paul was showing his followers that if they were going to continue this path and finish the course with joy, there would be much resistance. Remember, too, what Jesus said, *"Whoever finds their life will lose it, and whoever loses their life for my sake will find it."* (Matt. 10:39)

The apostle Peter said, *"Do not be surprised at the fiery ordeal that has come on you to test you, as though something strange was happening to you. But rejoice since you participate in the sufferings of Christ, so that you may be overjoyed when His glory is revealed."* (1 Peter 4:12-13)

*Life* is a test... Are you clay to the Potter? Read Jer. 18.

# The Elements of Being Born Again.
## (Part 1 of 2)

*"The founder of The Salvation Army, General William Booth, pointed out six dangerous doctrines he observed in the Christian church of his generation:*
*1. Works without Holy Spirit.*
*2. Christianity without Christ.*
*3. Forgiveness without repentance.*
*4. Salvation without regeneration.*
*5. Politics without God.*
*6. Heaven without help."\**

Too many churches today are guilty of not preaching many of these issues. When was the last time you heard a good old-fashioned, barn-burning, fire-and-brimstone gospel salvation message? Since Billy Graham had his homecoming in 2018, there doesn't seem to be many evangelists travelling in first-world nations (Daniel Kolenda is doing a great job in Africa after taking over from Reinhard Bonkke).

The result? Too many people are "pew warmers" that are not born again. What does being born again mean? "Jesus replied, *"Very truly I tell you, no one can see the Kingdom of God unless they are born again."* (John 3:3). Being born again means the rebirth of our spirit. *"Flesh gives birth to flesh, but the spirit gives birth to spirit."* (John 3:6) It is not about receiving forgiveness or being made righteous; those are separate issues, but still part of it. Being born again is about being transferred from death to life. It is a radical transformation of our character.

*"Yet to all who did receive him, to those who believed in his name, he gave the right to become children of God - children born not of natural descent, nor of human decision or a husband's will, but born of God."* (John 1:12-13) (Also, have a look at Eph. 2:1 - 5).

*L*ife is a test... Are you born again? See Romans 10:9.

\* "Christians going to Hell" by Seung Woo Byun. Creation House, A Strang Company. 2006. P.115

# The Elements of Being Born Again.
## (Part 2 of 2)

I have been reading a book already referred to yesterday called *"Christians Going to Hell"* by Pastor Seung Woo Byun. It's a scary book with a scary title. There is a story in the book from a hospitalized pastor, and God showed him a vision of heaven and hell. What is the population of hell he wanted to know from an angel. *"The ratio of people entering hell and heaven is 1000 to one."* * (Authors Note: That being said, in a city of 100,000, only 1000 are going to heaven.) Further, the pastor wanted to know from this angel what kinds of people were in hell. The angel replied, *"there are two kinds of people in hell. One kind is those who did not believe in Jesus. Those who did not believe in Jesus come to hell 100%. The other kind is the people who went to church who died without repenting."* *

This is pretty serious stuff. It has been said that if we get to heaven, we will be very surprised as to who is there and who is not. Here are some more scriptures for you to think about.

*"I will rescue you from your own people and from the Gentiles. I am sending you to them to open their eyes and turn them from darkness to light, and from the power of satan to God, so that they may receive forgiveness of sins and a place among those who are sanctified by faith in me."* (Acts 26:17-1)

*"Blessed and holy are those who share in the first resurrection. The second death has no power over them, but they will be priests of God and of Christ and will reign with him for a thousand years."* (Rev. 20:6)

We must remember that just because we are Christians, does not mean we are clean and never have to repent. I recommend daily heart checks during quiet times with God. Ask Him "Lord, is there any area of my life that does not glorify you?" If you sense anything, repent from it! His grace is sufficient each and every time we fall short.

*Life* is a test... Repenting is not a one-time deal. Have you checked your heart if it is clean and in need of repentance in any area lately?

* *"Christians Going to Hell"* by Seung Woo Byun. Creation House, A Strang Company. 2006. P. 45

# Hebrews 6: 1-6 (Part 1 of 3)

Years ago, Gillian, a dear friend, introduced me to Hebrews chapter six (particularly verse six), and I have studied it over the years. It repeatedly "rattles my cage." I will spend the last three days of this month dissecting it. I have deliberately chosen the Message translation partly because of "a little change in diet" and because it reads rather well. Check this verse in several different translations.

*"So come on, let's leave the preschool fingerpainting exercises on Christ and get on with the grand work of art. Grow up in Christ."*

Ouch! I see this repeated problem in our society; complete immaturity, whether people are saved or unsaved. The world is a mess because the Christian church didn't do anything to prevent it from becoming a mess. We are the only ones with all the answers to the world's problems, but too many Christians are sitting on their "blessed assurances" in church on Sunday, keeping the pews warm. Jesus needs to be the complete focus of our attention (our life!) as we grow up working out our salvation every day (Phil. 2:12). We are warriors in the spiritual army of God with assignments. Grow up - get trained and get busy!

*"The basic foundational truths are in place: turning your back on "salvation by self-help" and turning in trust toward God;"*

Right... The bookstores are filled with "self-help books." Look, we are too messed up and beyond help, so save your money, read the Bible, and surrender to Jesus. Life is not complicated; give it over to Jesus and live by faith. Simple stuff...

*Life* is a test... Is your bookshelf filled with self-help books? Replace them with Bibles!

## Hebrews 6 (Part 2 of 3)

*"Baptismal instructions; laying on of hands; resurrection of the dead; eternal judgment. God helping us, we'll stay true to all that. But there's so much more. Let's get on with it!"*

The point here is that yes, we do need to know the church's instructions, we do need to know about laying on of hands, we need to be actively connected with God who is helping us, etc. "all that is true..." But, don't stay on milk all your life; get on some solid meat! (1 Cor. 3:2) I see too many Christians doing the same thing in the same church, the same way, reading the same scriptures for 30 years. I recently asked a lady what her ministry was, and she told me that once a month, she helped with the projection equipment in her church. Seriously???? She had no clue of what I was talking about.

The root issue here is that Christians are more influenced by secular culture than their Bibles. This, of course, has led to the complete apostasy of some denominations. We look to man's wisdom for solutions to the world's problems instead of God's wisdom, and we are reaping a harvest of lawlessness. We accept just about any behaviour in our society if it feels good and doesn't bother anybody else, but Holy Spirit knows about it...

What do you do? The answers can be found in 1 Peter 2:9-12; Ex. 19:5-6; and 2 Chron. 7:14. I will leave you with some homework. Read these Scriptures in different translations to "get the gist."

*Life* is a test... How many different translations of the Bible do you own? Get some more.

# Hebrews 6 (Part 3 of 3)

*"Once people have seen the light, gotten a taste of heaven and been part of the work of the Holy Spirit, once they've personally experienced the sheer goodness of God's Word and the powers breaking in on us - if then they turn their backs on it, washing their hands of the whole thing, well, they can't start over as if nothing happened. That's impossible. Why, **they've re-crucified Jesus!**"* (Heb. 6:4-7)

**Two points:**

**1)** Once you are genuinely born again, filled with Holy Spirit, praying in other tongues, watching Gifts manifest in your life, how can you turn your back on that? Strangely enough, some people do, and they offend Holy Spirit which is quoted as one of the only unpardonable sins. As Mark puts it, *"but whoever blasphemes against the Holy Spirit will never be forgiven; they are guilty of an eternal sin."* (Mark 3:29) Not something that you want to do...

**2)** "re-crucified Jesus"??? Yes. The next time you sin, think about that passage and what just happened. Because you are saved and in bondage so to speak to Jesus, then when you sin, you drag Him along with you, and He gets nailed to the cross again because of you. (As my mother would say right about now, *"put that in your pipe and smoke it!"*) The bottom line is that Jesus loves you so much that He died for you, and redeemed you from your sin on the cross. When you sin, you put Him back on the cross. If you have watched *"The Passion of the Christ"* movie, you will recall the tremendous pain and torture that Jesus suffered on your behalf. Would you like Him to go through that again? He does when you sin.

*Life* is a test... Now you know why I said at the beginning of this lesson that Hebrews 6:6 "rattles my cage." Does it rattle yours too? Think about this verse the next time temptation comes to your mind...

## He's Your Best Buddy.

Occasionally I am asked how I develop ideas to write this daily devotional. It has simply been a fantastic experience and journey for me about how the Lord just puts things on my heart. I can read a verse in the Word, and suddenly, "it" starts pouring out of me, in which case I run to my computer and start typing. Sometimes I sit at my study desk in my bedroom, staring out on the street, enjoying the winter sunshine and just start writing. In the summer, I sit on the back deck enjoying my view of the mountains, and the Lord gets me going. Sometimes I forgo the computer and just start writing until my hand hurts. Today's idea I received (are you ready for this? Say "yes") while folding laundry!

We have this sort of idea in our society that if we're talking to ourselves, we've gone a little crazy. People will joke with us and say, "do you answer yourself back too?" I suppose the truth is that we probably all talk to ourselves. I used to do that, and yes, I answered myself back! However, since absorbing my life into the Word of God, I've made a slight change; I still talk, but I don't talk to myself; I speak to Him!

I do carry on conversations with God, and yes, He does answer me back. I just speak what comes to my head; I do that without even thinking about what I'm saying - just everyday things. It's the Gift of Prophecy in action. The Words come from the throne room of God to the prophet's physical body and then out their mouth, bypassing the brain filter. Considering that the bible says that we can all prophesy (1 Cor. 14:31), just do it! Just start a conversation with God and prophesy over yourself! I do it all the time, and no, I am not nuts! At least, I don't think so; others may think I am, but I don't listen to them anyway. God is beside you, in you and with you. Start taking to Him! Forget what others think!

*Life* is a test... Talk to Him! You're not nuts!

# Satan and his Demons. (Part 1 of 2)

(Note: When I originally wrote the copy for this next series, my editor got on my case and told me that I needed to have more of a preamble introducing the subject. He said that new Christians wouldn't know what I was talking about, and many church-going Christians would still need an introduction to the topic. So, as much as I hate it when my editor does his job (it creates more work for me!) I know that he is right. My editor Graeme has done an awesome job on these books, so far be it for me to argue with him! So "Ed" (as in "editor' - my nickname for Graeme) here is your pre-amble:)

When Satan rebelled against God, he immediately began trying to convince the rest of God's angels to follow him to help build his evil kingdom. He did a good job considering that Revelation 12:4 says that he managed to persuade one-third of all the angels to follow him and forgo God. He probably offered them a better job and a higher rank, but whatever it was, he succeeded. Even though this now rebellious army is corrupt, full of sin and rebellion, they are surprisingly well organized and do a great job of messing up our lives and our natural world. Satan operates like Hitler did (or is the other way round??) By fear, control, and severe punishment.

Just as God's holy angels (as opposed to satan's unholy ones) are organized into different ranks, satan uses the same system in his own evil kingdom. Demons are ranked in order and, as I said, do a good job. In Eph. 6:12, we see four different ranks of demons, each having other responsibilities.

The first one mentioned is "principalities" or "rulers." These bad guys are the "best of the best" and are chosen by satan to rule in the heavenly places over all the other demons. Think of them as generals in the army. They are part of a special task force with the job of influencing earthly rulers and governments. It is not hard to realize that governments can be controlled by demonic forces. Think about nations in the past affected by these powers: W.W. I and II Germany, and Somalia's, Cambodia's and Rwanda's genocides… the list goes on.

## Satan and his Demons. (Part 2 of 2)

Next to and under the "generals" are the majors, otherwise known as "powers." Their job is to spread the power of evil and darkness into any given area (a city, town, even a street) and into people's lives - both the saved and the unsaved. How did they do this? Most of their work involves messing with our heads - whispering thoughts and putting us into tempting positions.

The third group is called "the rulers of the darkness of this age" or "the world forces of this darkness." These demons manage all the junk in our society: superstitions, cults, spirits of Jezebel, witchcraft, fortune-telling, and spiritual blindness. I studied deliverance for ten years, and believe me, when you get into this stuff, it is intense and very, very disgusting (and don't think for one minute that it is not real!) If people understood Halloween, for example, they would have nothing to do with it and instead be on their knees praying about it. This group's biggest goal is to ensure that people do not hear the truth about God. Remember that satan's biggest goal is for you to think he does not exist.

Finally, the last group is called "wicked spirits in heavenly places" or "the spiritual forces of wickedness in the heavenly places." These guys are not any worse than any other demons, but they are powerful in persuasion and persuading us towards darkness. This is where the spirits of religion come from. They are demons who have joined the church, profess religion, know the Word, etc. Their whole aim is to attack Christians and get them off into heresy. All forms of modern heresy, cults, new-age spiritualism, and Christian Science result from these wicked spirits in the Heavenly places.

In summary, some demons rule and spread the power of evil, and some demons try to bring us into the darkness that invades our spiritual lives to get us off track. Satan and all his demons are organized against Jesus to lead us astray and destroy us. Jesus said, "The thief comes only to steal and kill and destroy; I have come that they may have life and have it to the full." (John 10:10) Demons seek to interact with us, control us, communicate with us, and to mess us up in every way that they can. They succeed when we give in to them; it is called "sin."

*Life* is a test... Are your eyes more open to the schemes of darkness? You'll hear more tomorrow.

# Familiar Spirits. (Part 1 of 5)

The term "familiar spirits" is not well understood in the church today, so I will introduce it with some scriptures to back up the rest of the series. The idea refers to demons that are close or familiar to a person, such as a medium or a sorcerer, mentioned nine times in the King James version.

*"Regard not them that have familiar spirits, neither seek after wizards, to be defiled by them: I am the LORD your God."* (Lev. 19:31 KJV) We are not to consult with mediums or fortunetellers. Lev. 20:6 states God's opposition to involvement with people who communicate with evil or familiar spirits: *"And the soul that turneth after such as have familiar spirits, and after wizards, to go a whoring after them, I will even set my face against that soul, and will cut him off from among his people"* (KJV). *"There shall not be found among you anyone that maketh his son or his daughter to pass through the fire, or that useth divination, or an observer of times, or an enchanter, or a witch. Or a charmer, or a consulter with familiar spirits, or a wizard, or a necromancer."* (Deut. 18:10-11 KJV) The term is used in connection with a fortuneteller, a practice forbidden from God's people under the Law of Moses, and still, we today must do any of these practices as they open doors to the demonic.

Saul had a double standard. He removed witches, wizards, and mediums from Israel and then went in desperation, seeking a medium so he could summon the spirit of Samuel for help during a difficult time. (1 Sam. 28:3 and 9) This decision took the life of Saul and his sons. King Manasseh's reign was described as evil because of witchcraft and child sacrifice (2 Kings 21:6; 23:24,) but then King Josiah's saved Israel once again by his decrees that included removing those who consulted familiar spirits.

Is. 8:19 says, *"And when they shall say unto you, Seek unto them that have familiar spirits and unto wizards that peep, and that mutter: should not a people seek unto their God? for the living to the dead?"* (KJV). Is. 19:3 adds, *"And the spirit of Egypt shall fail in the midst thereof, and I will destroy the counsel thereof: and they shall seek to the idols, and the charmers, and to them that have familiar spirits, and to the wizards"* (KJV). God foretold of judgment upon those who consulted evil spirits. God wants us to talk to Him!

Familiar spirits are evil spirits, or demons, that have no place in the life of a Christian. We are to live by God's Spirit and stand against the spiritual forces of evil as we seek to live for the Lord (Eph. 6:12). The bottom line is that we are not to have anything to do with this stuff!

## Familiar Spirits. (Part 2 of 5)

Perhaps you are "familiar" with the term "familiar spirit." (sorry I couldn't resist....) A familiar spirit is a demonic spirit that attaches to someone (including Christians). They are intimate by nature, so they are called "familiar" as they want to get close to us. These spirits know our thoughts, life and behaviour very well, including our "sinful side." They know us better than anyone except God, of course. Often a person has no clue that a familiar spirit is deceiving them. (See April 17th's message where I speak on satan's deception to get a better idea of what I mean.)

These demons are the ones that whisper things into your ear like, "Don't you feel so lonely today." "You know that guy at work that you don't like; he gave you a dirty look today!" "No matter what I do or say, nothing is ever right." "I would've been happier if I had married someone else." You get the point…

Then there are the plans and ideas that invade our minds. Some are God giving you a "download." That is how Holy Spirit speaks to us. Be on guard and don't get into the fantasy realm, especially when it has anything to do with money, sex, or success. The world of fantasy is not from God. You are spellbound under their power when you yield to these familiar spirits. The ONLY power we should be under is the power of God because since Holy Spirit is in you, that is the only Spirit you should have anything to do with and the only one you should be communicating with! 1 John 4:1 says, *"Dear friends, do not believe every spirit, but test the spirits to see whether they are from God because many false prophets have gone out into the world."* Most people have no idea where these thoughts come from and their power over someone. Again, we are deceived, and we don't even know it.

*Life* is a test... Most people who get into deception do so because they don't know what God says about certain issues and satan's schemes. So, are you reading your Bible? Praying?

## Familiar Spirits. (Part 3 of 5)

### How do you know if you have a familiar spirit?

**1.** Negative behaviour around others. Our speech can be so intensely negative. An example would be people with very foul mouths who don't realize what they're saying.

**2.** Doing questionable things in secret. Are you doing anything that you wouldn't want anyone else to know? Even your spouse? The world is filled with men, including pastors, that are looking at pornography, and with a quick click of a finger, their dirty secret disappears, and nobody knows. However, Holy Spirit knows! Heb. 12:1 says, *"Therefore since such a great cloud of witnesses surrounds us, let us throw off everything that hinders and the sin that so easily entangles. And let us run with perseverance the race marked out for us."*

**3.** Hidden thought patterns. Married couples need to be completely transparent with one another. Make time for "pillow talk" every night. Healthy boundaries are necessary with family, friends and co-workers depending on the relationship, but we must also be transparent within those perimeters (i.e., no lies, gossiping, bragging etc.)

Can you really be two people? Yes, you can. James 3:11 says, *"Can both fresh water and saltwater flow from the same spring?"* Yes, you can be filled with Holy Spirit, then when you have a familiar spirit whispering a thought in your mind, you can be foolish enough to accept it. That fight becomes temptation which leads to an action, and now it becomes a sin. That is why the apostle Paul adamantly said in 2 Cor. 10: 3-5, *"For though we walk in the flesh, we do not war after the flesh: For the weapons of our warfare are not carnal, but mighty through God to the pulling down of strongholds; Casting down imaginations, and every high thing that exalteth itself against the knowledge of God, and bringing into captivity every thought to the obedience of Christ;"* (NKJV)

*Life* is a test... Are you familiar with familiar spirits?

## Familiar Spirits. (Part 4 of 5)

### How do we identify a familiar spirit?

It's easy. What emotions do you feel? If a thought has love, joy, peace, patience, kindness, or gentleness, it is probably from God. If it does not, then you need to question the source. Instead of having loving thoughts of God within us, we could have familiar spirits giving us thoughts that prevent us from allowing Holy Spirit to pour out of us. Phil. 4:8 summarizes this well: *"Finally, brethren, whatever things are true, whatever things are noble, whatever things are just, whatever things are pure, whatever things are lovely, whatever things are of good report, if there is any virtue and if there is anything praiseworthy - meditate on these things. The things you learned and received and heard and saw in me, these do, and the God of peace will be with you."* (NKJV) So, put your thoughts to the test. Do they align with this passage in Philippians? Yes, Jesus defeated satan at the cross, but that is not stopping him from harassing you. When someone cuts you off in traffic what comes out of you?

### 1. Addictions
Any addiction is the result of a familiar spirit. They know your weaknesses and how to get you to do something that you should not be doing. The worst is that they will even help you justify your actions! "I need to work another 3 hours to get this project finished or else. _____ will happen!"

### 2. Gossip
One familiar spirit that is far too common and divisive is gossip. It manifests as a need for negative information about other people. I wrote about this a few days ago so that I won't repeat myself.

 is a test... Are you played with addiction? Pursue freedom!

## Familiar Spirits. (Part 5 of 5)

### 3. Mediums/Astrology/Witchcraft and other weird stuff!

The Bible is very clear about talking to the dead. Don't do it. Why? Because you're talking to familiar spirits. This is what the secular world calls a ghost. There is no such thing as a ghost; they are familiar spirits or familiar demons. Additionally, have nothing to do with witchcraft; this includes books about it, Halloween, horror movies, etc.

*"Do not turn to mediums or seek out spiritists, for you will be defiled by them. I am the Lord your God."* (Lev. 19:31)

*"Saul died because he was unfaithful to the Lord; he did not keep the word of the Lord and even consulted a medium for guidance, and did not inquire of the Lord. So the Lord put him to death and turned the kingdom over to David, son of Jesse."* (1 Chron. 10:13-14)

*"ßAnyone who does these things is detestable to the Lord; because of these same detestable practices the Lord your God will drive out those nations before you."* (Deut. 18:12)

We can decide whose thoughts we should yield in our hearts, minds, and actions. Start with your heart; that is where it all begins. *"As a man thinks in his heart, so he is."* (Prov. 23:7a). *"Out of the abundance of the heart, the mouth speaks."* (Matt. 12:34b) You can let your mind run rampant, or you can cast down these imaginations and turn them all over to God (2 Cor. 10:5). I know I'm beginning to sound like a broken record, but it's the same answer to the same old problems - "constant contact" with God.

 is a test... Commune with Holy Spirit, not an unusual spirit!

# What on Earth is God Doing? (Part 1 of 3)

Pun intended. 1 Chron. 12: 32 says, *"from Issachar, men who understood the times and knew what Israel should do."* Issachar was one of the 12 Tribes of Israel, and they were wise gifted men who knew what to do. We live in an Issachar time now as God is rebuilding His church.

From the fall of the Roman Empire in 486 to the start of the Resonance in the 1300s, a period known as the dark ages, there was only no church rebuilding, but widespread silence from Holy Spirit. It is interesting to note that from that point on to today, every time the church received more light of restoration truth from the Word of God, there was (is) a corresponding increase in technology, inventions, and culture in our world. We saw the most significant jump with Gutenberg's invention of the printing press in the 1400s. Interestingly, he wanted to invent a machine that could produce bibles!

Martin Luther changed the world with his Ninety-five Theses, which started the Reformation in 1517. Then in the 1900s, we saw the Welsh Revival, followed by the manifestation of Holy Spirit in Azusa Street in California, USA and later in North Battleford, Saskatchewan. This early Charismatic movement was promptly put on pause by the Second World War. However, God returned with a vengeance with the Protestant Movement in the 1950s. Healings and Evangelism were commonplace with great ministries like Oral Robert's tent meetings and international Billy Graham Evangelistic Crusades. The Holiness Movement of the 1960s brought teachings of faith by many people including Kenneth Hagin that re-established the importance of spiritual giftings back to the church. In the 1970s, the church moved from a Pentecostal service to Charismatic renewal, and we saw many great teachers rising in their giftings, and then there was megachurch growth. Canada saw great preachers like Len Lindstrom, David Mainse, Terry Winter and Peter Youngren. The 1980s established the office of the prophet (Bishop Bill Hamon), and there were intercessory prayer and prayer walks.

More to cover from the last 30 years in the next two days! God has been on the move recently in more ways to count. I'll do my best to cover the highlights of the modern evangelical church.

*Life* is a test... Do you see God moving throughout history with power?

# What on Earth is God Doing? (Part 2 of 3)

The age of the Apostle was established in the 1990s, and with the acknowledgment of Apostles and the alignment of the five-fold gifting. The period of the Spirit and the age of the 21st century Ekklesia started in 2001. Ekklesia (or Ecclesia) is the Greek word translated in the New Testament as "church." It comes from Ek, meaning "out from and to," and Kaleo, meaning "to call," and has to do with a group of people called out from one place and another. It is an assembly or a congregation to govern. In this case, this government is a worldwide one. For this reason, believers should be working towards and believing for more restoration instead of waiting for the rapture and easing up into the heavens. Apostles will be vital in helping transform believers from pew warmers to active participants. Victorious Christians will be those who come to know their calling, understand their Gifts and work towards the harvest.

The Saints Movement of the 2010s saw our Ekklesia congregations understand what has happened in the last 100 years and start to act upon it now that the 5-fold offices have been restored. This turned them into "the Army of God" (2015's). We teach about the "Seven Mountain Dominion Mandate" as we, the Ekklesia, attempt to establish Jesus' completed Kingdom here on earth. The whole world has been affected since the Apostles and Prophets were restored. They will be instrumental in determining the goat and sheep nations. * Acts 3:21 emphatically states that the second coming of Jesus Christ cannot take place until all things are restored. We are now in an apostolic movement that is sweeping the globe. He is coming soon…

* The nations are represented as sheep and goats. Jesus will separate them into these two groups for judgment. One group, the sheep nations, has demonstrated their love for Jesus by lovingly serving others. The other group, the goat nations, did not love Jesus or help others (see Matt. 25:32-33). In my opinion, because of past and existing governments in Canada, we are now a goat nation, which is why we need to intercede as prayer warriors!

*Life* is a test… What changes has your church made in the last years/decades?

*Life is a test...*

# What on Earth is God Doing? (Part 3 of 3)

Many of our churches have gone from "believing in Jesus" to being active with Holy Spirit in community transformation. We have transitioned from the age of the church congregation to the age of the Ekklesia.

Why has all of this happened and continues to do so? God wants to restore His church to the priorities and practices of Jesus and His disciples, as outlined in the Book of Acts. The Christian church is the largest organization globally and the fastest growing. According to a conference I attended in Texas, it was reported that there are over 29,000 conversions to Christ every day in China, 20,000 in the continent of Africa, and 35,000 in the continent of South America (yes, you read that correctly, that is every day!) Global estimates are that over 100,000 people give their lives to Christ daily. Al Jazeera news was bemoaning that the world is losing 17,000 Muslims a day. More Muslims have come to God in the last 11 years than in the previous 1400 years.

The governing Church (Ekklesia) needs more Issachar leaders* to continue to know the signs of the times and listen to Holy Spirit, pray and bring the Word of the Lord to the world.

**Doc's Book Club:** Read anything by Dr. Bill Hamon.

*Life* is a test... There are no tests for this lesson, but I have homework for you! Go back and make a study of The Book of Acts.. Know it, read about it, be part of the changes!

* Prophetic leaders that know the signs of the times as given to them by God.
(1 Chron. 12:32)

## Heros of the Bible.

When you have read the Bible several times, you may spot various appealing characters. You might fancy Esther, Deborah, David (but hopefully not Goliath!), Moses, Joshua, Gideon, Paul, any of the disciples, etc. For me, my hero is Joseph. Why? He and I have had parallel lives.

- He clearly had the Gift of Administration, as do I.
- We were both ridiculed and bullied as youths.
- We both went through so much pain that we wanted to die.
- Joseph spent 17 years in prison. I've never been in a physical prison, but I've certainly been in an emotional and psychological one.
- He was enslaved; in my younger days, I was a slave to my work.
- After his time in captivity, he went from the prison to the palace in 24 hours; I was self-employed for 22 years and then moved into career ministry after 11 years of additional secondary education. I'm supposed to be "retired," but I think that "retirement" is for old people or people without vision. I've never been busier because I don't know how a Christian can "retire." It's a bit of an oxymoron! Billy Graham wrote his last book at the age of 98. I'm like those ads on TV for the Ever-ready battery bunny; I keep going and going and going, and so should you!

*"And the Lord said, "My Spirit shall not strive with man forever, for he is indeed flesh; yet his days shall be one hundred and twenty years."* (Gen. 6:3 NKJV) - I have every intention of making it! You?

*Life* is a test... Who is your biblical hero? How have they inspired you, and what have you learned from them?

# Does God Interrupt Your Day?

Some of you might be thinking, "yes, God interrupts my day, and that's OK with me." If you believe that, you missed the point.

God is not the interruption of your day; He's supposed to be your day! From the time you open your eyes in the morning until you close them at night, God is the centre of your attention. He wants to bring His peace to you today. Yes, you have your well-planned schedule, but He wants to re-organize you to reduce the day's demands. He wants to make room for Himself in your day so that the two of you can spend time together, and He can reveal more of Himself by giving you guidance and direction.

Some people have this crazy idea that they can hide from God. Seriously? He created you, knows more about you than you do, knows the next thought you will think before you think it! Rather than run from Him when we sin, which our flesh wants to do, run to Him, where He will greet you with open arms. Then confess your sin and... *"If we confess our sins, He is faithful and just and will forgive us our sins and purify us from all unrighteousness."* (1 John 1:19 KJV). When you feel stressed or burned out, He will bring healing to your soul. When life overwhelms you with battles and things are out of control, shout out His Name! *"Come unto me, all ye that labour and are heavily laden, and I will give you rest."* (Matt 11:28 KJV) Look to God as the rock-solid foundation in your life when everything around you is unstable and falling apart. He is the centre of your day and the centre of your life.

*Life* is a test... Is God an interruption of your day, or is He the centre of it?

## You Don't Need to Watch the News.

When I was a kid, you could, and we did, trust the news media. They took their job seriously and wanted to get the truth about a story, and we, as readers of newspapers and watchers of the evening news on television, had complete and total confidence in them. How things have changed. Firstly, as our society has walked further and further away from God, our world has disintegrated, and we now have a culture that lacks integrity and honesty. Secondly, access to information (aka the internet) has not made people wiser. If anyone says something that someone else disagrees with, it can be twisted into lies. So, who and what are you going to believe?

**1.** Start with the bible. It is the only truth there is, it has stood the test of time, and Jesus said He is the truth (John 14:6). No one else has ever said that, and no one ever will.

**2.** Stop watching the secular news. They don't know what is going on as they do not understand Eph. chapter 6. Remember that their goal is to fill you with fear so that you will keep watching them. That way, they can keep selling advertising, which they are in the business of doing!

**3.** Your news should come from Christian and/or honest news outlets, and you should make every attempt to listen to the prophets of God. *"Believe in the Lord your God, and you shall be established; believe His prophets, and you shall prosper."* (2 Chron. 7:14) Some credible news articles and stations I read and listen to are: The Elijah List, Charisma Daily News and Breaking Christian News. There is not much international news on these sites because they are US-based, but they occasionally have stories about other nations. Locally I watch Rebel News, True North and read the weekly "Epoch Times."

**Doc's Book Club:** Read *"Compassionate Capitalism: A Judeo-Christian Value"* by Dr. Harold R. Eberle and "*Defeating Jezebel"* by Jennifer Leclaire.

*Life* is a test... Whose news are you listening to?

## The Month of Sivan (May/June - Part 1 of 2)

**Appointed Time:** Shavuot (Pentecost); the giving of the Torah (the first five books of the Bible) at Sinai

**Alphabet:** The letter is "ZAYIN." Receiving mercy for completion.

**Tribe:** Zebulun, the businessman's month; it is a time to prosper.

**Characteristics:**

- The time of Pentecost (provision).
- Wheat is harvested in Israel, so it is a time of harvest and giving.
- This is the month to pray the Prayer of Jabez! (1 Ch. 4:10).
- Watch the door of provision to open and ask God to enlarge your boundaries and bring you into the fullness of your destiny. It is the month to connect your talk to your walk (Prov. 10:9), making continuous, ongoing progress in moving from one level of strength to the next.
- God is saying this month, "Whatever you are willing to work for this month, I will give it to you. I will increase you if you ask Me."

**Constellation:** Gemini

**Colour/Stone:** White and clear quartz or "moonstone."

Jacob prophesied over Zebulon that he would dwell by the seashore, a significant centre for sea trade, and Moses prophesied that Zebulun would rejoice in going out to the sea to trade. He feasted on the abundance of the sea and the hidden treasures of the sand. The tribe of Zebulon was noted for its ability in business and faithfulness. Zebulun joined with both Deborah and Gideon to stand against the enemy during the Judges' time. Fifty thousand soldiers from Zebulun came to help David at Hebron and served him "with an undivided heart." Zebulon was a great tribe with promised potential.

**Understanding the tribe of Sivan and how to pray to be in alignment with God this month.**

Sometimes we look at God's Word over our lives, and it seems impossible! We don't have the provision we need to fulfill God's plans for us. Some people receive a prophetic Word and immediately start to list why it will never happen! That response to the promises of God is unbelief.

## The Month of Sivan (May/June - Part 2 of 2)

We lay the groundwork for future blessings by expanding our boundaries. If you want to do that, celebrate what God has already done; celebrate Pentecost! Celebrate God's physical provision by giving first-fruits and thank offerings. Welcome Him this month and be filled afresh! One prerequisite for new boundaries is being faithful to do what God called you to do in the old. Matthew 25:21 says, *"because you were faithful over a few things, I will make you ruler over many."* Zebulun's secret was faithfulness! *"To whom much is given, from him much is expected."* (Luke 12:48)

Earth and heaven are connected in a timed sequence. Do not let your Greek mindset keep things fragmented. God is moving through the months, not disconnecting them but tying them together. I am partial to this month because it is the one that I align with. If you're unsure what month you fall under, I just read the descriptions of each one, pray and ask the Lord what your alignment is.

We are gathering wisdom as we move forward into the fullness of God's plan. We waste many years, but God's redemptive, restorative power can restore what is lost quickly. The Bible says that the years the locusts have eaten can be restored (Joel 2:25). Once we get moving in God's time, restoration accelerates. Our restoration will double, quadruple or go seven times faster than your waste. If you wasted 21 years, you could recoup that in three years. This is an incredible principle to understand. Many people wander about in life like a ship without a rudder. Thomas Carlyle said, *"A man without a goal is like a ship without a rudder."* However, God can restore all that is lost or wasted. So, please don't give up on people (or yourself) who have made a mess of their lives; instead, remember how the temple workers rebuilt in 52 days what had been torn down for 70 years (read the book of Nehemiah).

*Life* is a test... Are you thanking God for His provision?

## You are here for a Reason...

A song I enjoy that Harry Connick Jr. sings *"It had to Be You,"* composed by Isham Jones, with lyrics by Gus Kahn and written in 1924. I was listening to it the other day, and all of a sudden, Holy Spirit rose in me with the following thoughts: Yes, it "had to be you." God chose you, He didn't choose anybody else, so it had (has) to be you. For what? For whatever He has called you to do.

God chose you before the earth was formed (Eph. 1:4) and gave you things He has not given to anyone else. You have your own unique body, voice, fingerprints, personality, DNA - the list goes on. Further, He chose you to make you whatever He did. White, black, brown, red; blue eyes, brown eyes, green eyes, etc. Then, He chose to place you where He wanted you, in a particular place and culture, born to parents of His choice, and you came blest with specific spiritual giftings. **You were not and are not, an accident!**

Ok, you are here, so now what? Your assignments, should you be willing to accept them, are to do the following:

**1.** Make Jesus the Lord of your life and live for Him, with Holy Spirit in you, helping and guiding you through life.
**2.** *"Go forth into the world and take dominion over it for the gospel of Jesus Christ being fruitful and multiplying everything that you do."* God is not into addition but multiplication. (Gen. 1:28)
**3.** *"Go forth in the world, preach the gospel, and make disciples of all men."* (Matt. 28:19)

Simple stuff...

*Life* is a test... Yes, it had and has to be you to do what you're called to. Is that okay with you?

# You are in it, but not...

*"They are not of the world, even as I am not of it..."* John 16:17

Remember that when you were born again into this world, you were not destined for the ways of the world, and yet we are still not part of it. Set your mind and heart on Jesus, sit back, and let the Holy Spirit refresh your soul. Don't keep looking around but rather look straight ahead, following the path Jesus leads you. Remember that He will give you the desires of your heart when you are focused on Him (Ps. 37:4). Don't give up. Remember that the enemy is no match for anyone in Christ. Live a life completely sold out to Jesus!

Remember that as you approach every day that you're in charge. You are the boss of your life, not satan. You decide. Of course, this decision is made in union with the great counsellor, Holy Spirit. Some days go smoothly, and you may be unaware of His sovereign presence ever watching over you. On the days when your plans don't go according to plan, that's when you are more likely to be on the lookout for Him. Perhaps you missed it by not following His direction or maybe He is deliberately taking an approach you don't want to go. However, you must communicate with Him in those times because His ways are higher and better than our ways (Is. 58:8-9). Don't try and figure out what's going on; trust Him because He knows!

*Life* is a test... Have you ever thought that things sometimes don't work out because God is protecting you? Often He's protecting you from yourself.

# You are a Winner, Not a Loser.

*"But thanks be to God, who always leads us in triumph in Christ, and manifests through us the sweet aroma of the knowledge of Him in every place."* (2 Cor. 2:14)

Did you know that you are a winner, and as a winner - you can know victorious outcomes in every battle you face in life? God calls us to be "overcomers." (1 John 5:4) Therefore, we need something to overcome! Not to worry! If it isn't obvious, life is full of opportunities to overcome! To help you along the pathway of life, it helps to have a positive attitude no matter what you are facing and to maintain the mind of Christ through the trials and tribulations of life. NOTHING is impossible with God. (Luke 1:17)

Remember that God is a God of restoration. When your family and friends abandon you, He will be there to step up to the plate and lift you to a higher level with Him. He will rescue you when you feel alone. He will return you to a place of honour (Is. 43:4). He will give you rest (Matt. 11:28). He will free your mind from negative influences, attitudes, opinions from others against you etc. The key here is to find and use the wisdom of God as clearly outlined in His Word. Remember that spiritual maturity doesn't happen automatically. All of life is about growth. We seek God's knowledge, put into place His commandments, communicate with Him, and discipline our flesh to stay out of the way, and grow up with Holy Spirit coaching us along the way.

You can be victorious in all your battles. We can overcome with faith-filled determination and a positive attitude that aligns with God's will and purpose. God will always cause you to win because you were created in His image to be a champion!

*Life* is a test... You're a winner!! Don't ever forget it...

# Blest to Be a Blessing.

We live in a world that says the only reason for prosperity is to have more belongings and a better quality of life. What makes the secular world go around is "greed." More and more Christians are not being deceived by this and see that God wants to bless us to be a blessing to others.

God wants us to go out in the world and *"make his disciples of all men"* (Matt 28:19), and He knows that we cannot do that if we don't have the cash in the bank to do it. Therefore, He said, *"And God is able to bless you abundantly, so that in all things at all times, having all that you need, you will abound in every good work."* (2 Cor. 9:8)

Beyond the five necessities of life, what is that other "need?" What is the desire in your heart to express your Gifts and finances and complete that great commission? Perhaps you want to be a missionary; it takes money. Maybe you want to buy Bibles for Ethiopia; it takes money. Perhaps you want to set up a scholarship fund for students going to Bible college; it takes money. Maybe you would like to start a soup kitchen to help the homeless. You get the point. If you follow God's economy of seedtime and harvest and forget about the greed of the secular society, then before you know it, God will have a plan for you and the funds to execute the project (Jer. 29:11).

*Life* is a test... What financial harvest are you believing to receive? What will you do with it?

The one that God gave you. Find out what He has called you to do, and do it, (hint: it will be something you like and that you are good at. If in doubt, ask Him.) If you don't like something in the world, then...

## Be an agent of change.

If you don't have enough time, shut off your phone, computer, and TV and plant your money into His Kingdom to help preach the Gospel (it isn't your money anyway). If you are looking for the love of your life, stop. You will find them when you start doing what God has called you to do. Jesus loves you, and that is all that matters. Meditate on His Word, do His Word and live His Word. Yes...

## It really is that simple.

Emotions are great, but keep them under His control. Look after your body - it is the temple of the Holy Spirit. Open your heart, life and money to people and let your light shine by doing good works. Live by God's faith. Help others to build their dream, and in doing so, you will build your own. Then you can...

## Travel & help.

It really is the best education in the world, and you will find your life if you lose it by doing the works of God. Life is not about finding yourself but rather about creating yourself in the image of Jesus and making the world a better place when you leave than when you arrived. The world does not owe you anything. You owe the world everything. Don't talk about your rights. Fulfill your duties and responsibilities. Don't protest, pray. Because...

## Life is short.

Billions of people are hungry, cold, poor, sick, hurt, at war, and going to hell because you haven't helped them and told them about Jesus. After all, your real calling in life is to go out and make disciples of all men. It is not about you. So...

## What are you waiting for?

The "This Is Your Life" Poster can be downloaded and printed in any size for $7.95 CAD.

www.newstartministries.ca

# What is your **Mission** Impossible? *(1)

A mission is a vision given and powered by God through impartation.

The spiritual replication of Jesus into you is the goal of your life.*(2) Any other goal is secondary at best and harmful at worst. God built you to be His Spiritual being and for you to live out your life from His Spirit in you, rather than from within your soul.*(3)

Your mission (should you be willing to accept it) is the biggest gift that God can give you. It will be all life-consuming and give you the clarity to know what your life is all about. When God gives you your mission (ask Him; He will tell you)*(4), then preparation will be next:

- · What will you have to do to fill the mission?
- · What character, knowledge and discipline will you have to do to develop the mission?

Problems are not from a lack of discipline but rather a lack of vision.*(5) If discipline is an issue, you have not received God's full impartation. Using your faith,*(6) God will give you the plans,*(7) resources*(8) and energy(9) to accomplish His mission for you.

Be guaranteed that you will be hit with obstacles*(10) - God's barbells build spiritual muscle. Sin in you, others and satan creates the barriers you must go through to transform you into being Christ-like. Human soulish will won't work, as it leaves you tired, angry, hurt and bitter.

## God → Vision → Mission → Obstacles → Transformation → Goal Achieved

Question: Are you willing to give up your life to another being (God) and lose it so that you can find it*(11) by Him working through you to accomplish the mission you're trying to find?*(12)

| | | | |
|---|---|---|---|
| *1. Mathew 19:26 | *4. John 10:27 | *7. Proverbs 8:12 | *10. 2 Corinthians 4:8-9 |
| *2. John 3:13 | *5. Proverbs 29:18 | *8. Deuteronomy 8:18 | *11. Mathew 10:39 |
| *3 .Romans 8 | *6. Hebrews 11:1,6 | *9. Galatians 6:9 | *12. Luke 19:17; 1 Corinthians 9:24 |

The "Mission" Poster can be downloaded and printed in any size for $7.95 CAD.

## The Fifth Fruit of the Spirit - Kindness
### (Part 1 of 2)

The Greek word for "kindness" is chrēstotēs. It means tender concern, uprightness." It is the kindness of heart and kindness of act. Synonyms include sweetness, patience, goodwill, goodness, and gentleness.

Romans 2:4 says, *"Or do you show contempt for the riches of his kindness, forbearance and patience, not realizing that God's kindness will lead you to repentance? God's motive for bringing us salvation is kindness towards us."* Titus 3:4-5 gives us another example: *"But when the kindness and love of God our Savior appeared, He saved us, not because of righteous things we had done, but because of His mercy. He saved us through the washing of rebirth and renewal by the Holy Spirit"*

You have to remember that God is a good guy! He is not some cranky grandfather sitting on His throne throwing lightning bolts at us whenever we mess up! He is the foundation and epitome of love, and He expresses that love through kindness. He takes very tender care of us and keeps us protected and close to Him.

*"How priceless is your unfailing love, O God! People take refuge in the shadow of your wings."* (Ps. 36:7)

There are repeated examples in the bible of God's unfailing kindness:

**1.** God expressed kindness when He provided for Elijah and the widow of Zarephath during a drought - and He showed more kindness later when He raised the widow's only son from the dead. You can read about it in 1 Kings 17:8-24.

**2.** When Sarah exiled Hagar and Ishmael, God was there with compassion and kindness (see Gen. 21:9-21).

# The Fifth Fruit of the Spirit - Kindness
## (Part 2 of 2)

**3.** Jesus was full of kindness at every turn. *"When Jesus landed and saw a large crowd, he had compassion on them, because they were like sheep without a shepherd. So he began teaching them many things."* (Mark 6:34)

*"Then they came to Jericho. As Jesus and his disciples, together with a large crowd, were leaving the city, a blind man, Bartimaeus (which means "son of Timaeus"), was sitting by the roadside begging. When he heard that it was Jesus of Nazareth, he began to shout, 'Jesus, Son of David, have mercy on me!' Many rebuked him and told him to be quiet, but he shouted all the more, 'Son of David, have mercy on me!' Jesus stopped and said, 'Call him.' So they called to the blind man, 'Cheer up! On your feet! He's calling you.' Throwing his cloak aside, he jumped to his feet and came to Jesus. 'What do you want me to do for you?' Jesus asked him. The blind man said, 'Rabbi, I want to see.' 'Go,' said Jesus, 'your faith has healed you.' Immediately he received his sight and followed Jesus along the road."* (Mark 10:46-52)

When we exhibit the kindness of God, we are tender, benevolent, and helpful to others. Every action and word we speak should have the flavour of grace and love. To maintain this attitude toward those we love is not easy, but then everything is easier with Holy Spirit in control. To express kindness toward those against us requires the work of Holy Spirit in you, pouring out of you.

*Life* is a test... What would happen to our world if everyone exhibited kindness? Can it start with you?

# What to look for in a Church.

It is rather obvious that it needs to be Bible-based. That means that the final decision and the final Word of God being taught in the church are from the Bible. Pastors can preach excellent, politically correct sermons but still go off the wrong road. Everything they say needs to be based on scripture. The head person in the church should be an apostle or a prophet (Eph. 2:20). The church's leadership needs to be based upon a five-fold leadership/ministry (Eph. 4:11) with all the 30 Gifts being used by the congregation. Next, there needs to be pastors, evangelists, and teachers. These can be from the congregation (see the Gifts poster following Feb. 1). All members must mutually submit to one another. No room in any church exists for disorder, unrepentant sins or abuses, scandals, gossip, and strife. If there is, root it out! Everything must be done with dignity as ambassadors of Christ. It should be an Ekklesia - a spiritual governmental assembly ordained by God with signs following and impacting the local community and nations. Jesus must be honoured above all principalities and powers.

The best churches I've seen are ones that have four solid foundations for beginners:

**1.** Strong Bible teaching. The Alpha program is excellent.
**2.** A strong foundation on healing and deliverance for everyone in the church.
**3.** A solid teaching of biblical economics.
**4.** The discovery and usage of Spiritual Gifts.
**5.** A strong teaching about sin, repentance, the cross etc.
All these teachings should be compulsory for every person in the church, and once they have learned them, they should discover where they can be "plugged in."

**Doc's Book Club:** Read *"Christians going to Hell"* by Seung Woo Byun

*Life* is a test... How does your church compare to these points?

## Leadership (Part 1 of 3)

Having been self-employed for +40 years, I know what "leadership" means. A "leader" is a servant. He serves the people (staff first and customers second)* and sets the standard of performance and behaviour. He must develop a calibre of excellence (Titus 3:8). All of this is exemplified by Jesus. He was the ultimate leader, wise as a serpent and gentle as a dove. We do not "serve" God, He is our Father, and we are His children, not His servants. We are to "serve" each other as fellow believers. Leadership is "servanthood" (e.g., Jesus washed His disciple's feet).

A good leader can often be recognized by his followers, and followers, as a rule, are very good at identifying talent, Gifts and anointing. If you go and tell people that you're anointed, you're probably not, and you're probably not a leader. Other people will call you out as they recognize your spiritual leadership gift in you. Chuck Pierce and Peter Wagner called me out as an apostle when I didn't even know what an apostle was! A sound leader is also a good manager of finances. He tithes give to the poor, looks after widows and orphans, commits time and resources to the church and keeps his debt at a minimum, if at all. *"But select capable men from all the people - men who fear God, trustworthy men who hate dishonest gain - and appoint them as officials over thousands, hundreds, the fifties and tens."* (Ex. 18:21)

*Life* is a test... Has someone "called you out" to a position, or have you called yourself out?

* If you don't look after the staff first, you won't have any customers!

## Leadership (Part 2 of 3)

Leaders not only handle change well but go and look for it. A leader does not follow the axiom, "well, we've always done it that way." His attitude is "more the reason that it should be changed!" Leaders know that they are being left behind if sitting on their "blessed assurances." In short, if you feel comfortable, you know you're missing it. A leader challenges himself and others. Good leaders do not deny reality but instead recognize the times of turbulence as an excellent time for growth and development, not only by their followers but also by themselves.

I belong to a private sports club in Calgary. Years ago, the CEO, who has no boss other than the Board of Directors, decided that he needed to have a performance review of himself. As the boss, he always conducted performance reviews of his General Manager and Executive staff, but who reviewed him? One day, he thought, "how do I know how good of a job I'm doing? What things can I improve?" So he decided to hire a consulting firm and then put together a questionnaire randomly sent to some of the members. Only a leader would do that and ask those questions! Quite an act of humility, wouldn't you agree?

*Life* is a test... Are you challenging yourself regularly to grow?

# Leadership (Part 3 of 3)

After I had written *"Life is a Test"* volume one, I gave it to one of my mentors and asked him to provide me with feedback. I wanted to know if I had said anything from a theological perspective that was "out to lunch." He graciously accepted my gift and said he would give me feedback, adding that "nobody ever asks me to do that." One of the critical ingredients for being a good leader is accepting constructive criticism and going and looking for it. If handled correctly, no, it is not a sign of weakness or insecurity; it is a sign of a leader's desire - he always wants to improve the operation, including himself.

A good leader knows when to ignore competition (threats), respect them or look them in the eye and stare them down. "Fear not" is in the Bible over 450 times, and I don't know of anything that can destroy a person more than fear. It seems that most bad decisions in life are based on a foundation of fear. We are not all called to be leaders, but we should support those who are.

Some of my favourite fear quotes:

*"It's not death a man should fear, but he should fear never beginning to live."* - Marcus Aurelius

*"The greatest mistake we can make is living in constant fear we will make one."* - John C Maxwell

*"Never be afraid of trying something new. Remember, amateurs build the ark; professionals built the titanic."* - Unknown

**Doc's Book Club:** Read any books written by John Maxwell. A former pastor, John is now "the leader in leadership" worldwide.

 is a test... Are you able to have humility and ask others to critique you or your work?

**www.newstartministries.ca**

# What is the Will of God for You?
## (Part 1 of 3)

People ask me at times, "how do I know the will of God. I just wish I knew the will of God. What's the will of God for my life?" My answer to them is, "you will know what to do." How? Start with things that tell you from the Word what to do. Examples include always rejoicing and always giving thanks.

When you don't know, start with what you do know. You have a Bible and know God's will when you study His Word. Therefore, start with what you know, which is what God says. Find those scriptures that say or indicate, "this is the will of God."

*"Rejoice always, pray continually, give thanks in all circumstances; for this is God's will for you in Christ Jesus."* (Thess. 5:16-18) *"...always giving thanks to God the Father for everything, in the name of our Lord Jesus Christ."* (Eph. 5:20)

Do what the Word says, "pray continually," which will open doors for you. Doors to what? Understanding. Do whatever steps you are to be taking. If you study the Word, you will get a deeper understanding of the will of God. Does this mean that we walk around and in prayer all the time? No, it means that you have God on your mind, and you can pray in tongues quietly at yourself all day long. Last week, on my way to the grocery store, I praised God and worshiped Him the whole time I was showering, getting dressed and driving to the store. Guess what happened? I received sales and discounts totalling 1/3 of my bill! Receiving deals and discounts is a normal way of life for me, just like hearing from God.

 is a test... He is revealing Himself 24/7; are you tapping into that?

# What is the Will of God for You?
## (Part 2 of 3)

From March 2020 to today, I have thoroughly studied COVID-19. Not only from an academic perspective but mainly from a spiritual side. As billions of people worldwide are in fear, I am sitting comfortably, not in fear of anything. Why? Because God tells me what my next move is, what to do and what not to do, I am confident in His voice. Instead of confessing, "I don't know what to do," acknowledge this instead, "I know what to do as the Lord leads me."

If you think whatever first thought comes to your mind at any moment, or worse yet, you then say that thought, it won't be something good nine out of ten times. We live in a very hostile world, so we say negative things. As soon as you hear yourself saying, "what are we gonna do?" you know that you are already in trouble. We react without thinking of the consequences of our words. Instead, speak your words in faith. "I know what to do. God is giving me ideas and solutions right now. Thank you, Jesus."

Jesus said, *"...If you hold to my teaching, you are really my disciples. Then you will know the truth, and the truth will set you free."* (John 8:31-32) When you know the truth about the wisdom of God, it will set you free.

*Life* is a test... Are you conscious of the words that you speak?

# What is the Will of God for You?
## (Part 3 of 3)

Did you know that you are the prophet of your own life? The wisdom of God about you is in the Word; just find it and confess it! God wants to reveal various truths to you. Be it about Himself, about yourself, about the world, or about taking care of others well. We are all called to have God-given prophetic vision as to how to live with wisdom each day. So, prophesy! Share His vision and love with others.

Who oversees the destiny of your life? You do! Just use the Word of God as your foundation and then speak those Words of wisdom about yourself. *"For I know the thoughts and plans that I have for you, says the Lord, ideas and plans for welfare and peace and not for evil, to give you hope in your outcome. Then you will call upon Me, and you will come and pray to Me, and I will hear and heed you. Then you will seek Me, inquire for, and require Me (as a vital necessity) and find Me when you search for Me with all your heart."* (Jer. 29: 11-13 AMPC)

The next time that you don't know what to do read the above scripture, the part where it says "seek Me" and "He has plans."

*Life* is a test... Are you prophesying over your own life?

## Dross

What is it? According to the Canadian Oxford dictionary, *"the scum separated from metals in melting. Foreign matter mixed with anything; impurities."*

What is God trying to do in all of us? Get the dross out. How? The same way it gets out of metal; by becoming molten metal. In other words, we must go through God's fiery furnace, called "life." It won't happen just once, either; get used to it...

We are born with a destiny and a plan. God's plan. Our job is to find out what it is and then do it. However, because we are "born into sin," we want to control and fight (intentionally or unintentionally) against Him; the guy who knows all things sees and understands all things. Essentially, that means that we "don't need to know." He knows, so why do we need to? What to do???

We must learn to live from within ourselves, talking and listening to Holy Spirit inside us. He resides in the deepest depths of our being in eternal union. At that deep level of connection, we find peace. The world is constantly in flux, disaster, death and decay. But inside us is a goldmine of wisdom, knowledge and peace, just waiting to be tapped.

Seek to love Him and others and ourselves, too and know Him how He loves and understands you. Seek to be in Christ, know Christ, and grow in Christ instead of constantly searching for answers in a world that has none (and never will). He has all the answers so just seek Him. Simple stuff…

*"Trust in the Lord with all your heart, And lean not on your own understanding."* (Prov. 3:5 NKJV)

is a test... Pray the brave prayer and ask God to refine the dross out of you.

## Rest; you deserve a break today...

*"For if Joshua had given them rest, God would not have spoken later about another day. There remains, then, a Sabbath-rest for the people of God; for anyone who enters God's rest also rests from their works, just as God did from his. Let us, therefore, make every effort to enter that rest, so that no one will perish by following their example of disobedience."* (Heb. 4:8-11)

Our society is too busy, our rest is too short, and fear plagues the time in between. Our minds are bombarded with lies every single day. Social media tells us that if we don't think, dress, or act a certain way, then we don't matter. In school, we are told that if you're not good at academics or athletics, or are not popular with others, then we don't matter. This world is full of lies, and we have believed many of them. However they're just not true. We are made in God's image, and part of His image is to rest. Not only are we to rest one day a week, but we can seek God's rest anytime we want during the week. We can stop and rest just as God says He did when He made the earth.

*"Come to Me, all you who labour and are heavily laden, and I will give you rest."* (Matt.11:28)

*"Praise be to the Lord, who has given rest to his people Israel just as he promised."* (I Kings 8:56)

I am writing this in April 2022, and I just experienced a bad case of burnout. Whose fault is that? Take one day off to spend with family and God and relax and get rested. Take frequent rest breaks during the week. Spend time with God first and your family second.

*Life* is a test... Are you resting?

## By Design:

- You were created before the earth was. (Eph. 1:4, Jer.1:5)
- You were created in His image. (Gen. 1:27)
- You were created to worship. (Is. 43:21) If it's not God you are worshiping, then it will be some other thing or narcissistic endeavour; it is God's nature for you to worship.)
- You were created to do good works. (Eph. 2:10)
- You were created to connect with Him; depend on Him moment by moment. (Acts 17:28)
- You were created to live in an "earth suit" here on this planet for a limited time to bring heaven into the earth (Matt. 6:10), and in doing so, your job is to go out into the world and make disciples of all men. (Matt. 28:19)
- You are to continue this life as soul and spirit only, in eternal heaven (paradise) with God. However, God gives you freedom, and that freedom is the ability to "choose" as to whether you live for Him now and with Him later. (Deut. 30:19, Jos. 24:15)

## Starting Life and Living it to the Fullest.

Years ago, an article in our local newspaper about a community building under construction to help the "bored youth." I wrote the following letter to the editor:

To our "bored youth." Here are some suggestions to help you with your problem: rake the lawn, plant a garden, paint the fence, clean the garage, wash the car, make some repairs around the house, learn to cook, sew, paint, build, or any of dozens of other hobbies; shovel the snow for a senior, give help to a pastor or priest, tutor someone, read to the blind, visit the sick or the senior's centre, coach a minor-league, become a Brownie or Scout Leader, learn to play a musical instrument, go to church, work on volunteer organizations, help a disabled person, go buy the groceries for people who are "shut ins," help your parents and a teacher, do your homework, start a fund raiser for charity, register for a continuing education course, participate in any of dozens of recreational activities that are in abundance in our community, get involved in politics, get a job, start your own business, surf the net and learn something, babysit, and if all else fails go to the library and read a non-fiction book! (note: a man I know started mowing lawns when he was 14. Here it is years later, and he has 35 staff.)

Your parents do not owe you entertainment, your community does not owe you recreational facilities, and the world does not owe you anything. On the contrary, you owe the world something - your time, energy, gifts, talents, and money so that no one will be at war, in poverty, sick or lonely again. Life is about making the world a better place when you leave than when you arrived. Don't be a protester; grow up and be an agent of change...

Billions of people are, cold, poor, sick, hurt, hungry, or at war because you haven't helped them. Life is not about you. So, what are you bored about and what are you waiting for?

The "Design" Poster can be downloaded and printed in any size for $7.95 CAD.

www.newstartministries.ca

# Faith

One of my joys in life is working out at the gym. Like everyone else, I was shut down during Covid, so I bought myself some equipment, and now I have my gym in the garage! I have a TV there, so I can watch several Christian programs that I like when I'm on my running track. I was watching the Believers Voice of Victory recently, and they referred to a book called "Christ the Healer" by F.F. Bosworth. This book is very famous and one of those "foundational books" that everybody needs to read about the subject of healing.

Here is a direct quote that summarizes the subject of faith quite well:

*"Faith begins where the will of God is known. If it is God's will to heal only those who need healing, then none have any basis for faith unless they have a special revelation that they are among the favoured ones. Faith must rest on the will of God alone, not on our desires or wishes. Appropriating faith is not believing that God can but that God will. Because of not knowing it to be a redemptive privilege for all, most people in our day, when seeking healing, add to their petition, "if it is your will."\**

There are no "ifs" when it comes to faith. "God can, and God does," if we learn to use our faith and receive His power.

*Life* is a test... Are you praying "ifs" or believing God can?

\* Chapter 2, page 43, original text written in 1924 and published by Whitaker House 2000.

*Life* is a test...

# What is

## FAITH?

**H**aving been saved by **FAITH**, *"If you declare with your mouth, "Jesus is Lord," and believe in your heart that God raised him from the dead, you will be saved."* (Rom. 10:9) It makes sense that we should continue to live by **FAITH**, *"The righteous shall live by faith."* (Rom. 1:17b) What does it mean to live by **FAITH**, though, and how do we do it? The Bible tells us, *"by the* **FAITH** *God has distributed to each of you"* (Rom. 12:3) so we all have **FAITH**. We increase our **FAITH** by hearing the Word of God. Consequently, **FAITH** *comes from hearing the message, and the message is heard through the word about Christ"* (Rom. 10:17), and we express **FAITH** by walking in love *"The only thing that counts is* **FAITH** *expressing itself through love."* (Gal. 5:6) Hebrews 11:6 tells us that if we are not living by **FAITH**, we are not pleasing God *"And without* **FAITH** *it is impossible to please God,"* and Rom. 14:23 confirms this by saying that *"everything that does not come from* **FAITH** *is sin."*

Therefore, we are to grab hold of the promises of God, stand on them, confess them, believe them, and exercise our **FAITH**, which is to *"calls into being things that were not."* (Rom. 4:17) Hebrews 11:1 tells us, *"Now* **FAITH** *is confidence in what we hope for and assurance about what we do not see." In Matthew, "When he had gone indoors, the blind men came to him, and he asked them, 'Do you believe that I am able to do this?' 'Yes, Lord,' they replied. Then he touched their eyes and said, 'According to your* **FAITH** *let it be done to you;' Their sight was restored."* (Matt. 9:28-29) Finally, we build our **FAITH** by praying in the Holy Spirit, *"by building yourselves up in your most holy* **FAITH** *and praying in the Holy Spirit."* (Jude 20)

The "Faith" Poster is part of the Christian Manifesto Poster series. Produced in Calgary, Alberta, Canada, by New Start Ministries Ltd. These posters are available for sale from: www.newstartministries.ca  COPYRIGHT 2022.

The "Faith" Poster can be downloaded and printed in any size for $7.95 CAD.

www.newstartministries.ca

## We are all Facades....

One of the worst consequences of the fall of man in the Garden of Eden is the elaborate and complex barriers that we all put between ourselves and others. Facades abound in the world, and the church, ironically, does not escape it. How often is there strife at home about going to church and being on time, and when the family gets there, the "Christianese smiles" come out, and everyone is just fine! Right... We cover our authentic selves with our Sunday clothes, smiles, hugs and warm greetings. Then when we get home, we feel such a relief from the strain of "forced fellowship." The church is often the last place where people feel free to be themselves.

The solution to this artificial atmosphere is practicing His Presence at church, that "constant contact" again. Let your primary focus be communing with Him, worshiping Him, and glorifying Him. Then you will be able to smile at others with His Joy and love them with His love instead of trying to force the Fruits of the Spirit out of your personality. Next time you go to church, just leave all your defences at home, rest in the Spirit and take Him all in.

*"If we claim to have fellowship with him and yet walk in the darkness, we lie and do not live out the truth. But if we walk in the light, as he is in the light, we have fellowship with one another, and the blood of Jesus, his Son, purifies us from all sin."* (1 John 1:6-7)

*Life* is a test... Can you disconnect, and leave all your junk at home and come to church to truly worship?

## "Performance Review."

When it comes to God giving you a performance review, I have good news - you don't need one! Why? Firstly, you can't live up to His expectations (*"for all have sinned and fall short of the glory of God"* Rom. 3:23). Secondly, He doesn't care to give you a review. He loves you regardless of how well you are "performing."

Granted, He's not a happy camper about your sin, but He is so filled with love and grace that as long as you are faithful in confessing your sin, He is gracious and forgives you.

*"If we confess our sins, He is faithful and just to forgive us our sins, and to cleanse us from all unrighteousness."* (1 John 1:9 KJV)

Why does He do this? One reason and one reason only - love.

*"For God so loved the world, that He gave His only begotten Son, that whosoever believeth in Him should not perish, but have everlasting life."* (John 3:16 KJV)

*"I have loved you with an everlasting love;"* (Jer. 31:3)

Your accomplishments and your Christian walk have no bearing on God's love for you. We want to assess our abilities and analyze how we are doing. That is OK as long it is not a daily ritual and/or obsession. Our limited human perspective and the condition of our hearts distort our review of ourselves. We won't get it right, so why bother?

The solution? Bring all your performance anxieties to God and put them at His feet and sit back and receive His unfailing love for you. Problem solved.

*Life* is a test... Are you evaluating yourself? Why?

*Life* is a test...

# Waiting upon the Lord. Do I have to??
## (Part 1 of 3)

Waiting is painful. We live in an instant world. I remember one of the first times that a significant change started towards instant things: the microwave oven! Dinner was ready in a few minutes! It was unbelievable at the time. Then the internet gave us an instant connection to the world, and now we have smartphones which are not just telephones anymore; they are mini-instant computers at our fingertips. We are so used to the "instant" factor and having it now that our society has lost its patience! "Suffering for Jesus" means having to wait!

Then, we must wait on God! No really? We cry, "Oh God, why are you not answering my prayers? I started praying on Friday, and today is Monday, and still, no answers! Ugh!

Remember that:

- David waited at least 15 years from the time he was anointed to be a leader until he became King.

- Moses waited 40 years in the wilderness before God called him into action.

- Sarah waited 25 years from the time God told Abraham he and his wife would have a son until the day Isaac was born. No wonder she laughed at the idea!

- Hannah endured years of barrenness waiting for her baby, Samuel.

When you are in a hurry and impatient, read what David said in Psalm 40:1. *"I waited patiently for the Lord; He turned to me and heard my cry."*

*Life* is a test... How is waiting on the Lord going?

# Waiting upon the Lord. Do I have to??
## (Part 2 of 3)

The interesting thing about prophecy and hearing from God is that there never seems to be a consistent date or time. I was given a prophetic Word in 1998 by a pastor/prophet from England, and I'm still waiting for it to come to pass. I believe it has in the supernatural but has not manifested yet in the natural. God promises and often reveals strategies and visions and sends provision and *"witty inventions"* (Prov. 8:1). However, He never says when, and usually, we have to go through some warfare ("Life is a Test!"), and this is a test of our faith to see if all these things will come to pass. God is not giving us "fortune-telling" words. What a prophetic Word from the Lord is, is something that can come to pass if conditions align with His Word. In short, whether it happens or not is often dependent on us. If a prophet says to you, "I see you working in the mission field in Africa...." It won't happen until you get some education about missions, the money to go etc. In other words, God's Words to us are what can happen if we live by faith (and *"faith without works is dead."* - James 2:17)

There is an excellent story in the Bible about Zerubbabel and Joshua (not the promised land conquering one, the other one!) The two men were commissioned to rebuild Solomon's temple after it was destroyed by Babylon (see the end of 2 Kings). They got "down in the dumps" looking at the ruins of Jerusalem. The job was overwhelming, the cost was over budget (no money anyway), and "employee" morale sucked. Then there were the bad guys out to get them. The familiar spirits (you know who they are!) became "too familiar" and worked overtime to make their lives miserable. A hopeless situation, but God heard their cry for help.

*Life is a test...*

## Waiting upon the Lord. Do I have to??
### (Part 3 of 3)

Along came good ole Haggi, the prophet who gave them a Word from the Lord. *"On the twenty-first day of the seventh month, the word of the Lord came through the prophet Haggai: 'Speak to Zerubbabel son of Shealtiel, governor of Judah, to Joshua, son of Jozadak, the high priest, and the remnant of the people. Ask them, Who of you is left who saw this house in its former glory? How does it look to you now? Does it not seem to you like nothing? But now be strong, Zerubbabel,' declares the Lord. 'Be strong, Joshua, son of Jozadak, the high priest. Be strong, all you people of the land,' declares the Lord, 'and work. For I am with you,' declares the Lord Almighty. 'This is what I covenanted with you when you came out of Egypt. And my Spirit remains among you. Do not fear.'"* Then in verse 9 *"'The glory of this present house will be greater than the glory of the former house,' says the Lord Almighty. 'And in this place, I will grant peace,' declares the Lord Almighty."* Talk about a morale booster!

God promises to labour with whom He calls. He doesn't give people visions and dreams without expecting them to get complete them. The Apostle Paul wrote: *"Being confident of this, that He who began a good work in you will carry it on to completion until the day of Christ Jesus."* (Phil. 1:6)

Remember Shadrach, Meshach, and Abednego? God didn't put out the fire. He just put Jesus in there with them, and they came out unsinged and without smoke. It's not about God stopping all the things that look bad; it's about who's in there with you. (see Daniel 3)

*Life* is a test... Ps. 46:10 says, *"Be still, and know that I am God."* How is that verse working for you?

## Who Would've thought...

The "Abraham Accord" was signed in August 2020 between Israel and its Arab neighbours. What has happened since? Relations between the two are flourishing:

- a signed joint venture to send an unmanned spaceship to the moon
- the Israel expo booth in Abu Dhabi was a smashing success
- airline routes between the two groups have opened
- Abu Dhabi has opened an investment office in Israel
- trade and sharing of technology is at an all-time high

The Arabs have realized peace is far better and more profitable than war.

Significance? Peace and booming economies are good, but ease also comes with preaching the gospel throughout the Middle East. In 1948 when Israel was formed, there were 30 (yes, three-zero) Christians. Today? In 2019 there were 177,000, and 3/4 of them were former Muslims. With doors opening to the Middle East, *"This gospel of the Kingdom will be preached in the whole world as a testimony to all nations, and then the end will come."* (Matt. 24:14)

*Life* is a test... Are you praying for reconciliation in the world? Are you studying Christian movements world wide? It's amazing stuff seeing what God's up to internationally!

## Know Who You Really Are. (Part 1 of 2)

You are a spirit, first and foremost. People don't think that way, but that is the truth. When you were born again, your soul came to life from being dead and was joined in union with Holy Spirit. In 1 Cor. 6:17, it says, *"But whoever is united with the Lord is one with Him in spirit."* What happened to you?

At the point of your salvation, you were knit together and reborn, cleansed, renewed, and a new life began. This born-again spirit (you) now had real power - not what the world calls power. The Bible calls it "the anointing."

You are a spirit first, soul second and body third. Let's put it another way; **you are a spirit, have a soul,** and live in a temporary "earth suit" (like an astronaut who wears a spacesuit) called a **body**. Why in this order? The human body is fragile and has a limited lifespan and time in space. It will last longer, however, if we don't abuse it.

Did you know that your body was a temple? *"Don't you know that you yourselves are God's temple and that God's Spirit dwells in your midst? If anyone destroys God's temple, God will destroy that person; for God's temple is sacred, and you together are that temple."* (1 Cor. 3:16-17) It amazes me how easily the enemy may sway people to pollute their temple (body) with cigarette smoke, excessive alcohol, excess sugar, no exercise etc.

Our soul consists of our mind, will, and emotions, which gives us our ability to think, our desires, happiness, fear, control, and sin. Your soul is supposed to be under the supervision of your spirit and not the other way around! Spirit and soul live forever (unlike your body); it's just a matter of whether you live in the "H place" or the other "h place," which, as I said before, is a choice you will make in life. At death it will be made for you if you didn't choose Jesus. "Hell is the enjoyment of our practice, forever."

*Life* is a test... Are you taking care of your temple?

## Know Who You Really Are. (Part 2 of 2)

1 John 2:27 says, *"As for you, the anointing you received from him remains in you, and you do not need anyone to teach you. But as his anointing teaches you about all things and as that anointing is real, not counterfeit - just as it has taught you, remain in him."*

This inner anoint-ing is used to keep you connected with God.

Acts 1:8 says, *"But you will receive power when the Holy Spirit comes on you, and you will be my witnesses in Jerusalem, and in all Judea and Samaria, and to the ends of the earth."*

This type of anointing is outward. It is the power of the Gifts that are active in you.

Isaiah 10:27 says, *"In that day their burden will be lifted from your shoulders, their yoke from your neck; the yoke will be broken because you have grown so fat."*

People in the Bible with this anointing were Moses, Joshua, Isaiah, Jeremiah, Ezekiel, Elijah, and Elijah. God used that to speak His Words to raise or destroy kingdoms. This type of anointing destroys the yoke of bondage like a spirit of religion, Jezebel or witchcraft etc.

How do you get these anointings to develop in you? Be hungry for them and ask for them. Walk in faith, and desire to have them. Most importantly, walk in love.

*Life* is a test... Which anointing are you most comfortable operating in? Inner, outer, or one that destroys bondage of the enemy?

# Yes God heals, but...

Since Jesus is the tree of life, in Him and only in Him can we be set free from sickness and disease. *"I am the Lord who heals you."* (Ex. 15:26). However, it comes with a catch; God's promises are conditional. He can only work through His laws (spiritual and natural laws), and His rules (ways) are recorded in His Word. His ways are higher than our ways (Is. 55:9). God says that He will perform what He has said in His Word, *"I will hasten My Word to perform it."* (Jer. 1:12) We are responsible for obeying all of God's laws and statutes as written in His Word (Ex. 15:26). If we do that, we can expect answers from God when we pray. However, if we are out of alignment with God (i.e., in sin), then we can't expect anything from Him - answers or healing.

The Word of God gives us life and life more abundantly (John. 10:10). The Word is alive (Heb. 4:12) and will make us successful in everything we do - if we apply it! The trouble is that billions of people have rejected God's instruction book. Mankind has an independent prideful streak in him (called sin) that says, "I can do it!" Not only is the Bible a book of wisdom, knowledge, direction, and instruction etc., but it's also a book of medicine. Where does so much wisdom regarding health/medicinal practices today come from? The book of Leviticus.

I have many of the books written by Dr. Don Colbert. He has dissected the Bible and found incredible information about health and nutrition, and he has written and taught these principles for years.

**Doc's Book Club:** Read any books by Dr. Don Colbert.

*Life* is a test... Are you looking after your spiritual and physical health?

## Politics (Part 1 of 2)

Even the mention of the word can make a person's blood pressure go up. As with all things in life, everything in this world needs to be filtered through the eyes of God. I regard politics as a potential worldly trap. We must keep things within a Godly perspective. Keep an eye on these eight points:

**1.** Don't mistake believing that any political leader can and will restore a nation. People get so caught up in this that they think that the body of Christ depends upon who gets elected and who controls the government. There is only one government, and that's the government of Jesus, (aka The Kingdom of God) who can work with and through any political party, assuming that they are listening. Of course, we want to be sensitive to voting for Godly capable leaders, but to think that a political leader being elected is the fate of a nation is just plain idolatry.

*"Peter and the other apostles replied: "We must obey God rather than human beings!"* (Acts 5:29)

**2.** We focus too much on change within a nation without the proclamation of the gospel. You must incorporate being the light of the world, preaching the gospel, and of course, your involvement in church. To fulfill that gospel, we must commit to community trans-formation, work with God, and trust in Him rather than putting our faith in political leaders. The gospel is first, and our elected governments are second.

**3.** We think the solution to the problem is political change rather than promoting the gospel, which we should be doing. Changing laws is good; promoting biblical public policies is good too, but that's not what Jesus called us to do. His golden rule was for us to seek His kingdom first. *"But seek first His Kingdom and His righteousness, and all these things will be given to you as well."* (Matt. 6:33) What does all mean? "All" means all, doesn't it? Therefore, that includes politics and all the levels of government regulating our nations.

## Politics (Part 2 of 2)

**4.** Pray for your government. *"I urge, then, first of all, that petitions, prayers, intercession and thanksgiving be made for all people - for kings and all those in authority, that we may live peaceful and quiet lives in all godliness and holiness."* (1 Tim. 2: 1-2). Never pray against your Prime Minister, President, Premier, Mayor etc. Pray for Jesus in their lives.

**5.** "A political party represents the Kingdom of God." Ah, no, they don't. Many Christians on both the left and the right think their party is the correct one and represents God. My experience of the left is that they are too socialist, which is not the Bible, and the right can go too far as well. What did Jesus say? *"My Kingdom is not of this world. If it were, my servants would fight to prevent my arrest by the Jewish leaders. But now My Kingdom is from another place."* (John 18:36)

**6.** When election time comes, you're sold out working on the election, going to rallies, and forgetting your responsibilities with your family and church. Church attendance during an election campaign should be doubling, not decreasing!

**7.** Never use the Bible as a political handbook to justify your political ideologies. Self-righteous Christians will preach fire and brimstone against political parties. Look, read your Bible, focus on you, work towards community transformation, evangelism, and making disciples of other men. Pray for political leaders and then go and vote.

**8.** There's nothing wrong with financially supporting political parties, but it must be way behind your giving into the Kingdom. Read Romans 13:1-7.

*Life* is a test... Are you radically into politics or exercising faith through prayer and voting for Godly politicians?

## Receiving Refreshment from God.

The beach is nice. Curling up in an easy chair and relaxing with friends is good too. TV works for a while. However, nothing compares to the refreshing time that we can have in the presence and anointing of Holy Spirit. Firstly, it can happen in a second, anytime, anyplace. Secondly, like the weather, God is free.

*"With joy, you will draw water from the wells of salvation."* (Is. 12:3)

There are times in our lives when we can get parched. But that is all our doing, not His, because the reality of the matter is that Holy Spirit never leaves or forsakes us. (Jos. 1:5; Deut. 31:6) What to do when we are dry?

**1.** Confess any known sin.

**2.** Just say this, "Jesus, I come into your presence by your blood." Remember that it's not your work that can get you into His presence. *"Therefore, brothers and sisters, since we have confidence to enter the Most Holy Place by the blood of Jesus."* (Heb. 10:19)

**3.** Ask and welcome Holy Spirit and let Him manifest and fill you up. Start praising God over and over.

**4.** Slip into a pattern of Thanksgiving. Praise God and thank Him for all the blessings in your life. Play some worship music.

**5.** Meditate on His Word. Hopefully, you have memorized some scriptures. Read your bible and rejoice in His Word.

**6.** Sit and just rest with Holy Spirit.

*Life* is a test... What is your standard solution when you are feeling dry?

## You are Nothing.*

Make the best of your time in life by strengthening yourself within the blessings and anointing of Holy Spirit. What does this require? Your undivided attention. In chapter 1, verse 8 of his book, Joshua said, *"Keep this Book of the Law always on your lips; meditate on it day and night, so that you may be careful to do everything written in it. Then you will be prosperous."* The foundation of your very life is this relationship with Holy Spirit, and everything else will spring from it. Without Holy Spirit, you are nothing; you do nothing, see nothing, and know nothing. Isn't that what Sergeant Schultz used to say from Hogan's Heroes? (I couldn't resist...)

The bottom line is that you have nothing apart from God. Rejoice that He cares for you and remember to humble yourselves under the mighty hand of God. Never forget to cast all your care upon Him for He cares for you (taken from 1 Peter 5:6-7).

The problem with our lives is that we allow circumstances to dictate our sense of well-being. We are happy when things are going well, and we are miserable when things are not going well. Talk about a roller coaster! Rather than go for this ride, refuse to allow your circumstances to dictate your sense of well-being. Stay strong and steady.

*"Yes, my soul, find rest in God; my hope comes from Him. Truly He is my rock and my salvation; He is my fortress, I will not be shaken. My salvation and honour depend on God. He is my mighty rock, my refuge. Trust in Him at all times, you people; pour out your hearts to Him, for God is our refuge."* (Ps. 62.5-7)

*Life* is a test... Are you living "your" life or His?

* without Jesus

# The Month of Tammuz (June/July - Part 1 of 4)

**Alphabet:** The letter is "CHET" (C is not pronounced) - Chet is the Hebrew number "8," which signifies new beginnings.

**Tribe:** Rueben - to hear; be concerned.

**Characteristics:** - The month to guard your heart and your eyes. (Deut. 11:26, 30:15-19)

- The letter Chet is a symbol of life, but sin is also a Chet word. This is a month we must be careful to choose correctly.

- The month where God destroys so He can reconstruct. Consider what you hear and decide how to develop a new level of discernment or oppose counsel and advice.

- Rueben was Jacob's firstborn. He had great potential but failed to excel because he didn't deal with his fundamental issues. This month, ask the Lord to help you deal with issues (sin) holding you back.

- This is the month when Moses's face glowed after being with the Lord. God wants you to draw close to Him to receive his glory! Rise and shine!

- The Jews call this the "filmstrip" month. It is a time to look at your life like a filmstrip and see how it progresses. It's a month you can stop and assess your life and then any necessary adjustments.

**Constellation:** Leo cancer (the crab); remove the shell from your body and declare every shell around you will break. (Deut. 11:26, 30:15-19)

**Colour/Stone:** Carnelian

*Life* is a test... Do you keep a diary so that you can measure your self development?

## The Month of Tammuz (June/July - Part 2 of 4)

Look back at the events of your life and see how they are linked. It is a month to discern God's plan for your life. You should see an increase. Remember the blessings God has brought into your life! If blessings are not increasing, ask God to show you anything that needs to change. This is a month to connect the individual scenes and begin to see where your story is going. So review your filmstrip this month and ask God what adjustments you need to make to move into the next phase of his blessing!

It is a month to worship and seek God! That is because Tammuz is a month with a snare! If you are not careful to worship and seek the Lord this month, you are in danger of building a golden calf. Anything you look to that is not God is idolatry; money, another person, excessive anything etc. God proved to the people of Israel that He could overcome anything in Egypt. However, the Israelites didn't believe him, and they made an idol. Whatever you hang on to for security is an idol, and idolatry brings a curse.

Idolatry brings problems because it is an abomination that causes desolation. Abomination means source of utter disgust* and desolation means emptiness, or barrenness. Idolatry brings a curse Deut. 27:15, *"cursed is the man who carves an image or creates an idle."* Idolatry causes God's presence to leave. Ezekiel 8:6, *"idolatry drove God's presence away!"*

*Life* is a test... If you were to struggle with idolatry, what area of your life would it be?

* (The bible says that to look upon the nakedness of a woman is an abomination unto the Lord which explains why pornography is so dangerous and addictive.)

## The Month of Tammuz (June/July - Part 3 of 4)

### What Causes Idolatry?

When you face the circumstances of life, there are two different paths you can take; fear or faith. Each leads to a different destination. If you follow fear, you become a control freak. Idolatry is the "attempt to use a power beyond yourself to gain control of life." Fear will always lead to idolatry because it is the foundation of anxiety which will never make you feel secure and always leads to frustration. You will never see the power of God. The alternative is faith! Fear and faith are opposite expressions of the same thing! Fear is the expectation of what evil may come.

Faith is the expectation of the good God will do! Fear is the expectation that God will not keep His promises, and satan will fill your mind. Faith is the expectation that God will keep His promises by meditating on those promises. If you live in fear, you are not in faith; you will not be in fear if you walk by faith!

If you have faith, you can trust God and put your life in His hands. Then you will yield control, and if you do that, you can submit to God's will. You will never walk in God's power and blessing if fear controls your life! Faith always releases power and anointing! "All things are possible to those who believe." (Matt 19:26) How do you move from fear to faith? Review your filmstrip! (your life)

*Life* is a test... Are you living in fear or faith?

## The Month of Tammuz (June/July - Part 4 of 4)

Gen. 35:22 says that Rueben committed adultery with his father's concubine Bilha. This incident changed the course of Rueben's life. His birthright was lost, and the double portion was taken away and given to Joseph. Leadership was taken away and given to Judah. The priesthood was taken away and given to Levi. Then, when Jacob blest the other sons, he pronounced a curse over Rueben. Why did Rueben do it?

Jacob's family had been through a traumatic period. They had fled from Laban and were saved only because God warned Laban not to harm Jacob. Escaping Laban, they faced a confrontation with Jacob's brother, Esau, who had vowed to kill Jacob. Entering Canaan, their sister Dinah was raped at Shechem, and two of her brothers massacred all the city men in retaliation. The Canaanites were enraged! Fleeing Shechem, Rebecca's nurse Deborah died and was buried, and then Rachel went into labour and died giving birth to Benjamin. The entire family had gone through a time of tremendous upheaval, violence and loss. Then, to top it all off, Rueben committed adultery with Bilha. He wasn't thinking about what blessings lay ahead or what he could lose. He just wanted comfort now! Bilha was his golden calf! Instead of turning to God, he needed comfort and security and sought them in Bilha. Unfortunately, the descendants of Rueben followed in his footsteps, and the tribes also lost their inheritance.

In the month of Tammuz, learn from Rueben! God had a great destiny for Rueben and his offspring, but he forfeited his future through a golden calf! God has a beautiful plan for you, so don't be seduced by what feels good now in this month of Tammuz. Don't settle for a golden calf! Accept your call and speak forth your destiny this month. The lesson from Rueben is the message of Paul in Phil. 3:13-14.

*Life* is a test... Do you have a golden calf in your life?

## Don't Be So hard on Yourself.

*"And we know that all things work together for good to those who love God, to those who are the called according to His purpose."* (Rom. 8:28 NKJV)

Seeing God's plans and purposes for our lives can be challenging, especially when we make mistakes. For this reason, it is a grave mistake for you and I to be so hard on ourselves. Good things may be a blessing and enjoyable, but they're not learning experiences. The best learning and the best growth come from our mistakes. *"Blessing doesn't mean that you'll never have a battle, but God will enable you to win."*\*

Our problem is that our finite minds tend to enjoy looking back, longing to fix the past, all those things that burden us with regret. This is a waste of time and energy, which does nothing but lead us into despair, anger and frustration. Remember that frustration is never faith. We have made mistakes and will continue to do so because we're human. If you keep thinking that one day you'll get it right and not make mistakes, then you're guilty of pride.

Instead, let your failures in life be a source of blessing. Look to God and trust with expectation, anticipating that He can make situations turn around and turn lemons into lemonade. Remember to humble yourself and give empathy to yourself and others for their weaknesses too. All of this is to realize how much we depend on Him, which is a good thing.

Please don't be so hard on yourself; let's face it, you were dumb when you did that, and you are no longer. You learned from it, so forgive yourself, forget, and move on. Life is too short to live with regret.

*Life* is a test... Do you enjoy beating yourself up by looking at your past mistakes? Why?

*\*"The King's Signet Ring: Uncovering the Significance of God's Covenant with You."*
by Dr. Chuck Pierce and Alemu Befftu. Chosen books. 2022 Page 22

# The Sixth Fruit of the Spirit - Goodness
## (Part 1 of 3)

Goodness is virtue and holiness in action. In other words, it's where "the rubber meets the road." Goodness is God in action and results in deeds motivated by righteousness and a desire to be a blessing. It's a moral characteristic of a Spirit-filled person. The Greek word translated "goodness," *agathosune*, is defined as "uprightness of heart and life." Agathosune is goodness for the benefit of others, not us.

Goodness causes a person to act selflessly on behalf of others. Giving to the poor, providing for one's children, visiting the sick, volunteering for church activities, being a prayer warrior. Confronting someone about a sin demonstrates goodness too. Goodness is a commitment to do good over evil and right over wrong. The fruit of the Spirit of goodness mentioned in Gal. 5:22 also includes generously doing good to others.

Goodness is not something that we can just conjure on our own. James 1:17 says, *"Every good thing is given and every perfect gift is from above, coming down from the Father of lights."* It comes from God and, as with all things from God, manifests itself in us through Holy Spirit. When others see our good works, they will praise our Father in heaven (Matt. 5:16).

Ps. 33:4-5 says, *"For the Word of the LORD is right, and all His work is done in truth. He loves righteousness and justice; the earth is full of the goodness of the LORD."*

Eph. 5:8-10 uses some of these synonyms: *"For you were once darkness, but now you are light in the Lord. Walk as children of light (for the fruit of the Spirit is in all goodness, righteousness, and truth), finding out what is acceptable to the Lord."*

God wants the earth to be full of His goodness. However, since satan took control of the planet, he and mankind have come up with their own definitions of goodness. Our society has largely decided what is right and wrong not based on what God has taught us but on whatever mood, feeling or biased "research" they've experienced on the matter. "If it feels good, do it!"

# The Sixth Fruit of the Spirit - Goodness
## (Part 2 of 3)

Psalm 107 reads: *"Oh, that men would give thanks to the LORD for His goodness, and for His wonderful works to the children of men!"* The rest of the psalm mentions many aspects of God's goodness, such as He delivered His people from distress and afflictions brought on by their sins and led them the right way (verses 6-8).

What is the opposite of goodness? Evil. John 8:44 says that satan *"was a murderer from the beginning, and does not stand in the truth, because there is no truth in him. When he speaks a lie, he speaks from his resources, for he is a liar and the father of it."* Satan lied to Adam and Eve, and he continues that today. Do you think he will tell you what goodness is and that you should do it?

What is the purpose of goodness? Well, it is good for us! We are to be a light showing what is truly moral and good. Where can we find a great example of goodness in the Bible? In 2 Chron. 29 through 32. You can read here about Hezekiah, who was a good dude after his father's wicked reign. Hezekiah cleansed the temple and restored his society to worship God. Another example is that King Josiah (2 Chron. 34 and 35) followed the same pattern as Hezekiah, purging the kingdom of pagan practices. He found God's Book of the Law written by Moses and restored the Church, including Passover. When others are not "good," we can set an example of goodness in our lives.

*Life* is a test... How do you see goodness in your everyday life?

# The Sixth Fruit of the Spirit - Goodness
## (Part 3 of 3)

A bad example would be Manasseh, who was Joseph's son. It's interesting to note the pattern of history here. There were so many problems with Jacobs's children; then Joseph became a shining light, then the pattern of sins started again with Manasseh, who has not known for his goodness. Although Manasseh later repented at the end of his life, he brought back all the disgusting pagan influences and practices to the land, including child sacrifice, sorcery, witchcraft and the occult. His repentance was too late because his son Amon encouraged these evil practices when he became King. We must evaluate this world's ideas of "good," and then think about Isaiah 5:20: *"Woe to those who call evil good, and good evil; who put darkness for light, and light for darkness."*

**"Goodness"** Test:
**1.** Whose standard am I using when I say that I am a good person? Societies or the Bible?
**2.** Do I walk in life with fairness and integrity?
**3.** Is goodness a way of life for me?
**4.** Goodness manifests itself by not being self-centered. Am I selfish?
**5.** Do people see the light of Jesus in me or do they just see me as another person in the world?
**6.** Am I obedient to God's commandments?
**7.** Am I generous in doing good to others?

How do we get more goodness? Read His Word and keep His Word. Learn how to focus on others instead of being your own "centre of the universe." Goodness pouring out of you will come back to you. *"Cast your bread upon the waters, for you will find it after many days."* (Ecc. 11:1)

*Life* is a test... How did you score on the goodness test?

# Tips for Being a Daily Success for the Kingdom. (Part 1 of 4)

I have written a great deal in this volume as well as the last one about wealth and prosperity. My conclusions are always that it is entirely biblical. Recently, I ran across a secular article entitled, "six rich people habits that will change your life." These habits are okay but definitely secular, so I will completely Christianize the information:

**1.** Get out of bed and get on with your day. God's Word clarifies that we are instructed to work hard and put our best effort forward. The Bible, especially in the wisdom-filled book of Proverbs, often speaks of the cause and effect relationship of hard work and rewards and the effects of laziness and ruin.

*"Lazy hands make for poverty, but diligent hands bring wealth."* (Prov. 10:4) *"Diligent hands will rule, but laziness ends in forced labour."* (Prov. 12:24) *"How long will you lie there, you sluggard? When will you get up from your sleep? A little sleep, a little slumber, a little folding of the hands to rest - and poverty will come on you like a thief and scarcity like an armed man."* (Prov. 6:9-12) *"The one who is unwilling to work shall not eat."* (2 Thess. 3:10)

**2.** Exercise and a proper diet.

*"Do you not know that your bodies are temples of the Holy Spirit, who is in you, whom you have received from God?"* (1 Cor. 6:19) You are not your own; your life and body are God's gifts.

What do you do when someone gives you a gift? Hopefully, you will look after it. The medical field is now saying that 65% of health issues could be eliminated if people were not obese. I deeply respect Dr. Henry's claims after studying over 10,000 cases that 80% of disease is self-inflicted either directly or indirectly.

**Doc's Book Club:** Read *"A More Excellent Way to Be in Health"* by Dr. Henry Wright.

## Tips for Being a Daily Success for the Kingdom. (Part 2 of 4)

**3.** Pray every day. Further, it would help you to connect with Holy Spirit moment by moment throughout the day.

*"Rejoice always, pray continually, give thanks in all circumstances; for this is God's will for you in Christ Jesus."* (1 Thess. 5:16-18)

Prayer is simply communicating with God - listening and talking to Him. Believers can pray from the heart, freely, spontaneously, and in their own words. Prayer develops our relationship with God. Our marriage relationship will quickly deteriorate if we don't speak to our spouse or never listen to anything our spouse might have said to us. It is the same way with God. You are married to God! Prayer - communicating with God - helps us grow closer and more intimately.

What do you need to have successful communication with God?

**A humble heart**
*"If my people, who are called by my name, will humble themselves and pray and seek my face and turn from their wicked ways, then will I hear from heaven and will forgive their sin and will heal their land."* (2 Chron. 7:14, NIV)

**Wholeheartedness**
*"You will seek me and find me when you seek me with all your heart."* (Jer. 29:13, NIV)

**Faith**
*"Therefore I tell you, whatever you ask for in prayer, believe that you have received it, and it will be yours."* (Mark 11:24, NIV)

**Righteousness**
*"Therefore confess your sins to each other and pray for each other so that you may be healed. The prayer of a righteous man is powerful and effective."* (James 5:16, NIV)

**Tips for Being a Daily Success for the Kingdom.** (Part 3 of 4)

### Obedience

*"And we will receive whatever we request because we obey him and do the things that please him."* (1 John 3:22, NLT)

**4.** Set Goals.

The Bible offers a balanced approach (like most things the bible says) to set goals that include making plans with wisdom, guidance and humility. Jesus said in Luke 14:28, *"Suppose one of you wants to build a tower. Won't you first sit down and estimate the cost to see if you have enough money to complete it?"*

However, just because we've completed our planning doesn't guarantee our goals will be met. The process of setting goals must be mixed with humility. James says, *"Now listen, you who say, "Today or tomorrow we will go to this or that city, spend a year there, carry on business and make money." Why, you do not even know what will happen tomorrow. What is your life? You are a mist that appears for a little while and then vanishes."* (James 4:13-14).

The Bible teaches against two extremes: never setting goals and setting goals with no thought of God. Everything we do in life must be wholly entrenched and involved with God. Again, James says in 4:15: *"Instead you ought to say, 'If it is the Lord's will, we will live and do this or that.'"* It is good to make plans if we leave room for God to change our plans. His goals take precedence over ours.

Setting goals is one way to faithfully steward the resources and gifts God gives us. In all our goal setting, we must be submissive to God. Our goals should align with His plans for us and the things He esteems in His Word. We must also be humble. We may think things will look one way, but God can change our plans to accomplish His greater purposes in and through us.

## Tips for Being a Daily Success for the Kingdom. (Part 4 of 4)

**5.** Read the Word. Considering that the Word of God is alive, it would make sense to have it wholly engrained into our souls and spirits. Bible study should be an integrated part of our everyday lifestyle. The Bible should not just be a book that sits on the coffee table or something that gets casually looked at during the week. Further, putting scripture to memory is a great place to keep it so that you can call on it when the trials and tribulations come upon you. Remember, *"A good man out of the good treasure of his heart brings forth good, and an evil man out of the evil treasure of his heart brings forth evil. For out of the abundance of the heart his mouth speaks."* (Luke 6:45 NKJV) The Word must be in your heart to speak it out.

*"All Scripture is God-breathed and is useful for teaching, rebuking, correcting and training in righteousness."* (2 Tim. 3:16)

*"Your word is a lamp for my feet, a light on my path."* (Ps. 119:105)

*"For the word of God is alive and active. Sharper than any double-edged sword, it penetrates even to dividing soul and spirit, joints and marrow; it judges the thoughts and attitudes of the heart."* (Heb. 4:12)

**6.** Love one another. I think that this one is relatively self-explanatory.

*"You have heard that it was said, 'Love your neighbour and hate your enemy.' But I tell you, love your enemies and pray for those who persecute you,"* (Matt. 5:43-44)

*"A new command I give you: Love one another. As I have loved you, so you must love one another."* (John 13:34)

*"Dear friends, since God so loved us, we also ought to love one another."* (1 John 4:11)

*Life* is a test... Which of these points are you doing that build life giving habits?

**www.newstartministries.ca**

## To Fast or Not to Fast; That is the Question. (Part 1 of 3)

What are the positives of practicing fasting in your life?

### Here's the Good stuff:
- It will renew your spiritual vision, and bring enhanced spiritual awareness allowing you to better hear God.
- Breaks you free from of you, putting your flesh under your foot and allowing God to speak greater direction into your life.
- Purifies, humbles, and refreshes you.
- Deepens your relationship with God, adding power to your prayers which make demons flee.
- Facilitates breakthroughs.
- Cleanses the physical body and sheds pounds.
- It will make you realize how addictive and dependent you have become on food in our glutenous society.
- It will free up your pocketbook and your schedule.

### The Bad stuff:
- It's a test, but then "Life is a Test" (so I heard one time...)
- You might think you're going to die, but you won't.

Why do it? Because the good stuff far outweighs the bad stuff, and Jesus simply told us to do it without explanation. (Matt. 6:16) Case closed...

*"Is not this the kind of fasting I have chosen: to loose the chains of injustice and untie the cords of the yoke, to set the oppressed free and break every yoke?"* (Is. 58:6)

**Doc's Book Club:** Jantezen Franklin has the best books about fasting.

*is a test...*

# To Fast or Not to Fast; That is the Question. (Part 2 of 3)

The Christian pollster George Barna has said that less than 10% of the body of Christ tithes. I suspect probably 90% pray, but I wonder how many people are praying correctly. Fasting? Your guess is as good as mine, but I'll bet it isn't even close to 5%. What does that mean, then? That only 5% of Christians are having significant breakthroughs?? Could be. Many healing pastors say that less than 5% of people are healed and retain their healing at altar calls. All I know is that Jesus *said in Matt. 6, "when you pray," ... "when you give," .... and "when you fast..."* It is not an option.

*"Is this not the fast that I have chosen: To loose the bonds of wickedness, To undo the heavy burdens, To let the oppressed go free, And that you break every yoke?"* (Is. 58:6 NKJV)

Sometimes, it can take a severe devoted fast to break through either the demonic stronghold or put yourself in a position to hear from God.

The Bible reveals several different kinds of fast that can be used to unlock breakthroughs and victory:

**1.** Daniel fasted for 21 days for a breakthrough while seeking God's purpose and vision for what God wanted for His people (read Daniel 1:5-21; 9:1-27; 10:1-23.

**2.** Queen Esther fasted for divine protection and supernatural direction against the evil plans of Haman, who wanted to destroy the Jewish state (read Es. 4:16; 5:2).

**3.** John the Baptist and the disciples fasted to grow in their relationship with Jesus and be effective in their ministry (read Matt. 9:14; Luke 4: 1-2; Mark 2:18).

# To Fast or Not to Fast; That is the Question. (Part 3 of 3)

**4.** Jesus fasted for 40 days and 40 nights for spiritual power and victory over satan, particularly in temptation (read Matt. 4:1-2).

**5.** When God's people were bound by idle worship and needed deliverance, God sent Samuel, the prophet and judge who fasted for his nation's repentance, revival and restoration. That certainly sounds like something that we should be doing today! (read 1 Samuel 7:6)

**How should we fast?**

**1.** A complete fast is abstaining from any kind of food, but make sure you check with your doctor and drink lots of water. The length? A day: 3 days, 7 days, 14 days, or go for 21! (make sure you take electrolytes)

**2.** A partial fast means abstaining from certain foods, usually sweets and meats. This is commonly called a Daniel fast, and many Christians like to do it in January after all the gorging over Christmas. Keep in mind that fasting is not to lose weight but to hear from God; losing weight is just an added bonus!

**3.** God might lead you to do a juice fast. Fruits and vegetable juices only and smoothies.

**4.** If you are a part of an intercessory prayer group, prayer warriors might often lead believers to fast together for some time, and what type of fast it is to be.

Your decision about how and when to fast is between you and God. I know some people in career ministry fast one day a week. As for myself, I do a full fast twice a year.

*Life* is a test... Have you discovered the joy of fasting? (sarcasm intended)

# Breakthrough; what brings it?

Well, fasting can! Holy Spirit was sent by Jesus to be our companion and our helper, to walk alongside each one of us every day in our Christian journey. His job is to equip us and then power us to defeat the devil and every one of his minions. Start your mornings with Holy Spirit! That will charge you in faith and give you the strength and boldness to do what God wants you to do during the day.

Have you noticed when reading the Gospels that Jesus was always talking to God in prayer? He would go out in the wilderness by Himself and pray even when the disciples fell asleep at the switch! When we commune with Holy Spirit, He reveals God's secrets to us. Psalm 25:14 says: *"The Lord confides in those who fear Him; He makes His covenant known to them."*

As a reminder of Jesus' sacrifice to us, Holy Communion was instituted as a method of remembrance of that sacrifice. Unfortunately, communion has become ritualized in many Christian churches today, which was not what Jesus had in mind.

**Here's a daily plan:**

Start your day with some praise and thanksgiving; move into asking the Lord to reveal the Word to you. Next, read the Word out loud; that way, you will hear it! Ask Him what He wants you to pray about. Do lots of listening for that still, small voice. Yes, you can petition Him with your requests and finally cap off your intimacy time with Holy Communion. Have some good worship music playing through your prayer time. About once a week, I listen to my CDs about the shofar (see October 25-26 of Volume 1 of *"Life is a Test"* for a teaching about this).

*Life* is a test... Do you have a devotional plan that you are putting it into action?

# July

# 1

## Happy Dominion (Canada) Day!

Spiritual DNA is the essence of who you are. It is what God has placed in your spirit - the very nature of your conscious mind. Just as we have a spiritual DNA, the same exists for a country. As I have mentioned in previous messages, God is very particular about land since He owns it and is compassionate about how His land is used. For example, whether the land is used for war and bloodshed or the growth and expansion of God's Kingdom, with multiplication and blessing, is needless to say, rather important to Him.

The supremacy of God is mentioned in the preamble to the Canadian constitution. God is also referenced in Canada's official name, the "Dominion of Canada." The term "Dominion" and Canada's motto: "A Mari usque ad Mari" both reference Psalm 72:8 - *"He shall have dominion also from sea to sea."* (NKJV)

The Dominion of Canada is our country's official title and was first applied to Canada on July 1 at Confederation in 1867, when our nation was formed due to Queen Victoria signing the British North America Act. Later entrenched in our Canadian constitution were the words, "*Whereas Canada is founded upon principles that recognize the supremacy of God and the rule of law,*" which is our country's very foundation.

Our country's spiritual DNA is that we have always been known as a peacekeeping nation. Canada has a reputation for sending peacekeepers to stressed international areas and being part of the United Nations peacekeepers as well. This is not to suggest that Canada doesn't fight; on the contrary, Canada joined forces with Britain in 1939 against Nazi Germany and was instrumental in the famous battles of Vimy Ridge, and the Somme in World War I. Most importantly, the British troops, a precursor to "Canadian" troops, defeated the invading USA troops and beat them in the War of 1812. If that had not happened, Canada would have become the 51st state of the USA!

Now the time has come for Canadians to lift our voices to God and say, "Oh God, do not pass us by!" Jesus wept over Jerusalem because they did not recognize the time of their visitation. My heart is that we would know the hour of visitation for our Nation of Canada. God bless Canada!

*Life* is a test... are you familiar with Canada's DNA or the DNA of your own country?

**www.newstartministries.ca**

# Be Pure.

Jesus said in Matt. 5:8 *"Blessed are the pure in heart, for they will see God."* "Purity" is not overly familiar or even understood today. Young people nowadays haven't got a clue what the word means. Instead, satan has cracked into the church through rejection, pride, insecurity, fear, and unhealed hurts and wounds inflicted on others, including family, friends, previous relationships, coworkers etc). This leads to identity problems and fear, and pain. People gravitate to anything in life that will relieve them of pain without thinking of the consequences.

Rather than fall into the traps of our secular culture where doing anything as long as it feels good is OK, come and return to Jesus. The comment that "well, everybody else is doing it" does not hold any light to the gospel; it is called sin.

*"...and in Christ, you have been brought to fullness. He is the head over every power and authority."* (Col. 2:10)

The more deeply grounded and rooted you are in the love of Jesus, the more you will be able to share His love with others who struggle with life. You need to know who and what you are and then teach it to others.

*"I pray that out of his glorious riches, he may strengthen you with power through his Spirit in your inner being, so that Christ may dwell in your hearts through faith. And I pray that you, being rooted and established in love, may have power, together with all the Lord's holy people, to grasp how wide and long and high and deep is the love of Christ, and to know this love that surpasses knowledge - that you may be filled to the measure of all the fullness of God."* (Eph. 3:16-19)

 is a test... Do you follow with the "crowds of life" or are you firmly rooted and grounded in Jesus?

## Age is a Number.

We live in a world full of vanity, where old age is frowned upon. I see Hollywood actors in their 90s who don't look a day over 60. Really? Whom are they trying to fool, other than themselves? Isn't it amazing what plastic surgery can do these days?

People live for "freedom 55," spending their children's inheritance (which is a sin), and worse yet, they start to wind down when they turn 60. (I did freedom 55 for a month and was never so bored, so I went back to work!) The danger of this mentality is that our seniors (like yours truly) have made mistakes that give them many learning experiences. They are now filled with wisdom and the ability to help the rest of society. Why do you think I'm writing these books? Like everybody else, I have spent a lifetime making mistakes, and now it's time to share the wisdom that we "old folks" have accumulated from life's lessons with the next generation.

Abraham is probably the biggest patriarch in the Bible and was rich in wisdom and all things of God. He lived to be 175 and did not spend his time playing golf for five months every winter. Read through Genesis and the book of Joshua and see the legacy Abraham left the future generations.

We do not have to believe society's lies that say we are "over-the-hill" when we hit 40 and ready to be put out to pasture when we're 60. The senior years are our prime years when we should be getting busy and working harder than ever to improve the world. Instead of golfing for five months, try going to Belize, for example, to build housing or volunteer with YWAM or Mercy Ships. Keep working, keep thinking young, take communion every day, stay in the Word constantly, keep busy, exercise your body, spirit and mind, and never grow old. Life is about doing for others. Billy Graham wrote his last book at age 98. What are you waiting for? Death?

*Life* is a test... Are you growing older or younger?

# Waiting, Trusting, and Hoping (faith).

Not exactly Friday afternoon after work light conversation…

Life is a Test and a challenge, and these three, waiting, trusting and in faith, will keep you busy for your entire life. They are woven together like fine thread until they get bigger and then are braided into a three-strand rope.

What does God want from us more than anything else? Trust. Why? Because it is the main bond that ties us together with Him. Living by faith is trust. Waiting for Him to move in a certain area with our eyes and hearts focused on Him is what He wants. The mistake we can make all too frequently is to say, "I trust you," and then, with fear and anxiousness, we go out and do exactly what we want (fear) to do. We just voided our own spoken words.

How to overcome this? Persevere. *"Now faith is the substance of things hoped for, the evidence of things not seen."* (Heb. 11:1 NKJV) Faith is not "wishing" faith is knowing. Knowing what? That God will be faithful to His Word. Therefore, the thing that we are standing on is His Word. What to do? Find the Words in the Word that give you the thing you need. If you need healing, find the healing scriptures and decree them out loud, thanking Him that healing has come to pass. If you need finances, read 3 John verse 2 and all the other financial scriptures (tithing is a requirement) and then decree and stand.

You belong to Him, and you don't need to sit around passing the time, waiting for God to move. He did already 2000 years ago. Decree it and stand in faith.

*Life* is a test... Are you decreeing His Word?

## Quote Day (Part 1 of 2)

I write a lot of notes. I make notes at every church service, seminar, and course I attend. Every few months, I review my notes, which I did today sitting in the beautiful summer sunshine. Here's a miscellaneous list of "knock 'em dead quotes" from the last six months that are in my notes:

"You are called to spread God's goodness, not criticize the media."

"Alignment with God restores what you have lost."

"We are called to plunder (satan) or else be plundered."

"The definition of marriage is the death of two wills, then the covenant of one."

"Hurt people want healing, and offended people look to hurt others."

"The storm that is approaching you can be stopped by worship. You will know how to suppress the storm when you are in and with Him."

"Without love, your accomplishments in life amount to nothing."

"When you have had a setback, you can't step back but move forward to your comeback."

"When a prophetic word is given, it needs to shake you." (my thoughts are if the words don't shake you, then question the source.)

"We can't have revival without repentance."

 is a test...  Note some of these that stand out to you. Write one out and reflect on it.

*Life is a test...*

## Quote Day (Part 2 of 2)

"Declare what God has said."

"People are desperate for hope; consequently, the world is ripe for revival."

"Church is not about religion; it is about a takeover! Jesus went to hell and back to get the keys the devil stole, and He gave them to you!"

"I need people that can handle big blueprints; there are no small blueprints in Heaven." (a prophetic Word, and I don't remember the source).

"God never shows you anything that does not belong to you."

"Get the devil out of your life and start building using Words."

"You want to be sent out, but first, humble yourself, listen to Me and come to a higher place. Then you will be deep in the spirit. I will unravel scrolls and send Words you have never heard, and I will unravel problems you want deliverance from. My presence brings you answers." (a prophetic Word, and I don't remember the source).

"Whatever God gives you will be multiplied under His anointing."

"Every time you don't extend grace to someone, you have established a barrier."

"Don't allow friction around you to irritate you beyond your peace."

*Life* is a test... Note some of these that stand out to you. Write one out and reflect on it.

## He Speaks; I type...

I feel Holy Spirit sensing me just to type as He will speak, so tighten your seatbelt. I never know where Holy Spirit is going to have me go!

*"You are not waiting for Me to move, I am waiting for you!"*

God's Word declares your potential, which He established in you before the earth was formed. (Eph. 1:4). He made you with Gifts (Eph. 4:11-12) and established your destiny (Eph. 1:11) which He wants to bring you into. Rather than bungle your way through life missing the mark, remember this: His work will be performed in your life as you believe it and as you listen to Him and exercise the authority He has given you to execute your right of way and power over the enemy (Luke 10:19). Satan is out to steal, kill and destroy (John 10:10) and God is out to bless and prosper you in every way (1 John 1:2; Matt 6:33). Just believe and declare that you can rise up in the Spirit of God and defeat whatever has established itself against you (Eph. 6). *"Submit yourselves, then, to God. Resist the devil, and he will flee from you."* (James 4:7). Confess your sin that sets you free (1 John 1:9), and then act in and with the authority God has given you (Luke 9:1). Ok, now my part…

*"Life is difficult. This is a great truth, one of the greatest truths. It is a great truth because once we truly see this truth, we transcend it. Once we truly know that life is difficult - once we truly understand and accept it - then life is no longer difficult. Because once it is accepted, the fact that life is difficult no longer matters."*

This quote is from Scott Peck. He was not a Christian, and I suggest that reading the Word is much better than reading any secular works. However, this is still a good quote. I would add that the truth to seek is *"Jesus, the truth the light and the way."* (John 14:6), and once we receive Him, life is not nearly as difficult...

 is a test... Is life difficult? Learn to receive Jesus each day, and life won't feel so heavy.

**www.newstartministries.ca**

## Let Your Life Shine.

*"Arise, shine, for your light has come, and the glory of the Lord rises upon you. See, darkness covers the earth and thick darkness is over the peoples, but the Lord rises upon you and His glory appears over you."* (Is. 60: 1-2)

We must always remain connected to God and reflect His interest in our lives and in how we treat others. It's a good idea daily to evaluate yourself and the activities you are involved with and ensure that you are on track with His purposes in mind.

We must also remember to make room in our lives for the Spiritual Gifts that He has implanted in us. In other words, be prepared for God to work through you by activating those Gifts. How? Allow Holy Spirit to work through your issues so that whatever may be holding you back from your destiny will be overtaken by His will and purposes. Just as we would equip ourselves with materials, equipment, even clothing as in a uniform, to accomplish a task, we must use the elements described in Eph. 6 every waking moment.

*"Therefore put on the full armour of God, so that when the day of evil comes, you may be able to stand your ground, and after you have done everything, to stand. Stand firm then, with the belt of truth buckled around your waist, with the breastplate of righteousness in place, and with your feet fitted with the readiness that comes from the gospel of peace. In addition to all this, take up the shield of faith, with which you can extinguish all the flaming arrows of the evil one. Take the helmet of salvation and the sword of the Spirit, which is the word of God."* (Eph. 6:13-17)

 is a test... Did you remember your armour today?

## Secret Places (Part 1 of 2)

It is fun to keep surprises from your spouse or your children, like birthday and Christmas gifts or a special date or holiday. Since we are God's children, He likes to do that too!

There is an immense hidden treasure to be found in God simply by listening to Him. He pours blessings upon us, but some of His blessings must be actively searched until we find them. God likes to reveal a little bit of Himself and then hopes we will search further for more truth than more blessings.

*"For in the day of trouble He will keep me safe in His dwelling; He will hide me in the shelter of His sacred tent and set me high upon a rock."* (Ps. 27:5)

We know that God is a revealer of secrets (*"The king said to Daniel, 'Surely your God is the God of gods and the Lord of kings and a revealer of mysteries, for you were able to reveal this mystery.'"* Dan 2:47), but whom does He reveal to? Two different groups of people:

*"Surely the Sovereign Lord does nothing without revealing His plan to His servants the prophets."* (Amos 3:7)

2 Chron. 20:20 says, *"believe His prophets, and you shall prosper."* (NKJV) This is why we must listen to and believe His prophets.

The second group is anyone that fears God (remember that fearing God is to hate sin - Prov. 8:13)

Ps. 25:14 says, *"The secret of the Lord is with those who fear Him."*

 is a test... Have you searched the scriptures for God?

## Secret Places (Part 2 of 2)

I think one of the greatest tragedies of this world is that there are very few people that will enter into the secret places of the Lord because they are unaware of its existence, or they won't bother to look for them. Additionally, there's a price to be paid for finding any secrets; cultivating a lifestyle that reflects Jesus and not the world. That is probably the biggest personal revelation I've had as a Christian. The more I study the Bible, the more I discover how rich it is, and the more I realize how much more I want of it!

Studying God's Word is like going on a treasure hunt. There's a new game out there in recent years called "geo-caching," where people use a GPS device or an app on their phone and look for pre-hidden caches put there by other people for anyone to find. Think of the Bible in the same way, and many scriptures point to the secret places of the Lord. Ps. 91:1 says, *"He who dwells in the secret place of the Most High Shall abide under the shadow of the Almighty."* Ps. 81:7 says, *"You called in trouble, and I delivered you; I answered you in the secret place of thunder; I tested you at the waters of Meribah."*

This concept of a secret place is not us moving off to a monastery! Nor does it mean that we are to live a secret Christian life. No, having a secret place is an intentional decision to establish a routine that includes time with God reading the Bible, praying, and listening to Him. That is where and when we meet Him. Check out these passages: John 14:21; John 15:4 - 5; Romans 12:2; and 1 John 2:5 - 6.

Abiding in God is where we find shelter, refuge, and fortress. It is in the secret place that we are most vulnerable with God and will most deeply experience His intimate love, guidance, and wisdom.

 is a test... Do you go into your prayer closet daily and seek the Lord?

## Rest

Our natural physical bodies need rest. Hopefully, you get some every 16 hours. Our internal organs don't function properly without adequate rest, and our overall health deteriorates. If you lack rest, you lack energy and the ability to think clearly. There is also another kind of rest that you need: spiritual rest.

One of the hardest lessons I've learned in life is "six days shalt thou labour." I used to work six days a week, attend church on Sundays, perhaps take some time off in the afternoon, and then start working in preparation for another week on Sunday night. I remember one time when I was running two businesses, I worked six months without a day off. However, since studying the Word of God, I discovered that God is not a happy camper if we don't take a day off and spend it with Him. Further, if we recharge our spiritual batteries in addition to our physical bodies, we can accomplish more in the other six days of work in the week and have fewer problems and headaches. Isn't it an interesting "coincidence" (or as I like to say, a "God incident") that if we take a day off, life goes so much better? Duh…

Where is our mistake? In our crazy, high-paced society, we miss this: *"Casting all your care upon Him, for He cares for you."* (1 Peter 5:7)

Here's some more: *"Cast your burden on the Lord, And He shall sustain you."* (Ps. 55:22) *"Come to Me, all you who labour and are heavy laden, and I will give you rest."* (Matt. 11:28) *"Be anxious for nothing, but in everything by prayer and supplication, with thanksgiving, let your requests be made known to God; and the peace of God, which surpasses all understanding, will guard your hearts and minds through Christ Jesus."* (Phil. 4: 6-7)

*Life* is a test... Here is a hard question for you; if you don't have time to rest one day a week, how do you have time to watch TV or browse social media? (or anything else of that nature).

## Lesser But No Less Significant Prophets.

Some of the least-known Prophets are in the "minor prophet" section of the Bible, beginning with Hosea and going to Malachi. There you will find more famous stories, such as Jonah, but not as often talked about stories with great promise and hope, such as Haggai, which I am writing about today! Haggai is a story co-occurring with Ezra's in his book and speaks about what was happening when the Israelites returned to their land after their exile in Babylon.

*"Now Haggai the prophet and Zechariah the prophet, a descendant of Iddo, prophesied to the Jews in Judah and Jerusalem in the name of the God of Israel, who was over them. Then Zerubbabel, son of Shealtiel and Joshua, son of Jozadak, set to work to rebuild the house of God in Jerusalem. And the prophets of God were with them, supporting them."* (Ezra 5:1-2)

God called Haggai and his partner Zechariah to encourage the Israelites as they rebuilt the temple while much opposition was going on against it (detailed in Ezra and Nehemiah). They were responsible for seeing God's Spirit sent out among the people.

*"Then Haggai, the Lord's messenger, gave this message of the Lord to the people: "I am with you," declares the Lord. So the Lord stirred up the spirit of Zerubbabel, son of Shealtiel, governor of Judah, and the spirit of Joshua, son of Jozadak, the high priest, and the spirit of the whole remnant of the people. They began to work on the house of the Lord Almighty, their God."* (Haggai 1:13-14).

Haggai was a messenger of hope and encouragement to people in need, and so are we called to be messengers of hope & encouragement to the same people - people battling opposition and in need of hope. I encourage everyone reading this to read this great and often overlooked story in the Bible!

 is a test... Are you reading the "small" books of the Bible? It's all God inspired!

# Death; Everyone's Favourite Topic.
## (Part 1 of 2)

Let's talk about funerals. Are you having a bawling/squalling service when you die? I like to believe there is no such thing as a "funeral" for a Christian. At least, not in the traditional sense. After all, it really is a "Homecoming Celebration."

We Christians are an odd bunch. We spend much time getting people into heaven through missionaries, evangelists, and ourselves by following and doing Mark 16:15-16 *"And He said to them, "Go into all the world and preach the gospel to every creature. He who believes and is baptized will be saved, but he who does not believe will be condemned."*

Then when someone goes to their new home in heaven, we have a "funeral" where we gather for crying, balling, grieving etc. Yes, there is a time for healthy grieving. Jesus did that when Lazarus died, but then there is a time to move on. Let's look at what Ps. 116:15 says about it: *"Precious in the sight of the Lord is the death of His faithful servants."* (NKJV)

Why would God take pleasure in the death of your body? With your body gone, you are now set free to go home. God is celebrating because you're coming into Heaven and not into satan's kingdom. That's definitely worth celebrating! Don't forget, when you get to Heaven, you will see your friends and family that are saved, but you will also move into your mansion. *"In My Father's house are many mansions; I would have told you if it were not so. I go to prepare a place for you. And if I go and prepare a place for you, I will come again and receive you to Myself; that where I am, there you may be also."* (John 14:2-3 NKJV)

*Life* is a test... Have you planned a funeral or a homecoming?

## Death; Everyone's Favourite Topic.
### (Part 2 of 2)

In addition, you are now set free from the devil's attack and set free from this place called Earth that pales in comparison in every way to Heaven. Remember that Earth is simply a temporary place where God puts us as a place of schooling and testing. Life is a test...

What we need to do is control what we think about death. "Death" is only the death of our bodies, and life is released as our souls and spirits "get out of Dodge" and go to be with the Father! I have left instructions in my will for my family to have a "Homecoming Service" celebrating my life and celebrating my entrance into heaven. Then my children are instructed to book a party room at the club that I belong to in Calgary for a party with food, drinks and celebration! Then later, there will be a "reading of the will" and my children will find out how much they will get! Party time! However, because of Gen. 6:3, this is another 50+ years away for me! :) (sorry kids!)

I have read biographies and heard many testimonies from people that had what is referred to as a "near-death experience." Their bodies died, and they went to heaven. They met Jesus, who told them they needed to return, usually because they had unfinished business. Every testimony I have heard has had the same thing in common; the people never wanted to come back. Heaven is too much of a fantastic place, and once you're there, you won't want to come back because it is so much better there than life here.

**Doc's Book Club:** Read *"Heaven is for Real"* by Todd Burpo.

*Life* is a test... Are you excited about heaven? How do you feel about this time on Earth one day ending?

# The Month of Av  (July/Aug - Part 1 of 5)

**Alphabet:** The letter is "TET" - resembles a womb.
- a month when the earth contracts.
- the secret of pregnancy moves into the earth realm.
**Tribe:** Simeon - to hear; be concerned.
**Characteristics:** - This month you metamorphose or disintegrate. The month the Lion roars (Amos 3:8). The month is where God destroys so He can reconstruct. Consider what you hear and determine how to develop a new discernment level, or you can oppose counsel and advice. Listen carefully! You will hear key impressions this month.
- This is the month to decree a season of "completion & release."
- That which has held you, shake it off.
- We decree that God's people are coming through, and the battle will be turned.
 God's move is in our midst, so be still and know that He is God.
- It is a critical month, a time of "dire straits." You are either going to "make it or break it this month."
- It is a time to humble yourself and make changes in your life. It is a time of transition, which means a time that brings death, which is a good thing.
**Constellation:** Leo (the lion) - the divine will of the Father is executed
**Colour/Stone:** Green/Emerald

   This month is the "low point" of the Jewish calendar. The 9th of Av was when the people of Israel chose to receive the negative report of the ten spies and refused to enter the Promised Land. This date was also marked by the destruction of both the first and second Temples in Jerusalem.

## The Month of Av (July/Aug - Part 2 of 5)

If you study the history of the Jews, you discover that the Jews are caught in a cycle of destruction. Every year on the 9th of Av, a window of destruction opens over them. On the 9th of Av, Israel chose to listen to the voice of UNBELIEF!

Av 9 - 587 BC - The armies of Babylon destroyed Solomon's Temple.

Av 9 - AD 70 - The Romans destroyed the 2nd temple.

Av 9 - AD 135 - The Final Defeat of Jews by Rome.

Av 9 - AD 1095 - The 1st Crusade is launched, killing thousands of Jews.

Av 9 - AD 1290 - The Jews are expelled from England.

Av 9 - AD 1492 - The Jews are expelled from Spain.

Av 9 - AD 1942 - The Jews were deported from the Warsaw ghetto to the death camps.

The month of Av was initially intended to be the month that Israel entered the Promised Land. God had planned that Av would be a month to celebrate His goodness every year. However, the people agreed with unbelief instead of believing in God and gave a negative confession. They said: "The enemy is too strong for us. We will all die!" They tasted the fruit of the land but refused to enter. They held back in unbelief, and they put themselves under a curse by doing that. Because of their sin on that date, Israel spent 40 years in the wilderness. At the end of that time, God, in His grace, gave them a second chance to enter (God is the God of second chances). However, they never truly repented of their sin. So, every year, the cycle comes back, and the window of destruction comes again. When you don't repent of past sins, satan is free to bring the curse of that sin back around you, and he has the legal right to keep the door of destruction open over your life.

A curse brings a decrease in what is good, beneficial, and pleasant. The curse takes what is flourishing and makes it barren. It takes what has life and releases sickness and death. It takes abundance and reduces it until there is poverty and lack. A curse is an open the door to the devil in your life! The devil is always looking for an opportunity to suppress you. He wants to steal, kill and destroy. A curse gives the devil the legal right and opportunity to do that.

## The Month of Av (July/Aug - Part 3 of 5)

Where do curses come from? God brought Israel out of Egypt in the Exodus by His mighty power. At Passover, He broke the power of slavery and released them from their enemies and oppression. He led them through the Red Sea and showed them His power in the wilderness. He taught them at Sinai and revealed His glory. Then, in the month of Av, He brought them to Kaddish Barnea at the border of the promised land. Twelve spies entered the land and searched it. The spies brought back the fruit of the land for them to see and taste! They all agreed it was just what God had promised it would be, but they disagreed on whether they could trust God to give them the land. Ten spies said we can't take the land; the enemies are too strong for us we will all die. Two spies said God will give us a land God has brought us this far; let's move forward in faith and take the land.

On the ninth day of Av, they chose to listen to the voice of unbelief! God had opened the door to the future, but they refused to go in. So instead of Av being a month of blessing, it turned out to be a month of mourning and destruction. They received a curse instead of a blessing, and spent 40 years in the wilderness, never repenting. Consequently, that cycle repeats itself every year.

Av can be a month to enter the blessing or experience the curse! However, curses can be repented of and broken.

**Curses:** Constant sickness, addictions, mental and financial problems, confusion/depression, barrenness and reproduction issues, break-down of marriage, family alienation, being accident-prone, a history of suicide and premature death. The solution? Decree that all curses are broken.

### Seven things to put you under a curse:
Racism, robbing God, robbing man, dishonouring your parents, self-destructive words, covenant-breaking and broken relationships.

# The Month of Av (July/Aug - Part 4 of 5)

Galatians 3:13-14 says that Jesus redeemed us from the curse by becoming a curse for us. Jesus paid the price to break every curse by shedding his blood, but we must repent and receive that by faith! To deal with a curse, first, repent of the sin that caused the curse to come, and then receive Jesus's authority and break the curse off your life. Receive His Promise and mix it with FAITH this month!

The Hebrews associate Av with a new level of discernment. This month, you are developing a new discernment level or opposing counsel and advice. If you look back on your life, you can identify times when people gave you counsel and advice; but you thought you knew more than anyone else and did not act on the advice. Use wisdom and allow the Lord to guide you and hone your discernment for these critical days ahead.

Simeon and Levi had the same sin and, consequently, the same curse but with incredibly different results. Simeon's tribe was scattered in the North, but Levi prospered. Why? Levi reversed the curse by repenting and seeking God wholeheartedly, and Simeon never did. The early church realized that people turning to Jesus from a pagan background brought much baggage. As a result of their lifestyle in pre-Jesus days, many new believers still carried feelings of guilt and shame. Many were tormented by demons and lived under a curse. They could never enter into a relationship with Jesus until those things were dealt with.

Consequently, when someone became a Christian, they were first assigned a teacher. They were taught who they were in Christ, how to walk with God and experience blessing. They were taught how to exercise Spiritual Gifts and function as part of the body of Christ. They gained a new identity and knew who they were in Christ Jesus. Next, they were assigned to a deliverance minister to set them free from all their past baggage. Then after they went through deliverance, they were baptized. They came up out of the water declaring, "I am a new creature" - and they really were! Reflect upon how healthy our churches would be if we did the same as the above!

## The Month of Av (July/Aug - Part 5 of 5)

Most Christians are never taught how to walk in God's blessing, and they are not set free from their past. Instead of being set free, more burdens are added! On top of their other burdens, they now have religion, ritual and legalism! They never experience the joy and freedom that God promises. This is what's wrong with our church today, a lack of understanding and training.

That was never God's plan! The good news is that God is restoring his church and breaking off dead religion. He is also restoring the deliverance ministry in a big way. You can be delivered! You can walk in freedom, experience the joy God wanted you to have, and move forward to fulfil your destiny on earth. God wants you to be free! God wants every curse broken so you can walk in the fullness of his blessing. Many Christians suffer the effects of the curse without even knowing it.

Now would be an excellent time to clean your home and consecrate your property. Objects that represent false gods, pagan worship, or that promote evil: pornography, R & X rated and horror movies, dream catchers, idols like Buddhas, Ouija boards, anything to do with witch-craft, masks/idols from foreign countries, witchcraft books/toys, Halloween paraphilia etc. - in short anything that does not glorify God. Repent of these things and decree the curses gone.

**Doc's Book Club:** Read *"Set Yourself Free: A Deliverance Manual"* by Dr. Robert Heidler

*Life* is a test... Are you under a curse? Now you know what to do about it.

# The Seventh Fruit of the Spirit - Faithfulness (Part 1 of 3)

Faithfulness has two different meanings. Firstly, there is the faithfulness of God or Jesus, which refers to steadfastness, honesty, firmness, and His unchanging character. Secondly, human or natural faithfulness refers to our steadfast commitment to God and trust in Him. Faithfulness means that we are full of faith, and faith is created within us when we allow Holy Spirit to "go to work" in us. While these definitions of faithfulness may sound beyond us in our natural life, they guide thought, habits, patterns, and the heart for a relationship with God, which can be developed within us by seeking Holy Spirit. Remember that all the Fruits of the Spirit are tied to Holy Spirit. These fruits are characteristics that God grants us when we accept Him and grow with each passing season we experience - if we continually keep going deeper in our relationship with Him.

Faithfulness is the conviction that the scriptures mean what they say they mean. Biblical faithfulness simply means believing in and of God - His existence, works, and character. He does exist, and He means what He says as written in His Holy Word. Faithfulness is the result of Holy Spirit working in us, which is our witness to God's promise that if we accept the truth about God, He will save us and do all He says He will do.

Faithfulness is believing that God is Whom He says He is and continuing in that belief despite the situations in our lives and what we see in this world called "life." We trust what God says in the Bible, not necessarily what the world or our own eyes tell us. We trust He will work out everything for good. We trust He will work His will in us. We trust that our situation on earth is being worked out for our good. The only way we can have such faithfulness is through Holy Spirit in us. He testifies to the truth and tells us to seek God. The Spirit of God gives us faith and makes us faithful.

*"John Wesley said that the fruit of faith that comes from God has the power to overcome sin. First, it is the power to overcome external sin, such as evil speech and actions. Next, it is the power to overcome interior sin because faith purifies our hearts from unholy lust and fleshly nature. Therefore, no matter how much we claim to have faith, he is not a true worshipper if his heart is in pure."* \*

\* *"Christians Going to Hell"* by Seung Woo Byun. Creation House, A Strang Company. 2006. Page 64

## The Seventh Fruit of the Spirit - Faithfulness (Part 2 of 3)

Faith protects us from fear, and fear destroys faith. Eph. 6:13-17 lists all the armour of God. Faith, "in addition to all," is the shield to keep us safe from the fiery arrows of the devil.

If we are full of faithfulness, we believe in God; it is as simple as that, no questions asked. We trust that He always has our best interests at heart and is there for us in the struggles of life, even when we do not understand Him. We believe and accept that He loves us (John 3:16), He wants to be with us (John 14:2), He desires to save us (John 14:6), and He is working in us (Phil. 1:6) and wants nothing but the best for us (3 John 1:2). We live with the confidence that we will receive God's promised blessings, especially when we are obedient to His Word.

When do we need faithfulness? When God's promises seem to contradict what we see entirely. We use faith and call things not as though they were (Rom. 4:17). When God's ways are hidden from us (Is. 45:15), when the devil is on our case, when tragedy comes one right after another, we need Holy Spirit to produce His fruit of faithfulness in us.

The character of Jesus, the thing that we have faith in, is disclosed in John 16:13-14: *"But when he, the Spirit of truth, comes, he will guide you into all the truth. He will not speak on his own; he will speak only what he hears and tell you what is yet to come. He will glorify me because it is from me that he will receive what he will make known to you."*

Therefore, we also have faith and faithfulness that Jesus is our saviour, and the Holy Spirit testifies that very fact in 1 John 5:6-8 *"This is the one who came by water and blood - Jesus Christ. He did not come by water only, but by water and blood. And it is the Spirit who testifies because the Spirit is the truth. For there are three that testify: the Spirit, the water and the blood; and the three are in agreement."*

## The Seventh Fruit of the Spirit - Faithfulness (Part 3 of 3)

Heb. 11 is the faith chapter and the heroes of faith, which I have written about before (Jan. 24, Ap. 13-14). It has a long list of faithful men and women in the Old Testament who trusted God and lived by faith. Abel's understanding of God made his sacrifice genuine and authentic. Noah trusted God's Word about the coming flood and God's promise to save his family (Gen. 6-9). Abraham and Sarah believed that they could and would have a child in their old age (Gen. 21:1-34). Rahab trusted God to protect her family when the Israelites destroyed the city of Jericho (Jos. 6).

Faith, or a faithful commitment to whom God says He is, is the foundation of our relationship with God. As Jesus travelled, He responded to people's faith and curtailed His involvement where there was no faith (Mark 6:1-6). As with all the characteristics of the Spirit's fruit, the first and best place to begin is with Jesus. Jesus, through His sacrifice, allowed us to access the Holy Spirit, to lead us, just as He had led God's chosen for generations.

Mark 4:35-41 tells the story of Jesus calming the storm. After being roused by the terrified disciples, Jesus stopped the wind and the waves and said, *"Why are you so afraid? Have you still no faith?"* (Mark 4:40). Jesus did not bring a storm to teach the disciples a lesson or anything like that. He didn't even consider the situation worthy of bothering with. So much so that at the time, He was having a nap! The disciples were in fear because they had no faith. However, as they grew in their training with Jesus, they grew in faith, and you can see a whole set of "new" disciples in the Book of Acts as they were praising God while in a prison cell! (Acts 16:22-25) Faith in God means not fearing worldly troubles, not just because God is God, but because we *"count all things to be loss given the surpassing value of knowing Christ Jesus."* (Phil. 3:8)

*Life* is a test... Would you have responded like the disciples?

# God Didn't Do It.

A few weeks ago, I attended a breakfast meeting that had three guest speakers as the meeting's program. The last one gave a testimony about how his wife had passed away six months prior after dying of cancer. His testimony was about her life, the battles she fought, how he tried to see God through all of this, etc.

He repeatedly remarked about how God killed his wife; he even used the word "murdered." "I don't understand why God took my wife." His remarks stunned me, and the audience sat there, and said nothing. I guess in the interest of good decorum and sensitivity, no one spoke out against him. However, his comments were completely wrong.

Let's set the record straight. God does not kill people! This lady died from cancer, and the author of cancer and, for that matter, all sickness and disease is satan.

The speaker said they had prayed for healing, but God didn't want her healed. Nothing could be further from the truth. God healed this lady 2000 years ago when His son went to the cross and took all of our sins, sickness, disease etc., on Him. So why did she die? It is a complex answer and not within the confines and restrictions of a daily devotional. I have studied healing for 40 years, and in the words of Kenneth Hagin, most of the time, when people are not healed, it's because of an issue of unforgiveness. There are many other issues as well; genetic, fear, wrong medicines, but God does not kill people. He welcomes Christians to their new home when their bodies fail.

**Doc's Book Club:** Read *"Christ the Healer"* by F.F. Bosworth.

 is a test... Have you blamed God for something? Confess your sin and repent.

## Which World Are You In?

*"Now about your love for one another we do not need to write to you, for you yourselves have been taught by God to love each other. And in fact, you do love all of God's family throughout Macedonia. Yet we urge you, brothers and sisters, to do so more and more, and to make it your ambition to lead a quiet life: You should mind your own business and work with your hands, just as we told you, so that your daily life may win the respect of outsiders and so that you will not be dependent on anybody."* (1 Thess. 4:9-12)

*"Lead a quiet life..."* Really? I would suggest to you that nothing in this world is quiet. Further, there have been more wars fought in the world since the end of the second world war than in the entire history of mankind. The United Nations has been utterly dysfunctional in promoting its mandate of peace. The governments didn't have a clue about how to handle the Covid "feardemic," and at the time of this writing, Ukraine is being bombed, the price of oil is setting record highs, and 95 million additional people around the world are in poverty because of Covid and lockdowns. (Note that a "quiet life" does not mean sitting and doing nothing. It means not being in strife with others.)

Did you catch that part in the first paragraph? *"You should mind your own business."* Wouldn't it be nice if the social media giants and the people contributing to them would do that?

What's my point? The world has no answers, and Jesus has every answer. If you are born again and walking in the fullness of Holy Spirit, you are now a decoder. Study the Word, and Holy Spirit will reveal Himself to you on a scale you can't even imagine. We are to be in this world but not part of it (John 15:19 and John 17:14-16. Rom. 12:2; Eph. 4:22-24; 1 Thess. 4:1).

*Life* is a test... Are you living a quiet life surrendered to Him?

## Grief (Part 1 of 2)

Grief has no place in our lives. Grief can bring sickness and disease because disease is a companion of death. Grief is a killer. What to do about it? When you start dealing with grief, or if it comes to you in the future, say this: "in the Name of Jesus, I bind the spirit of grief, I bind the spirit of death, I bind the spirit of fear and I rebuke you. I command you to leave me and go to dry places away from me. (Matt. 12:43). Do not return and do not send any other demons to replace you. (Matt. 12:45) Now you leave, and I plead the blood of Jesus over me." (further references: Mark 16:17-18; 1 Peter 5:8; Eph. 6:10-18).

What does it mean to "plead the blood?" "Plead" is a legal term. You plead your case in a court of law. There is a courtroom in heaven where satan accuses us of our sins. However, every time we confess our sin and admit to being guilty as charged, we then plead our case which is that we are covered by the shed blood of the lamb of God. Every time without fail, that squashes the prosecutor's (satan's) case.

*"I, even I, am he who blots out your transgressions, for my own sake, and remembers your sins no more."* Is. 43:25

*"If we confess our sins, he is faithful and just and will forgive us our sins and purify us from all unrighteousness."* I John 1:9

Not only does God forgive us but He also forgets about it. Confess your sin, plead your case, (the blood) bind the devil (Matt. 16:19) repent which means stop doing the sin (James 4:7) and then forget about it and move on (Rom. 8:1). You are now washed clean so don't bring it back to God which is rehearsing your sin because He has "plum forgot" about it (1 John 1:7).

**Doc's Book Club:** Read ***"Operating in the Courts of Heaven"*** by Robert Henderson.

 is a test... Are you controlling grief or is grief controlling you?

## Grief (Part 2 of 2)

Now we can walk in the fulness of the spirit because we have confessed our sin, which gives us peace, and that peace puts the devil in his place, which is under our foot. *"The God of peace will soon crush satan under your feet."* (Rom. 16:20). We are to overcome the devil (Eph. 6:12), so be an "overcomer" by the Word of His testimony. *"They triumphed over him by the blood of the Lamb and by the Word of their testimony; they did not love their lives so much as to shrink from death."* (Rev. 12:11)

Finally, forget about it, and forget about satan. Frankly, we give him too much attention anyway, and he doesn't deserve it. Then just live your life - loving Jesus and loving others. There is healing, deliverance and joy in Christ when you do that. Now you know who you are, your authority, and what you can do, so do it! It all belongs to you if you are in Christ Jesus. Simple stuff...

All of what I have written is not to suggest that we do not minister to others who are going through grief. Of course, we should. We are to extend love and empathy to anyone going through grief. We can even help them *"walk through the valley of the shadow of death"* (Ps. 23:4), but those measures are temporary because eventually, we all must walk by ourselves. We must be very conscious that we're not on the "pity pot." If you lose someone, take time to grieve, and if you feel yourself unable to shake the loss after some months or a year, shake it off and give it to God!

Additionally, take a grieving course through your church. It's about processing reality. I have seen or heard of too many people losing their spouses and remarrying in less than a year. Often it is a case of using someone to fill the void in a person's life, which is not a healthy situation. In short, they have never dealt with the grief.

*Life* is a test... Are you grieving anything? Have you in the past? Give it to God.

## Why Is He Attacking You?

I spent about ten years studying healing and deliverance. Then I thought I would start a deliverance ministry but realized it was not my calling (I'm just not pastoral enough.) It was still an excellent education and certainly gave me insight into the world of spiritual warfare.

Occasionally, I run across upset people complaining that they're "under attack by the devil." My standard pat answer is, "why are you allowing him to do that?" Firstly, we're under attack most of the time because of our sins, so why are we sinning? Sometimes we can be attacked because we're doing an excellent job of the Lord's work. Sometimes sickness comes simply because we live in a fallen world. However, regardless of the situation, it is still a matter of perspective. You are not under attack; the attack is under you! The enemy is under your feet, and you are seated over top of him in heavenly places. Of course, that's assuming that you're taking control of the situation.

What's the answer? Change your perspective. The enemy is exceptionally good at what he does, but that should never stop you from doing yours. Besides, when we use our authority, which is the key, we don't ever lose! Read the Book of Revelation and find out who wins. We do! Don't forget that *"For it is written: 'As I live, says the Lord, Every knee shall bow to Me, And every tongue shall confess to God.'"* (Rom. 14:11) By the way, that includes satan and all his "minions," too. Their days are numbered...

 is a test...  You should be attacking demons, not them attacking you. Are you?

## You Are an Influencer.

The Bible promises you a glorious future no matter what is happening around you and in the world. You were created to make a difference, leave the world a better place than when you arrived and bring light into darkness. You are the influencer in the world; the world does not influence you.

People tend to have life backwards. They think they were born on this earth as physical beings, and then if they "make it to heaven," they will float around in the sky with some white wings attached. No, the truth is that you are a heavenly being living for a short time on the earth in an "earth suit" (aka body) and not an earthly being trying to get into heaven. While you are here, you have a mission to accomplish, and if you live your life according to God's will, He will bless you with His presence, protection, love, provision - everything! Jesus warned us that there would be problems in this world but that we could still rejoice because through Him we have overcome the world (John 16:33). Remember that although you are in this world, you are not of it (John 17:16). You are a heavenly child with a great future, blest going in and blest going out (Deut. 28:6), living life to the fullest without fear, (2 Tim. 1:7) having the anointing of Holy Spirit (1 John 2:27) and the power to kick the devil's butt anytime you want (Eph. 6:11).

Life is good...

 is a test... Are you influencing or are you being influenced?

## You Are Covered?

After Adam and Eve sinned in the garden, they saw their nakedness and were ashamed. God made clothes for them. Another time God provided for Aaron and his sons, covering their nakedness as well. When the priests stood in the Holy place on behalf of themselves and their nation, they had to ensure they were covered. Otherwise, their iniquity would speak against them, and they would die.

Much the same applies to us. Through confession of sin, repentance and humility, we ask for the blood of Jesus to cover our iniquity, which then covers all of our sins. We also like to keep our confessions to God confidential because we don't want to expose our shame and disgrace. *"And above all things have fervent love for one another, for "love will cover many sins."* (1 Peter 4:8)

God, in His mercy, provides a covering for us; the atonement through His son's blood so that we can stand tall and righteous before God just as a priest did in the Old Testament. For this reason, we need to have a regular reminder of God's covering and protection over us, and we do that by having communion.

*"For I received from the Lord that which I also delivered to you: that the Lord Jesus on the same night in which He was betrayed took bread; and when He had given thanks, He broke it and said, 'Take, eat; this is My body which is broken for you; do this in remembrance of Me.' In the same manner, He also took the cup after supper, saying, 'This cup is the new covenant in My blood. This do, as often as you drink it, in remembrance of Me.' For as often as you eat this bread and drink this cup, you proclaim the Lord's death till He comes."* (1 Cor 11:23-26)

*Life* is a test... God has freed you of your shame and iniquity. Have you received that?

## Story and Moral.

**Story:**

One day a farmer's donkey fell into a well. The animal cried piteously for hours as the farmer tried to figure out what to do. Finally, he decided the animal was old, and the well needed to be covered up anyway; retrieving the donkey wasn't worth it.

He invited all his neighbours to come over and help him. They all grabbed a shovel and began to shovel dirt into the well. At first, the donkey realized what was happening and cried horribly. Then, to everyone's amazement, he quieted down. A few shovels loads later, the farmer finally looked down the well. He was astonished at what he saw. With each shovel of dirt that hit his back, the donkey was doing something unique. He would shake it off and take a step up.

As the farmer's neighbours continued to shovel dirt on top of the animal, he would shake it off and take a step up. Pretty soon, everyone was amazed as the donkey stepped up over the edge of the well and happily trotted off!

**Moral:**

Life is going to shovel dirt on you, all kinds of dirt. The trick to getting out of the well is shaking the dirt off and stepping up. Each of our troubles is a steppingstone. We can get out of the deepest wells by not stopping, never giving up! Shake it off and take a step up.

**Remember the five simple rules to be happy:**
**1.** Free your heart from hatred - forgive.
**2.** Free your mind from worries - most worries never happen.
**3.** Live simply and appreciate what you have.
**4.** Give more. (why do we give the waitress 15 or 20% but struggle to give the church 10%?) Ouch!
**5.** Expect less from people but more from yourself.

*Life* is a test... What do you instinctively do when life shovels dirt on you?

**www.newstartministries.ca**

# You are an Ambassador.

*"We are therefore Christ's ambassadors, as though God were making his appeal through us."* (2 Cor. 5:20-21)

When you were born again and made Jesus the Lord of your life, you became a citizen of His Kingdom (His army), which gives you full access to His benefits, but it also means you are in boot camp, the military, and you have work to do. Ambassadors represent the government of the nation from which they are from, to which they are sent. They have diplomatic immunity because they are governed by the laws of their own country and not the laws of the country they live in.

The same applies to the Kingdom of God, whom you now represent. These laws are governed by love, and you have Christ's authority to use His power to change things in the natural world. You are commissioned to represent Jesus here on earth, and this is what He told you to do:

*"Jesus called his twelve disciples to him and gave them authority to drive out impure spirits and to heal every disease and sickness."* (Matt. 10:1) *"As you go, proclaim this message: 'The Kingdom of heaven has come near.' Heal the sick, raise the dead, cleanse those with leprosy, and drive out demons. Freely you have received; freely give." (*Matt. 10:7-8) *"He said to them, "Go into all the world and preach the gospel to all creation. Whoever believes and is baptized will be saved, but whoever does not believe will be condemned. And these signs will accompany those who believe: \* In my Name they will drive out demons; they will speak in new tongues; they will pick up snakes with their hands; and when they drink deadly poison, it will not hurt them at all; they will place their hands on sick people, and they will get well."* (Mark 16:15-20)

The point? Use the power given to you as an Ambassador.

 is a test... \* If you do not see signs, and don't speak in tongues, then are you a believer?

# You Can Only Handle So Much and God Knows That.

*"No temptation has overtaken you except what is common to mankind. And God is faithful; He will not let you be tempted beyond what you can bear. But when you are tempted, He will also provide a way out so that you can endure it."* (1 Cor. 10:13)

*"When tempted, no one should say, "God is tempting me." For God cannot be tempted by evil, nor does He tempt anyone."* (James 1:13)

I met a lady who lived her life in a complete state of being overwhelmed. She would start laundry on Mondays and still be working on it by Friday. She said one time that she didn't like flossing her teeth because it was just another thing for her to have to remember! She had lived most of her life bogged down in confusion and constantly being overwhelmed with every detail. However, the truth is that God will not put more on you than you can handle. Therefore, if we feel overwhelmed, it is often self-inflicted. The pressure in your life is coming from yourself, or the enemy of your soul is getting you all in a fester. Remember that he is out to steal, kill and destroy your joy and everything else in your life (John 10:10). We must remember to reject the pressures of man, the forces that we create ourselves, and rise above the sea of frustration and shake off the enemy's threats.

If you're feeling overwhelmed, well, there is something for you to work on. When you feel overwhelmed, sit down for a moment, and meditate on Jesus. Trust Him to deal with whatever pressures you are going through, whether it's being placed on you or just thoughts festering in your head. Cast them down (2 Cor. 10:5) and focus on Jesus. Ask Him for help with whatever is overwhelming you.

*Life* is a test... What will you do the next time you feel overwhelmed?

# The Coven's Plan to Wreck the Church.
## (Part 1 of 2)

There are eight main points of attack used by satanists when attempting to breach a church's defences and try to neutralize it.

**1. Profession of Faith.** They often pretend to become saved to gain credibility. (1 John 4:1-3; Luke 21:8; Matt. 7:21-23)

**2. Build Credibility.** Through regular attendance and helping with church projects, they discover the committed members of a church fellowship and who are not.

**3. Destroy the Prayer Base.** Establish alternative prayer groups which divide or cancel the most powerful prayer meetings.

**4. Rumours.** Gossip and rumours can be easily spread once the prayer cover has been destroyed. (1 Thess. 5:22)

**5. Teach and Change Doctrines.** Through Sunday School, youth and other groups will try to bring in teachings intended to divide and confuse people. Examples include:

- making prayer complicated so people will doubt their relationship with God (Heb. 4:14-16).

- they will twist scriptures to make false doctrines look legitimate.

- "Loving rather than judging." There comes a false belief that we aren't permitted to judge false teaching etc., which is not Biblical. We are to test the spirits and render righteous judgement, deal with sin in the church, and more. God loves people but hates their sins, so we need a balance in the "loving" of people.

**6. Break up Families.** The unity of both church and nation is based on unity in the family. Children and teenagers need to hear the preaching of the Word of God with their parents, yet many churches run programs for their younger members simultaneously. This means that the younger family members miss out on the serious preaching of the Word of God. What they receive instead is often not as useful for family spiritual maturity, resulting in the teenagers wanting to avoid church attendance and the alleged boredom of the younger ones. It also means the satanists often get into "teaching" the Sunday School to children because, in most churches there is usually a shortage of available and competent people for such roles. Anyone who appears sincere and at least partly capable is often given the task.

*Life is a test...*

# The Coven's Plan to Wreck the Church.
## (Part 2 of 2)

**7.** Stop accurate teaching about satan. Scriptures such as 2 Cor. 2:11; Hosea 4:6; 1 Peter 5:8; John 3:19. A lot of junk is spread by satanists to ensure this happens, including "We don't want to give satan any glory by talking about him" and the like. Disciples of Jesus Christ are commanded to be aware of satan's schemes so we can circumvent them. It has been noted by former coven members that church members who complain the loudest against teaching about satan are probably members of a local coven trying to protect their boss.

**8.** Direct attacks on Church Leaders. Any Church leader who takes a stand in public for the Lord Jesus Christ; (and, by implication stands against spiritual darkness) will be targeted by the enemy's agents. That is why they need our ongoing and committed prayer support. That is a significant part of why prayer support is targeted early - to remove the protective shield over a church or ministry. At the end of every letter Paul wrote, he appealed for ongoing prayer cover from the believers.

When you suspect enemy agents are at work in your church, the first step is to pray. Alert the leaders and the Intercessory Team of the need to protect the church congregation. This prayer protection should be regular and ongoing. If things are getting out of order, then a particular season of prayer might be appropriate.

There are many exceptions, but often coven members sent in to wreck a church congregation are single men and women who recently "moved into the area" and frequently know the Bible better than the pastor. (This is why preaching the gospel to a Jehovah's witness is so difficult. They know the Bible better than most Christians do.)

*Life* is a test... Have you considered being part of the prayer team at your church? Every church needs a covering from all forces of the enemy.

Note: With thanks to www.jubileeresources.org

## Take Jesus' Voice Seriously, Not Satan's.
### (Part 1 of 2)

Satan is very cunning but has limited powers and is a bit of a twit. He loses the final battle (read the Book of Revelation - we win!), but he keeps trying. As I repeatedly have written in these two devotionals, WE have authority over him on the condition that we use the power of Jesus given to us (Matt 9:8, 10:1, Luke 10:19, Mark 6:7) when it is needed. Keeping satan bound from hurting you and your family is easy; don't sin. *"Submit yourselves, then, to God. Resist the devil, and he will flee from you."* (James 4:7). When we do sin, then repent to God, thank Him for cleansing us, use that "God-given" authority and cast the devil out, then move on with life (and as Jesus said, *"go and sin no more."* John 8:11). We control satan and his minions; they do not control us unless we allow them to.

The last sentence is critical, there. No power that satan or his minions has can last if we don't give them room to. Satan can speak and jibber-jabber all he wants, but he won't get anywhere. His voice is not the one we should be most worried about.

Jesus, however, didn't pull any punches when talking about what the Kingdom of God demands from us. There's one particular in Matt. 7 we'll look at tomorrow, and Jesus is rather intense with sin. Whether plucking out our eyes (Matt. 18:9) or cutting off our hands (Matt. 5:30), these metaphors show the severity that sin can cause and the level we ought to go for to avoid sinning.

*L*ife is a test... Whose voice do you pay more attention to?

## Take Jesus' Voice Seriously, Not Satan's. (Part 2 of 2)

It has been said that the three scariest words in life are "you have cancer," and the four most frightening words are "I want a divorce." True, those are words that we never want to hear however, these words are not nearly as scary for us. Why? Jesus can heal anything. Divorce? Perhaps separation might be needed for a cooling down period and for couples to come together with scriptures to mature, grow - "work it out," etc. *"God hates divorce."* (Mal. 2:16) Both scary situations can be overcome with repentance, forgiveness and the love and light of Jesus' healing. However, let's look at these scary words from Matt 7: 21-23:

*"Not everyone who says to me, 'Lord, Lord,' will enter the Kingdom of Heaven, but only the one who does the will of my Father who is in heaven. Many will say to me on that day, 'Lord, Lord, did we not prophesy in your name and your name drive out demons and in your name perform many miracles?' Then I will tell them plainly, 'I never knew you. Away from me, you evildoers!'"*

What do we do with this? To quote the disciples, *"Who can be saved?"* (Luke 16:26) The answer is hidden in these verses. *"He who does the will..."* Is your heart "sold out" to Jesus? He said that the greatest commandment He wanted us to do was love. First, your "vessel" (you) needs to be clean of sin, then surrender and allow Holy Spirit to resonate through you and out of you with the nine fruits of Him (now you know why I taught you about them!) *"Love the Lord your God with all your heart and with all your soul and with all your mind and with all your strength. The second is this: 'Love your neighbour as yourself. There is no commandment greater than these."* (Mark 12:30-31 NKJV)

Still, those verses are scary stuff. People that are sure they are saved and will get into heaven might be in for a big disappointment. How do we "know Him"? Surrender and repentance means to change and love. Loving Him, which is to do His will and love others, is His greatest commandment. *"Love your neighbour as yourself.'* There is no commandment greater than these." (Mark 12:31) (Also, read 1 John 4:7-12)

*Life* is a test... How do you feel reading Matthew 7:21-23?

# The Climate of You & Your Home.

God expects us to take dominion over the world and shift the spiritual atmosphere around us. However, before we do that, we must make sure we have turned our atmosphere to Him. That means creating a spiritual climate that sets the stage for God to move in our lives.

Option A: your climate is one of strife, indifference, anger, complaining, frightened, jealousy, frustration, selfishness, bitterness - you get the idea. I think strife is probably the worst of all of these in this list because it fuels all the rest. Keep strife out of your life at any cost. *"The tongue also is a fire, a world of evil among the parts of the body. It corrupts the whole body, sets the whole course of one's life on fire, and is itself set on fire by hell."* (James 3:6)

Option B: your climate is one of worship, hope, generosity, forgiveness, no, selflessness, peace, prayer, joy, etc. Most importantly Holy Spirit is present.

Option A is self-explanatory. It's all a result of sin. How do we eliminate this? Confession of sin and repentance. Forgive others and forgive yourself. The key to option B is simply the fruit of Holy Spirit in our lives that rejects the works of the flesh. When we do this, we position our hearts into a fruitful atmosphere of harvest and blessing. *"Blessed is the one who does not walk in step with the wicked or stand in the way that sinners take or sit in the company of mockers, but whose delight is in the law of the Lord, and who meditates on his law day and night. That person is like a tree planted by streams of water, which yields its fruit in season and whose leaf does not wither - whatever they do prospers."* (Ps. 1:1-3)

*Life* is a test... What climate are you under?

## Conformity vs Morality.

I once heard two contrasting words that really stuck with me. The contrast was between two words: conformity and morality. The definitions were that conformity is doing what everybody else is doing, regardless of what is right. That morality is doing what is right, regardless of what everybody else does.

Sometimes in our lives, we may come to a crossroads like this one, where we must choose between going with the majority or going after what is right (or what we've been commanded to do!) Take a second in your mind to think about what the Bible says about this idea of conformity vs morality.

The Bible speaks that we must live differently from the world, allowing ourselves to be *"transformed by the renewing of our minds"* (Rom.12:2) and that we are to be a *"city on a hill for all to see"* (Matt. 5:14). Israel was placed in the crossroads of the Earth for a reason - everyone had to pass through it for trade! This allowed God's people to show the world there was a different way to live and that their gods were not the true God. The challenge was for the Israelites to not conform to what was around them, though unfortunately, we know that proved very difficult.

Choose morality, folks. If you know what is right, stick to it! Be bound to it and stick to it if you must. We must not be conformed to the patterns of this world and instead allow ourselves to live through the lens of morality for all to see that there is something different available - true life with Christ.

*Life* is a test... Are you more likely to go after conformity or morality?

## It's in "The Book!" (Part 1 of 2)

Let's look at Gen. 6:3. God said (I will paraphrase) I will not have men live so long anymore (like 900 years), so their average lifespan will now be 120 years. Next, we see in the Book of Leviticus all the things man is not supposed to eat. Why? Because God wants to teach us healthy eating habits to make it to 120 years! No cancer, no disease, just health and long life.

I find it ironic (downright amusing) that medical science has concluded that the human body should live to be 120 years. They said that all on their own. Gee, if they had read the Bible, they could've found it there! The Book of Leviticus teaches many things that people today could still learn practically and medically. One study showed that much of Pakistan, up to 80%, does not have a flush toilet, so they suffer from disease frequently. Well, the Book of Leviticus explains what to do to avoid disease, including purifying and cleaning your hands!

All the scientists and medical doctors who claim God's hand is not present everywhere they look will reconcile themselves with the Bible one of these days. It's all there; all they must do is read it. It is correct, and the answers to human life are there too. However, it is a codebook and needs to be spiritually discerned. By whom? By those in Christ who receive the wisdom of God and His Word through the spirit of man and not man's mind. Therefore, if you are not born again, your heart is dead, and you cannot receive any coded wisdom.

*"The god of this age (aka satan) has blinded the minds of unbelievers so that they cannot see the light of the gospel that displays the glory of Christ, who is the image of God."* (2 Cor. 4:4)

*Life* is a test... Have you read the Book of Leviticus?

## It's in "The Book!" (Part 2 of 2)

Divine healing is a spiritual thing you receive through your spirit, not your mind. God's covenant is to live 120 years, so do that! People struggle with that, saying they don't want to live that long. However, we must not lose the perspective that we have a job to do, *"He said to them, "Go into all the world and preach the gospel to every creature. He who believes and is baptized will be saved, but he who does not believe will be condemned."* Mark 16:15-16 What else are you planning to do? Sit at home and watch TV shows?

Jesus said this in John 10:10: *"The thief does not come except to steal, kill, and destroy. I have come that they may have life and have it more abundantly."* The scripture is the dividing line of the Bible. It's the basic summary and foundation of the entire Word of God. Why? Because the greatest gift that God gave us is the gift of choice, and the option is which side of the dividing line, in other words, which side of the fence are you going to sit on?

There is a lot in the Bible that we may not be familiar with just because we don't sit down and read it. It's all in the Book, folks! Try to read through the New Testament every year and allow the words to sit deep in your heart, meditating day and night on it (Joshua 1:8).

*Life* is a test... Are you in the Word enough to know the Word?

## How to Hear from God. (Part 1 of 2)

**1.** Get alone. Go to your "prayer closet" - your bedroom, den, office, etc.- and close the door!

**2.** Play worship music so your mind can focus and get off everything else you are thinking about.

**3.** Talk to God about what is on your heart. Give Him your burdens because prayer is the exchange of obligations. If you prayed and are still burdened, you didn't do the exchange, which means you whined instead of sincerely giving Him your baggage. Ask Him what He wants you to pray about.

**4.** Read some scripture and write down what you think a particular passage is saying to you. Draw out what God has written in His Word. *"Counsel in the heart of man is like deep water, but a man of understanding will draw it out."* (Prov. 20:5 KJV)

The ability to hear God is natural; we are born with it. Why? How? Firstly, God created us to worship, and if people are not worshipping Him, they will worship someone or something else by their nature. We also learn through classes, practice and Spiritual Gifts how to hear. The good news is that you can listen because we are sheep, and *My sheep listen to my voice; I know them, and they follow me."* (John 10:27)

Just as a child at age two or three has immature speech and is then taught to speak as an adult, we must and can't do the same with how we pray.

*Life* is a test... Have you tried these four steps listed above?

*Life* is a test...

# How to Hear from God. (Part 2 of 2)

**Quieting Yourself so God Can Speak.**

Sometimes people can go down the wrong road and think that they're hearing from God when it's their flesh. Be careful of the following:

**1.** You are constantly "hearing" about every detail of everything in your life. "Nada".... - that is your flesh talking. God gave us brains and expects us to use them. Yes, we want "constant contact" (that is a relationship), but we are to "work out our salvation," which means growing up. *"Therefore, my dear friends, as you have always obeyed - not only in my presence but now much more in my absence - continue to work out your salvation with fear and trembling."* (Phil 2:12) God expects us to grow up in communicating with Him. Should you be having constant contact with your son? Yes, perhaps when he is two years old, but not when he is 30! Remember that we are God's children, and like every parent, He expects us to grow up - in Him and His Word.

**2.** Don't be foolish and do the "fate thing" where you lose all control of your Bible reading and go down the road of being a martyr and then blame God when He doesn't deliver. Again, be mature in your walk and reading and hearing. I don't believe that "everything happens for a reason;" it's too much of a "Que Sera Sera" attitude. I think that the two worst anti-God songs ever recorded were "Que Sera Sera" by Doris Day and "My Way" by Frank Sinatra. Lovely songs, I suppose but evil lyrics.

*Life* is a test... Is it your flesh that is hearing God or your spirit?

## Get a New Heart.

Too many people are tuned into the earth's natural realm and the news and activity of what they hear and see, which, because the world is filled with sin, they are believing worldly lies. The antichrist system has its minds bound to this world instead of being tied into God's heavenly realm. Consequently, many of the world's people live in fear, and their hearts become stony as they lose their love for each other and God.

*"I will give you a new heart and put a new spirit in you; I will remove from you your heart of stone and give you a heart of flesh. And I will put my Spirit in you and move you to follow my decrees and be careful to keep my laws."* (Ezk. 36:26-27)

The solution, as always, is our connection to God. We must tune in to heaven's frequency, where we will see and hear something very different from what we are watching and visiting here in the world. Repentance and turning our lives over to God releases the sound of great rejoicing. Set your affections on things above, not on the things of the earth. Learn to live in both spiritual realms but focus on what Jesus has called us to be and do, His bride and the light of the world to others.

*"For our light and momentary troubles are achieving for us an eternal glory that far outweighs them all. So we fix our eyes not on what is seen, but on what is unseen, since what is seen is temporary, but what is unseen is eternal."* (2 Cor. 4:17-18)

*"Do not conform to the pattern of this world, but be transformed by the renewing of your mind. Then you will be able to test and approve what God's will is - his good, pleasing and perfect will."* (Rom. 12:2)

*Life* is a test... Are you focused on Jesus or the world?

## Take the Narrow Road!

Following yesterday's theme, we live in a very challenging and changing world, and things are happening quickly. This requires a mind of flexibility and adaptability in our natural world. It also puts us in a position where we need to be more sensitive to His leading and be ready to make changes to ensure we are where we need to be.

*"But small is the gate and narrow the road that leads to life, and only a few find it."* (Matt. 7:14)

Who are the ones that find it? The ones that show up! If you were standing at a fork in the road and one was wide, where most of the people were going down, and the other was narrow, which was God's path, would you see that narrow path and walk down it? Yes, you would if you were smart, but you'll never get to that fork in the road, that choice to make unless you show up! How do you do that? You become born-again, start seeking God and start looking for answers!

It is obedience that is the key to walking with Him. Rom. 6:16 says, *"Don't you know that when you offer yourselves to someone as obedient slaves, you are slaves of the one you obey - whether you are slaves to sin, which leads to death, or to obedience, which leads to righteousness?"* Yes, it is OK to be a slave to Jesus, and then look for His path and that fork in the road of life and then, choose the narrow one.

*"... choose for yourselves this day whom you will serve..."* (Jos. 24:15)

*Life* is a test... Did you choose today? Which path?

## Fear and Phobia.

*"Do not allow the world's atmosphere to weigh you down and create fear. "For God has not given us a spirit of fear, but of power and of love and of a sound mind." (2 Tim. 1:7)*

Looking back at the "covid season" now, it's quite noteworthy to me how so much fear there was and how much it affected society. At the start, there was so much unknown about it, so we were all curious about how it would pan out. As months became close to two years of restrictions, a few things became clear to me:

**1.** The hyperbole of the media and government can potentially be very damaging, and it showed through how much fear was transmitted each day in the news and through media.
**2.** Selfish people and corrupt companies will try to take advantage of people even in trying times. "Selling" bad news is a money maker to these guys.
**3.** We must lean on the hope of Christ first before we listen to the media outlets, as there is a frequent tendency for the voice of the world to be louder in the media than the one of Christ.

You have the right and are commanded by God to prosper in life, but you have to choose it. Alternatively, you could choose fear in life if you wish. So, throw your burdens and the things that trouble you onto Him.

*"For My yoke is easy and My burden is light." (Matt; 10:30)*

*"Trust in the Lord with all your heart and lean not on your own under-standing; in all your ways submit to him, and he will make your paths straight." (Prov. 3:5-6)*

*"Know that the LORD is God. It is he who made us, and we are his; we are his people, the sheep of his pasture." (Ps. 100:3)*

*Life* is a test... Whose voice were you listening to more during covid? God's, or the worlds?

# The Month of Elul (Aug/Sept - Part 1 of 3)

**Alphabet:** The letter is "YUD" - appointed mercy from the hand of God and known as the month of repentance and forgiveness.
**Tribe:** Gad
**Characteristics:** The month that "the King is in the field." He is beside you as you work, so approach Him and allow His countenance to shine on you. This is the month to fix what has been broken.
- The month of God's favour.
- The month to find your place in the company of the Lord.
- Is the mother month, the month of nurturing.
- The King is in the field!
- This is the month to be with God; it's a special time to be with Him.
- God is seeking your heart and wants His relationship with you restored.
- Ask yourself, "is there any part of my life that I have not put into God's hands?"
- Gad was a warrior tribe. It is the month to put on your spiritual armour and let God train your hands for battle.
- Stand in the gap for your family and ask God for His intercession in their lives.
**Constellation:** Virgo (the Virgin)
**Colour/Stone:** Grey/Jasper or Hematite
**Scripture:** 2 Sam. 10:1

Elul brings transition! It is a season of change! What was true in the past season will not be true in the season ahead. This month we go from a narrow place (Av) to a broad place! (Elul) We go from oppression of the enemy to the favour of God, and it is one of the most joyful months. Elul is the month of preparation for the "high holy days" in the next month, Tishri. This month is when Moses assented to Mount Sinai to receive the second tablets of the covenant. These days, God revealed Himself to the Jewish people with great mercy during Elul.

## The Month of Elul (Aug/Sept - Part 2 of 3)

This is a transitional month, the last month of the old year, which precedes the "fall feasts." The days from the Feast of Trumpets to the Feast of Tabernacles are the holiest in the Biblical calendar. These are times to prepare ourselves to come to God's presence and glory. However, before the feasts start, we have Elul. For most of the year, a King lived in palaces protected by armed guards and iron gates, and a person would have to have an audience and make an appointment etc. However, one month each year, the King left his palace, went out among his people, and set up a tent near a small town. The announcement was made, "the King is in the field!"

God is especially assessable to you during Elul. This month, God is saying, "open up for Me the eye of a needle, and I will open for you the most expensive corridors of the Great Hall!" Find a place in your life to dedicate to Him and let Him prove Himself to you.

Elul is the "point" month. We need to understand how something starts and can get to its end. If we don't know how we got to where we are, we won't know how to move on to the next place. You must come to a point in your life where you recognize how you got into your mess and that God has appointed this month to get you out of your mess. Ask God to show you how you got there and where you need to be. He might have a dream that jars you loose from a bad situation, a revelation from a scripture, or a prophetic Word from Holy Spirit that gives you insight.

On the battlefield, you can be hard-pressed by the enemy. However, when things look dark, God comes with an army of angels. So, this is a month of deliverance from the enemy's power! This month, God will meet you on the battlefield and lead you to victory.

*Life* is a test... Are you prepared to meet the "King of Kings and the Lord of Lords" this month??

**www.newstartministries.ca**

## The Month of Elul (Aug/Sept - Part 3 of 3)

This month there are three Biblical patterns: Jehoshaphat (2 Chron. 19). - He lived in Jerusalem and went out among the people from Beersheba to Ephraim and turned the people back to the Lord! Then, he appointed judges in the land. He told them, "Let the Lord's fear be upon you.... with the Lord our God, there is no injustice, partiality, or bribery." As Jehoshaphat turned the people back to God, God is seeking your heart this month too. God's heart is yearning for you! He wants your heart to return to Him. This month means, "I am my beloved's, and my beloved is mine!" God wants His relationship with you restored. As you come out to meet Him, His countenance shines on you, and you are shown favour! God wants to come near, and He desires to bring you into His character's experience. He wants to manifest His justice, His righteousness, and His love.

Another Biblical example is Melchizedek. When Abraham was weary from war, Melchizedek was there in the field, and he came to bless Abraham. When God comes into the field, He comes to bless you. He wants to fix what is broken. He wants to overcome the emotional drain that has removed your strength. He wants to nurture you, and restore you to health and prosperity.

A third example of the King in the field is, of course, Jesus! According to the first chapter of John, it was the Word of God becoming flesh, and that flesh came down and He was in the field to meet the people. He was "God made accessible." You could quickly come to Him with a question or request and receive what you need. He came to manifest God's goodness, love, and righteousness to heal and deliver. He came to draw us into an intimate relationship with God. Elul is a picture of the earthly ministry of Jesus. He had lived here in a field in a tent of mortal flesh for 33 years. So, what do we do? We run to Him! Throw yourself into His arms, be lost in His embrace, and give yourself to Him. Put your life in His hands.

Ask yourself, "is there any part of my life I have not put completely into God's hands?" What have you been worrying over that you can entrust to Him? Look at the cares and anxieties that have drained your strength and cast those carers totally on Him. Then allow Him to shine His favour on you.

*Life* is a test... Can you do 1 Peter 5:7?

## Truth or Lies? (Part 1 of 2)

Many Christian parents tell their children about Santa Claus, the Easter Bunny, Halloween, the Tooth Fairy and then also throw in God around the same holiday times. Consequently, when those children learn that Santa is their parents and not real, when they know that the Easter Bunny doesn't lay chocolate eggs that Halloween is a celebration of witchcraft and death, and the parents are the natural Tooth Fairy; they assume that Jesus is also a lie and so give up on God. And we wonder why?

Too many people are tuned into the earth's natural realm and the news and activity of what they hear and see, like all these pagan festivals and practices. They believe in lies as the world is filled with evil and then teach those lies to their children. Instead of being bound into God's heavenly realm, the antichrist system has its minds attached to this world. Consequently, these lies and the world's evil lead people to fear, and their hearts become stony as they lose their love for each other and God.

*"Because of the increase of wickedness, the love of most will grow cold."* (Matt. 24:12)

However, turning to God will do this:

*"I will give you a new heart and put a new spirit in you; I will remove from you your heart of stone and give you a heart of flesh. And I will put my Spirit in you and move you to follow my decrees and be careful to keep my laws."* (Ezk. 36:26-27)

 is a test... Are you believing or teaching lies?

## Truth or Lies? (Part 2 of 2)

The solution as always is our connection to God. We must tune in to heaven's frequency, where we will see and hear something very different from what we are watching and seeing here in the world. Repentance and turning our lives over to God releases the sound of great rejoicing.

*"Set your minds on things above, not on earthly things. For you died, and your life is now hidden with Christ in God. When Christ, who is your life, appears, then you also will appear with him in glory. Put to death, therefore, whatever belongs to your earthly nature: sexual immorality, impurity, lust, evil desires and greed, which is idolatry. Because of these, the wrath of God is coming."* (Col. 3:2-6)

Learn to live function both spiritual realms but set your focus on what Jesus has called us to be and do, His bride and the light of the world to others. Our spiritual senses need to be focused on Jesus and not on the things of this world.

*"For our light and momentary troubles are achieving eternal glory that far outweighs them all. So we fix our eyes not on what is seen, but on what is unseen, since what is seen is temporary, but what is unseen is eternal."* (2 Cor. 4:17-18)

*"Do not conform to the pattern of this world, but be transformed by the renewing of your mind. Then you will be able to test and approve what God's will is - His good, pleasing and perfect will."* (Rom. 12:2)

*"Create in me a pure heart, O God, and renew a steadfast spirit within me."* (Ps. 51:10)

*Life* is a test... Do you tune into heaven's frequency and see the world from heaven's perspective?

**www.newstartministries.ca**

## The Eighth Fruit of the Spirit - Gentleness
### (Part 1 of 3)

Gentleness is the eighth fruit of the Spirit. Gal. 5:22-23 says that the Holy Spirit works in us to be more like Christ, and gentleness is part of that. Gentleness is also translated as "meekness," which does not mean weakness but involves humility and thankfulness toward God. In essence, polite, restrained behaviour toward others. The opposite of gentleness is anger and revenge. Gentleness is not commonly used in our everyday language, and in the New King James version, it is only used ten times.

The Canadian Oxford dictionary describes gentleness as *"essentially the act of being gentle, the opposite of being rough, severe, or drastic."* We don't often think of gentleness as strength, but it takes much power to be gentle. It is easy to be angry and harsh, which is a weakness, not a strength.

We speak words that help or hurt, and we choose what influences those words and the actions we take. Left uncontrolled, we are powerful with our words and easily hurt others and ourselves. To be gentle is to recognize that God's ways and thoughts are better and higher than ours. (Is. 55:9). If we maintain a level of humility in our lives we will not be shaped by sin and the world, and then we can reflect gentleness towards others.

When we are filled with the Spirit's fruit of gentleness, we will correct others "gently" instead of arguing in resentment and anger and putting others down. We will forgive readily. Competition and envy will disappear as the goal becomes less about us and more about preaching the gospel (Phil. 1:15-18).

Gentleness also means giving up the right to judge others and us (Rom. 8:1). Gentleness means that we accept that the rain falls on the *"just and the unjust"* (Matt. 4:45) and that God may use methods usually difficult for us to understand to reach others.

## The Eighth Fruit of the Spirit - Gentleness
### (Part 2 of 3)

To live in a spirit of gentleness toward God is to accept His judgment on people and issues. We think it is gentle to go easy on people and try to justify actions that God has called sin. Nada! Paul says, *"If someone is caught in a sin, you who live by the Spirit should restore that person gently."* (Gal. 6:1). This doesn't mean to be so soft that the sinner doesn't realize he has sinned; it means to confront the brother gently - to be mild, loving, and encouraging. Jesus gave us the perfect picture of gentleness: *"See, your king comes to you, gentle and riding on a donkey"* (Matt. 21:5), and now He offers us His gentleness as a gift. If we allow Holy Spirit to lead us, we will be filled with the fruit of gentleness.

Jesus was not a wimp and was not without righteous anger. He overturned the tables of those misusing the Temple of God and referred to the religious people as *"a brood of vipers"* (Matt.3:7), yet… there was a gentleness about Him. He let the children come to Him; He did not deny the Gentile woman who begged Him to heal her demon-possessed daughter. In all things, He walked in gentleness, doing nothing but the will of His Father.

*"Now Jesus called His disciples to Himself and said, "I have compassion for these people; they have already been with me three days and have nothing to eat. I do not want to send them away hungry, or they may collapse on the way."* (Matt. 15:32)

God is love, and we were made to love, to be kind, to be gentle and yet, to have this character does not mean that we are never attacking the enemy - only that we need to be in alignment with God, walking in gentleness daily, yet overturning the enemy if God wills us to.

*"A gentle answer turns away wrath, but a harsh word stirs up anger."* (Prov. 15:1

*"Let your gentleness be evident to all."* (Phil. 4:5)

## The Eighth Fruit of the Spirit - Gentleness
### (Part 3 of 3)

Jesus did not attack the Pharisees when they tried to challenge Him, but rather He answered with Godly wisdom and gentleness, trying to get them to think. Consequently, His accusers never had a case against Him. Even when standing before His accusers, He did not claim His innocence in anger, instead choosing to remain silent. Even when He was beaten and then on a cross, He did not call down the Angels to destroy His accusers. Instead, out of His love and gentleness, He accepted our iniquities upon Himself so that we might be saved. Jesus walked in gentleness.

We can build our character in it by practicing gentleness in every situation. As with all the Fruits of the Spirit, it is subject to Holy Spirit operating in us and us practicing the fruit. Through communing with Holy Spirit, through spending time in the Word - listening to God's voice in it and us - we open ourselves more and more to the fruit of the Spirit. As we walk in each fruit, we find that our ability to use them increases.

Sometimes, we reach a point where we think we have "made it." Where we had begun to think of ourselves as walking in it fully, only to discover through some tests that while yes, our daily walk improved, there is still room for improvement. After all, "Life is a Test!" Yet, God never tests us beyond what we can endure (1 Cor. 10:13). We can always choose to grow closer to God and stronger in Him in all the Fruits of the Spirit.

The different Fruits of the Spirit make us realize how imperfect we are and how much more work we must do. But that's OK; God is there with us to help us as He knows what imperfect vessels we are. The more we humbly realize that the more we reach out to Him.

*Life* is a test... When the intense moments of life come, do you remember to walk in gentleness?

## Set Backs; We All Have Them.

*"So do not fear, for I am with you; do not be dismayed, for I am your God. I will strengthen you and help you; I will uphold you with my righteous right hand."* (Is. 41:10)

Society has this unrealistic expectation that happiness is the goal of life and an entitled rite of passage. That explains why the millennial generation "has an attitude" - one of "entitlement." Then, when setbacks come (which is the truth of life), too many people can't handle them (i.e., life's problems).

Having a setback does not mean that our forward motion has been sabotaged. It does not mean that life is over, our project is finished, or our marriage is gone. Setbacks are times to analyze, reflect, pray, seek God for wisdom, etc. This is not a time for weeping, discouragement, or losing hope. Satan is trying to mess with your head, and if you allow him in, well, you will reap what you have sown (Gal. 6:7). Don't give him the pleasure and satisfaction of doing that! Instead, put them under your feet (Rom. 16:20).

The power and strength you need come from Holy Spirit, so depend on Him. Your energy is in moving forward! Just keep moving and never quit. God sees us, is with us, and anxiously waits to give us ideas (Prov. 8:12) and wisdom. (Job 28:28, Prov. 8:12, Prov. 9:10) "Chill," and ask. Simple stuff…

*"Never give in. Never give in. Never, never, never, never - in nothing, great or small, large or petty - never give in, except to convictions of honour and good sense. Never yield to force. Never yield to the apparently overwhelming might of the enemy."* Sir Winston Churchill

*Life* is a test… How will you handle your next setback?

## God's Design. (Part 1 of 3)

By design:

- You were created before the earth was (Eph. 1:4, Jer.1:5).
- You were created in His image (Gen. 1:27).
- You were created to worship. (Is. 43:21) - and if it's not God that you are worshiping, then it will be some other thing or narcissistic endeavour. It is God's nature for you to worship Him.
- You were created to do good works (Eph. 2:10).
- You were created to connect with Him, so depend on Him moment by moment (Acts 17:28).
- You were created to live in an "earth suit" here on this planet for a limited time to bring Heaven into the earth (Matt. 6:10), and in doing so, your job is to go out into the world and make disciples of all men (Matt.28:19).
- You are to continue this life in eternal Heaven (paradise) with God as soul and spirit only. The catch is that God gives you freedom and that freedom is the ability to "choose" whether you live for Him now and with Him later (Deut. 30:19, Jos. 24:15).

That's life in a nutshell, and it is nothing more complicated than that. Simple stuff...

However, our society seems "hell-bent" (pun intended) on living a narcissistic, entertainment-filled, egotistical self-satisfying, "successful" life. "It's all about me." Living in this technologically crazy-driven world has brought everyone towards needing an addictive "fix." All in the interest of solving boredom, while 2/3 of the world lives at or below the poverty line. Bored? Get a life.... *

 is a test... Seriously, are you bored? Keep reading...

(It's a cute expression, but actually, you should be losing your life - not to yourself but to Jesus!)

## God's Design - Bored? Really??? (Part 2 of 3)

Years ago, there was an article in our local newspaper about a community building under construction to help the "bored youth." I wrote the following letter to the editor as a response:

*"Your parents do not owe you entertainment, your community does not owe you recreational facilities, and the world does not owe you anything. On the contrary, you owe the world something - your time, energy, gifts, talents, and money so that no one will be at war, in poverty, sick or lonely again. Life is about making the world better when you leave than when you arrive. Don't be a protester; grow up and be an agent of change.*

*Billions of people are cold, poor, sick, hurt, hungry, or at war because you haven't helped them. Life is not about you. So, what are you bored about, and what are you waiting for?"*

It's essential for the "bored" younger generation to be empowered and know they can make a change. Skills are essential to have and using online tools, it's so easy today to gain practical skills. Learning about mechanics, baking, computers - anything - is available at the click of a button. Make use of it! It's an incredible gift people my age didn't grow up with. Remember that education is something that can never be taxed or taken from you.

*Life* is a test... Are you making use of online tutorials and remote skills acquisitions? I have included a couple of posters for you to check out. You can buy them on my website!

## This is your LIFE.

The one that God gave you. Find out what He has called you to do, and do it. (hint; it will be something you like and that you are good at. If in doubt, ask Him.) If you don't like something in the world, then...

## Be an agent of change.

If you don't have enough time, shut off your phone, computer, and TV and plant your money into His Kingdom to help preach the Gospel (it isn't your money anyway). If you are looking for the love of your life, stop. You will find them when you start doing what God has called you to do. Jesus loves you, and that is all that matters. Meditate on His Word, do His Word and live His Word. Yes...

## It really is that simple.

Emotions are great, but keep them under His control. Look after your body - it is the temple of the Holy Spirit. Open your heart, life and money to people and let your light shine by doing good works. Live by God's faith. Help others to build their dream, and in doing so, you will build your own. Then you can...

## Travel & help.

It really is the best education in the world, and you will find your life if you lose it by doing the works of God. Life is not about finding yourself but rather about creating yourself in the image of Jesus and making the world a better place when you leave than when you arrived. The world does not owe you anything. You owe the world everything. Don't talk about your rights. Fulfill your duties and responsibilities. Don't protest, pray. Because...

## Life is short.

Billions of people are hungry, cold, poor, sick, hurt, at war, and going to hell because you haven't helped them and told them about Jesus. After all, your real calling in life is to go out and make disciples of all men. It is not about you. So...

## What are you waiting for?

The "This Is Your Life" Poster can be downloaded and printed in any size for $7.95 CAD.

www.newstartministries.ca

# The Ten Stages in the Life of a Christian
# ENTREPRENEUR

1. **I THOUGHT IT** – God gives you the vision, and you have a flash of euphoric inspiration. (Prov. 8:12)

2. **I CAUGHT IT** – You start to get excited about the vision but make the mistake of telling your family and friends, and they tell you that you are crazy and that your idea will never work. (Proverbs 29:18)

3. **I BOUGHT IT** – You consider the cost of the vision, pay the price and get nothing but discouragement, but you decide to live by faith. (Romans 1:17; Galatians 3:17)

4. **I SOUGHT IT** – Nobody can talk you out of it, but despite that, you lose money and begin to second guess yourself. Then you remember that God is bigger. (Philippians 4:13)

5. **I FOUGHT IT** – To keep from "losing it" while others are mocking you. You want to quit. (Psalm 27:14)

6. **I WAS FRAUGHT WITH FEAR** – but I persevered. (Isaiah 41:10)

7. **I GOT IT** – YOU MEET WITH SUCCESS! You actually possess the dream and are glad you paid the price. (I Samuel 18:14)

8. **I HAD AN ONSLAUGHT** – Suddenly, everyone wants to be your "best friend," and your family completely supports you. (Ezekiel 16:14) So,

9. **I TAUGHT IT** – You pass it on to the next generation. (Matthew 5:19)

10. **I HAVE AN AFTERTHOUGHT** – and realize that God was with me all the time. (Deuteronomy 31:6b)

The "10 stages in the life of a Christian Entrepreneur" Poster can be downloaded and printed in any size for $7.95 CAD.

www.newstartministries.ca

## God's Design. (Part 3 of 3)

We were born before the beginning of time; we live in an "earth suit" for a limited period and then go to the "H place" or the other "h place" depending on the decision that we have made. While living in this natural world, it is governed by physical laws as established by God from the foundation of the world. In addition, He has also established certain spiritual laws for us to abide by and to bless us with. Blessings come to those who put the spiritual laws into practice.

From the foundation of the chromosomes in your DNA to the size of the stars, everything is made well and in order. His design is literally divine! (*"And God saw that it was good"* - see Gen. chap. 1). Everything He does works in complete harmony and balance.

What causes things to go out of sync, and what are the consequences? Lucifer was one of God's favourite angels, but he got proud one day and decided to leave a took a third of the other angels with Him (see Ezekiel 28). Adam and Eve were tempted, and the rest is history. Jesus came back as the second Adam to repair the mess. (Rom. 5:14, I Cor. 15:25 - 22). Then Jesus called us to carry on His job by:

**1.** Calling heaven down to the earth. (Luke 11:2)
**2.** Living life through God using the 10 Commandments and the Beatitudes as our foundation.
**3.** Loving our neighbours as ourselves and keeping ourselves free of sin.
**4.** Going out preaching the gospel. (Mark 16:15-16 )

If we let sin in our lives, we become out of balance with the spiritual laws, which then don't work anymore, and we open ourselves to sickness, disease, financial problems, and relational problems the list is endless. So, stick with God's design and laws. Simple stuff...

*Life* is a test... Can you see the design that God has made and how really simple life is? Just follow the laws.

**www.newstartministries.ca**

## Ethics (Part 1 of 2)

Ethics in the Bible refers to a system or ideology produced by the study, interpretation, and evaluation of Biblical morals. We call this a moral code or standard; principles, conscience, values, behaviours, rules of conduct that we choose to live by as written in God's Word. Ethics are principles that govern a person's actions. Ethics define right and wrong behaviour. The words "ethics," "morals," and "morality" may be applied in different contexts, but they have essentially the same meaning. Our laws written in our western/modern civilization have come from the Bible. The Ten Commandments (Ex. 20:1-17) were the standard of conduct and essentially the foundation of all our societies from the Garden of Eden to today. Even the roots of "civil law" all stem from the Bible.

Jesus did not abolish the moral and ethical laws that had been in effect from the time of Moses, but instead, He affirmed and expanded those principles. God is concerned about how we live our lives from the inside (attitudes and motives) rather than any show of religion on the outside. This is where the whole issue of living under a facade comes into play. We must be moved by our hearts, not by our heads. It is for that reason that Jesus calls the Pharisees of His day a "brood of vipers." (Matt. 12:34) They were holy men on the outside but wolves in sheep's clothing on the inside. Reflect on these scriptures:

*"Let integrity and uprightness preserve me, For I wait for You."* (Ps. 25:21 NKJV)

*"Therefore, whatever you want men to do to you, do also to them, for this is the Law and the Prophets."* (Matt. 7:12 NKJV)

*"And whatever you do, do it heartily, as to the Lord and not to men."* (Col. 3:23)

*Life* is a test... What barometer are you using to measure your own ethics? How about using the Bible?

## Ethics (Part 2 of 2)

Jesus told us to humble ourselves to God and then love and demonstrate that love to others. (Matt. 22:34-40, Mark 12:28-31, Luke 10:25-28, John 13:34-35).

The 10 Commandments were not simply a list of rules and regulations, but the more significant issue is that we should not even entertain these sins in our hearts, let alone manifest them.

Jesus gave many examples of applying His ethical teachings in His "Sermon of the Mount" (Matt. Chap. 5-7).

### The Beatitudes

"* *Blessed are the poor in spirit, for theirs is the Kingdom of heaven.*
* *Blessed are those who mourn, for they will be comforted.*
* *Blessed are the meek, for they will inherit the earth.*
* *Blessed are those who hunger and thirst for righteousness, for they will be filled.*
* *Blessed are the merciful, for they will be shown mercy.*
* *Blessed are the pure in heart, for they will see God.*
* *Blessed are the peacemakers, for they will be called children of God.*
* *Blessed are those who are persecuted because of righteousness, for theirs is the kingdom of heaven.*" (Matt. 5:3-10)

Sadly, our world has turned so far from ethics that many people don't even understand the word's meaning. It's now entirely socially acceptable to cheat the government out of taxes when Jesus said, *"Render to Caesar the things that are Caesar's..."* (Mark 12:17). I recently had a chat with my stockbroker. He said the number one problem plaguing his industry was money laundering and fraud.

*ife* is a test... Read The Beatitudes (or "be attitudes" as some people like to call them!) in several different translations and you'll get a better understanding.

## Families and Sunday.

God is not a happy camper when we don't take one day a week to stop work and spend time with Him and our families. It is so important to Him that it is listed as number four from the top in the list of the big ones (aka The Ten Commandments - see Ex. 20).

I can remember when Sunday was a big day in our family: church /Sunday school, followed by visiting my grandparents, lunch and then family time either at home or at our sports club. The day was further enjoyed by "Sunday dinner" and more family time (watching the Wonderful World of Disney* followed by Ed Sullivan!) It's hard to imagine now, but all the banks and stores were closed on Sunday (banks were only open from 10 am until 3 pm Monday to Friday, and there were no ATMs. Plus, most people used cash!) The day was about God and family, the entire foundation of any society.

Then in the 70s, the government, in its infinite wisdom (sarcasm intended), decided to allow everything and anything to be open on Sunday. Society loved their newfound freedom. Now compare that to today when Sunday is often the busiest shopping day of the week! When is the day of rest observed?

It is a sad and tragic observation to note that our families and society have become more fragmented since Sunday store openings. Not only are our families not meeting on Sunday and honouring the Lord, but most families do not eat together at least once per day during the week, and if they do, inevitably, the TV is on! We then wonder why society is in a mess. We have reaped what we have sown.

*"Therefore say to them, 'Thus says the Lord of hosts, "Return to Me,"* *declares the Lord of hosts, "that I may return to you," says the Lord of* *hosts."* (Zech. 1:3)

*Life* is a test... How are you spending your Sundays?

* Look at many of the shows that Disney is producing now....

**www.newstartministries.ca**

# The Fundamentals of Prayer.

You will notice two things about Jesus' prayer methods when you read the Bible. Firstly, He prayed all night and secondly, He prayed alone. Then He taught His disciples to pray fervently as He did. In Luke chapter 18, verse one, He used an example of a woman constantly nagging a judge for justice. Finally, the judge relinquished and gave it to her desires. Jesus's point was to keep praying until you get a breakthrough.

Fire has always fascinated me, as it does many people. Indeed, wilderness survival manuals will always say that the first thing you should do in a survival situation is to start a fire. It provides warmth and light, but it also affects our psychological well-being. Life always seems better around a roaring warm fire! It takes three things to start a fire: fuel, oxygen and a spark. We need His Word, power, and prayer; prayer is our oxygen, the Word is the fuel, and passion is our spark. We need to pray with complete fury and intensity - as if it was the essential thing in your life (and sometimes it is!)

Some Christians fail to receive answered prayer because they don't understand God's purpose for prayer. They think that prayer is all about getting something, which is why some people fast - to get God to move. We are missing and need to understand that prayer goes far beyond petitioning Him for our daily needs. It encompasses a divine call to become passionate prayer intercessors with God and pray through the things He desires us to pray about. Our prayers can (and will) move heaven and earth if we pray according to His will and direction. Prayer will take on a whole new meaning, purpose, and power as you partner with God for things in His heart and not just the stuff in ours. Be passionate in prayer, embrace what He wants you to pray about, and watch Him give you the breakthroughs you desire.

*Life* is a test... Are you a passionate intercessory prayer warrior?

## Faith in the Prayers that we Pray.

Faith is the most powerful tool and weapon in the entire universe. God Himself used faith to build the universe. Simply.... *"faith is the substance of things hoped for, the evidence of things not seen."* (Heb. 11:1) Prayer uses our faith to believe in God for supernatural things that you foresee in the heavenly realms, which are not seen in the natural. Prayer puts faith to work as faith expects, contemplates, predicts and reaches out for things to come into reality from the heavenly realms.

Remember the story of the woman that had a blood disease for 12 years? (see Luke 8:42-47) She had faith to believe that this man, Jesus, the Son of the living God, walking down the street in front of her, could heal her. She had an expectation and knew in her heart that Jesus could do that for her. She spoke by faith within herself and said if I could just touch the hem of his garment, she would be healed. *"She came up behind him and touched the edge of his cloak, and immediately her bleeding stopped. "Who touched me?" Jesus asked. Peter said, "Master, the people are crowding and pressing against you when they all denied it." But Jesus said, "Someone touched me; I know that power has gone out from me." Then the woman, seeing that she could not go unnoticed, came trembling and fell at his feet. In the presence of all the people, she told why she had touched him and how she had been instantly healed. Then he said to her, "Daughter, your faith has healed you. Go in peace."*

Now here is the crucial point: Jesus said that it was **her faith** that made her whole. Our healing begins with belief (in Jesus) and faith (in Jesus). We must do that before we call upon our Lord and Saviour to heal us.

*Life* is a test... *"The just shall live by faith"* (Heb. 10:38) Are you?

*Life is a test...*

## Wait...

When you don't know what to do, do nothing. Take a second and wait for peace to come. Peace comes through wisdom and is obtained in the Lord's Word (James 3:17). Peace is God's continuous gift to us. It flows abundantly from His throne of grace.

Remember when the Israelites were out in the desert, and they were hungry? God sent them manna and told them not to store it but wait for a fresh batch each day (see Ex. 16). Why? Because God was trying to teach them not to live on their self-sufficiency but trust Him each day. If God permanently gave us peace and independence, we would fall into self-control and autonomy. He wants us to depend on Him daily because that requires us to live by faith. *"The just shall live by faith."* (Rom. 1:17b, NKJV) Heb. 11:6 tells us that if we are not living by faith, we are *"not pleasing God,"* and Rom. 14:23 confirms this by saying that *"whatever is not of faith is sin."*

When in crisis mode, the devil intends to bring confusion into your soul and take your mind off God. What to do? Take a deep breath and get some clarity about the situation you are dealing with. Satan always wants us to run ahead of God by giving us confusion, stress and strife with others with the inevitable hope that we will make a bigger mess and more mistakes. Instead, resist satan and his temptations and he will flee from you. Don't go down that road!

*"Be still and know that I am God."* (Ps. 46:10)

*"Wait for the Lord; be strong, take heart, and wait for the Lord."* (Ps. 27:14)

*"The Lord is good to those whose hope is in Him, to the one who seeks Him."* (Lam. 3:25)

*Life* is a test... Are you in peace or fretting??

**is a test...**

## Angels (Part 1 of 3)

Angels or *"ministering spirits"* (Heb. 1:14) are assigned by God to help us. They have greater power and ability than humans (2 Peter 2:11) but are not greater than humans. God made them servants to serve mankind. They exist in heaven and the spirit realm (1 Kings 8:27; John 6:38). God created the angels individually, and they do not marry and reproduce (Mark 12:25). Instead, each "son of the true God" was individually made (Job 1:6).

Angels were created before the earth existed. When God created the earth world, the angels *"began shouting in applause"* (Job 38:4-7), which means they were there before the earth was. We do not know how many angels there are, as the Bible does not give an exact figure, but we know that there are many of them! John had a vision in Rev. 5:11, and it seems that he saw hundreds of millions of angels.

Angels are ranked, and the angel who is the greatest in both power and authority is Michael, the Archangel (Jude 9; Rev. 12:7). Seraphs are high-ranking angels, and they are stationed near God's throne (Is. 6:2, 6). Cherubs are another high-ranking order of angels, and they have unique jobs. For example, they guarded the Garden of Eden entrance after Adam and Eve were expelled (Gen 3:23, 24).

God uses angels as He directs His servants to preach the gospel's good news (Rev. 14:6, 7). Angels help keep the Christian church free of evil spirits and evil people (Matt. 13:49) and are used by God to protect those faithful to God (Ps. 34:7; 91:10, 11; Hebrews 1: 7, 14).

*Life* is a test...  Have you ever seen angels at work in or around your life?

# Angels (Part 2 of 3)

To give more context to angels and these curious heavenly beings, I think it's good to dispel some related myths. Here are four false ideas about angels:

**Myths about angels:**

**1.** All angels are good.

Not all of them. When Lucifer the Archangel left heaven and became known as satan, he took a third of the angels with him, and they are what we call demons. They are known as *"the wicked spirit forces"* and *"the angels who sinned"* (Eph. 6: 12; 2 Peter 2:4).

**2.** Angels are immortal.

Wicked angels (demons), including satan, will be destroyed (Jude 6).

**3.** People become angels when they die.

Nope. Angels are a separate creation of God, not resurrected humans (Col. 1.16). People whose bodies have died and know Jesus go to heaven and receive the gift of eternity (1 Cor. 15:53, 54), and are ranked above the angels (1 Cor. 6:3).

**4.** Angels exist to serve humans.

Yes, but… It's one of the reasons that God created them, but they answer to Him, not us (Ps. 103:20, 21). Jesus acknowledged that He would call God for help, but not directly to the angels (Matt. 26:53). We do not pray to angels or anything or anyone else (including Mary); we pray to God or Jesus. Prayer to God is part of our worship, which belongs to God (Rev. 19:10). We should pray only to God through Jesus. Angels stand ready to do whatever God Commands them to do.

## Angels (Part 3 of 3)

There are lots of examples of angels in the Bible:

**1.** An angel told Mary that she would have a son who would forgive people of their sins (Luke 1:28-33).

**2.** An angel strengthened and encouraged Jesus the night He was betrayed (Luke. 22:43).

**3.** In the Book of Acts, we see that an Angel rescued Peter and the other apostles (Acts 5:19-20).

**4.** An angel came for Elijah and brought him some bread and water. (1 Kings 19:5-7)

We can activate angels by praying to God. For example, when we pray binding and loosening prayers (Matt. 18:18), the prayers go to God, and then He instructs the Angles to do what is needed. These battles in the heavenly realms are between good and evil.

We should never forget to pray for heaven's agenda, like *"calling things that be not as though they were"* (Rom. 4:17) and calling *"heaven into the earth"* (Matt. 6:10). We will encounter powerful results when we cultivate a worshipping heart in conjunction with heaven's agenda. We must never stop praying and ask the Lord to send angelic help. Remember that the *"prayers of the righteous are powerful and effective"* (James 5:16).

Daniel did not stop praying until his prayers were answered; it took 21 days! He knew how to get results. Remember that breakthrough answers to prayer are hanging in the balance between heaven and earth. Angels who are God's assistants will deliver answered prayers to you as you partner with God and *"pray without ceasing."* (1 Thess. 5:17)

*Life* is a test... Did you know that you have angels with you 24/7?

## Refining

Why do bad things happen to good people? It's one of the ironies and tragedies of human existence. But God has a plan...

He will use every bad and unwelcome situation in our lives to refine our character and get our attention if we allow Him to do that. When the painful things of life happen, we have two choices: 1. complain, cry, react in anger, or even retaliate in revenge or 2. we can choose to sit in the company of Holy Spirit and tune in to Him and find the grace that we need to get through the situation. (*"My grace is sufficient for you..."* - 2 Cor.12:9) Instead of asking, "why Lord is this happening to me?" A better question might be, "Lord, what is it that you're trying to teach me in this situation?"

As I mentioned before, on May 12th, Joseph is my personal biblical hero. One of the reasons is that I see so much of myself in his life. Perhaps you can relate to him as well. He did so many right things and yet suffered so much mistreatment. But it was in that prison cell that he learned how to rule over his flesh nature so that God could break him of himself and eventually had the skill, talent and humility to rule over others well. You see, it was God's plan for Joseph to save his family - God's children, the Israelites - from the famine, but Joseph had to be broken of his pride before he could be used.

I have repeatedly seen in the church and the secular world that that path is often the same for many people. The call to greatness always leads us through the worst part of our lives, where we face our most significant weaknesses, insecurities and true motivations. There's nothing like a good bout of pride and pain to reveal our true natures. Remember, in every situation in life, whether positive or negative, there's an opportunity to work out our salvation and grow more like Jesus.

*Life* is a test... Do you allow God to refine you when you're in troubled times?

# Follow the Protocols.

If you are invited to a function at Buckingham Palace, you will be briefed by a protocol employee on the proper procedures when you meet the Royal family. Governments employ full-time protocol staff! The same applies if we meet a judge, President, Prime Minister etc. By acknowledging the correct protocol, we recognize the seat of authority -position - that this "high-level" person represents.

As Christians, we must be conscious of the protocol we need to use to approach God's throne room when praying. We enter the King of King's courtroom with hearts of thanksgiving and praise regardless of how we might feel at the time.

*"Shout for joy to the Lord, all the earth. Worship the Lord with gladness; come before Him with joyful songs. Know that the Lord is God. He made us, and we are His; we are His people, the sheep of His pasture. Enter His gates with thanksgiving and His courts with praise; give thanks to Him and praise His Name. For the Lord good and His love endures forever; His faithfulness continues through all generations."* (Ps. 100)

Remember that prayer is just you chatting with God, and it places you in a position to communicate very closely with Him. Praise opens the door, and He ushers you into His presence. God inhabits the praises of His people (paraphrased from Ps. 22:3). Partnering with God through prayer and praise creates a euphoric spiritual atmosphere for blessings, healing, deliverance, and salvation - whatever you need.

*"Praise be to the God and Father of our Lord Jesus Christ, who has blest us in the heavenly realms with every spiritual blessing in Christ."* (Eph. 1:3)

*Life* is a test... Are praise and worship part of your daily routine?

*Life is a test...*

# The Mind - God's Greatest Invention.

Man is the pinnacle creation of all the things that God has made. He was having a good day when He made you and I. The pinnacle of the creation of the entire universe is the human being, specifically the brain. Interestingly, scientists claim that we only use 13% of it! If that is true, it is even more amazing when we look at the talent of some people. Michelangelo, Leonardo da Vinci and Albert Einstein are excellent examples. Einstein said one time that he never actually invented his theory of relativity. Instead, he said that God gave it to him. I wonder how often that happens to incredibly bright and creative people. We are all blest to do great things; it's just a matter of believing in God and tapping into Holy Spirit's directions and His creativity. He is the one that paints pictures and invents computers.

*"The mind governed by the flesh is death, but the mind governed by the Spirit is life and peace."* (Rom. 8:6)

God wants to control our minds. Why? It is God's creation, but because of sin in the world, the mind becomes the most restless and unruly part of our makeup. The mind constantly wants to "ride shotgun" on our lives, overruling the work of Holy Spirit. When we say, "life is a battle," it truly is! The battle is between our will and Holy Spirit.

God risked everything and gave us the freedom to think for ourselves. This is a privilege which sets us apart from animals and robots. Don't forget that we are made in God's image (Gen. 1:26-27).

Though the shed blood of God's Son on the cross which redeemed us, our minds are the last stronghold of complete rebellion. We need to open ourselves to the fullness of Holy Spirit because when He is controlling our minds, we are filled with life and peace.

*Life* is a test... Are you controlling yourself, or is He controlling you?

# Wisdom and Money.

*"The Spirit of the Lord is on me because he has anointed me to proclaim good news to the poor. He has sent me to proclaim freedom for the prisoners and recovery of sight for the blind, set the oppressed free, and proclaim the year of the Lord's favour."* (Luke 4:18)

It was wisdom that enabled Jesus to speak the Word about poverty. Many people do not understand what poverty is, or they fail to see that it is more than just a lack of money (and consequently they think that the solution is to get more money!) Millions of wealthy people in this world are poor; poor in spirit, poor in knowing God, poor in knowing the wiles of the devil, etc.

Money gained outside of wisdom often brings sorrow and even loss. *"The blessing of the Lord it maketh rich and addeth no sorrow with it."* (Prov. 10:22 KJV) Note that wisdom is righteously connected to the obtaining of wealth and prosperity. 2 Chron. 9:22 says this about Solomon: *"King Solomon was greater in riches and wisdom than all the other kings of the earth."* No matter how you look at it, *"wisdom and riches are the same."* Look what 1 Kings 3:11-13 says about Solomon: *"So God said to him, "Since you have asked for this and not for long life or wealth for yourself, nor have asked for the death of your enemies but for discernment in administering justice, I will do what you have asked. I will give you a wise and discerning heart so that there will never have been anyone like you, nor will there ever be. Moreover, I will give you what you have not asked for - both wealth and honour - so that you will have no equal among kings in your lifetime."*

As we hunger for God's wisdom, it produces God's favour, guidance, direction, strategies, etc., to gain wealth. Why? To build the Kingdom of God (Deut. 8:18). Your job is to go out and make disciples of all men (Matt. 28:19), and it takes money to do it.

*Life* is a test... Are you getting wisdom and understanding? (Prov. 4:5)

## Two Responses to Problems.

Too many people live their lives unaware of God's involvement. It is like they are sleepwalking their way through life. Then one day, they walk right into a problem. It stares at them in the face, and it is so overwhelming that they have no clue how to address the situation.

When (not "if") this happens to you, you have two responses; one will take you up, and the other will take you down, possibly destroying you as you fall. If you fight, reject, complain, get into fear, lash out at God or others over your difficulty, and start resenting and feeling sorry for yourself, it will take you down a road of self-pity. Or there is response number two:

You can choose to look at the problem as a challenge, perhaps a "God-sent" one (it could be!); an opportunity to have a "perspective lifter" - a fresh view of the situation. Go with God to look at your problem and ask Him for wisdom and guidance - what His opinion is on the deal. Once your view is highlighted from His perspective, life never seems so wrong. "Bad things are an opportunity in drag..."

Look at life through His eyes, not yours. Turn towards Him and see the light of His shining presence all over the situation. Seek Him. Find the answers to what He wants you to do.

*"Come to me, all you who are weary and burdened, and I will give you rest. Take my yoke upon you and learn from me, for I am gentle and humble in heart, and you will find rest for your souls."* (Matt. 11:28-29)

*Life* is a test... How do you respond when the crunch of life comes?

# Did You Remember Jesus? (Part 1 of 3)

*"Anyone who listens to the word but does not do what it says is like someone who looks at his face in a mirror and, after looking at himself, goes away and immediately forgets what he looks like." (James 1: 23-24)*

There is no point in reading this book, the Bible, or any other book if you are not applying what you are learning. *"Reflect on what I am saying, for the Lord will give you insight into all this." (2 Tim. 2:7)*

We need to consider what Jesus said, so it is a good idea to pray for a few minutes before your daily Bible reading. Holy Spirit, who inspired the Bible, is in you, so ask Him to open your eyes to what God wants to reveal.

Verse 8 says from 2 Tim 2 says, *"Remember Jesus Christ, raised from the dead, descended from David."* It seems like an odd statement. Remember Jesus? How could we forget Him! But we do; We forget Jesus in the heat of the moment.

Distractions come with busy schedules, the guy who cuts you off in traffic, the poor service at a restaurant, the tax notice from the government, not getting the job or pay raise you wanted - the list goes on and on. We all have "the stuff of life," and it is a response to that "stuff" that is so crucial. Whichever answer we choose separates us from the world since we are to be in the world but not part of it.

*Life* is a test... How well do you remember Jesus when feeling your temper or emotions well up?

*Life is a test...*

# Did You Remember Jesus? (Part 2 of 3)

How often are we faced with a "stress moment" and respond with fear, panic, anger, blame etc.? Well, did you remember Jesus then? Did you stop and pray? Did you ask Jesus for some help? How about His wisdom? He does know how to handle it; after all, He is God...

The irony and tragedy of life is that we spend our time with God in our daily devotions, and then when the pressure points come and "it" *hits the fan, we have our "Jesus moment." Or do we? "A good man brings good things out of the good stored up in his heart, and an evil man brings evil things out of the evil stored up in his heart. For the mouth speaks what the heart is full of."* (Luke 6:45)

My point is, what is coming out of your mouth when the pressure moment happens? "Jesus, I need your help" or "@4#!9&$*!" and the negative emotions that rise with it?

In verse 8; (2 Tim. 2), Paul tells Timothy to *"remember Jesus Christ, raised from the dead...."* OK, let's do that:

**1.** Remember Jesus because the gospel is about Him.
**2.** Remember Jesus because He is the world's best role model.
**3.** Remember Jesus, who died for us on the cross but didn't stay there.
**4.** Remember Jesus because He came back, turned the Kingdom over to us, left, and sent Holy Spirit for you and me.
**5.** Remember Jesus, the Alpha and the Omega, the Lamb of God, the Bread of Life, Holy One, the Redeemer, King of Kings, Lord of Lords, Lion of Judah, Messiah, God with Us, Our Peace, Wonderful Counselor, Prince of Peace and many more…

Note: This is why I have a personal dislike for Roman Catholic crucifixes. I find them to be offensive. He was on the cross but isn't anymore. Further, I don't like using the cross symbol because it was such a horrific way of punishment and death. My choice is the Ichthys Fish symbol. More on that later.

## Did You Remember Jesus? (Part 3 of 3)

Remember Jesus at work, home, in relationships, at church - all of life. Remember Jesus as you labour for the gospel, battle temptation, and endure pain and persecution, remembering that it is but for a season (Heb. 11:25).

Jesus is our hope, the only hope. Build a habit through the constant connection of remembering Jesus every waking moment and pattering your life to be like Him. This is what Paul wrote about for 2/3 of the New Testament; this is the gospel, our gospel and our hope.

If we die to Jesus, which means dying to ourselves - to sin - then we live forever, now and later. It is estimated that over 200 people die every day as martyrs to Jesus and live forever with Jesus. If we stay here and endure suffering for the gospel, we too shall get our just reward and live forever with Him. If we reject the world and live a life for Him, standing through faith in His Word, then we will receive our just reward both now (*"in this time"* - Mark 10:30) and later. If we are faithful to Him, He is loyal to us. If we deny Him, He will deny us. So, choose. Remember, "Life is a Test." Will you make the right choice?

*"Whoever acknowledges me before others, I will also acknowledge before my Father in heaven."* (Matt 10:32)

Paul writes in Romans 6:6, *"We know that our old self was crucified with Him so that the body ruled by sin might be done away with, that we should no longer be slaves to sin."*

*Life* is a test... Are you remembering Jesus?

## What's the Delay?

You have prayed, fasted, cleaned up the sin, and nothing happens. Here are two possibilities for why your answers are delayed: God or satan.

Satan creates delays so that we will miss divine seasons of break-through, blessings of God's favour, and significant opportunities to advance the Kingdom of God. Don't forget, that satan is on your case 24 /7 every day. It's just a matter of how much he gets into your life which is up to you. In addition, he still has the authority to create strongholds through you falling for his temptations which then block the anointing of God, which are designed to lead us to walk in disobedience and go around in circles like a dog chasing its tail. They are intended to wear us down and make us believe that God's promises will never be obtained. We get stuck like a mouse in a cage running on one of those exercise wheels. We run like crazy, but we never get anywhere. Sound familiar?

Alternatively, there may be divine delays sent by God. He sends things to protect us, teach us, and make our point toward Him. Perhaps it might be a pause in time where He can fill us with wisdom etc. His goal is to teach us humility, obedience, prayer and perseverance. The key here is to know who the author of the delay is. If you cannot determine a divine delay from a demonic one, you'll fight against God's preventative and protective measures. Christians often have a "blame everything on the devil" attitude, and sometimes that is not the case.

Every decision we make should be backed by the Word of God under the direction of Holy Spirit. We need to see God at any cost; otherwise, we continue to run through a maze of confusion, frustration and disappointment. We must be obedient and trust that He will lead us to the correct path of blessing and prosperity.

*Life* is a test... Is your spiritual radar active and strong enough to differentiate between God and satan?

# Don't be a Drama Queen (or King).

When I was a little boy, my dad would tell me if I were upset about something, "there's nothing in life that a good night's sleep won't cure" (not exactly something a five-year-old wants to hear!) Life always looks better tomorrow. In other words, we must remember to hold our peace in that moment of stress. The worst thing we can do is start making decisions when we're under the gun. Chill, and pray about it. Tomorrow is another day, and your mind will be clearer.

When all hell is breaking loose against us, the enemy will back off quickly if we keep steady. He will often strike hard and then, like a coward, disappear before we get our armour and sword of the spirit ready to fight back. The key here is not to get sucked into the drama that he wants you to have and the drama that other people may be displaying. This is where the rubber hits the road, and we have to choose to believe wholeheartedly that God is a better option. The bottom line is that He cares for you, and all He wants is you - 24/7.

*"And we know that all things work together for good to those who love God, to those who are the called according to His purpose.* (Rom. 8:28)

I must admit that that is a hard scripture to remember in the heat of the moment. Here are two more like it:

*"So then, my beloved brethren, let every man be swift to hear, slow to speak, slow to wrath."* (James 1:19 NKJV)

*"...casting all your care upon Him, for He cares for you."* (1 Peter 5:7)

The last thing you need to hear is somebody preaching the scriptures to you when your blood pressure is going up. That is why we need to have them easily accessible in our hearts when we need them.

*Life* is a test... How are you handling the pressure points of life?

**www.newstartministries.ca**

# The Month of Tishri (Sept/Oct - Part 1 of 2)

**Appointed Times:** Feast of Trumpets, Atonement, and Tabernacles; it is the month of God's most important appointed times.

**Alphabet:** Letter is "LAMED" - signifies the aspiration to return to your absolute source.

**Tribe:** Ephraim - "be fruitful and multiply."

**Characteristics:** Starts the New Year; - Tishri is the month of the fall feasts, when we are to return to God and experience His glory. This is the 7th month, and all 7s are essential. It is a month of "completion and fullness."

- **Feast of trumpets:** this is a wake-up call!
- **Days of Awe:** for ten days after the first of Tishri - draw close to Him.
- **Atonement:** turn and return to God and put your sins under the blood.

**Constellation:** Libra (the scales) - where the deeds of man are weighed and judgment is released

**Colour/Stone:** Black Onyx or Agate

**Scripture:** Matt. 9

- Tishri is associated with the constellation Libra the scales, which pictures the deeds of a man weighed and judgement released. This is a month to concentrate more on the justice system.

- Starts with a blast of the Shofars, which is a wake-up call. We are to turn and return to God (see October 25-26 of Volume 1 of *"Life is a Test"* for a teaching about the Shofar).

- Day of atonement - for all of our sins; be restored. Fast and thank God, and this will restore our relationship with Him.

- Ephraim was the second son of Joseph, and he was blest by Jacob instead of Manasseh. He was given good land and became the dominant tribe of Israel. Joshua and Samuel were both descendants.

- When Judah split, they became the dominant tribe, but they messed up!

- Ephraim rebelled against David via Jeroboam and reintroduced the golden calf. They forgot God, and though some repented in 2 Chron. 30, it was only temporary, so the Assyrians destroyed them.

- In 2 Kings 22, Josiah turns Judah back to God via Josiah, and there is a revival that affects Ephraim in 2 Chronicles 34. The Assyrians had been a wake-up call to Ephraim, and they were restored.

## The Month of Tishri (Sept/Oct - Part 2 of 2)

God wants us to recognize His redemptive plan for each month. This is not fortune-telling. The heavens declare God's redemptive plan, and we must walk this plan out in the earthly realm. The Word of God is on a circuit and circles the earth. Ps. 19:6 talks about this. The heavens declare the glory of God, and the Word circles the earth (the sun makes a circuit) and we must begin to pull the Word down and see the manifestation in our midst.

The Tribe of Ephraim later became known as Samaritans. What Jesus said to the woman at the well (a Samaritan) was significant as she led others to the Lord and became an Evangelist.

As the seventh month, Tishri is the month of the Head of the Year, Rosh Hashanah. All 7s are dear to the Lord and are dedicated to the Lord, so this month is the most special. We have already come through two feast cycles and are ready to enter another when we get to this time of the year. God has declared a time for us to feast at The Head of the Year, which provides revelation for the year ahead. Divine providence creates a new beginning. God will release specific revelations that will start your new beginning in a new way.

Tishri is the month of reflected light, different from what we see in April when we have the sun's light. This is the moon's light, which changes our environment, how we process time, and the timing of crops and harvest.

The story of the tribe of Ephraim is the story of what the fall feasts are all about. They sinned, had a wake-up call, repented, and rejoiced.

Note: In the Roman calendar, the first month or Head of the Year is January. In God's calendar, the Head of the Year is Tishri's seventh month. I am writing more about Tabernacles on September 22.

*Life* is a test... Are you using this time to draw closer to God?

# Knowing the Heart of God

As I have been teaching in these two volumes, we must know the Word of God, His voice and His will. However, knowing His heart is just as important. Since we were created in His image, He has emotions, too. Where He differs though is that the access to His heartstrings is through communion with Holy Spirit and our worship. God wants to reveal His heart and Himself to us. He desires and wants intimacy with every one of His children (all 8 billion of us!)

The central part of our body is our heart. People think that that's a figurative expression because emotions are in the brain. Recent scientific and medical studies have led doctors to believe that the same type of emotional cells and nerve endings in the brain are also in the stomach and the heart. That explains why we feel butterflies in our stomach when we get nervous or stressed. Likewise, God's heart is the foundation of who He is, His thoughts, will and purposes.

*"Keep your heart with all diligence, For out of it spring the issues of life."* (Prov. 4:23 NKJV)

Getting to know the heart of God comes simply by studying His Word regularly (like daily!), hearing His voice and spending time in prayer and worship. Knowing what Jesus would do helps too! Christians like to wear these little bracelets around their wrist that spell the acronym "W.W.J.D?" - what would Jesus do? I have witnessed all too often the irony and tragedy of this. Some Christians fail to find out what Jesus did; if they do, they don't do it anyway. Therefore, what's the point of wearing the bracelet?

The more time we spend with God, the more we begin to think as He does, and the fundamental nature of His heart is revealed to us.

*Life* is a test... Do you know His heart?

## The Fish.

The Christian fish symbol, called the Ichthys or Ichthus, has two parts: the double line, which forms a fish symbol and an acronym of the first letters of five Greek words. These first five letters are: Iesous, Greek for "Jesus"; Christos, Greek for "anointed"; Theou, Greek for "God's"; uios, Greek for "Son"; and soter, Greek for "Savior." Together, this spells ICTHUS, which as an acrostic means "Jesus Christ, God's Son, the Savior."

Several of Jesus' disciples were fishermen to whom Jesus said, *"Follow me, and I will make you fishers of men."* (Matt. 4:19; Mark 1:17) Jesus also fed five thousand people with five small loaves and two fish (Matt. 14:17). He compared the Kingdom of Heaven to a net thrown into the sea and gathering fish of many kinds (Matt. 13:47). After His resurrection, Jesus appeared to His disciples in bodily form and made them breakfast; bread and fish (John 21:9–14).

The early church was hotly persecuted, so Jesus' followers communicated via this fish symbol. For example, if a house was friendly to Christians, it might have a fish on the doorframe. Or, when meeting someone on the street or at the beach, they would draw a half-circle or arc in the dirt or sand. If the other person was not a believer, the person was observed drawing in the dirt. If the other person was a believer, they would complete the fish symbol on the ground. With a stick, one person draws the arc, then the other person uses the same starting point, but draws an upside-down arc, thus making a complete IXTHUS symbol. Therefore, two believers would then have the fellowship of knowing each believed in IXTHUS.

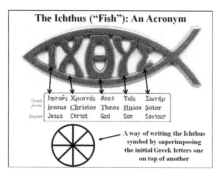

# The Cross.

The "Christian" use of the cross did not begin until the time of Constantine, three centuries after Jesus was born. Archaeologists have not found any Christian use of the symbol before that time. The cross was a torture tool used by the Romans and was a well-known symbol used to describe the power of Rome and what would happen to those who became an enemy of Rome. The cross as a "Christian" symbol was most likely adopted somewhere in the 3rd century.

While the New Testament does make clear mention that Jesus was crucified, there are only a few specific mentions that it was on a cross (John 19:25, Mark 15:30). Other times in the New Testament, such as Acts 5:30, 10:39, and 13:28-29 refer to it as a "tree." The Greek word xulon, translated as "tree," can mean various things like a stick, club, tree or stake in these verses.

There is no evidence that God's original early church used the cross symbol. Nowhere does the Bible explicitly command its use. We see analogies such as picking up our crosses and following Him (Luke 9:23), but it's never said we are to use the cross symbol. It surely would if God expected this of Christians.

I choose not to use a cross as a personal symbol for myself. Why? Because it is a symbol of a prolonged and painful death. Further, I feel somewhat offended by crucifixes that still have Christ on the cross. He's not there anymore! I prefer and use the fish symbol.

*Life* is a test... How do you see the cross as a Christian symbol?

## The Ninth Fruit of the Spirit - Self-control - (Part 1 of 2)

Self-control is the last of the Fruits of the Spirit, but certainly not least in importance. It is essential when it comes to living a Godly and disciplined life. We need to be an excellent example of Christ living in us. Let your light shine! Self-control also qualifies us whether we can be in any supervisory position in the church and be an example to others. It is also one of the qualifications listed for elders in the local church. *"An elder must be blameless, faithful to his wife, a man whose children believe and are not open to the charge of being wild and disobedient. Since an overseer manages God's household, he must be blameless - not overbearing, not quick-tempered, not given to drunkenness, not violent, not pursuing dishonest gain. Rather, he must be hospitable, one who loves what is good, who is self-controlled, up-right, holy and disciplined. He must hold firmly to the trustworthy message as it has been taught so that he can encourage others by sound doctrine and refute those who oppose it."* (Titus 1:6-9).

There are several Biblical applications to self-control. Remember that in Christ, our bodies are temples of the Holy Spirit. He lives inside of you, so why would you pollute your temple with a poor diet, obesity, addictions etc.? *"Do you not know that your bodies are temples of the Holy Spirit, who is in you, whom you have received from God? You are not your own;"* (1 Cor. 6:19) It takes much self-control, especially in our modern first world society to look after our temple and not succumb to the peer pressure of this gluttonous narcissistic society. We must be masters over our bodies.

This includes marriage too. Our society expects that premarital sex is the accepted norm, but that's not what the Bible says. Hebrews 13:4 says, *"Marriage should be honoured by all, and the marriage bed kept pure, for God will judge the adulterer and all the sexually immoral."* Sex before marriage is called fornication, and sex after marriage with a different person is called adultery. There's nothing more to say about it than that! Self-control must be practiced with people both inside and outside of marriage.

## The Ninth Fruit of the Spirit -
## Self-control - (Part 2 of 2)

The tongue is next. James 3:2-10 summarizes this the best: *"When we put bits into the mouths of horses to make them obey us, we can turn the whole animal. Or take ships as an example. Although they are so large and are driven by strong winds, they are steered by a very small rudder wherever the pilot wants to go. Likewise, the tongue is a small part of the body, but it makes great boasts. Consider what a great forest is set on fire by a small spark. The tongue also is a fire, a world of evil among the parts of the body. It corrupts the whole body, sets the whole course of one's life on fire, and is itself set on fire by hell. All kinds of animals, birds, reptiles and sea creatures are being tamed and have been tamed by mankind, but no human being can tame the tongue. It is a restless evil, full of deadly poison. With the tongue, we praise our Lord and Father, and with it, we curse human beings who have been made in God's likeness. Out of the same mouth come praise and cursing. My brothers and sisters, this should not be. Can both fresh water and saltwater flow from the same spring? My brothers and sisters, can a fig tree bear olives or a grapevine bear figs? Neither can a salt spring produce fresh water."*

Another issue is our emotions. Proverbs 16:32 says, *"Better a patient person than a warrior, one with self-control than one who takes a city."* As you can see, self-control responds to people or circumstances in a controlled fashion versus reacting in anger. How? (see July 19 of Volume 1 of *"Life is a Test"*)

**1.** Raising your voice never works. Give it up for lent!
**2.** See it coming. We all have "buttons" - have a strategy ready.
**3.** Make positive plans about how you will react and speak about a situation before it happens.
**4.** It is crucial that you vent your anger correctly. *"In your anger do not sin. Do not let the sun go down while you are still angry."* (Eph. 4:26)

*Life* is a test... Self - control is life's greatest challenge. How's it going for you? Ask God for help.

This is the last of the nine fruits. Remember this, the Fruits of the Spirit are more dangerous to the devil than the Gifts of the Spirit.

# The Restoration of the Church. (Part 1 of 3)

One of the most exciting things that God is doing in His church today is the restoration of the Biblical Feasts.

**1.** Passover is usually held in April in our Roman calendar; it is about redemption and cleansing.

**2.** Pentecost, a few weeks later, is about God's provision.

**3.** Tabernacle's is held in September. It is to do with God's glory.

There is a parallel with the Tabernacle of Moses, which had the outer court (redemption and cleansing), The Holy (provision) and The Holy of Holies – a place where only the priests were allowed and where there was the presence of God's glory. God's yearly cycle is a journey into the presence of experiencing Him. It was like walking into Moses' Tabernacle; the outer court, the inner court and then the Holy of Holies.

The High Point of the year in Biblical terms is Tabernacles which starts with the "Fall Feasts," of which there are three. There is a 21-day countdown designed to bring you into an experience of His presence. By following this countdown, you have a taste of revival every year!

The starting point is the "Feast of Trumpets" and it is the first day of the seventh month of God's calendar. It starts with the blast of the Shofar (trumpet), which is a call to "awaken." It literally is a wake-up call - the first step to revival! An example of that was when Argentina lost the Falklands war, and their economy collapsed (a wake-up call), which led to an amazing spiritual revival. However, God designed a less painful way to get our attention; the sound of the shofar is intended to pierce our soul and get our attention.

# The Restoration of the Church. (Part 2 of 3)

Ten days after the Feast of Trumpets is "The Days of Awe." The message here from God is "turn and return to Me." It is a time to turn from anything that hinders your relationship with God (i.e., sin). Draw close to God and ask Him how you need to get closer to Him. Then you are ready for "The Day of Atonement" – a day to be restored. This is the day to put all your sins under the blood of the Passover Lamb (Jesus) and be entirely stored to God and His purposes. Fast, seek God, and confess all your sins (Is. 44:32).

Finally, after these "countdown feasts," there is the big one; "The Feast of Tabernacles" - a whole week of joyful celebration! It is the time of God dwelling amid His people to celebrate our return to Him, and we celebrate being in His presence! It's party (revival) time!

**Summary:**
**1.** Wake up - the sound of the shofar.
**2.** Turn and return - draw near to God.
**3.** Be restored to Him.
**4.** Rejoice and party!

### How do we experience Tabernacles?
Seek His face and call Him for a fresh outpouring of His glory and Holy Spirit in our lives as we start a New Year. He promises a special blessing if we do this. Follows these practical steps:

**1.** Set aside time to meet with Him.
**2.** Spend relaxing, reading and studying His Word.
**3.** Get together with family and friends.
**4.** Share testimonies of His goodness!
**5.** Eat your favourite food and party! Praise Him and thank Him for His blessings.

## The Restoration of the Church. (Part 3 of 3)

Now people would say, "isn't all this just Jewish stuff?" People fail to understand that we are adopted into the family of Abraham according to the Book of Hebrews, which makes us Jewish. The irony and tragedy here is that we do not celebrate the Biblical feasts in the Bible. Instead, we celebrate secular holidays like Christmas and Easter, the celebration of which is not in the Bible.

Zec. 14:16-19 says, *"the time will come when people from among the Gentiles will worship the King, the Lord Almighty and celebrate the feast of Tabernacle's."* That time is now, which is why God is restoring this to the Christian church. So if you were a gentile (a non-Jewish person) who worships the God of Israel, this feast is for you!

### Celebrating Tabernacles:

- Remember God Tabernacles with His people.
- Enjoy the fun of celebrating with God.
- Anticipate God in His glory to come and tabernacle with us again and again.
- God wants to draw you into His presence so you can experience His glory.

### Doc's Book Club: Read *"The Apostolic Church Arising"*
by Dr. Chuck Pierce and Dr. Robert Heidler and *"The Messianic Church Arising!"* by Dr. Robert Heidler.

*Life* is a test... Connect with Glory of Zion and you will learn all about the Apostolic Church. www.gloryofzion.org

## Two Masters.

*"No one can serve two masters. Either you will hate the one and love the other, or you will be devoted to the one and despise the other."* (Matt. 6:24)

Just as Deut. 30:19 says, you must choose; an intelligent person would choose God because truly He is our master. If pleasing people is your goal in life, you will become a slave to that. People can be a more challenging task masker than God because they manipulate and control you with their power, otherwise known as witchcraft.

Since God is our master, He is also our first love in life because that is what we are to Him. Our love is grounded in His immense unconditional love for us. The more we humble ourselves to Him, the more He will uplift us to a closer personal and intimate relationship with Him. The joy of living in His presence outshines any other pleasures of life.

So today is the day, like every single day. You have a decision to make. Who will be in the driver's seat of your life for the next 24 hours? God or you? God rejoices in our victories, successes, and accomplishments and is there to hold us and weep with us as we go through the struggles of life.

*"Come near to God and He will come near to you."* James 4:8

*"I pray that out of His glorious riches He may strengthen you with power through His Spirit in your inner being, so that Christ may dwell in your hearts through faith. And I pray that you, being rooted and established in love. may have power, together with all the Lord's holy people."* (Eph. 3: 16-17)

*Life* is a test... What choice will you make today??

# Get Wisdom and get Understanding.
## (Part 1 of 5)

The biggest thing that has amazed me in writing the first and second volumes of *"Life is a Test"* is how God has directed me to write something and how much I have learned from what He has said to me. Yes, I understand this book is for you to read, but since I was the first student of these books, I can assure you I have learned a great deal. Now that the first volume is published, yours truly reads it daily! (and I will be reading this one daily, as well)!

This is how God has directed me to write the next five days: a scripture about wisdom and some commentary pouring out of my spirit through the Gift of Wisdom. I am unsure where He is going with this, but we will find out. Enjoy the ride; here it goes…

**1.** *"If any of you lacks wisdom, you should ask God, who gives generously to all without finding fault, and it will be given to you."* (James 1:5)

Well, if you don't know something, ask. It seems pretty straightforward. "but I don't hear from God," you say. Well, get into a position to hear. We have been on this journey before:
 - quiet your thoughts and emotions, cast down the junk spinning in your head (2 Cor. 10:5)
 - start thanking, praising, and worshiping
 - read scripture out loud
 - present your issues
 - then, focus on Him, visualize Jesus sitting next to you because He is, and then listen

**2.** *"But the wisdom that comes from heaven is first of all pure; then peace-loving, considerate, submissive, full of mercy and good fruit, impartial and sincere."* (James 3:17)

Where are you getting your wisdom from? The world? "Give it up for lent!" Read the Word and forget the dumb self-help books and save your money. (Aren't you glad God is more patient with you than I am?)

## Get Wisdom and get Understanding.
### (Part 2 of 5)

**3.** *"Blessed are those who find wisdom, those who gain understanding, for she is more profitable than silver and yields better returns than gold. She is more precious than rubies; nothing you desire can compare with her. Long life is in her right hand; in her left hand are riches and honour. Her ways are pleasant ways, and all her paths are peace. She is a tree of life to those who take hold of her; those who hold her fast will be blest."* (Prov. 3:13-18)

Do you remember when God asked Solomon a question? *"That night, God appeared to Solomon and said, "Ask for whatever you want me to give you."* ( 2 Chron. 1:7) I suppose many of us would've asked for money, better relationships, and better health; the list is endless. But no, Solomon's very wise response was, *"Give me wisdom and know-ledge, that I may lead this people, for who is able to govern this great people of yours?"* He didn't want the wisdom and knowledge for himself. He wanted it for his people. God's reply to this was, *"God said to Solomon, "Since this is your heart's desire and you have not asked for wealth, possessions or honour, nor for the death of your enemies, and since you have not asked for a long life but for wisdom and knowledge to govern my people over whom I have made you king, therefore wisdom and knowledge will be given you. And I will also give you wealth, possessions and honour, such as no king who was before you ever had and none after you will have."* (verses 11-12) Talk about having your cake and eating it too! Talk about being supernaturally blest because you were wise enough to give the correct answer. The greatest thing you can have in your life is wisdom, and according to James 1:5, all you have to do is ask for it.

**4.** *"The fear of the Lord is the beginning of knowledge, but fools despise wisdom and instruction."* (Prov. 1:7) "Fear" is not to be "fearful" of God, but rather fear of being in sin (Prov. 8:13). A fool doesn't want to learn anything and many people in this world are like that.

# Get Wisdom and get Understanding.
## (Part 3 of 5)

**5.** *"Be very careful, then, how you live - not as unwise but as wise, making the most of every opportunity, because the days are evil. Therefore do not be foolish, but understand what the Lord's will is."* Eph. 5:15-17) The world has no answers, and everything they try to do has failed. Why? Because the root and foundation of man is sin. We are all born into this world in sin (John 9:34). Yes, that cute little child or grandchild that was just born into your family is filled with sin (they're not called the terrible twos for nothing!) Unless man redeems himself by repenting of his sins and confessing Jesus as Lord, this cute baby will be a sinner for the rest of his life and contribute to the world's destruction. The only answer is salvation and the wisdom that comes from Jesus.

**6.** *"Let the message of Christ dwell among you richly as you teach and admonish one another with all wisdom through psalms, hymns, and songs from the Spirit, singing to God with gratitude in your hearts."* (Col. 3:16) Want some wisdom? Got a problem you need solved? Then start singing songs and hymns and worship God out of your spirit, and He'll speak to you. Simple stuff...

**7.** *"Do not be wise in your own eyes; fear the Lord and shun evil."* (Prov. 3:7) Ah, this one hurts; it is about pride. We get so smug sometimes because we think we're so intelligent. Ha! Here we are as little mortal humans using less than 13% of our brain, and we believe we are smart. We have all the answers; we "have it together!" Right...The biggest thing I've learned in life is that the more I study the Word, the more I realize I don't know anything. All this education and all these books I've written have done nothing but make me hungrier for the Word. Pride is listed first on the seven things that God hates (Prov. 6:16-19). Why? Because pride is about arrogance and control, and control is the one thing that God wants you to give to Him. He'll let you be the co-pilot of your life, but He is the navigator and the pilot. Listen...

# Get Wisdom and get Understanding.
## (Part 4 of 5)

**8.** *"Then you will know the truth, and the truth will set you free."* (John 8:32) Jesus said that He was the truth, the light and the way and that no one comes to the Father except through Him. (John 14:6) Mohammed didn't say that, and neither did Buddha, the 10,000 Hindu gods, the New Age gods or any other demonic thing. Why? Because they can't. Both Mohammed and Buddha were men, not deities and not God. The 10,000 Hindu gods don't even exist other than being demons, and the same goes for the New Age gods or whatever they are. My point is that wisdom comes from truth and the only truth is Jesus.

**9.** *"By wisdom a house is built, and through understanding it is established; through knowledge its rooms are filled with rare and beautiful treasures. The wise prevail through great power, and those who have knowledge muster their strength. Surely you need guidance to wage war, and victory is won through many advisers. Wisdom is too high for fools; in the assembly, at the gate, they must not open their mouths."* (Prov. 24:3-7)

Don't build your house, business, or anything else in life without getting the wisdom you need to do that from God. Get this power and strength from God so that you will have the knowledge that you need. When you're loaded with this Godly wisdom, you will defeat your enemies and accomplish your goals and God's purpose for your life. And if you don't do any of this, well, you're just plain dumb...

*"Words from the mouth of the wise are gracious, but fools are consumed by their own lips."* (Ecc.10:12)

You can usually tell when a man is speaking wisdom because the Words of the Lord coming through him are sweet and divine, and at the same time, you can usually hear the foolishness of an unwise person. If you are unsure, ask Holy Spirit to guide you and direct you to what is being said.

# Get Wisdom and get Understanding.
## (Part 5 of 5)

**10.** *"All Scripture is God-breathed and is useful for teaching, rebuking, correcting and training in righteousness, so that the servant of God may be thoroughly equipped for every good work."* (2 Tim. 3:16-17)

Being rebuked and corrected by the Word of God will provide you with wisdom, having your mind entrenched in the Word will provide you with wisdom, and getting all of this will make you equipped to do what God has told you to do. If you don't know what to do, ask Him.

**11.** *"This is what the Lord says: Let not the wise boast of their wisdom or the strong boast of their strength or the rich boast of their riches."* (Jer. 9:23)

Ah, yes, we are back to that pride thing again. The root of boasting is insecurity, and insecurity is fear. The Bible says over 400 times to fear not. "Fear" is the number one thing that defeats all of us. They say that the most common fear of man is the fear of public speaking! If you want to boast, you can; boast about what the Lord has done for you and that the "secret to your success" is Jesus.

*Life* is a test...

You have just gone four days without having to do a test! I must be slacking off! Now I'm going to lower the boom on you and give you some homework. Buy yourself a concordance if you don't already have one, or you can use one online as I do. I like www.biblegateway.com. Search the word "wisdom," find every scripture on this subject and record it in your journal. There is nothing I can think of that is more critical in life than the wisdom of God.

$\mathcal{L}ife$ _is a test..._

# Halloween; why would anyone do this?

(Note: This message was moved from October 31 to today, so you can read about it in advance and prepare. I don't know of a month that needs more intercessory prayer than October! Get busy...)

Halloween is a demonic festival. I wrote about this on October 6 in Volume 1 of *"Life is a Test,"* so I won't repeat myself, but suffice to say that Halloween is the most demonic anti-Christian event today. Activities like torturing black cats, child kidnappings and child sacrifices still occur in our modern world. Why then, would anyone want to glorify and celebrate this day?

The greatest tragedy of human existence is to not know what you don't know. In other words, to be so blinded that you don't know that you are blinded. Think about it; if you knew that you were deceived, you wouldn't be deceived anymore, would you? So how do you know that you're not??? This is how cults operate.

Our society is laced with deceptions. People are controlled by evil spirits, media, and governments (think Germany 1935); they are brainwashed by curses, behaviours, social media, and sins and don't know they are. Every October 31st, people go overboard to "celebrate" a demonic Festival. Seriously???

The bottom line: NEVER celebrate, glorify, or enjoy ANYTHING that does not exalt God. Halloween is not "harmless fun." If you think that, then you are horribly deceived.

**Doc's Book Club:** Read *"Exposing the Enemy: Simple Keys to Defeating the Strategies of Satan"* by John Ramirez and *"Halloween - Trick or Treat with The Festival of Death"* by Col. Tom McKenny (available from www.jubileeresources.org)

$\mathcal{L}ife$ is a test... Go back and read April 17th.

# My Church Pet Peeves. (Part 1 of 8)

I have decided to spend the next few days talking about a few of my personal pet peeves with the church. I'm open to feedback on these. You can reach me on my website if you want further discussions! I am not sure where this will go, but we'll all find out!

**1. There is no such thing as a "Christian."**

Back in the days of the Bible, there were not a lot of people on the planet that worshiped God. There were a few, and one of them was a man by the name of Abram, whom God recognized as being faithful to Him, so He changed his name to Abraham and started a new generation of people called Hebrews or Israelites. They worshiped God, and one day a few generations later, child was born among them who was the Messiah. Therefore, Jesus was Hebrew or what we today call Jewish. In other words, He was not a "Christian." As Jesus taught the Jews, some became followers of Him and were known in the Book of Acts as *"followers of the way."* Later they became known as "Little Christs," which evolved into the word "Christian." There were now three groups on the earth: the Jews, the followers of Jesus, and everybody else. It was Constantine in 300 AD that cemented the use of the term "Christian," and we've been called that ever since. So, what/who truly are we? According to Gal. 3 6-7, *"we are adopted into the family of Abraham,"* which makes us *"adopted Jews."* Abraham put his trust in God, which made him right with God. Remember that all men who trust God are "the sons of Abraham." Ninety-nine verses in the Bible talk about how we are adopted into the family of God, and Abraham started the family under God's direction.

The problem is that the word "Christian" can mean so many different things in our pluralized society. On top of that, people use the term "born-again Christian," an oxymoron. I just like to say I am a follower of Jesus and leave it at that.

*Life* is a test... Who are you?

**www.newstartministries.ca**

*Life* is a test...

# My Church Pet Peeves. (Part 2 of 8)

**2. Why do Christians celebrate Easter, Halloween and Christmas but not the festivals in God's Word?**

Easter is a festival never mentioned in the Word and does not come from a Christian foundation. No one in the Bible ever celebrated Easter. Constantine outlawed Passover and ordered Christians to celebrate Christ's resurrection during the spring fertility festival to appease the pagans and keep everyone under his control. In other words, Christ's resurrection was taken from its Biblical context and celebrated in the context of a pagan feast. Pagans held a feast in spring to honour the goddess of fertility, whose symbol was an egg. Here is how the word "Easter" developed: Canaanites: ASHERAH; Persians: ASTARTE; Babylonians: ISHTAR; Britons: EASTRE

By the end of the fourth century, Pagan sacrifices were outlawed, and pagan shrines were changed into Christian churches. Some pagan priests even became Christian priests. Pagans were told they lived in a Christian empire and that it was their responsibility to live as Christians. The trouble is, they didn't know Jesus; they were still pagans. Their beliefs had not changed!

- By the year 600, paganism had inundated the church.
- Most early Middle Ages (500-800 AD) church leaders were unbelievers.
- Those resisting were persecuted as enemies of the empire.
- By the Middle Ages, the common people and many kings and priests were illiterate. Even those who could read were often denied access to the Bible. Bibles were written in Latin - a language people couldn't understand, and the Bibles were chained to the pulpit where they couldn't be read except for those in priestly and above roles.
- Superstition and idolatry were rampant.
- Salvation was by good works, pilgrimages, and financial contributions.
- The Church became a powerful and wealthy political organization.
- When Rome crumbled, the Church stepped in to fill the vacuum, becoming a great military power but losing the supernatural power of God it had once known.

Thank goodness for Martin Luther's reformation on October 31, 1517!

*Life* is a test...  Do you celebrate God's festivals?

# My Church Pet Peeves. (Part 3 of 8)

Christmas was never celebrated until the 17th century, and its roots aren't originally Christian either. What do presents, lights, Santa Claus, decorated trees, or glutinous turkey dinners have to do with the birth of Christ, who was not born in December? Jesus never celebrated His birthday, and neither did anybody else. Before Constantine, the holidays of the Ekklesia (what we call "church" * today) were the Biblical Feasts. The Ekklesia never celebrated the birth of Jesus - it wasn't important. The Romans celebrated December 25th as the birthday of Mithras, the founder of a Roman demonic cult. Constantine took many of the ideas of this cult and used them as a foundation for his new "church of Rome." Some of this demonic symbolism is still in that church today. The unconverted pagans rushed into the "new church" but didn't want to give up their holiday, so they declared December 25th to be the birthday of Christ and gave the church a new holiday called "Christmas."

Jesus told us to do what He did and that we would do more than He did. So, what did He do? He celebrated Passover, and so should we. He observed Tabernacles, and so should we. Jesus also celebrated the Feast of Dedication (Hanukkah), so perhaps we should do that too! Jesus did not celebrate Easter, Christmas or Halloween. Jesus told us to follow Him and His example, so why does the church look so different from God's clear commands? Look at the following:

| The Bible & Ekklesia | The Church |
|---|---|
| • Passover | • Easter |
| • Unleavened Bread | • Palm Sunday |
| • First Fruits | • Good Friday |
| • Pentecost | • Advent |
| • Trumpets | • Halloween |
| • Atonement | • Lent |
| • Tabernacles | • Christmas |

**Our Churches are teaching us the wrong stuff!**

* "Church" is a pagan word meaning a place where pagans gathered in a circle to worship their god.

**Doc's Book Club:** Read **"Romes Anathemas: Insights into the Papal Pantheon"** by Dr. Selwyn Stevens.

www.newstartministries.ca

# My Church Pet Peeves. (Part 4 of 8)

### 3. We are using the wrong calendar.

I realize that we all live in this world, and if we're going to catch our airplane on time, then we had better use the Roman calendar. I get that, but at the same time, the Bible and Hebrew Calendar is the one God originally had His people use. What to do? Use both. Download God's calendar to your computer calendar here: www.heb.cal.com (and it is free!) Use the Roman calendar to get you to the correct gate at the right time to catch a plane, make meetings on time, and get to work on time. Then use God's calendar and celebrate His festivals and months so that you align with Him and receive all His Words, wisdom, and blessings. Now you know why I have written about each month of God's calendar on the 15th of every month.

### 4. "Five-fold ministry."

These words are used in the Bible, but it has been misinterpreted to mean that there are only five Gifts of the Spirit: Apostle, Prophet, Evangelist, Teacher, and Pastor. Many people conclude that the pastor is the "minister" and the others are the "laymen." Nothing could be further from the truth! Peter Wagner, whom I have mentioned many times and regarded as the father of Spiritual Gifts since he was the first one to write about them, didn't like the five-fold ministry term because people thought there were only five Gifts and ignored the rest of the Gifts. Secondly, if someone in the church does not have one of the five, they tend to think that they are not Gifted, or worse yet, they feel like a second-class Christian because they're not anointed. That is why Peter does not use that term and I don't, either. I struggled with this for years, and then I received a "download" about it one day. I checked with the Dean of my Theology school and Peter, and they acknowledged my theory. The Gifts can be classified as follows:

*Life* is a test...

# My Church Pet Peeves. (Part 5 of 8)

Each of the 30 recognized Spiritual Gifts can be categorized under the main "five-fold" gifts, which are: Apostle, Prophet, Evangelist, Teacher and Pastor.

| Apostle | Prophet | Evangelist | Teacher | Pastor |
|---------|---------|------------|---------|--------|
| Apostle | Prophet | Evangelist | Teacher | Pastor |
| Leadership | Discernment | Faith | Wisdom | Administration |
| Giving | Exhortation | Miracles | Knowledge | Hospitality |
| Celibacy | Intercessor | Healing | Mercy | Service |
| | Tongues & | Missionary | Preaching | Help |
| | Interpretations | Deliverance | | Worship Leader |
| | Musician | | | Voluntary Poverty |
| | | | | Craftsman |

To *"equip the saints"* (Eph. 4:12), we must know what we will equip them with. Or, more accurately, we must discover what Gifts each saint has. We can learn what Gifts Holy Spirit has assigned each person through Spiritual Gift surveys, strength finder tests, and other personality tests. On average, 37% of a church's congregation has the Gift of Pastor, and the remaining four categories are divided amongst the rest of the congregation. The job of the lead person in the church (who should be an Apostle and not a Pastor) is to then "raise up" (i.e., teach, train, impart etc.) each of his parishioners. A church will not grow with a Pastor in charge, as church growth is not his gifting. A Pastor needs to be "tending to his sheep" - doing his job (and he is not interested in growing the church as that gives him more work to do). The position of "growing" is for the Apostles, who, with the support of the Prophet and Evangelist lead the church to grow, mature and finally fulfill the great commission. Administrators (who are under the Pastor classification) work alongside the Apostle to carry out his orders. In short, the Prophet hears from God, the Apostle works with him, and they create the vision between them, and the Administrators get the work done with Service and the Helps people.

*Life* is a test... Do you know your Spiritual Gifts? If you don't, what do you think you may have from the list above? Take a Gifts survey!

# My Church Pet Peeves. (Part 6 of 8)

## Goals of the Five-fold Categories

**Apostle:** - a burning desire to see people work together in unity
- always sees the bigger picture but doesn't usually know
- makes declarations about people and is very visionary
- how to get there; that's what Prophets and Administrators do

**Prophet:** - their sole purpose in life is to ask, "how can I hear God
- clearly"
- subscribes to dreams and visions
- wants to know his or her heart and purpose
- wants to draw his or herself and others into intimacy with God

**Evangelist:** - burning passion for those who do not know Jesus
- always looking for an opportunity to witness
- shares easily with others; is a salesman
- bored easily in church unless there is a message about salvation

**Teacher:** - loves the truth in the Word
- never compromises as they're full of integrity
- has a hunger for education and teaching others

**Pastor:** - has genuine concern for others; empathy and compassion
- really wants to know how others are doing and wants to help them

Every Gift under these categories will have many of the same characteristics. Here is the plan for church growth:
- the Apostles/Prophets establish the church.
- they locate (after testing etc.) the Pastors and commission them.
- they locate the other pastoral gifts (Admin., Helps, Hospitality, etc.) and commission them.
- they locate the Teachers to start educating the body of Christ and commission them.
- they locate the Evangelists and commission them and send them out.
- they continue the cycle by identifying and "raising up" new leaders.

*Life* is a test... Where do you see yourself in the Ekklesia?

**_ife is a test..._**

# My Church Pet Peeves. (Part 7 of 8)

The Ekklesia should be emerging, changing, reconfiguring ahead of the world, and relevant as they do their work. Since we (not the world) have anointed Prophets, we know what's going on before it happens (2 Chron. 20:20b). The Ekklesia should never be an old wineskin.

Too many Christians believe the church is a building; a place for them to go on Sunday and receive, whether it be a good message or for fellowship and socializing with others. They do not understand or appreciate that the day they entered the Kingdom of Heaven (became born again, assuming that they are), they entered boot camp, and their role was to be trained as a warrior. In the meantime, many churches don't teach this, and too many preachers preach apostasy. Consequently, today's church has as many problems and sad statistics as the rest of the world (divorce, financial issues, ill health etc.) We are the ones that have the answers and are to live in health, happiness, purpose, joy, fulfilment, success etc. Sadly, much of the Christian church does not (see Deut. 28:13).

As an example: I attended one of the local churches in my community last year, and this is what I experienced:
- next to no signage and no greeting by anyone
- there was no "worship," just a few unsmiling faces singing some songs
- 10 minutes of music, 10 minutes of church announcements, 10 more minutes of music and then a weak unfilling message with the pastor acknowledging that the weather was so lovely and that he would not talk too long so that everyone could be home on time for lunch (true story).
- no vision about the Church, its local, national and international ministry
- no one acknowledged my presence as a guest before or after the service
- no altar calls, no healings, no prophetic Words

In short, it was dull. I should have stayed home and watched the paint dry. That would've been more exciting.

The solution? Develop apostolic Ekklesias that follow the Book of Acts.

**_ife_** is a test... Does this example sound like your church?

*Life* is a test...

## My Church Pet Peeves. (Part 8 of 8)

Jesus never prayed for the sick. He prayed to His Father, stopped praying, and simply ministered to the sick person. He never asked God to heal the sick but proclaimed to them that they were healed (in some cases He also said that "their faith" made them whole).

That being the case, why does the church pray for the sick? Jesus never did, and we are supposed to do what He did! He prayed, and then He ministered. Instead, we have groups that go to the hospital to "pray for the sick." Why? How about going to the hospital and casting out a few demons, if need be, and then just do what Jesus did? Minister to the sick, lay hands on them and declare them healed.

There is one place in the Bible that speaks of using oil when ministering healing:

*"Is any sick among you? Let him call for the elders of the church; and let them pray over him, anointing him with oil in the name of the Lord: And the prayer of faith shall save the sick, and the Lord shall raise him up; and if he has committed sins, they shall be forgiven him. Confess your faults one to another, and pray one for another, that ye may be healed. The effectual fervent prayer of a righteous man availeth much."* (James 5: 13-16 KJV)

Years ago, I heard a testimony about a Christian orderly working in a mental institution. Each day when he visited the patients, he would quietly sing to them the words "Jesus loves me, this I know." He kept doing it constantly, daily, and after a couple of weeks, the patients began to smile. Eventually, they started to sing with him, and in six months, 80% of the patients were discharged. My point? Constant contact with Jesus keeps demons away.

*Life* is a test... Ok, enough about me; what are your pet peeves with the church today, if you have any? How can you be a part of the solution?

*ife* **is a test...**

# How to Receive a Breakthrough?
## (Part 1 of 2)

*"So he said to me, "This is the word of the Lord to Zerubbabel: 'Not by might nor by power, but by my Spirit,' says the Lord Almighty."* (Zec. 4:6)

We attempt to make changes/improvements, solve problems, be "successful," etc. However, if we're looking for a real breakthrough in our lives, remember that it is by God's Spirit and not by our human endeavours that we will accomplish what we are looking for.

The first mistake we make is surrendering our peace to the enemy. We have a goal that's causing us stress, a problem we wish to resolve, etc. Our human nature is to take it upon ourselves to use our analytical thinking and come up with all these solutions and ideas. Now we have added more stress to stress! However, here in Zechariah, God says to His prophet not to use his might but rather the might and power of God. He has put His Name above all others. *"Therefore God also has highly exalted Him and given Him the name which is above every name."* (Phil. 2:9)

This power from God cannot be earned as it is a gift to those whose hearts turn towards God. Faith in His Word, His love, His truth and His power is all we need. Like a mouse running on one of those exercise wheels in a cage, we run like crazy, but we don't get anywhere with our plans, schemes and solutions, and then cry out to God when things don't work out.

God's power for us is free once we surrender to Him and live our lives for Him. Simple stuff...

*ife* is a test... Whose power are you using; yours or His?

*Life is a test...*

# How to Receive a Breakthrough?
## (Part 1 of 2)

Are you waiting for God to move in your life? Need a miracle? Breakthrough is a process, and here are the steps:

**1.** Make your claims to Him backing them with scripture. Don't whine!

**2.** Spend time with Him and allow Him to convict you of any sin, then repent, forgive others and forgive yourself.

**3.** Allow your mind to be transformed and renewed on the things of God.

**4.** Spend time in the Word, pursue the things of God and don't quit!

**5.** Worship, worship, and worship some more and then praise and thank Him for what He is about to do. (and then do some more worship!)

Breakthroughs happen when we least suspect it. They happen when you are doing something God told you to do (i.e., being obedient) that probably has nothing to do with your breakthrough. Examples:

- you bless someone, either spontaneously or when He tells you to
- you forgive
- you choose to love others when they hurt you
- you pray for people that you don't even know
- you return your tithe to God (it is worship)
- you give an offering when you had other plans for that money
- you respond in peace when your spouse is hurtful
- you pray for the person that cut you off in traffic
- when you love others enough to cover their sins
- you are home in your prayer closet and open a spiritual portal through praise and worship
- you are reading your Bible, and then suddenly...

*Life* is a test... Do you need a breakthrough? Just do these steps.

# Who is in Control?

*"For with God, nothing will be impossible."* (Luke 1:37)

*"Now to Him who is able to do exceedingly abundantly above all that we ask or think, according to the power that works in us."* (Eph. 3:20)

*"The Lord is my shepherd; I shall not want."* (Ps. 23:1)

The most significant factor in our lives is learning to give up our control and turn our life over to Him. Some of us have a sense of peace by being in fear and worrying. Why? Because it "assures us" that we are in control of the situation and know what we are doing. Right...Isn't it ironic that some people feel safer driving their car than getting into a commercial aircraft, and a plane is safer than a car by a long shot! Why is that? Because in an airplane, they have no control over their destiny, whereas they "feel" that they are in control when driving their car. Go figure…

Try this: Pull your mind away from your problems and focus on Jesus. To start with, if nothing else, this will at least give you a break from all the stress you're putting yourself through! When I say, "focus on Jesus," I don't mean dumping all your fears and junk on Him. What is He supposed to do with that? No, focusing on Him means just being still, listening, and worshiping Him. Anxiety attempts to get us off track and fill our minds with negative thoughts. Remember that He is God, who will and does take care of you. Rather than try and maintain control over your life, could you give it up? Abandon yourself to Him. This may not be easy, and I agree it takes practice, but you have your whole life to do just that. So, get busy….

*Life* is a test... Can you give "it" up?

# The World offers, God gives....

| The World | God |
|---|---|

**The World**

- fame
- fortune
- health
- good looks, body beautiful
- happiness
- acceptance

In short, "success" and the price you pay is striving, work, and eternity in hell when your body dies.

*"What is your life? You are a mist that appears for a little while and then vanishes."* (James 4:14)

**God**

- surrender to Him and He will give you all that "the world" has according to His perimeters and "work/sorrow" is not involved.

*"Delight yourself also in the Lord, And He shall give you the desires of your heart."* (Ps. 37:4 NKJV)

*"The blessing of the Lord makes one rich, And He adds no sorrow with it."* (Prov. 10:22 NKJV) (I think "work" could be inter-changed in this verse with "sorrow.")

What God offers that the world cannot is the power of the Kingdom of God at your disposable 24/7, eternal life in heaven (or you can have eternal life in the other "h" place), peace, joy, thankfulness, protection, healing, forgiveness etc. etc.

Joining in agreement with Jesus puts us in a position to receive a blest and prosperous life. The blessings of God make us rich in a way the world has no comprehension of. We may not always get our way or what we want, which is often a good thing, but we will carry the understanding that God is sufficient. Nothing else matters when we know that God loves us and we love Him.

*Life* is a test... Which one of these options makes sense to you?

# Oct    14

## The Mistake that Christians Make.

We measure ourselves by our performance because we live in a performance-based culture. We need to remember that God does not measure our success by how much money we make, by how many people we impact with the gospel (e.g., how big we grow our churches), how extensive our offering and firstfruits are or how many missionaries we support.

When we stand at the pearly gates and receive judgment, Jesus will ask us only one question: how well did you love? Anything we do that is not motivated by love is worthless today and will be useless and worthless to us then.

The most critical thing we need to concentrate on in our limited time here on earth (*"life is but a vapour"* James 14:4) is how we love, the degree to which we love, and the kind of love we exhibit to others. Let Jesus teach you how to operate in love, for love's sake, asking for nothing in return. We must always love in this way and learn to be more like Jesus every day and in every way. Jesus was the essence, the epitome, and the foundation of love. Jesus calls us to love, His greatest commandment. Start by loving Him and allow yourself to receive His love, purity, and power. We must pour ourselves into Him as an offering, allowing every part of Him to seep inside us.

*"A new command I give you: Love one another. As I have loved you, so you must love one another."* (John 13:34-35)

*"Love must be sincere. Hate what is evil; cling to what is good. Be devoted to one another in love. Honour one another above yourselves."* (Rom. 12:9-10)

*Life* is a test... What will you say when Jesus asks you, "how did you love"?

**www.newstartministries.ca**

*Life is a test...*

# The Month of Cheshvan (Oct/Nov - Part 1 of 2)

**Alphabet:** The letter is "NUN" - symbolizes the Messiah
**Tribe:** Manasseh - to forget, to leap, up and away
**Characteristics:** - Manasseh means God has made me forget my sufferings, forget the pain of the past, and find new beginnings.
- The only month that has no holidays. The Jewish people believe this month is reserved for the time of the Messiah's arrival.
**Constellation:** Scorpio (the scorpion) - tread on serpents and scorpions
**Colour/Stone:** Onyx
**Scripture:** Matt. 9

- This was the month of the great flood, which brought judgement and new beginnings.
- This is the month of the tribe of Manasseh, who was the first son of Joseph. A tribe of warriors and Gideon was one of them; they were very blest and rich in the promised land. They were given the largest piece of land, one section east of the Jordan and the other on the west of the Jordan. However, when the ten tribes rebelled, they joined them and turned from God. Many prophets warned them that they did not listen, and the Assyrians conquered them and took them away. In their captivity, they repented and turned back to God. Therefore, it is a month to repent. See how you messed up in the past and repent.
- Revelation 7:6 says that in the last days, Manasseh will be restored.
- It is a month to celebrate the goodness and faithfulness of God.
- Invite Jesus Christ to integrate through the darkness in your life.
- You cannot move forward without forgiveness.
- Manasseh became the lost tribe in India.
- God judges sin and is full of grace. Even if you messed up, restoration is possible through repentance.
- The Jews believe the soul responds in this month in unusual ways. This is a month to smell the awe of God and a month when the fragrance of the Holy Spirit begins to emanate so a move of the Holy Spirit can begin.

# The Month of Cheshvan (Oct/Nov - Part 2 of 2)

Many people with the "Greek mindset" think that God is dealing only with spiritual issues, and they do not make the connection between body, soul and spirit.

Being a Christian does not exempt us from going through bad times. However, as we present ourselves as living sacrifices to God, we are transformed by renewing our minds in Christ. If you are in the world and you are a child of this world, then you are a son of Baal, and all you can do is conform to the image of this world. If you live in the image of Christ with the blood of Jesus flowing through you to purge your soul, you cannot be conformed to this world.

This is the month that you must war with words. Words that are not spoken correctly go into the inward parts of your stomach. Lots of stomach problems are the result of receiving wrong words. It would help if you yelled from your inner being, "I am satisfied," and pushed out anything in you that is dissatisfied.

The constellation associated with Cheshvan is Scorpio, the scorpion. The scorpion and snake are symbols of this month. We need to understand the snake of Eden. Remember that God gave us authority to tread on serpents and scorpions, so this is a crucial month to stand in authority. Satan wants to get the upper hand in your life, but this is the time to plant your heel on the enemy's plans to transform you into his image. Instead, as you deal with your trials and difficulties through the anointing, you will be changed into Christ's image.

*Life* is a test... Are you blowing away the negative experiences of your life to change you into a new creation in Jesus?

# Life is Easy; Just Make Wise Choices.

When you choose to worship God over watching sitcoms on TV, you're making a good choice. Granted, there's nothing wrong with entertainment in limited amounts (although I can think of better things to watch than sitcoms), but worship should always be a priority. When you choose scripture over a fiction novel or prayer over texting and chatting with friends, it pleases and moves Holy Spirit.

*"But seek first the kingdom of God and His righteousness, and all these things shall be added to you."* (Matt. 6:33 NKJV)

What happens when you seek Him? You will find Him! *"You will seek Me and find Me when you seek Me with all your heart."* (Jer. 29:13 NKJV) It's not rocket science, is it?

The mistake that many people make is that they are looking for some supernatural encounter. They're doing it backwards; seek the Kingdom first, and then you'll find the supernatural. "Life is a Test," and life is simple. Choose worship, scripture, prayer, and Jesus and Holy Spirit because they have chosen you. They made you! Isn't it sad and tragic that we make life so complicated when it is merely so easy? Just choose Jesus. Talk to Holy Spirit all the time. Simple stuff...

Case in Point. I recently went to Canadian Tire for some gardening supplies, some picnic tables, etc. I got deal after deal after deal. I just let Him do the shopping and tag along, watching Him make things happen. It's called "the favour of God," and it can happen to anyone that stays connected with Jesus. Life can be very easy. Just let go!

**Doc's Book Club:** Read *"The Favour of God"* by Dr. Jerry Savelle

*Life* is a test... Do you walk in the favour of God?

# God is Your Friend. (written in the first person)

"You are my child, and I am your Savior and Lord, but I am also your friend. I like hanging out with you and hearing about the things that are on your mind. Talk to Me more often! I like it! I love laughing with you, watching you create stuff (we are a good team!), working with you, and being by your side when you need Me.

I like to love your personality; I mean, after all, I gave it to you, so I know what makes you tick, and I want to hear you laugh, and I like it when you ask questions too.

I am your Dad and I love watching you grow and learn; yes, making mistakes is part of life and growing up. Remember that I am there for you when you make them. I am your role model, so get to know Me better!

When you sin, don't pull away from Me; run to Me! It is best if you confess it right away; then, I will help you to move on. I am here to judge your sin but not your weaknesses. I am your biggest cheerleader and number one fan! Remember that...

I can give you strength when you need it and courage too! I can help you to overcome fear and pain. Just ask…

So, come and enjoy the sweetness of our friendship, and I will share the secrets of My heart with you. You are not My servant; you are My child, and I long, like any parent, to have a close intimate relationship with you. I love you, and, oh, have a great day!"

*Life* is a test... Reading this, does any part of it make you want to pull away or harden your heart? He's a good Father.

## *Life is a test...*

# Planning is Good but...

Planning is good; as the expression goes, if you fail to plan, you will plan to fail. I get all that, and I'm sure you do too, but sometimes we can plan too much. God wants to bring peace to us in the process too. You will not find peace by engaging in excessive planning, with which you try to control your life. When we need to walk in constant planning, it's a form of unbelief. You end up with your mind spinning around with multiple plans to ensure all your bases are covered to the extreme. You figure that you'll have peace if you get your schedule completely organized, but peace is never obtainable, although within your grasp.

We seem to pride ourselves on being prepared for all possibilities, but suddenly, out of the blue, something unexpected throws everything into confusion. God did not design the human mind to figure out the future, let alone dwell on it, for that matter. Frankly, from God's perspective, the future is none of our business. It is simply beyond our capabilities. Besides that, if we knew the future, we wouldn't have to live by faith, would we? Since the Bible says that it is impossible to please God without living by faith (Heb. 11:6), if we knew all the answers, we would never need faith, and therefore we wouldn't be pleasing God! So, what is the solution?

"Constant contact." Bring all your needs, hopes, dreams, fears, and everything and commit them to God for His care, not yours. Turn from the pathway of constant planning to the way of peace.

Hold your plans loosely. It is okay to have an outline but make room for God to perfect those things concerning you. He will lead the way if you allow it. Or you can stubbornly cling to your desires and ideas. Just remember that you cannot predict how things will work out. Be flexible. Ps. 138:8 says, *"The Lord will perfect that which concerns me; Your mercy, O Lord, endures forever; Do not forsake the works of Your hands."*

*Life* is a test... How are you doing at planning in balance?

# Put on the Garment of Praise.

*"...to bestow on them a crown of beauty instead of ashes, the oil of joy instead of mourning, and a garment of praise instead of a spirit of despair."* (Is. 61:3)

Here God is reminding believers of His love and good plans for us. (Jer. 29:11 and 3 John 1:2). We can also see His desire for us to be joyful and worshipful - to put on a garment of praise.

When we are going through difficult times and challenging circumstances, it is the time to set our minds and hearts on God and to give praise. Remember that He is our rescuer and comforter, constantly moving through the issues of our lives, working out the best for us in the long term. It's a dichotomy, isn't it? Praising God when we are going through a personal hell. What is a "garment of praise"?

A "garment" represents a person's inner attitude. God wants us to exchange our garments and thoughts for a new crown and robe to show the drastic change He can do in someone's spirit.

Essentially, He wants to replace our faulty thoughts with truth and turn our pain into joyful worship of Him. Being aligned with these "new clothes" - His plans and purposes, not ours - leads Him to fulfill all His promises in the Bible, of which there are over 8000!

Today is a new day that the Lord has made and a perfect time to shake off the heaviness and the problems of life and clothe yourself with a garment of praise. Tell depression to leave, and then get out your Bible and worship the Lord!

*Life* is a test... Can you praise Him when times are tough?

# The Psalms. (Part 1 of 2)

The Psalms were primarily written by King David and contained great wisdom and comfort. The Psalms expressed the deepest passions of humanity. In this book, we can hear the psalmist's desperate cry in the wilderness amid despair and the enthusiastic and tremendous praise of God, his provider, and Jesus his comforter. Other authors of the Psalms include the sons of Korah, Ethan, Asaph, Solomon, and Moses.

On hope, David speaks to his soul in Ps. 42:5: *"Why, my soul, are you downcast? Why so disturbed within me? Put your hope in God, for I will yet praise him, my Savior and my God."*

I decree Ps.103: 1-5 every day: *"Bless the Lord, O my soul; And all that is within me bless His Holy name! Bless the Lord, O my soul, And forget not all His benefits: Who forgives all your iniquities, Who heals all your diseases, Who redeems your life from destruction, Who crowns you with lovingkindness and tender mercies, Who satisfies your mouth with good things, So that your youth is renewed like the eagle's."* (Ps.103 NKJV) And Ps. 1:1-4, as well: *"Blessed is the man who walks not in the counsel of the ungodly, Nor stands in the path of sinners, Nor sits in the seat of the scornful, But his delight is in the law of the Lord, And in His law, he meditates day and night. He shall be like a tree Planted by the rivers of water, That brings forth its fruit in its season, Whose leaf also shall not wither; And whatever he does shall prosper."* (Ps. 1 NKJV)

If you are having trouble sleeping at night, read aloud these Psalms: *"I laid down and slept; I awoke, for the Lord sustains me."* (3:5 NKJV) *"I will both lie down in peace, and sleep; For you alone, oh Lord make me dwell in safety."* (4:8 NKJV) *"It is vain for you to rise up early, to sit up late, to eat the bread of sorrows; for He gives His beloved sleep."* (127:2 NKJV)

*Life* is a test... Have you read the Book of Psalms? Find your favourites and memorize them.

# The Psalms. (Part 2 of 2)

God responds to your voice! *"In my distress, I called upon the Lord, and cried out to my God; he heard my voice from His temple, and my cry came before Him even to His ears."* (18:6 NKJV)

When you need to praise God, decree this: *"Let them shout for joy and be glad, who favour my righteous cause; and let them say continually, 'Let the Lord be magnified, who has pleasure in the prosperity of His servant.' And of my tongue shall speak of your righteousness and of Your praise all the day long."* (35:27-28 NKJV)

Remember these psalms: *"Delight yourself also in the Lord, and He will give you the desires of your heart. Commit your way to the Lord trust also in Him and he shall bring it to pass. He shall bring forth your righteousness as the light, and your justice as the noonday."* (37: 4-6 NKJV) and *"the steps of a good man are ordered by the Lord, and He delights in his way. Though he fall, he shall not be utterly cast down; For the Lord upholds him with His hand."* (verse 23-24)

Psalm 46 is known as the "warfare psalm," 51 the "confession psalm," and 57 is the "comfort psalm." Use them when you need to. Don't forget the "protection psalm," which is number 91.

I have been very blest to have spent my life trail riding and hiking in Banff and Kootenay National Parks and Mnt. Assiniboine Provincial Park as well; the most beautiful country in the world (check out the images of these places on Google). Consequently, this psalm is my personal favourite: *"the mountains shall bring peace to the people."* (Ps. 72:3 KJV) And they do!

*Life* is a test... Do you express to God how you feel as the Psalmists did?

# Freedom

We hear a great deal about "freedom" in today's world, but I sometimes wonder if people truly understand what the word freedom involves. Freedom is not the right or privilege of doing whatever you want, whenever you want and however you want. As we have seen with the start of the fall of the Roman empire, "too much of a good thing," this so-called "freedom," leads to complete and utter disaster. Complete freedom destroys us and our societies by the nature of who we are and how sin has infected that nature. In short, we cannot live in a world of lawlessness. God established rules in the book of Deuteronomy and other books throughout the Bible that lay a foundation that essentially protects us from ourselves. That being the case, what is freedom?

Freedom is the ability and choice to live in perfect unity with God with our complete reliance upon Him. How do we get this? It comes from surrender and a whole lifestyle of submission. Not a form of request that comes from duty, obligation, fear, rules and regulations, but rather a simple yielding of every aspect of our lives out of love. Every action thought, word and desire must be wholly surrendered to him. When we do this, nothing can hijack our peace. This does not mean that we will not experience trials and temptations; it simply means that we don't have to be tormented anymore by them. Merely surrender and stop trying to make things happen on your own. Releasing all this pressure gives you peace that surpasses all understanding. This is true freedom.

*"Do not be anxious about anything, but in every situation, by prayer and petition, with thanksgiving, present your requests to God. And the peace of God, which transcends all understanding, will guard your hearts and minds in Christ Jesus."* (Phil. 4:6-7)

*Life* is a test... Are you free?

*L*ife
is a test...

## Are You a Pew Warmer or Transformer?

Do you see or want to see God moving inside the confined walls of your church or outside the walls of it? Is it time for you to say, "no longer my denomination, my friends, my church, but rather it's His people, His church and His world?"

God called Adam to *"have dominion over the fish of the sea, and over the fowl of the air, and over the cattle, and over all the earth, and over every creeping thing that creepeth upon the earth..."* (Gen. 1:26) Jesus (the second Adam, 1 Cor. 15:45) continued this mission by bringing the Kingdom back to earth (Matt 6:9-13). Then, He called us to do what He did and more (John 14:12) and told us to go out and take the gospel to the world (Mark 16:15).

Are we "the church" accomplishing this as we "huddle down" and stay in our locked-down mentality behind the walls of our church building which will and can be mistaken for "the church" aka Ekklesia, aka the body of Christ? No, the gospel, the Ekklesia, the body of Christ, tells us to "go out!"

Yes, we need a local church. Why? It is a place to: gather the body of Christ, worship, serve others, teach and mainly equip. Eph. 4: 11 - 13 says, *"so Christ Himself gave the apostles, the prophets, the evangelist, the pastors and teachers to equip His people for works of service, so that the body of Christ may be built up until we all reach unity in the faith and the knowledge of the son of God and become mature, attaining to the whole measure of the fullness of Christ."* Our churches are our training grounds. However, lay down your "church agenda" for God's agenda which is to train and send out.

Where to start? Have everyone in our church complete a Spiritual Gift survey, divide people into groups, and start knocking on doors. Ask what you can do: repair, clean, mow grass, shovel snow, wash windows, listen, pray, teach if they are open, do they have food - the list is endless. Finally, introduce yourself and say that you are part of a group of people that follow Jesus from ABC church and leave a trac and invite them to come to church on Sunday.

*L*ife is a test... Is your church a transformer one??

**www.newstartministries.ca**

# Whom Are You Going to Believe?

Gen. 21 says, *"Now the Lord was gracious to Sarah as He had said, and the Lord did for Sarah what He had promised."* Sarah became pregnant and bore a son to Abraham at the very time God had promised him that. (verses 1-2). It continues in verse 5 saying that Abraham was a hundred years old when his son Isaac was born to him." (verse 5)

We have a nasty habit of deciding what God is going to do, what He can do and what He will do. Don't you think it's odd that we, as mere mortals decide what God will do? Really???

The Bible is filled with hundreds and hundreds of promises; all we need to do is dig out those promises and let our faith arise! It's time to shake off unbelief, fear, complacency, and discouragement and get excited about what God has said in His Word. When you're feeling depressed, read the last two chapters in the Book of Job, and discover all the things He can do and has done. We can't do any of those things, not even close, but an all-powerful, all-knowing miracle working God can do anything, and all He is waiting for is for us to believe who He is and whom He says He is.

Jesus looked at them and said, *"With man this is impossible, but not with God; all things are possible with God."* (Mk. 10:27)

*"The just shall live by faith"* (Heb. 10:38), and *"faith is the substance of things hoped for the evidence of things not seen."* (Heb 11:1). So let faith arise in your life!

*Life* is a test... Have you ever stopped for a moment to think about what God has done, what He has created?

# Invite Him and Keep Inviting Him.

Some people make the mistake of inviting Jesus into their lives, thinking that it is a one-time event. We should be asking Him moment by moment every day with every single activity. This will surprise many, but He is just as interested in the mundane things we do as the essential things. We tend to plan our day and live our own lives without Him until we get into trouble and have a crisis on our hands, and then we cry out to Him with our needs. Maybe if we spent time asking Him to help us plan our day, we wouldn't have gotten into trouble in the first place!

Wouldn't it be better if we took time every morning to spend time with Him and then invite Him into every event we participate in during the day? Converse with Him all day long as if your best friend was standing right next to you - because He is, and He is!

Jesus longs to fill the void in each of us. Trials will come and go, and blessings will come to those who are connected to Him, but He is the same yesterday, today and tomorrow (Heb. 13:8), wanting to be the main focus of our lives.

Therefore, choose Him when distractions come, fear rages, isolation and rejection follow, people hurt you, and also when He loves you, blesses you, and celebrates with you. He should be part of every waking moment of your day. There is no "mystery of life" as the world maintains, but instead, just love Jesus and others. What else is there? Simple stuff...

*"And surely I am with you always, to the very end of the age."* (Matt. 28:20

*Life* is a test... Do you invite Him in, daily?

**www.newstartministries.ca**

# How to Minister to the Sick. (Part 1 of 5)

We must keep in mind several vital points when we minister healing:
- Keep trying and don't give up even when healing does not manifest.
- Don't let the devil frustrate you.
- Keep in mind the reason for healing: to fulfill the great commission, to rebuke demons, and to demonstrate signs and wonders (which follow the teaching of the Word) which bring people to salvation.

So many people are reluctant to minister healing to others because of fear. What if they don't get healed, they say. Well, what if they do??? God honours us when we step out in faith, and we must have confidence in knowing that Jesus wants to recover as much as He wants to forgive. *"Jesus went about preaching, teaching, and healing..."* (Matt: 9:35), and we must do the same. Self-control instantly believes what Holy Spirit has told us to do, so we must overcome fear, or God cannot use us. God is the source of all power, but He refuses to be the channel; it is up to us to be the channel, the conduit pipe.

**Now I'll describe what's called the"L prayer."**
**1.** As a prophetic sign, lift your right hand (the vertical part of the letter "L"), pray to the Father, and claim Matthew 10:1. *"Jesus called his twelve disciples to him and gave them authority to drive out impure spirits and to heal every disease and sickness."*

**Example:** "Thank you, Lord, for this lady. Thank you, Lord, for Matt. 10:1, thank you for giving your disciples power to heal the sick and cast out demons. I claim that promise right now and thank you for healing her. I know that it is not your will for her to be sick. Thank you for using me as a conduit pipe." (Remember that we have authority, which is the freedom to exercise power when needed.)

**2.** Then, stop praying to the Father. You do not need to go on and on praying, and never beg, plead or bawl.

# How to Minister to the Sick.
## (Part 2 of 5)

**3.** Lay both hands on the sick person, thus forming the horizontal part of the letter "L" with your arms and attack the sickness with Words of faith and rebuke the devil as necessary.

**Example:** "In the Name of Jesus, I command sickness and disease to leave this body. Satan, I command you to take your hands off this lady now in the Name of Jesus."

### How can we justify using the "L prayer?"

**1.** God gave us the power to perform miracles (Acts 1:8).

**2.** We have the person of Holy Spirit (speaking in tongues) within us.

**3.** We are commanded to lay hands on the sick, and they will recover (Mark. 16:18).

**4.** We have authority from heaven (i.e., "The Name of Jesus").

**5.** We have the Word of God and our disposal. *"He sent His Word and delivered them of all the inflictions."* (Ps. 107:20)

**6.** We have Holy Spirit. We cast out demons by the power of the Holy Spirit, and by doing so, the Kingdom of God has come to us (Matt. 12:28).

**7.** We have authority by the blood of Jesus. (Communion)

### Points to remember when ministering to the sick:

**1.** Be friendly and full of grace (John 1:14), look the person in the eye, and wait for God to speak to you.

**2.** Ask the sick person, "what would you like Jesus to do for you?" (Matt. 20:29)

**3.** Ask the sick person where the pain is without getting into too many details.

**4.** If healing does not come immediately, ask the person how long they have had the symptoms and when it started. By doing this, you are looking for the blockage of the healing and where a door has been opened to the devil.

# How to Minister to the Sick.
## (Part 3 of 5)

**5.** Keep looking at the person and encourage their faith level. Look for faith; you will know when they are ready. This is why teaching healing before laying on the hands builds a person's faith. When they come for the altar call, they will have expectant faith. Ask them is there is someone that they need to forgive.

**6.** Ask them to do something they couldn't do before. For example, if they have a sore shoulder, ask them to move it now.

**7.** When healing comes (Luke 17:17), give thanks and praise and ensure they are born again.

**8.** Administer "aftercare." It is best to hand out a booklet explaining to them about healing and how to keep it by claiming versus and rebuking the devil if symptoms return. Tell them to go home and tell their friends and family what Jesus has done for them!

**9.** If there is no manifestation of healing, repeat all the procedures and ask more questions. Find another person to agree with you for the sick person's healing (Matthew 18:19). Encourage the ill person to agree with you and encourage them to come to another meeting. Remind the sick person that sometimes healing takes time. They might, for example, be healed on the way home or several days later. Generally rule, sick people often have terrible confessions. *"Life and death are in the power of the tongue"* (Prov. 18:21), so it may be necessary to educate the sick person and tell him to change the words that they are speaking. *"By your words you are justified by your words you are condemned."* (Matt. 12:37) *"God's Words are life unto those that find them, and health to all their flesh."* (Prov. 4:20)

**10.** When praying in a hospital, make sure you get permission, have courtesy and respect for people around you, and it is a good idea to bring a CD with scriptures on it and/or index cards.

*Life* is a test... Memorize these steps so that when you need to minister healing you know exactly what to do.

# How to Minister to the Sick.
## (Part 4 of 5)

### Roots of Sickness

One of the best ways Christians should look at life is to think of our lives as a long hallway. On the left and right sides of the hallway are doors. Holy Spirit functions well throughout the corridor when these doors are closed, keeping us safe, prosperous, and in good health. Opening any of the hallway doors allows the devil to mess up our lives. Some people think the devil cannot harass us because we are born again. This is not true; demons can be cast out of the saved just as much as they can be thrown out of the unsaved. There are four reasons why we get sick:

**1.** What opens the doors in the corridor? Firstly, we must remember the three reasons why Jesus came to the earth: to forgive sins, to reveal the works of God, and to destroy the works of the devil. The doors in the hallway are opened by sin, the deadliest virus in the world!

**a)** individual sin
**b)** the sins of a nation
**c)** the sins of leaders
**d)** the sins of past family generations

**2.** The failure of our bodies which consist of our body, spirit, and soul (mind, will, and emotions.) If our flesh (i.e., body) is making all the decisions in our life, and the soul follows it, then our spirit is not connected to God. Our bodies lead us into sin, opening the door for our bodies to fail physically. This is where chronic illness comes from.
**3.** Curses; we may have generational curses, but we can also curse ourselves through our sinful activities and words. *"There is no curse without a cause."* (Prov. 26:2)
**4.** The fragility of our bodies. They wear out with age.

*Life* is a test... Are you a victim of curses? Repent and break them in Jesus Name.
**www.newstartministries.ca**

*Life is a test...*

# How to Minister to the Sick.
## (Part 5 of 5)

Our mistake in praying for healing is that we cry out to God, asking Him to do something about it. He already did 2000 years ago when His son was on the cross. God is telling us to be conduit pipes, connect with His power, and minister it to other people through faith. The main reason people do not administer healing is fear, but we must remember that we have confidence that Jesus wants to heal as much as He wants to forgive. When I minister healing, I use these three prayers in this order: (you can use these before or after using the "L prayer" or in con-junction with it.)

### 1. Oil Anointing
*"As you are outwardly anointed with this Holy oil, so may our heavenly Father grant you the inward anointing of Holy Spirit. Of His great mercy, may He forgive you your sins, release you from suffering, and restore you to wholeness and strength. May He deliver you from all evil, preserve you in all goodness, and bring you to everlasting life; through Jesus Christ our Lord. Amen"*

### 2. Authority
*"Thank you Lord, that you love us so much that it is not Your will that we should endure pain. Thank you for the power of Matthew 10:1, which says that You gave us authority over sickness, disease and demons. Give us faith for that right now, Lord, and thank you for Your anointing. Holy Spirit, we welcome You to move here according to Your will. We invite Your healing power over every sickness, pain, and demons. In Jesus Name."*

### 3. Command Healing
*"Body, I speak the Word of Faith to you. I command every internal organ and every part of this body to function in the perfection to which God created it to function, for it is the temple of the Holy Ghost; therefore, I charge this body in the Name of the Lord Jesus Christ and by the authority of His Holy Word to be healed and made whole in Jesus' Name."* (Prov. 12:18) Amen

P.S. Hopefully you were having nothing to do with Halloween today other than praying and interceding against it. Go back and read April 17 and October 1st.

## The World's "Wisdom?"

I have previously written about ensuring we receive "wise counsel." Whose? Frankly, "the world" doesn't know what is going on. It responds by telling us the "news," but it is everything and anything that will sell newspapers (usually something fearful; remember the toilet paper hoarding during covid?) Look at what King David said in Ps. 1:1-3:

*"Blessed is the man Who walks not in the counsel of the ungodly, Nor stands in the path of sinners, Nor sits in the seat of the scornful; But his delight is in the law of the Lord, And in His law he meditates day and night. He shall be like a tree planted by the rivers of water, That brings forth its fruit in its season, Whose leaf also shall not wither; And whatever he does shall prosper."* (NKJV)

I will dissect this passage from a 2021 perspective. Stop listening to the evening news and social media, for that matter. The "world" has no idea what is happening because they are not tuned into God's plan. Any counsel that you receive should be from Godly people. Don't listen to people that scorn or condemn you. Stand up for what is truth and Godly - the Bible. The world doesn't know what true truth is. The wisdom of God should be the one telling you whether to get medical treatments, not the government.

Remember this: God's wisdom is pure, peaceful, gentle, reasonable, and leaves you feeling relaxed and calm. You can feel the Spirit's Fruits pour from Holy Spirit onto you. God's wisdom doesn't waver, and He has no double - standard of hypocrisy. If you study His Word long enough, you will "just know" His thoughts before asking Him anything. Yes, it takes practice; work on it daily. You have the rest of your life to get to know Him better, and the sooner you do, the better your life will be. *"But the wisdom that is from above is first pure, then peaceable, gentle, willing to yield, full of mercy and good fruits, without partiality and without hypocrisy."* James 3:17 NKJV)

*Life* is a test... Where and who are you receiving wisdom from?
Read 2 Chron. 20:20b.
**www.newstartministries.ca**

*Life* is a test...

## Identity Crisis.

Gosh, we live in an exciting world, don't we? When I was a kid, boys were boys, and girls were girls. Now there seems to be much confusion about that. As with all things in life, the solutions are pretty simple. On the practical side, if you are unsure who you are, here's a simple solution. Drop your drawers, bend over and look between your legs. What you see or don't see will tell you everything you need to know!

Anything you "feel" differently about what I have just said is an attack on your soul. As I have written earlier, everything in the world is either Christ (anointing) or anti-Christ (no blessing). You were created before the world was born (Eph. 1:4), in the perfect image of God (Col. 3:10), male or female (Gen. 5:2). So, what do you do when your soul gets attacked by a devil trying to tell you something else? (Not to get into another whole lesson but the demonic spirit behind this identity stuff is Jezebel who uses familiar spirits. Read about her in 1 Kings and 2 Kings).

Do not despair when you have an identity crisis and are unsure what you are, who you are, where you belong or what you should be doing. Get back to your foundation, which is God. Then, place yourself firmly on the solid rock of God's Word and stand in faith, trusting that since He is the same yesterday, today and forever (Heb. 13:8) that He will continue to love you, support you, guide you, and direct every facet of your life if you continue to surrender to Him. If you have serious identity issues, find people specializing in deliverance and inner healing and be set free. If you are not born again, then get born again. If you don't know the Word, then read the Word. If you want to hear the Word of God, read the Bible out loud. Simple stuff…

**Doc's Book Club:** Read **"The Spiritual Warriors Guide to Defeating Jezebel; How to Overcome the Spirit of Control, Idolatry and Immorality."** By Jennifer LeClaire.

*Life* is a test... Life is not complicated when your foundation is Jesus. What's your foundation?

## Taste God.

*"Taste and see that the Lord is good; blessed is the one who takes refuge in Him."* (Ps. 34:8)

God is everything! He is the creator of this amazing planet and universe. Look at all the millions of species and varieties of animals and plants. Then there are billions of stars and planets. How about His most incredible creation? You! It was a good day for Him when He made you, just as you are!

God desires and gives us complete intimacy with us. He wants to be a part of every single issue of our lives. Even the tiny things we think He is too busy for (like finding a parking spot!) He blesses us continually, even in those things that we believe are painful and nothing but trouble. Just as a parent disciplines a child, He brings things into our lives to help us grow more like Him - to help us cleanse ourselves of sin and pride and make us more reliant on Him.

We desire to be in control, so we constantly seek in life "understanding" when what we need to be doing is trusting Him as that keeps us close - which is where He wants us to be. Why? The closer we are to Him, the better He can comfort, direct, and bless. He wants to bless us; we must surrender and live for Him, not ourselves. Spend your days praising and thanking Him! Tune in to Him, leave all the other voices and junk spinning around in your head behind, and walk in His peace. *"Come near to God, and he will come near to you."* (James 4:8)

*"Let the peace of Christ rule in your hearts, since as members of one body you were called to peace. And be thankful. Let the message of Christ dwell among you richly as you teach and admonish one another with all wisdom through psalms, hymns, and songs from the Spirit, singing to God with gratitude in your hearts. And whatever you do, whether in word or deed, do it all in the Name of the Lord Jesus, giving thanks to God the Father through Him."* (Col. 3: 15-17)

*Life* is a test... Are you drawing closer to Him every day?

# The Reality of Life.

Jesus said that there would be trials and tribulations in our lives.

*"These things I have spoken to you, that in Me you may have peace. In the world you will have tribulation, but be of good cheer, I have overcome the world."* (John 16:33 NKJV) Much of this will be from people that will come against you. They will persecute you because you are a Christian and believe in Jesus. *"Yes, and all who desire to live godly in Christ Jesus will suffer persecution." (*2 Tim. 3:12 NKJV) Or they will fight with you about some other issue.

So, what to do?? Well, WWJD? He would manifest His love towards the people that are coming against Him. Remember that we are supposed to be like Him and do what He did. (Ouch!) Therefore, do that very thing.

Pause for a moment, and then turn the anger you feel rising in you into prayer power. Instead of being offended over the negative words being spoken to you, which are starting to get you upset, break the word curses by the authority of Jesus. Then go on the "counter-attack" by getting into prayer. Jesus told us to pray for our enemies (Matt. 5:44). Bless those that curse you and don't get caught into a "ping-pong" match where the ball of accusation goes back and forth and back and forth - they curse, and you curse back, and they curse and on and on it goes. Words are said that you will often regret later. So, why say them? Instead, move into a Spirit opposite of that - whatever is moving against you.

*"Bless those who curse you, pray for those who mistreat you."* (Luke 6:28)

**Doc's Book Club:** Read ***"The Bait of Satan"*** by John Bevere. This is another must-read book for every Christian. It will definitely wreck you.

*Life* is a test...  Easier said than done isn't it?

# You Are a Pot Made Out of Dust.

*"And the Lord God formed man of the dust of the ground, and breathed into his nostrils the breath of life; and man became a living being."* Gen. 2:7 *"Therefore if anyone cleanses himself from the latter, he will be a vessel * for honour, sanctified and useful for the Master, prepared for every good work."* (2 Tim. 2:21 NKJV)

We are vessels of God, made by Him from dust. In a nutshell:

- He made us to worship Him; He wanted kids!
- He made us before the world was formed (Eph. 1:4).
- He has plans for us to prosper (Jer. 29:11).
- He told us to take dominion over the earth (Gen1:26).
- His son told us to heal the sick, cast out demons and make disciples of all men (Luke 9:1 and Matt. 10:1; 28:19)

In the meantime, we are to be vessels of His heavenly glory, carrying Holy Spirit within us. This way, we will know the depths of His love and be able to interact with Him. The catch is that we must want this and purify ourselves to get it. The troubles of life want to take us away from this. If we can't sense Holy Spirit's presence, it is because we have yielded ourselves to these troublesome thoughts. So *"cast all your care on Him"* (Ps. 55:22; 1 Peter 5:7) and let your thoughts bask in thoughts of Him. Keep in "constant contact" with Him, and all these troublesome thoughts you have will melt away.

*Life* is a test... Is your "vessel" pouring in Holy Spirit and then pouring it out to others??

* Synonyms: pot, basin, bowl, receptacle. Also, check Jer. 18:4, where the example is used about us being on the potter's wheel.

*Life* is a test...

# It Can Come Back and Bite You.

I think the most significant issues I see lacking in society today are character and integrity. To put it bluntly, there is too much cheating and trickery.

Do you remember how Jacob, with his manipulative mother's help, cheated on his brother and father? It came back to bite him because Laban consequently tricked him! (aka *"you reap what you sow!"* - Gal. 6:7). You can read about these stories in Genesis 25 and 29.

Sometimes we ask ourselves what went wrong; why did God allow this to happen to us? God will do whatever is necessary in His wisdom to see our character flaws. He will lead us into a bad situation where we can witness our ungodly reactions as He puts a mirror in front of our face, revealing the truth about ourselves. Cry out to Him, and He always gives us the option to cast out our weaknesses and exchange them for His strength and His righteousness. In short, we need to "give it up." Give up what? Our selfishness, control, disobedience, sin - you name it.

Just as the Pharisees did, we can put up a grand façade, go to church, be seen with all the right people and say all the right things, but only God knows our true hearts. We can make "sacrifices for Jesus" and do all kinds of religious stuff, but the reality of the matter is that God is the one that knows our hearts. What He's looking for is obedience. Be careful that you don't "know of God" but don't "know God."

*"Obedience is better than sacrifice."* (1 Sam. 15:22)

*Life* is a test... Character and integrity are everything. Have you considered yours?

# Clean the Junk out of Your Life and Home.

*"Nothing in the world is more dangerous than sincere ignorance and conscientious stupidity."* - Martin Luther King Jr.

We live in a world where people do not know what they don't know. Case in point: I walk into people's homes, and I see dream catchers, Ying-Yang symbols (one of my neighbours has one on their front lawn), Ouija boards, Zodiac symbols, horror and R-rated movies, children's fantasy books about witch-craft (you know whom I mean) - the list goes on. Further, people are involved in activities that they think are harmless but have demonic spiritual connections. We must remember two things: everything in this world is either anointed of God (Christ) or not anointed (anti-Christ), and secondly, all items in our lives need to glorify God in all ways.

If they don't, then why are we keeping them? I encourage people to go through their house once a year and make sure there's nothing in it that isn't honouring God in some way. It would take me days and days to write a comprehensive list of things we Christians should not be involved with, so instead, I will give a list of three books that I would highly recommend and leave you to do more research in this area if you wish.

**Doc's Book Club:** Read: *"Signs & Symbols: Cults, New Age and Cultic Insignias and What They Mean."* by Dr. Selwyn Stevens. *"Deliver us From Evil"* by Cindy Jacobs. *"Deliverance Training Manual"* by Dr. William Sudduth.

*Life* is a test... What's in your house (life) that does not honour God?

## Devotion, not Religion.

Many people are radically devoted to a set of rules and communities that are supposed to bring eternity closer to some sort of "divine unity." I met a lady one time who told me that she believed in God, believed in angels but didn't go to church. Huh? Jesus taught and showed pure loyal devotion to God. Life as we know it is a forward motion. Either be caught up in the commotion of this crazy world or move forward in faith in Jesus. Real natural religion is to love others how you want to be treated as you love God with all your heart, soul and mind (Luke 10:27) because He made you! Something must make nothing into something, and that was God. (not some spark or bang in a sea of void...)

Natural religion is to be whom God created you to be. Model yourself after Jesus. Each day the choices you make determine the faith you need to get through the day etc. What are you standing on? The Word or what society tells you?

*"Do to others as you would have them do to you."* (Luke 6:31)

*"Do not love the world or anything in the world. If anyone loves the world, love for the Father is not in them. For everything in the world - the lust of the flesh, the lust of the eyes, and the pride of life - comes not from the Father but from the world. The world and its desires pass away, but whoever does the will of God lives forever."* (1 John 2:15-17)

*"Do not conform to the pattern of this world, but be transformed by the renewing of your mind. Then you will be able to test and approve what God's will is - His good, pleasing and perfect will."* (Rom. 12:2)

*"They are not of the world, even as I am not of it."* (John 17:16)

*Life* is a test... Whose world are you living in? His or his?

# Keep Focused on Heaven.

*"Since, then, you have been raised with Christ, set your hearts on things above, where Christ is, seated at the right hand of God. Set your minds on things above, not on earthly things. For you died, and your life is now hidden with Christ in God. When Christ, who is your life, appears, then you also will appear with him in glory."* (Col. 3:1-2)

What the scripture means is that we should be focused on heaven and what God is doing instead of focusing on what's happening here on earth. Firstly, we're only here for a short time, and all of these problems and issues are temporary. Secondly, you will have less trouble with your troubles and experience far less fear and condemnation in your life if you look at life through God's eyes instead of your own and the world's.

What is the most significant single element people are looking for in life? Peace. Yet it is so hard for 95% of the world to obtain. The world has nothing to offer us except the opposite of peace. There is no peace without Jesus.

*"There is no peace, saith the Lord, unto the wicked."* (Is. 48:22 KJV)

Would you describe yourself as a person of peace? If there are areas in your life where peace isn't present, is there any part of that area that isn't devoted to God? We must live holistically, always giving every aspect of our lives to Him, or else leave room for the enemy to take away God's peace in our lives.

*Life* is a test...Are all areas of your life lived through a lens of peace?

# Standing Up for Your Beliefs.

*"If you are silent about your beliefs because you are worried someone will be offended, then your beliefs are not that important to you, but rather what people think about you is. When you stand up for what's right and true, you will receive both hate and love, but everyone will know what you're fighting for."* This quote arrived on my Facebook page one day and was from "America's Best Pics and Videos," without reference to who wrote it.

The problem with the Christian church today, in my opinion, is that it is not vocal enough and does not take a stand. Furthermore, you can blame the Christians if you want to blame someone for the mess. Where were they when the governments took prayer out of the schools? Where were they when abortion and sodomy laws were passed? If you do not like your government, well, you elected them. Too many Christians will not become involved with politics. Why?

Remember that it was the people who elected Adolf Hitler!

**Quotes from Dietrich Bonhoeffer:**

**1.** Silence in the face of evil is evil itself.
**2.** Not to speak is to speak. Not to act is to act.
**3.** Your life as a Christian should make non-believers question their disbelief in God.
**4.** Being a Christian is less about cautiously avoiding sin than about courageously and actively doing God's will.

https://en.wikipedia.org/wiki/Dietrich_Bonhoeffer

*Life* is a test... Do you stand up for what you believe in?

*Life* is a test...

## Remembrance Day.

Remembrance Day has been observed in Commonwealth member countries since the end of the First World War to honour armed forces members who have died in the line of duty. Following a tradition inaugurated by King George V in 1919, the day is also marked by war remembrances in many non-Commonwealth countries as well. In most countries, Remembrance Day is observed on November 11th to recall the end of First World War hostilities. Hostilities formally ended "at the 11th hour of the 11th day of the 11th month" of 1918 by the armistice signed by representatives of Germany and the Entente between 5:12 and 5:20 that morning. The First World War officially ended with the signing of the Treaty of Versailles on 28 June 1919.

Here is a prayer for today:

"Father God, we thank you for the freedom you gave us and for the price that was paid by Christ so that we could live free. Today, we remember the great sacrifice paid by our military and civilians. We thank You for the brave men and women who have fought and continue to fight so courageously for our nation. We ask for Your support and blessing for our military, veterans, and their families. We pray that You will be gracious and encircle them with your peace. We pray for your great favour and goodness to be evident in their lives.

We thank you that Canada is a leader in peacekeeping worldwide and has the DNA of being a nation that heals other countries. We ask that You provide your protection, that You would be their guiding force who leads the way and keeps them safe from behind. We ask that You draw them to Yourself amidst the dangers they face in a dark world, for You, Jesus are the Truth, the Way, and the Light."

*Life* is a test... Are you remembering today?

*L*ife *is a test...*

## Faith Under Pressure.

Nothing seems to wreck a person more than reading The Message translation of the Bible (and that is a good thing!) Check this out:

*"Consider it a gift, friends, when tests and challenges come at you from all sides. You know that under pressure, your faith-life is forced into the open and shows its true colours. So don't try to get out of anything prematurely. Let it do its work so you become mature and well-developed, not deficient in any way."* (James 1:2-3)

Don't you just need to hear that? It is not what we want! In this paraphrase, the Apostle James says, "be happy and consider it a gift." Right... a gift? When "stuff happens," it is a gift. OkeeDokee...An old expression goes like this "you will find out what you are made of when it hits the fan..." It is easy to "live by faith" and to "count it all joy" when things are going well. But that is not the reality of life. No one ever said that life was or would be easy. Jesus went so far as to say that there would be storms. No kidding... The real question is, what will we do, how will we react, WHEN, not IF, the storms come?

When I reflect on this, I think, "what do people do that don't have Jesus in their life?" Who or what did they fall back on? The world has just come through one of the biggest tragedies since the second world war - covid. The biggest, most significant contributing factor to this was not so much virus but it is what the entire thing did to people. Fear... the Bible speaks over 400 times about not being in fear, yet is that precisely what didn't happen to 90% of the world? Toilet paper hoarding? Seriously? What is the fundamental basis of fear? Fear of death. That's one of the greatest joys of being a Christian; we have no fear of death. Paul says in Phil 1:21, *"For to me, to live is Christ and to die is gain."* Why? Because when our bodies die, we are out of here! And if we know Jesus, we are then with Him forever.

*L*ife is a test... What are you in fear about?

# Grace is Power.

*"My grace is all you need, for My power is greatest when you are weak."* (2 Cor.12:9)

This verse is powerful (no pun intended) and the body of Christ so often misses it. In a nutshell, His grace gives us power. Essentially, God is saying to the Apostle Paul, *"When you can't do it in your natural ability, step aside; my empowerment, works best in this situation. You can't do it, but I can't. That's my job so trust Me."*

Further down in this chapter, we come to this part: *"I have worked harder than any of the other apostles..."* (sounds like Paul is on an ego trip, but keep reading...) *"No it was not really my own doing, but God's grace working with me"* (1 Cor. 15;10). Paul is boasting about God, not himself. He had a fantastic mission and excelled at it, including writing a good portion of the New Testament. Here, in this passage, his acknowledgment is that his success was because of God's grace.

Do you have an assignment? Of course, you do; that's why God created you, and He even prepared you for the tasks that He gave you. Eph. 2:10 says, *"For we are God's handiwork, created in Christ Jesus to do good works, which God prepared in advance for us to do."* That job, that destiny, admittedly is beyond our natural ability, which is why we need God's grace, faith and Gifts. Additionally, if we could do it or even some of it without Him, we would be able to share in His glory, which He will not allow. *"What I do is done for my own sake - I will not let my name be dishonoured, or let anyone else share the glory that should be mine and mine alone."* (Is. 48:11)

*Life* is a test... Are you able to boast in God and not yourself?

## The Church in Crisis.

I see two significant problems in the church today. The first is apostasy which I thoroughly examined in Volume I of *"Life is a Test"* (September). The second problem is that the church lacks a dream. Not just a dream for itself (which it lacks) but it also does a lousy job of helping young people achieve a goal for themselves.

When we don't have a dream, we criticize and knock-on others who do! Oh, the irony of it! And the people that are against you are usually in your own home! *"...a man's enemies will be the members of his household."* (Matt. 10:36) There is more irony; when you have a dream, and it materializes, those same people against you are often suddenly your best buddy!

Years ago, when the dinosaurs lived, according to my children, (yes, they think I am that old even though they're all in their 20's now) I had an idea to start a commercial printing business, and I knew nothing about printing. My family and friends thought I was nuts. I bounced the picture off a few businesspeople and they thought it was a great idea. It turned out to be all Holy Spirit based, and 18 years later, when we sold it, we were the second-largest printer out of 22, stretching from Calgary to Vancouver. I'm also happy to say that we won 37 regional and international awards for our work. My point? Dream! Dream big and dream with Holy Spirit playing a very active role in those dreams. *"Delight yourself also in the Lord, And He shall give you the desires of your heart."* (Ps. 37:4 NKJV)

*Life* is a test... What are you dreaming about? Put it at His feet.

# The Month of Kislev (Nov/Dec - Part 1 of 4)

**Appointed times:** The beginning of Hanukkah

**Alphabet:** Letter is "SAMEKH" - trust, support; a circle or ring; a repeating cycle. Words: turn, go around, surround, encompass, to come full circle.

**Tribe:** Benjamin, gifted with the art of the bow; the only child of the 12 born in the Promised Land, so watch Israel this month.

**Characteristics:** - A month to develop your warfare strategies: to have a prospective revelation for war.
 - A month to enter a new level of trust and rest.
 - To declare your life experiences filled with tranquility and peace; ask for the rivers of life to flow.

**Constellation:** Sagittarius (the Archer) - a time to fight against empires and cultures.

**Colour/Stone:** Opal or Rainbow Jasper.

By examining our hearts and motives during this time each year, we can break up and out of old patterns of mistrust.

The month of dreams. We are to receive God's direction through dreams. Kislev is the month of second chances, so do not forget to take advantage of this. Remember, those old enemies are here too! It is the month of darkness, but the days also grow lighter.

**Types of Dreams:**
 - flying dreams - you have risen above
 - chasing dreams - running from fear
 - naked dreams - you are feeling vulnerable
 - test streams - you fail
 - is a time for visitation from the Angels

**Why does God speak in mysteries?** To draw us closer to Him.
 - When God shows us a mystery, He wants us to find the answer.
 - God wants us to pray, to seek and gain an understanding of Him!
 - Reading a good mystery holds our attention! God wants to captivate us!
 - His promise? If we draw near, He will reveal His meaning.

*Life* is a test...

# The Month of Kislev (Nov/Dec - Part 2 of 4)

Kislev is associated with the Tribe of Benjamin. He was the youngest son of Jacob and his favourite after Joseph was presumed dead following him being sold to Egypt. Benjamin was constantly protected by the other tribes, which was not God's plan. He was to be a warrior but was too protected by his brothers to come into his destiny. He could not drive out the Jebusites and was noted for violence and perversion. Some have wondered why God has let us face such brutal battles. We question, "why didn't God shelter me from those difficult situations?" God wants you to know that He had a purpose for overcoming difficulties. He wants you to gain strength. He wants you to learn to overcome and be victorious.

The Tribe of Benjamin eventually did overcome and finally came into its destiny. Several great people came from the tribe of Benjamin: Esther, Mordecai, and the Apostle Paul. Most of the New Testament books were written by descendants of the tribe of Benjamin. How did Benjamin learn to overcome? The turning point came with Jonathan's covenant with David. David was from Judah, and Jonathan was from Benjamin. Jonathan's father, Saul, was Israel's first king and was very much a Benjamite. He was ruled by fear and wanted to be protected. The time came for him to be anointed King, but he was afraid! He ran and hid amongst the caves.

In 1 Sam. 13, Saul's father caused him to disobey God, and he forfeited the kingship. However, when David arrived and led Israel to victory against Goliath, Saul's son Jonathan saw David's courage, and something snapped inside him. He said, "that's what we are supposed to be!" Consequently, Jonathan cut a covenant with David. He rejected fear; instead of wanting to be defended, he was willing to lay down his life to protect David. Then, David and Jonathan extended the covenant to the House of Jonathan (Benjamin) and the house of David to Judah.

Eventually, Benjamin "came to his own" with where he should have been in the first place. The northern tribes rebelled and formed the northern Kingdom of Israel, but the tribe of Benjamin stood with Judah, took part in revivals, repaired the temple and had restoration to their entire tribe.

# The Month of Kislev (Nov/Dec - Part 3 of 4)

Kislev is an important month to take a stand against the enemy! It is a month of destiny and a new identity. Interestingly, a famous Benjamite was renamed… made into Saul of Tarsus, who had been named after the ungodly King Saul. As King Saul did with David, he tried to hunt down and kill God's people. But "Saul" wasn't the identity God wanted for him. So, God changed his name to "Paul," a Gentile name, to equip him to be an apostle to the Gentiles. Sometimes life circumstances have branded you with an identity that isn't what God chose for you. For some of you, how you view yourself is not how God views you! This is a month you can come into your new identity.

(Note: Technically, Paul's name wasn't changed because God told him to change his name. His name was simply Saul to the Jews, but Paul was his "Gentile name" if you will. To Gentiles he was Paul, to Jews he was Saul. His name wasn't formally "changed." You can see this in Acts 9).

Another example is that Jesus renamed Simon, called him Peter, and gave him the identity of the rock. Ask God to show you habit patterns and ways of thinking that have held you in an old cycle. There are certain things every year that you want to make a spiritual locator and say, "I am not going through that again."

Kislev is the month that Hanukkah begins. Hanukkah is the only holiday in the Jewish calendar, which connects two months, starting in the month of Kislev and concluding in the month of Tevet. The message of Hanukkah is that amid destruction, there is mercy. The issue with Hanukkah was that the light would not go out. Amid any destruction, God will find a way to impart mercy to you. No matter what aspect of destruction you are dealing with - external, internal, physical or spiritual.

God has a way of imparting mercy to build the future. His grace is sufficient, and His love is everlasting. Kislev is the month of cleansing, ask God to bring you to your true new identity!

# The Month of Kislev (Nov/Dec - Part 4 of 4)

Kislev is associated with the constellation Sagittarius, the Archer. This month is a time to fight against empires and cultures. This is a must to shoot straight and move quickly. Cut your losses and move on. Review your support system this month, including who is supporting you and whom you are supporting. Consider who your friends and associates are and why you are connected with them.

Last month we had the month of the flood, so this is the month of the rainbow. Examine what you have warred through in the past year to come to a place of peace. God makes a covenant with us so that we will not have to war with those things again, which was the rainbow's symbolism. In this month of tranquility and peace, you may still have warfare. Many people do not understand this aspect of war. This means that amid the warfare, you are on the offensive so that you have peace amid the conflict. When we get tangled up and out of our alignment with God, we get into trouble. Therefore, keep God close to you in all things.

Note: Hanukkah is observed for eight nights and days, starting on the 25th day of Kislev. The story of Hanukkah is preserved in the books of the First and Second Maccabees, found in the Apocrypha, a collection of books written in the four centuries between the Old and New Testaments. Though the Apocrypha is not Scripture, many Protestants have historically, theologically, and spiritually found this helpful scripture. Discerning readers of the Apocrypha gain a fuller understanding of first-century Judaism, including the messianic fervour that led, in part, to Jesus's passion. I quite enjoy reading it.

**Doc's Book Club:** Read, *"Hanukah Devotional Book - the Miracle of Hanukah"* by Curt Landry.

*Life* is a test... Make a list of what you've been fighting spiritually in the last year, and simply say to yourself, "I don't want to go through this anymore." Then, make the necessary changes.

# Jesus' Resume. (Page 1 of 2)

My name is Jesus -The Christ. Many call me Lord! I've sent you my resume because I'm seeking the top management position in your heart. Please consider my accomplishments as outlined in my resume:

**Address:** Ephesians 1:20
**Phone:** Romans 10:13
**Website:** www.thebible.com
**Keywords:** Christ, Lord, Savior, and Jesus

**Qualifications:**
I founded the earth and established the heavens (Prov. 3:19).
I formed man from the dust of the ground (Gen. 2:7).
I breathed into man the breath of life (Gen. 2:7).
I redeemed man from the curse of the law (Gal. 3:13).
The blessing of the Abrahamic Covenant comes upon your life through me (Gal. 3:14).

**Occupational Background:**
I've only had one employer (Luke 2:49).
I've never been tardy, absent, disobedient, slothful or disrespectful.
My employer has nothing but rave reviews for me (Matt. 3:15 -17).

**Skills Work Experiences:**
Some of my skills and work experiences include:
- empowering the poor to be poor no more
- healing the broken hearted
- setting the captives free
- healing the sick
- restoring sight to the blind
- setting at liberty them that are bruised (Luke 4:18).

I am a Wonderful Counselor (Is. 9:6). People who listen to me shall dwell safely and not fear evil (Prov. 1:33).

Most importantly, I have the authority, ability and power to cleanse you of your sins (1 John 1:7-9).

# Jesus' Resume. (Page 2 of 2)

**Educational Background:**
I encompass the entire breadth and length of knowledge, wisdom and under-standing (Prov. 2:6). In me are hid all the treasures of wisdom and knowledge (Col. 2:3).
My Word is so powerful it has been described as a lamp unto your feet and a light unto your path (Ps.119:105).
I can even tell you all the secrets of your heart (Ps. 44:21).

**Major Accomplishments:**
I participated actively in the greatest Summit Meeting of all times (Gen. 1:26).
I laid down my life so that you may live (2 Cor. 5:15).
I defeated the archenemy of God and mankind and made a show of him openly (Col. 2:15).
I've miraculously fed the poor, healed the sick and raised the dead!
There are many more major accomplishments, too many to mention here. You can read them on my website, which is located at www:thebible.com

Now that you've read my resume, I'm confident I'm the only candidate uniquely qualified to fill this vital position in your heart. In summation, I will properly direct your paths (Prov.3:5-6) and lead you into everlasting life (John 6:47). When can I start? Time is of the essence (Heb. 3:15).

**References:**
Believers and followers worldwide will testify to my divine healing, salvation, deliverance, miracles, restoration and supernatural guidance.

*Life* is a test... Would you hire this man? Why wouldn't you? Why don't you?

Note: Many thanks to my dear friend Peter Enns. Check out his great website! www.godtalk.ca

## Feeling Weak?

That is OK. Emotions and times of feeling low does not mean something is wrong. God created them, and He put them in us. Feelings can be good, even great! However, at the same time, we can use negative emotions destructively. Jesus wept. He probably felt sad at times as well. He did get angry (in the temple, John 2:13-16), but you will notice that His emotions never took Him to a place of being out of control and to the point of sin.

What are we to do when we feel weak? Rejoice! Why? Well, because He said, *"My grace is sufficient for you, for my power is made perfect in weakness."* (2 Cor. 9:12). The problem is that we see ourselves as a "work in progress," which is OK because it keeps us moving forward. However, God does not look at us that way. What He sees is a work of art! A masterpiece, a complete winner! You may see your failures, but He doesn't because you have been washed clean by the blood of His most precious son. What to do, then? Call on Him to give you strength when your emotions tell you, you are weak.

Keeping our emotions productive and not destructive has a lot to do with this verse. *"When I was a child, I talked like a child, I thought like a child, I reasoned like a child. When I became a man, I put the ways of childhood behind me."* (1 Cor. 13:11) It's a polite way of saying that we need to grow up, a lifelong process...

*Life* is a test... Have you grown up into maturity with your emotions?

# Do Unto Others....

How we treat others usually comes back to us, one way or the other. Getting others to treat you how you want to be treated is not as difficult as it sounds if you love yourself the way God loves you. We hear that expression that says, "hurt people, hurt people," and it's true! People treat others poorly because they have been treated poorly and are in some pain. So, they hurt, and consequently, they injure others.

What is the solution? It's the same answer that solves every problem in life - God! If we sit down every morning to spend some time praising and worshiping and allowing the love of the Father to flow over us and pour into us, then as we go through the day and remember that love, and then we pour it out onto and into others. So, let Him love on you, love Him back, love yourself and then spend the rest of the day loving others.

*"Do to others as you would have them do to you."* (Luke 6:31)

*"A new command I give you: Love one another. As I have loved you, so you must love one another."* (John 13:34)

*"And hope maketh not ashamed; because the love of God is shed abroad in our hearts by the Holy Ghost which is given unto us."* (Rom. 5:5 KJV)

*Life* is a test... Are you learning to receive His love for you so that you can pass it on?

## What is Power? (Part 1 of 2)

One quote about power that's always stuck with me is that power is the ability to create. God has this power to create, as do we. We must remember that satan does not have the power to create but will use what's been created for evil. This implication means we have power over him (no pun intended)! So, what are you worried about? You control him; he does not control you unless you allow him to enter your life ("sin" opens the door for him).

Read through Genesis chapter 1. God said nine times, "Be," and it was. "Yeah, but He is God." Let me finish... The Bible says we are co-creators with God. Hmmm. Jesus said that we were to not only do what He did but that we would do greater things! This is coming from a guy who raised people from the dead and controlled the weather, and yes, we have the same power in us! *"Most assuredly, I say to you, he who believes in Me, the works that I do he will do also; and greater works than these he will do, because I go to My Father. And whatever you ask in My name, that I will do, that the Father may be glorified in the Son. If you ask anything in My name, I will do it."* (John 14: 12-14 NKJV)

I have not raised anyone from the dead (yet) only because I haven't had the opportunity, but my pastor friends in Rwanda have, and they think nothing of it. People say you can't control the weather; well, yes, you can; I see it done all the time. For example, I was skiing with my daughter recently, and when we arrived at the ski hill, it was cold, cloudy and windy. So, I went to work. I kept praising God and thanking Him for a beautiful sunny day. By the time we had finished skiing, about 80% of the day was sunny and warm. Coincidence? Sure, I'll give you that, but all I know is that when I quit praying (and using my authority) the so-called "coincidences" quit happening...

*L*ife is a test... Do you understand the power you have in Christ Jesus?

# What is Power? (Part 2 of 2)

Merriam-Webster defines it as: *"the ability to act or produce an effect; physical might; mental or moral efficacy; political control or influence."* The word is translated from the Greek word "dynamis," from which we get the word dynamite. There are different usages of the word in the Bible: a state of moral excellence, influencing and having authority that results from affluence, and the authority for performing miracles.

When do we need God's power? I wouldn't lay hands on anyone and minister healing to them without checking in with God first! I remember hearing Benny Hinn say on one of his broadcasts that he's never healed, anybody! He said his definition of healing was to tell people to take two aspirin and call their doctor in the morning! We are just conduit pipes; we connect to God, taking in the power of Holy Spirit in one hand, letting Him flow through us and dishing that power out from the other hand as needed.

We need God's power for ourselves when we need to be strengthened and built up or empowered. The devil is on our case, trying to get us depressed and drag us down all the time, 24/7. For example, after I wrote volume one of *"Life is a Test,"* I assumed that the project was over. Little did I know He wanted me to write volume 2. I told Him I could not do that, and He said, "I know - I'll do the writing, and you do the typing." That is power! Now I know how preachers prepare a sermon on Sunday. It's the power of God.

*Life* is a test... Are you relying on Him and asking for His power when needed?

# It is all about Intimacy.

Intimacy with God is the precursor for ministry - the very foundation for everything else in life. Why? Because all of us that are born-again are in full-time ministry! If you try to depend on your own strength and knowledge to reach others, you will be guilty of working in the flesh instead of by the Spirit.

Saturate yourself with God's presence daily, and it will "leak" out of you everywhere you go. Jesus said in Mark 8:34: *"Whoever wants to be my disciple must deny themselves and take up their cross and follow me."* What cross? The cross of self-sacrificing yourself to live His life in you. That is called you loving Him. When you are one with Him, you will feel His compassion for the people around you. Don't let your fears, attitudes, opinions and judgements of others get in the way of your Holy partnership. Submerge your will into divine passion, and He will take out the dross, purify you, bless you in every way and make you prosperous.

*"Beloved, let us love one another, for love is of God; and everyone who loves is born of God and knows God. He who does not love does not know God, for God is love. In this the love of God was manifested toward us, that God has sent His only begotten Son into the world, that we might live through Him. In this is love, not that we loved God, but that He loved us and sent His Son to be the propitiation for our sins. Beloved, if God so loved us, we also ought to love one another. No one has seen God at any time. If we love one another, God abides in us, and His love has been perfected in us. By this we know that we abide in Him, and He in us, because He has given us of His Spirit. And we have seen and testify that the Father has sent the Son as Savior of the world. Whoever confesses that Jesus is the Son of God, God abides in him, and he in God. And we have known and believed the love that God has for us. God is love, and he who abides in love abides in God, and God in him."* (1 John 4:7-12)

*Life* is a test... How intimate are you with God?

# Jesus is the Prince of Peace.

Jesus rules over stress and strife when we make Him the Lord over our thought life. It is that a control issue again, Him or you? Since anxiety and peace can't coexist, then let the peace of Jesus "do its thing."

Our problem is that we overthink and respond to every single stimulus. The younger generation is addicted to cell phones, video games and social media; they need that constant "fix." Consequently, our minds are so busy and full of "stuff" that, without realizing it, we push Jesus away and out of our thoughts. Our hearts may yearn for Him, but our heads are too busy. What to do?

Firstly, if your heart is yearning for Him (as it should be), then the good news is that He will respond. He longs to love us and have a relationship with us. He's our dad; isn't that what dads like to do with their kids?

Secondly, exalt His presence. As Christians, we are powerful enough to choose what we think about. We can control our thoughts if we choose to.

Thirdly, just put your "junkie thoughts" on an altar of praise. Lay your concerns at the feet of the King of Kings and Lord of Lords. Quietly say His Name to yourself, and then let some praises come out of your mouth. Sink deep into the stillness of His peace. Trust Him to take care of them.

*"Peace I leave with you; my peace I give you. I do not give to you as the world gives. Do not let your hearts be troubled and do not be afraid."* (John 14:27)

*Life* is a test... Are you able to turn "it" over to Him?

# Prosperity

*"The condition of being successful or thriving especially: economic well-being." (Merriam-Webster)*

Next to the word "deliverance," I don't know of a word that has more of a problematic connotation and gets more people up in arms than the word "prosperity." Ironically, every parent wants their child to be prosperous, but adult Christians fail to understand that they are children. We are God's children, so why wouldn't He want the best for us?

Prosperity is the product of choices that give us a certain quality of life by being aligned with God's Word. Prosperity is an ongoing lifestyle, not a fleeting moment that results from thinking the way God thinks. It produces complete "wholeness" in your walk with God, giving you success in every form of life. Remember that "prosperity" includes every facet of your life, not just your finances.

Too many people get to a point where they realize they've made so many mistakes that they can't possibly be prosperous. They forget that God can redeem lost time, waste and all the screw-ups we've made in life out of pride and ignorance. It's old-fashioned stubbornness that keeps us from believing God can restore us. We can repent by asking for help, and He is faithful to forgive and restore to us all that was taken.

*"If we confess our sins, he is faithful and just and will forgive us our sins and purify us from all unrighteousness."* (1 John 1:9)

*"I will repay you for the years the locusts have eaten."* (Joel 2:25)

*Life* is a test... Are you stuck in religion that says the Christians can't be prosperous?

# WEALTH.

## Jesus was beyond WEALTH.

Without the obligations of managing/owning a vineyard, Jesus turned water into wine, and it wasn't even His water! Not just wine, but "the best wine," without even paying for it! (John 2:10)

As an inside trader in the fishing industry, He had prior knowledge in respect to the location and volume of catch that would make any futures trader on the New York Stock Exchange a millionaire in 30 days. (John 21:6)

Of the twelve businessmen He dined with on one occasion, Jesus could predict which one could not be trusted, right down to the time that the betrayal took place (Matthew 26:21), as well as which of the twelve would deny Him, even after publicly confirming a vote of confidence in favour of Jesus' leadership. (Matthew 26:34) Any executive demonstrating such insight into people's character as Jesus possessed could easily demand a "mega salary" to chair the board meetings of any multinational conglomerate corporation and they would be to willingly pay.

When it came to paying taxes, He was able to extinguish His liability simply by having a fish pay the tax for Him! (Matthew 17:27)

He could heal the incurable diseases of His day with just a touch and no medical costs. (Luke 5:13)

When He wanted to travel into town, without so much as a phone call, He had a donkey waiting that He had never bred, never fed, never stabled, or ever trained, and He never had to worry about parking when He arrived at His destination! He received a voluntary "red carpet" reception. (Matthew 21:7)

If "knowledge is wealth," Jesus tops the list again as the intellectuals of His day marveled at His knowledge. (Luke 20:26; John 7: 14-15)

His Father owns the largest cattle ranch on the planet (Psalm 50:10), the whole Earth itself, and everything in it. (Psalm 24:1)

Jesus' house contains many mansions, and the road on the main street in His neighborhood is constructed with gold. (Rev: 21:21)

He was able to multiply assets exponentially! In the case of the feeding of the 5,000 men, if we conclude that one person would have eaten half a loaf of bread and one fish, then Jesus' "food fund" showed a capital growth rate of 50,000% per day (bread) and over 250,000% per day (fish)!

Jesus was a unique dresser, so much so that after His death, rather than cut up His coat and divide it four ways as a souvenir, the soldiers decided to draw straws for this trophy and keep this quality seamless garment as one piece. (John 19: 23-24)

His burial was that reserved for the very, very rich. In this case, the mega rich merchant Joseph, from the town of Arimathea, donated the tomb that Jesus was buried in. Jesus didn't even have to pay a dime for the tomb! (Matthew 27:60)

Jesus was beyond wealth, because you clearly can't give what you haven't got, and you can't lead from behind, so when Jesus' Father promised to give wealth, He could only do so if He first possessed wealth (Ecclesisatis 5:19). You would, therefore, not be surprised to discover that this same Jesus was able to teach His wealth techniques to the "apprentices" that followed Him and do the things that He did with His power, which He said we could also do – and even greater things! (Deuteronomy 8:18; John 14:12)

## Jesus was clearly beyond wealth!

### (and He is willing to teach it to us. Are you willing to learn it?)

The "Wealth" Poster can be downloaded and printed in any size for $7.95 CAD.

www.newstartministries.ca

# MONEY.

What God says about

There are over 2480 scriptures that refer to money or stewardship. The words "rich" or "riches" are in the Bible 186 times. "Money" is in the Bible 114 times. Jesus spoke more about money and stewardship than any other subject. The purpose of money is to build up the Kingdom of God (Deuteronomy 8:18) so that the great commission can be fulfilled. (The gospel is free – it just takes money to preach it.)

Jesus was born rich into royalty and said we were to be like Him. The Magi's gifts were worth $400 million in today's dollars.* Jesus owned a house (John 1:38-39), paid taxes (Matthew 17:24), was on the lecture circuit at age 12 (Luke 2:47), ran a business with his dad, had a treasurer, had a staff of 12 and later 72 (Luke 10:17), had people giving financial support to His ministry (Luke 8:2-3), wore designer clothes (John 19:23-24), and became poor once in His life for us on the cross (2 Corinthians 8:9). His first miracle was one of luxury in a setting of wealth (John 2: 1-8) and He had the skills to supply lunch for 5,000 men and their families (John 6:7).

Success is the ability to endure pain; wealth is the ability to obtain what is immediately required,* and prosperity is having enough provision to complete God's instructions.

Money may not bring happiness, but it brings more joy than poverty ever did! Tithing is not a method of getting money from you but a method of getting money to you.

Money is the answer to everything. (Ecclesiastes 10:19b)

Poverty is not a financial problem. It is a spiritual one - a curse (Deuteronomy 28: 1). Worldly wealth is all about financial accumulation for self. True prosperity is all about economic expansion for God, who wants you to use it for distribution to others.

Meditate on the Word, and you will be prosperous (Joshua 1:8).

The greatest tragedy of human existence is not knowing what you don't know. Now you know...

So what are you going to do about it?

The "Money" Poster is part of the Christian Manifesto Poster series. Produced in Calgary, Alberta, Canada, by New Start Ministries Ltd. These posters are available for sale from: www.newstartministries.ca COPYRIGHT 2022 (*Dr. Peter J. Daniels with permission).

The "Money" Poster can be downloaded and printed in any size for $7.95 CAD.

www.newstartministries.ca

# How to be RICH God's way

Tithe 10% of your gross income to your local church. It is not yours or yours to keep. Plant financial seeds into His Kingdom through alms to the poor (like missions) and firstfruits to your church and other ministries. Use cash (not credit or debit cards) as much as possible (when you see money slipping out of your fingers, you will think twice about spending it.) Pay credit card balances immediately when they are due.

Reduce your consumer spending. Learn how to be thrifty and economical in your shopping. Buy used as much as possible.

Pay down the mortgage on your house, which should have a basement suite or some rental income to it. Payments should be weekly, starting on Monday.

Get a retirement plan started when you are 18. Invest wisely in solid "blue-chip, dividend-paying stocks."

Establish an education fund for your children. When they reach college age, they buy a house with the education fund in their name. They get rent-paying roommates to pay the mortgage and pay their own tuition.

Buy term life insurance to care for your loved ones.

Save 10% of your gross income for emergencies. If there is something that you want to buy, learn to save for it by putting 20% of your money away to save for significant expenditures.

Get all the education that you can to get a good, well-paying job with excellent benefits and be a good employee.

Establish a trust fund for your grandchildren.

Start this plan when you are 18, and by retirement, you will be a millionaire.

The "Rich" Poster can be downloaded and printed in any size for $7.95 CAD.

www.newstartministries.ca

# Pray for the Church.

*"But you are a chosen people, a royal priesthood, a holy nation, God's special possession, that you may declare the praises of Him who called you out of darkness into His wonderful light."* (1 Peter 2:9)

We, the church - the Ekklesia - need to remember that we are chosen! God chose us before the earth was formed (Eph. 1:4); for what? To be His army. We are the ones that are to spiritually engage the enemy and stand firm concerning issues of justice, peace, honesty and righteousness. The church is to be the spiritual climate of a nation. We set the tone, not politicians (many with demonic agendas). This being the case, why is our society such a mess? Simply because we have not done our jobs.

However, as we repeatedly see in the Old Testament, God is a God of second chances. He is keen on us rising up, realizing our mistakes, repenting, and turning from our wicked ways (Act 3:19). It is vital that we, the church, are trained, educated in the ways of the Word and active. We are to take dominion against this world, bringing heaven into the earth (aka Thy Kingdom come...). When we work together, we become unstoppable. *"Again, truly I tell you that if two of you on earth agree about anything they ask for, it will be done for them by my Father in heaven. For where two or three gather in my name, there am I with them."* (Matt. 18:19)

**1.** Pray that the church would be one (Phil. 2:2) and live by faith (Rom. 1:16).
**2.** Ask God to remove double-mindedness so that the church does not waiver in prayer and does not compromise the Word (James 1: 6-8).
**3.** Remember, *"if my people, who are called by my name, will humble themselves and pray and seek my face and turn from their wicked ways, then I will hear from heaven, and I will forgive their sin and heal their land."* (2 Chron. 7:14)

*Life* is a test... Are you praying for the church and your church?

# What is Holy Spirit Doing in You?

**1.** He is rebuilding you. We don't fix our lives; we are powerless to do that. He does that in us if we allow Him to. We are all broken vessels that need repair so let Him do His work.

**2.** Holy Spirit is called *"the Spirit of truth"* (John 16:13), and knows how to bring us to maturity by teaching us. He speaks to us with His still, small voice, revealing mysteries and giving guidance. He also brings situations and circumstances to pass, like getting the right people to us at the right time.

**3.** When we allow Him to, He is helping us to subdue our flesh. Our willpower is just not enough. Look what Rom. 8:13 says; *"For if you live according to the flesh, you will die; but if by the Spirit you put to death the misdeeds of the body, you will live."* The spirit of God can put to death the bad stuff in us. Jesus defeated the power of sin once and for all. Rom. 6:6 says, *"For we know that our old self was crucified with him so that the body ruled by sin might be done away with, that we should no longer be slaves to sin."*

**4.** God does not anoint us once and then leave us hanging on a limb. He constantly renews us and sends out a fresh anointing whenever we ask Him. His favourite thing is to reveal His glory through us! Since Holy Spirit is in us, we are to be a mirror and be transformed into the same image from glory to glory. The result: We *"are being transformed into His image with ever-increasing glory, which comes from the Lord, who is the Spirit."* (2 Cor. 3:18)

*Life* is a test... Is Holy Spirit in you so that you can be rebuilt and renewed?

*Life is a test...*

## The Abundant life.

The new is now because we are living in a new era. The start of every month is a time called Rosh Chodesh, where if we pray and seek God, He will give us prophetic Words of guidance and direction for the rest of the month. Then if we step daily into that new era, we can walk in the fullness of God's blessings!

"New" can be something that has never been before or a better quality of what you have been developing, accomplishing and embracing.

It is also the end of a month (in the Roman calendar) so ask these questions:

**1.** What is the greatest desire stirring in you?
**2.** What do you want to take with you into the next season and what do you want to leave behind?
**3.** How has your life improved in the last 30 days? If it hasn't, why not? Then ask yourself what you'll do about it so that it doesn't repeat itself.
**4.** What will you be watching?
**5.** What will you be occupying your time and your mind with?
**6.** How will provision be coming so you secure your future and so that you can be a blessing to others?

If you are not growing, you are not living; if you are not living, you are slowly dying. Jesus came to give us an abundant life, so what changes are you making to ensure that the next month is better than the one you are leaving?

Grab ahold of life and live it to the fullest!

*Life* is a test... Are you living or slowly dying?

**www.newstartministries.ca**

*L*ife *is a test...*

# "A Still Tongue Makes a Wise Head."

This is an expression that my dad used to use. I recall another one too that goes something like this, "better to keep your mouth shut and people to think that you are a fool than for you to open it and confirm their thoughts."

We tend to unload our problems on others. Why? It comforts our flesh. Next thing you know, they are giving us advice. The problem is that well-meaning people can give advice - even good advice - that does not reflect God's will. It seems that so often in life that His wisdom and will are the opposite of what we are thinking (and the people giving us "advice") and what we want to do. Additionally, this is how gossip and rumours start, by you telling other people your troubles.

We need to remember that God is the Spirit of truth. He said that He would lead and guide us into what we needed. So, what part of this are we not getting? Why do we go to others to "unload" when God is there to lead us? Always remember that He is there 24/7, speak to Him. A still tongue does make a wise head sometimes when dealing with others.

*"Be and know that I am God."* (Ps. 46:10 NKJV)

*"The Lord will fight for you, and you shall hold your peace."* (Ex. 14:14 NKJV)

*"A fool vents all his feelings, But a wise man holds them back."* (Prov. 29:11 NKJV)

*L*ife is a test... Do you stop and think about what you're going to say before you say it?

# You Are An Altar.

*"Then come, let us go up to Bethel, where I will build an altar to God, who answered me in the day of my distress and who has been with me wherever I have gone." (Gen. 35:3)*

**Let's start with the basics again:**
**1.** You were created before the world (Ep. 1:4).
**2.** You were born into sin (Ps. 51:5).
**3.** Jesus said you must be born again to be part of His Kingdom (John 3:3, 16; Rom. 10:9).
**4.** Jesus said, "receive the Holy Spirit" (John 20:22; Acts 1:8).

Let's assume that you have completed all these points. What are you now? A Holy temple of God. You are the house of God! You are an altar of devotion. You are becoming (working through your salvation Phil 2:12) a reflection of Jesus.

Just as water can be purified by being forced through a filter, we can do the same with our thoughts. Every morning surrender the junk in your head that you accumulated yesterday - fear, worry, hurts etc. - to the holiness of Holy Spirit who resides in you. Being constantly aware of God's presence and grace in our lives keeps us out of sin and submissive to Him and opens the door to blessing. The bonus is that others can see His grace in us.

Without realizing it, you can become a living witness and testimony of God's grace. We are tested in life to have a testimony. You can't have one without the other! People will take note of your countenance and how you handle opposition and see the joy and peace that you release to others (as opposed to strife). Let your light shine!

*Life* is a test... How is your witness going?

## "Where there is no vision, the people perish: but he that keepeth the law, happy is he." (Prov. 29:18 KJV)

*"Then the Lord answered me and said: "Write the vision And make it plain on tablets, That he may run who reads it." (Hab. 2:2)*

Without vision, we have no passion. Without passion, we live a boring life that accomplishes nothing. God put us here to live a life of accomplishing His will; to take dominion over the world and make disciples of all men. Passion is what drives us, so get lots of it! We need to stay relevant and keep our eyes on the high calling in Christ (Phil 3:14).

Our world teaches us to "think out of the box." Why? We were not born into one! No, think like Jesus. He knows us as He created us and knows all the answers before we have even figured out the questions! Think like the world? Seriously? They haven't got a clue what will happen, but we do; just read Matt. 24: 3-14. Think out of the box? Not on your life! Just think like Jesus. Simply put, we must guard our hearts and not let the world pollute our minds with it's garbage.

*"Keep thy heart with all diligence; for out of it are the issues of life." (Prov. 4:23 KJV)*

*"Be careful for nothing; but in every thing by prayer and supplication with thanksgiving let your requests be made known unto God. And the peace of God, which passeth all understanding, shall keep your hearts and minds through Christ Jesus." (Phil. 4:6-7)*

*Life* is a test... Are you guarding your heart?

# What is a Disciple?

Jesus had 12 of them, and the term "disciple" isn't used again following the gospels. We don't seem to use it in our modern vernacular, so we ought to ask, what is a disciple? According to the Canadian Oxford dictionary, a disciple is *"a follower or pupil of a leader, teacher, philosophy, etc. 2. a professed Christian."*

Well then, we need to become disciples - a learner of God's ways. Becoming a Christian is not a one-time event. Firstly, we are to *"work out our salvation"* (Phil. 2:12). Secondly, we are to be renewed on the Word daily (Eph. 4:23). Thirdly, we can't live without faith (Rom. 1:17b) nor can we please God without faith (Heb. 11:6) and we get confidence by hearing the Word (Rom. 10:17). Finally, we are to be *"learned ones"* meditating on this Word, day and night (Jos.1:8).

I have been studying the Bible for 40+ years, and I have many scriptures in my head (I must, too, be able to write these books!) However, what amazes me about the Scriptures is that the more you read, the more revelation that comes, and the more you learn and grow. Honestly, there are days when I feel that I have not even scratched the surface of the Bible!

The happiness that society seeks so fervently is not found in our circumstances. It is discovered when we unearth the richness of the Word. Peace and contentment are found not in things and pleasures but with the intimacy of His Word. Sit with Him daily, and He will become the treasure the world seeks. Then you will find joy unspeakable, peace unsurpassable and love inseparable.

*Life* is a test... Are you becoming a disciple of Jesus?

# Wrecked for God. (Part 1 of 6)

It is August 15/22 today, and I'm sitting outside at the picnic table on my deck. It has been a hot summer, but today it's a bit cooler. Generally, I write on my computer, but sometimes I sit with a pad and pen and just write what Holy Spirit puts into my spirit. I'm going to start a series called "Wrecked for God." I don't know what this will be about or how long it will take. I know that Holy Spirit has "stuff" stirring in me, and I need to "get it out." So tighten your seatbelt, hang onto your hat and let's see where Holy Spirit will go. With the title "wrecked," who knows, it might hurt!

Mother Theresa was the Roman Catholic nun famous for compassionately ministering in India to the poorest of the poor in the slums of Calcutta. When asked why she did what she did, she responded that she saw Jesus in every person she ministered to. Not only did she serve them, but she dignified every person she saw. She knew that by serving others, she was serving Jesus.

*"For I was hungry and you gave me something to eat, I was thirsty and you gave me something to drink, I was a stranger and you invited me in, I needed clothes and you clothed me, I was sick and you looked after me, I was in prison and you came to visit me.'*
*Then the righteous will answer him, 'Lord, when did we see you hungry and feed you, or thirsty and give you something to drink? When did we see you a stranger and invite you in, or needing clothes and clothe you? When did we see you sick or in prison and go to visit you?'*
*"The King will reply, 'Truly I tell you, whatever you did for one of the least of these brothers and sisters of mine, you did for me."* (Matt. 25:35-40)

*Life* is a test... What does this Scripture stir in you?

*Life* **is a test...**

## Wrecked for God. (Part 2 of 6)

Yesterday's writing begs the question. How do you (me) react when:
**1)** The checkout line moves slower than usual because the cashier is "in training?"
**2)** The employee at the drive-through forgets to put Ketchup packs with your order of French fries?
**3)** You realize that you're thinking the person driving 20 km/h slower than the speed limit is "an idiot" and the guy driving 20 km over the speed limit is "a maniac"? (of course, you're never a maniac when you're speeding because you never speed. Right...)
**4)** Someone takes "your" parking spot at church and then sits in "your" pew? You get the point...

Some related quotes I have collected:
*"The insignificance of daily life are the tests of humility, as they prove what is the spirit that possesses us (i.e., don't sweat the small stuff; and it's all small stuff)."*
*"The humble man feels no jealousy or envy."*
*"Being occupied with self can never free us from self as the deeper we sink in humility before Him, the nearer He is to fulfill every desire of your faith."*
*"Look upon every man who tries or vexes you as a means of grace to humble you."*

Do we live by contempt or compassion? With love and patience or irritation and frustration?

Holy Spirit wants to re-order our thinking. He wants to challenge us to view every person we meet respectfully regardless of our judge mentalism and contempt. Yes, even Christians fall into the "holier than thou" attitude of dispensing judgement and criticism. Jesus called us to see every person as a beautiful thing, made in the image of God. Why? Because that is what 8 billion other people are.

*Life* is a test... We are all guilty of judge mentalism. What are you doing about yours?

*L*ife *is a test...*

## Wrecked for God. (Part 3 of 6)

Let's refer back to the true definition of love: *"Love is patient, love is kind. It does not envy; it does not boast; it is not proud. It does not dishonour others, it is not self-seeking, it is not easily angered, it keeps no record of wrongs. Love does not delight in evil but rejoices with the truth. It always protects, always trusts, always hopes, always perseveres."* (1 Cor. 13: 4-7)

*"A new command I give you: Love one another. As I have loved you, so you must love one another."* (John 13:34 NIV)

Jesus, in this passage, is telling us to be radical. Exercise patience, kindness - the works - to the people that don't like us, the homeless, our annoying workmates, strifeful family members, the incompetent staff, the crooked media and politicians and the guy who cuts us off in traffic. Right... The Passion translation says it best in Luke chapter 6:

*"Are you really showing true love by loving only those who love you? Even those who don't know God will do that. Are you really showing compassion when you do good deeds only to those who do good deeds to you? Even those who don't know God will do that."* (ver. 32-33)

*"Rather love your enemies and continue to treat them well. When you lend money, don't despair if you are never paid back, for it is not lost. You will receive a rich reward and you will be known as true children of the Most High God, having his same nature. Be like your Father who is famous for his kindness to heal even the thankless and cruel. Overflow with mercy and compassion for others, just as your heavenly Father overflows with mercy and compassion for all." Jesus said, "Forsake the habit of criticizing and judging others, and you will not be criticized and judged in return. Don't condemn others and you will not be condemned. Forgive over and over, and you will be forgiven over and over."* (ver. 35-37 TPT)

*L*ife is a test... Are you walking in love?

## Wrecked for God. (Part 4 of 6)

The problem with our judge mentalism is that God does not use it the same way we use it. We are always looking at the outward appearance of a person - the flaws, weaknesses and even strengths. However, Jesus does not look at us that way at all. He is looking at the inside of us - what's in our hearts. He sees whether your heart is plugged into Him, and if so, it moves His heart.

You see, God the Father, God the Son and God Holy Spirit all love us very much, more than we can even fathom, and they are always looking at what is in our hearts. If you know what's in there, and something doesn't glorify Him, give it over to Him. It's from a place where we are fully understood and transparent with God that we can receive more of His fullness, including the best He has for us. Being "wrecked for Jesus" is a symptom of surrender.

*"Let us draw near to God with a sincere heart and with the full assurance that faith brings, having our hearts sprinkled to cleanse us from a guilty conscience and having our bodies washed with pure water."* (Heb. 10:22)

*"And so we know and rely on the love God has for us. God is love. Whoever lives in love lives in God, and God in them."* (1 John 4:16)

**Doc's Book Club:** Do you really want to get "wrecked?" Read any books or listen to any CD's by Graham Cooke. www.brilliantperspectives.com

*Life* is a test... Does your current heart posture allow you to be wrecked for Him?

## Wrecked for God. (Part 5 of 6)

We are wrecked. Now what? Let the Word seep deep into your heart (meditate on the Word - Jos. 1:8). The seed of compassion of Jesus' love will take root in due time and birth the nine Fruits of the Spirit. Only by being connected with Him can this happen. Before long, "in the flesh" is just impossible. Learn to see others through the eyes of love, mercy and compassion instead of through our eyes of judgment, mentalism and criticism.

Here is a tip for you that I have been using for years. My goal every day is to make at least one person either smile or, better yet, laugh. I tease, I thank, I compliment, crack a joke - whatever it takes to get the response I am looking for. Here is another tip. Put yourself in the place of the people that you see. Be thankful for the person at the fast-food restaurant who is getting minimum wage for pouring you a "double-double" coffee. Praise God for the people who clean your hotel room, dry your clothes, wash your dirty restaurant dishes, etc. Be thankful for cashiers, retail clerks, receptionists, policemen, truck drivers, medical staff, and yes, even politicians, and lawyers! (in my next book I'll give you some of my favourite lawyer jokes!)

Dare you try this? Ask Jesus, who lives inside of you, to help you see and love others, just as He does. Look past their mistakes, ethnic background, weight, gender, job, education and social status or lack thereof, and just let Jesus "do a number on you." Let's face it, He made every one of us, so who are we to criticize His craftsmanship? Does this mean that we accept their sin? No, we accept them as broken vessels in need of Jesus.

*"Love your neighbour as yourself."* (Rom. 13:9b)

*Life* is a test... What can you do today to bring a smile to some one's face?

# Wrecked for God. (Part 6 of 6)

We are wrecked. Now what? Start celebrating who Jesus is all the things He has done for you, all He has made you be, and the fact that you're alive and breathing now. Not easy, I know, but that is where the discipline comes in, and it is called "living by faith." We can choose to rest and rejoice in Him (Matt. 11:28). We can believe what our hearts say and confess with our mouths that Jesus is Lord (Rom. 10:9) It's there He can take residence, living and reigning in our lives regardless of the situations and circumstances that we face.

The bottom line is that we do need to believe this! The problem in our world is that it tells us that we must seek significance. People want to go to the world and "find themselves." Why? Are they lost? Well, yes, they are! They have not found Jesus, who is the only one that has ever said, *"I am the way, the truth, and the life."* (John 14:6). He is right there to help us as we go to search for significance in all kinds of religions, cults, New Age, fitness, and body beautiful, the lust for money, yet nothing fills that emptiness in our lives... except Jesus. This has become so complex and entrenched in our society that "Who am I and why am I here" has become its religion! An idol unto itself. This is what fuels so much of our social media. Some people must take pictures of themselves and their various activities and post them for friends to see to feel significant. Really? What is the root of that? Insecurity, fear, the need to be loved, the list goes on. Nothing, experience, or asset can solve any of that, for it is all vanity. Only Jesus is the answer, not religion or lust.

*"And I saw that all toil and all achievement spring from one person's envy of another. This too is meaningless, a chasing after the wind."* Ecc. 4:4 (also read Ecc. 5:10 and 5: 18-20)

*ife* is a test... Are you wrecked for Jesus? Have you kicked the Spirit of Religion out of your life?

*Life* is a test...

## Do You Practice What You Preach?

I don't think there's any concept that can put a pastor or teacher under a table more than this one. Sometimes the struggle can be so intense that pastors don't want to stand behind the pulpit. I, like many people, have the same problem. When you're writing non-fiction work intended to be educational, you often feel like the world's worst hypocrite for telling people to do things that you struggle to do yourself. I read this devotional every day, because I have to work at this stuff just as much as you do! Some pastors and public speakers go through painful depression after speaking, even when their presentation is good!

How do we fix this? We need to utilize and express a great deal of humility and grace upon ourselves. Before our presentation, we need to enter into some pretty solid prayer and ask for all of Him and none of us. Then listen in the Spirit and let Him lead you. Another thing that I do is recognize an old expression that says "the best way to learn something is to teach it to someone else." You, the readers, are my students, but I am the student of Holy Spirit who has been completely instrumental in writing this project. I cannot begin to tell you how much I have learned! Hopefully, you have too!

Yes, you should practice what you preach, but the next time you don't, forgive yourself and don't beat yourself up; you're not perfect. Besides, if you were, you wouldn't have anything to work on when you get out of bed tomorrow!

*Life* is a test... What are you "preaching" and not doing yourself? Be kind to yourself.

# Find Balance.

Life has its ups and downs. Disappointments come and go, as do blessings. Either one of these situations can distract us from spending time with God.

Disappointments leave us focused on ourselves, and our pain; we pour our heart out onto other people etc. It puts distance between Jesus and us. The same happens when life is a bowl of cherries, and the blessings are poured out; we tend to forget about God. We must remember that nothing separates us from His love, but these disappointments and blessing distractions can crush our awareness of His presence and love. All our emotions, whether healthy or unhealthy, can cause us to drift away from the one who is with us, in us and loves us more than anything. We're back to constant contact again…

Busyness is OK since we are all called to work. (2 Thess. 3:10; 1 Tim. 5:8) and we are all called to minister to others. However, satan will use busyness, even ministry, to get us off track. We can feel so self-righteous about working incredible hours "serving God" that we forget that we are not respecting the Sabbath and not spending enough time with Him because we are "too busy." Worse yet, we come up with these brilliant ideas and then rush off to do them in our impatience, perhaps remembering to pray to God with "please bless my plans." What to do?

Delight yourself in Him, and He will delight Himself in you. Keep God entirely in the centre of your heart and your plans; He will guide you through every area of your soul.

*Life* is a test… Remember to reflect on Him in the good times and the bad.

# What to do When You Are Attacked.

When your enemies (especially your family!) choose to attack you with criticism and judgement in areas of your life that you are struggling with and are still "working out your salvation," refuse to receive it. The most significant burden that people (both saved and unsaved) are burdened with in our culture today are shame, guilt and condemnation. It is hard to deal with these issues because "good intending" family and friends can point out our faults and mistakes. Of course, satan and his minions get there "like a dirty shirt" to exasperate the situation and pour salt into your emotional wounds. That's their job and they are good at what they does.

However, don't accept it! Remember that God sees us as complete in Christ, accepted, and we are His beloved. Besides, what do other people know? God knows you better than you do, so why listen to others? Look at this from God's perspective. He sees us through the eyes of love as growing in grace. We are and will be transformed through the revelation of God's love and grace, not by man's criticism. What to do? As always, focus on Jesus. Forget about what others say.

*"...and you are complete in Him, who is the head of all principality and power." (Col. 2:10)*

*"There is therefore now no condemnation to those who are in Christ Jesus, who do not walk according to the flesh, but according to the Spirit." (Rom. 8:1)*

*ife* is a test... We are His beloved. Do you let others take that away from you?

## I Will Never Leave You or Forsake You. (Heb.13:5)

Too many people in this world live a very lonely life. What we need to understand is what the bottom line is. When you come into your relationship with Jesus, very simply, you're in a relationship with Him! We are *"labourers together with God."* (1 Cor. 3:9)

He very clearly said that He would never leave us or forsake us. We, together with Him, are battling to establish His will on earth. He will always lead us to the best possible pathway we should take, even if that means a long journey through the wilderness. Jesus walked one; for 40 days without food and then went through the test of His life!

These desert walks and dry times in life (yes, we will have many of them) often include spiritual warfare. Remember that satan is on your case, looking for an opportunity to exploit a situation in your life every chance he gets since he walks around like a roaring lion (1 Peter 5:8). Jesus may even be silent for a while so that you can't even feel His presence (but He is still there…) However, the simple fact and reality is that He is 100% committed to you. He is dedicated to seeing His will activated in your life. What is His will? He wants nothing but the best for you.

We are in this thing called "life" together with Him. Therefore, never think anything beyond that. Jesus is not going anywhere; He is here for us 24/7! We might as well have His Word and Him; why not? The truth is that HE IS THE TRUTH! (John 14:6) He made you, loves you, will lead and guide you, answer all your questions, and never leave you. What's not to like? Why would anyone not want Him? "Ask, and it will be given to you; seek, and you will find; knock, and it will be opened to you." (Matt 7:7)

**Doc's Book Club:** Read **"God, Where Are You?!: Finding Strength and Purpose in Your Wilderness"** by John Bevere.

*Life* is a test... Do you ever been in a wilderness?

## The Month of Tevet (Dec/Jan - Part 1 of 2)

**Alphabet:** Letter is "AYIN" (means eye); Let your good eye see. War with the evil eye of others and break the power of evil watchers.

**Tribe:** Dan; to judge, grow up and mature.

**Characteristics:** - a month of holy anger or righteous indignation; be angry at sin.
- This month is the time to pray for your commander-in-chief.
- Review education for initiation into the next phase of life.
- This month is a good time to fast and purify the blood, so your brain and heart function properly.

**Constellation:** Capricorn (the goat) - be aware of making wrong alignments.

**Colour/Stone:** Dark Blue or Turquoise/Sapphire

**Scripture:** Eph. 4:26 to 27

Tevet is associated with the constellation of Capricorn, which pictures a goat. This is a dangerous time because you will see nations that are not allies of the covenant, the goat nations, take a wrong turn. This is a month to leap forth and review your education for initiation into the next phase of life.

Dan was the fifth son of Jacob. The word Dan means to rule, judge, and execute judgement. Unfortunately, Dan went into idolatry and perversion. Dan failed to achieve his destiny and was not restored from revelation like the other tribes. Samson and Esther were both called by God to save Israel. Both were tempted away from their call but, in the end, succeeded, although Esther died with success and Sampson died in failure. Sampson lived to satisfy his passions, and he did not honour his call to God. During the time of the judges, the tribe of Dan went back and forth between sin and then not sinning and then back again. They had this cycle seven times, and his downfall was when he was attracted to Philistine women. He was gifted by God but did not have a heart for God. No praying, no worship, but rather rash, self-seeking, and controlled by lust. Spiritual Gifts will still work even if you're not following God. The danger is that you don't seek the Lord.

## The Month of Tevet (Dec/Jan - Part 2 of 2)

### What went wrong for Dan?

- They would not stay in their land because they would not take the land of the Philistines as they were told to.
- They never got what God had for them.
- They made the city of Dan and worshiped idols.
- In 722 BC, the Assyrians carried them into captivity; it is a month to learn from Dan's mistakes.
- Emotions controlled Dan. This month make sure your emotions are submitted to God. Obey; don't be controlled by feelings.
- Don't give into Jezebel; instead, get into a position to receive power from God.
- It's a month to give your life totally to the Lord.
- Reject idolatry!
- Seek God with all your heart! Jer. 29:12 *"you will seek me, and you will find me when you seek him with all your heart."*
- Pay attention to the prophetic Words over your life this month, so you do not miss your destiny.
- Be willing to war when God calls you to war and stand for your inheritance; don't back down.

### Which path are you on in Tevet?

(see Eph. 1:11, Eph. 2:10, Jer. 1:5, Jer. 29:11)
- This does not mean there is no struggle. God is working through all things. If you seek Him, all things will work together (Rom. 8:28).
- This is the month to look at your life and ensure you're on track for your destiny.
- Some people do not get there! They miss their destiny as Dan did!
- The month that you are to see clearly.
- A time to seek God with all your heart.
- Do not be controlled by fear but instead live by faith.
- Learn the lessons from Dan!

*Life* is a test...Are you missing your God-given destiny? It's never too late!

# The Old Covenant and the New Covenant. (Part 1 of 2)

Aren't you glad that you don't live in the days of the Old Testament? Before Jesus came to the earth, God required many different sacrifices to do with blood from His people. Why blood? This miraculous fluid that runs through our bodies is the basic foundation of our operation. It is the river of life that the entire body feels; if it fails, it dies. God decreed that blood was sacred and not to be consumed as it is life itself. (Deut. 12:33).

In the Old Testament, butchering animals, splitting their carcasses in half, pouring blood on an altar etc., was how sin was washed out of mankind. Using an animal as a "scapegoat," the blood of the dead animals atoned for the people's sins. Atone or atonement means to make amends. God wants blood, the "river of life," to be shed to make amends for sin.

Thank goodness that Jesus came onto the scene! He went to the cross of His free will and became the Passover lamb. His shed blood replaces the butchered goats and sheep. Aren't you glad? Then Jesus asked us to sacrifice our whole hearts to Him. He sacrificed His life for us; now, we surrender our lives to Him.

In the Old Testament, there were strict protocols for approaching God. Only the priests were allowed to enter the Holy of Holies in the temple, and they only did that once a year on the Day of Atonement.

When Jesus died on the cross, a critical happened: He said, *"it is finished."* (John 19:30). What did he mean by that? Among many things, one was that animal sacrifices were no longer needed. Phew...

## The Old Covenant and the New
## Covenant. (Part 2 of 2)

That meant the blockage to the "Holy of Hollies," the blockage to God Himself, was over. As a symbol of this, the curtain in the temple that separated the Holy of Holies suddenly ripped in half when Jesus died (Matt. 27:51). Now, there was no curtain blocking the people from the very presence of God.

Today, Jesus invites you to come boldly to His throne of grace to receive His mercy, His life inside you. This happens when we confess our sins and repent of them, and then He is faithful and forgives us of our sins and remembers them no more (1 John 1:9). We ask Him into our hearts, and we are born again (John 3:3). Next, He sends Holy Spirit (John 16:7 - although we do need to ask) as a comforter to lead and guide us through the challenges and storms of life. Now we are in a position where no special preparation (butchering of animals) is needed to approach God. Jesus's blood has washed us clean, so we now are in a place to come to God. How? Just stop, focus on the Name of Jesus, praise and worship for a few seconds and guess what? He's there! (Actually, He's there all the time. It's just that you're now connected with Him).

**The Old Covenant** - animal sacrifices, blood, obedience, preparation, sometimes fear, atonement, (making amends) once a year on the Day of Atonement.

**The New Covenant -** Jesus has done it all at the cross! All we need to do is confess, repent and receive. It is simple and "finished," as Jesus said it was on the cross.

Worship Him in truth and sincerity of love. We praise and worship, and He shows up which is all we need to go deeper into our relationship with Jesus.

*Life* is a test... Read Hebrews chapters 8-10 for an in-depth study of this!

## Take the Narrow Road!

Following yesterday's theme, it's a very challenging and changing world we live in, and things are happening quickly. This requires a mind of flexibility and adaptability in our natural world. Still, it also puts us in a position where we need to be more sensitive to His leading and be ready to make changes to ensure we are where we need to be.

*"But small is the gate and narrow the road that leads to life, and only a few find it."* (Matt. 7:14) Who are the ones that find it? The ones that show up! If you were standing at a fork in the road and one was wide, where most of the people were going down, and the other was narrow, which was God's path, would you see that narrow path and walk down it? Yes, you would if you were smart, but you'll never get to that fork in the road if you don't show up! How do you do that? You become born-again, start seeking God and start looking for answers!

It is obedience that is the key to walking with Him. Rom. 6:16 says, *"Don't you know that when you offer yourselves to someone as obedient slaves, you are slaves of the one you obey - whether you are slaves to sin, which leads to death, or to obedience, which leads to righteousness?"* Yes, it is OK to be a slave to Jesus, and then look for His path and that fork in the road of life and then, choose the narrow one. *"...choose for yourselves this day whom you will serve..."* (Jos. 24:15)

*Life* is a test... Did you choose today? Which path?

# Perception or Discernment? (Part 1 of 2)

When I was a child, I realized that I was developing the skill of perception. I was exceptionally good at observation. I could walk into a room, perhaps a hotel lobby, and notice everything! As I grew, "I decided" (my first mistake) that this was a gift from God. I have since learned that "perception" is not a gift, but discernment is. What is the difference?

Perception comes from your flesh; discernment comes from Holy Spirit through your spirit. It is one of the 30 Spiritual Gifts. In short, perception is not reality. What we perceive about other people is not always accurate, and what they perceive about us is often inaccurate. Therefore, stop depending on your five senses, including what others tell you (gossip?), to form a conclusion. Nine times out of ten, you will be wrong. Wrong perceptions lead to presumption, and presumption ruins relationships. Truthfully, perceptions are a trap by satan to mess with your head. Turn those thoughts over to God and leave them alone.

*"Judge not, that you be not judged. For with what judgment you judge, you will be judged; and with the measure you use, it will be measured back to you. And why do you look at the speck in your brother's eye, but do not consider the plank in your own eye? Or how can you say to your brother, 'Let me remove the speck from your eye', and look, a plank is in your own eye? Hypocrite! First, remove the plank from your own eye, and then you will see clearly to remove the speck from your brother's eye."* (Matt. 7:1-5 NKJV)

*"Stop judging by mere appearances, but instead judge correctly."* (John 7:24)

*Life* is a test... Are you the judge and jury of others?

# Perception or Discernment? (Part 2 of 2)

What then is discernment? The dictionary meaning is to *"sense something by intellect."* True, but our own discernment as Christians is supernatural. Like all Spiritual Gifts when discernment is active in you, it is supernatural; you become like Superman! Strength in the Gift that you are operating in comes from God.

The Gift of Discernment is referred to in the Bible as the "discerning of spirits." Notice that it is plural which means bad spirits and good ones. Too many Christians have used this gift for detecting demons and the motives of people they believe are wrong. All Spiritual Gifts must be used correctly. People who operate in this one tend to give too much credence to the enemy instead of God. Spiritual Gifts operate from love, not judge mentalism or flesh power.

By definition - *"The Gift of Discerning of Spirits is the exceptional power that God gives to Christians to know whether certain behaviour purported to be of God is in reality divine, human or satanic."* (Matt. 16:21-23; Acts 5:1-11; Acts 16:16-18; 1 Cor. 12:10; 1 John 4:1-6)"*

*"And this is my prayer: that your love may abound more and more in knowledge and depth of insight so that you may be able to **discern** what is best and may be pure and blameless for the day of Christ."* (Phil. 1:9-10) *"...to another the working of miracles, to another prophecy, to another **discerning** of spirits, to another different kinds of tongues, to another the interpretation of tongues."* (1 Cor. 12:10)

*Life* is a test... If you have this gift, are you operating it correctly and out of love?

\* Quoted from the Spiritual Gifts Poster available on my website.

*Life is a test...*

# What is God doing???

**He is rebuilding us.** We are under construction - a work in progress - and He has strategically placed roadblocks - tests - in areas of our lives. Why? To help us to grow stronger in faith and His Word. We don't fix our lives; we are powerless to do that. Just chill and let Him do it!

**He is teaching us.** *"But the Advocate, the Holy Spirit, whom the Father will send in my name, will teach you all things and remind you of everything I have said to you."* (John 14:26) He allows us to hear His still, small voice and reveals His mysteries so we can know Him intimately. He will bring teachers, encouragers, and prophets into our lives who will guide us as needed.

**He is renewing us.** He does not anoint us once and then put us on a shelf. Holy Spirit sends fresh anointing when we are tired and or discouraged. *"Come unto me, all ye that labour and are heavily laden, and I will give you rest."* (Matt. 11:28 KJV). *"He saved us through the washing of rebirth and renewal by the Holy Spirit."* (Titus 3:5)

**He is subduing our flesh.** Willpower does not work! Rom. 8:13 says, *"For if you live according to the flesh, you will die; but if by the Spirit you put to death the misdeeds of the body, you will live."* Holy Spirit destroys the enemy in our lives. In the face of temptation, we can feel weak, but we must remember that He has defeated the power of sin once and for all on the cross. We must yield to His work in us.

**He is revealing His glory in and through us.** *"And we all, who with unveiled faces contemplate the Lord's glory, are being transformed into his image with ever-increasing glory, which comes from the Lord, who is the Spirit."* (2 Cor. 3:18). Fix your eyes on Jesus, and not on your mistakes. When you focus on yourself, you will be disappointed. When you focus on Him, you will be changed into His image.

**He is refining us**. Holy Spirit is a fire, and He wants to burn up anything that does not resemble Christ. Remember the dross? I wrote about it on May 30th. Don't be afraid when the Spirit turns up the heat. *"Consider it pure joy, my brothers and sisters, whenever you face trials of many kinds, because you know that the testing of your faith produces perseverance. Let perseverance finish its work so that you may be mature and complete, not lacking anything."* (James 1:2-4) God uses our problems for His miracles.

*Life* is a test... What is He working in you right now?

## Problems, Problems and More Problems.

It is called "life" - get used to it. If we didn't have problems we would be bored. Problems get us out of bed in the morning and give us purpose, meaning and fulfillment. Problems also teach us to trust Him; it is just a matter of perspective. Call them "challenges to overcome" and God made us overcomers! (1 John 4:4) Firstly, turn every "challenge" over to Him. *"Casting all your care upon Him, for He cares for you."* (1 Peter 5:7) When you cast your cares you will step into a new level of freedom that you've never experienced before. It is not our job to mentally assess every situation and try to be a "fixer." No amount of worry will change anything. *"Therefore I tell you, do not worry about your life, what you will eat or drink; or about your body, what you will wear. Is not life more than food, and the body more than clothes? Look at the birds of the air; they do not sow or reap or store away in barns, and yet your heavenly Father feeds them. Are you not much more valuable than they? Can any one of you by worrying add a single hour to your life?"* (Matt. 6:25-27) We can move forward with solutions with the guidance of Holy Spirit *"Faith without works is dead"* (James 2:17) so God calls us to move since we are conduit pipes of Holy Spirit, but only as He leads.

The problem in society is that we think and analyze too much. Sometimes God is working on others or other situations and circumstances that need to come to pass. Sometimes He's waiting for us to grow in certain areas. We will never stumble upon the answers to problems by racking our brains out, holding onto them with worry and fear. None of these problems are ours alone. "The team" - Father, Son and Holy Spirit are with us always. We must release "the stuff" to them, step back, quiet ourselves, worship and listen. We must believe that He loves us and wants to bless us and give us the answers. That wisdom comes from peace; (James 3:17) and it passes all understanding (Phil 4:7).

*life* is a test... Are you a problem-seeker or a problem-solver?

## You are Here for a Time Like This!

*"Before I formed you in the womb I knew you; before you were born I sanctified you; I ordained you a prophet to the nations."* (Jer. 1:5)

*"But you are a chosen generation, a royal priesthood, a holy nation, His own special people, that you may proclaim the praises of Him who called you out of darkness into His marvelous light."* (1 Peter 2:9)

Our core identity is "chosen in Christ"! We are spirit first, eternal, and our souls are conformed to His image. As we seek first the Kingdom - His will - it causes everything to then fall into place. His vision for our lives becomes our vision.

Everyone has been chosen for the here and now or is to be born. We are a chosen generation, fashioned by God for HIS pleasure, a royal priesthood whose sole purpose is to love others and serve the Kingdom in this hour. We are to help people, feed them, clothe them, educate them in the things of God, stand up to tyranny - the list goes on. The world is not dull and it will get more interesting as we enter the end times. We are seeing Matthew 24 come to pass right before our very eyes. We are seeing Ezekiel 38 come to pass as well. This generation has been chosen for this notable season of history, handpicked by God! Think about it; you are alive today - living where you are - because God handpicked you to be here right now. You are a part of the glorious harvest that's about to take place before Jesus comes back.

When we know that we are chosen, we will understand the reason for our existence and the dynamics of our call. Holy Spirit will take the blinders off our eyes, and we will see His will and His mission in life that He has for us. Then everything will flow in the right direction.

*Life* is a test... Why do you think God specifically chose you to be alive today?

# A Good Day to Pray.

Every day, whether we are with our families or not, whether we are celebrating holidays or not, whether gifts are being exchanged or not… God is on the throne. Whether today is your favourite day of the year, or you may fall more under my beliefs for today, * it is a special day because God made it and wants to be closer to you.

Today is a good day to talk about family. Whether you're surrounded by them today, on your own, or somewhere in between, God wants to be involved with you and your family. As a loving Father does not give snakes to those who ask for bread (Matt. 7:9-11), so He will not move away from you if you ask Him to be close today.

Remember today if you are with family, many are without… pray for those people. Remember today that many are in destructive families… pray for those people too. Remember those in the world that do not have the five basic necessities of life… pray for those people. Remember those who have suffered hardships and pain in the past over the holiday season, and then this year, they'll be reminded of it… pray for them too.

We must remember to lift our brothers and sisters up today! I pray on this day, for it's on these days that the roots of the enemy can grow deep. I would invite you all in between festivities today to do as Paul told the Thessalonians - *"pray without ceasing."* (1 Thess. 5:16)

Enjoy today, whether you are celebrating or not!

*Life* is a test... Have you ever tried to "pray without ceasing" for a day? Try it!

*I have expressed my views about Christmas and Easter etc., so I won't repeat myself. I want you to know that my editor, Graeme Henderson, wrote today's devotional. Thanks "Ed!" Great job! Merry Christmas to you.

# Hope (Part 1 of 4)

Jer. 29:11 says, *"For I know the plans I have for you,"* declares the Lord, *"plans to prosper you and not to harm you, plans to give you hope and a future."*

God put you here with a specific job to do and the Gifts to it. He then gives you the vision and sends you out! You have a God-ordained destiny that is unique to you, and no one else can achieve it but you. This journey, called life, is about God's hope in you. Jesus is presented in the Bible as our "blessed hope" in Titus 2:13. *"while we wait for the blessed hope - the appearing of the glory of our great God and Savior, Jesus Christ."*

Paul said In Rom. 5:2, *"through whom we have gained access by faith into this grace in which we now stand. And we boast in the hope of the glory of God."* Hope overcomes despair and discouragement because it generates excitement and enthusiasm. Romans 12:12 says, *"be joyful in hope."*

Revelation 22 says that Jesus is coming back soon. That was said 2000 years ago, so when is it soon? The Bible says that 1000 years is like a day unto the Lord (2 Peter 2:38), meaning that Jesus walked the earth two days ago! That means today is soon, just two days from when He said that! Jesus is coming soon, so what are you worried about? The media doesn't know what is happening, so why bother to listen to them? All they will do is fill you with fear. Instead, read the good news of Jesus Christ found in His Holy Word, which tells you that we are the bride of Christ with power over every evil thing. However, we have lots of hope because we know the truth!

There is only one definition of faith in the Bible, which is in Hebrews 11:1 *"Now faith is the substance of things hoped for, the evidence of things not seen."* If you take away hope in your life, you succumb to mere existence. The people with the greatest hope are farmers; they always believe that a bigger and better crop is coming next year!

## Hope (Part 2 of 4)

Without hope, life becomes bleak, joyless, a burden, painful, and filled with depression and despair. Life has no meaning without hope. Why did the suicide rate go up during the season of Covid? Because people lost hope. If you have no hope, your heart will break. You will have a joyless walk through a life of pain without hope.

Many people are searching for hope. The Bible's message is this: there is hope in Jesus. That is the only place you'll ever find it in a book of 8,810 promises. Hope is not wishing. The hope in the Bible is alive, real, available, powerful, and eternal and gives us exceeding joy. Just like the Word, the Bible says it is *"sharper than a two-edged sword"* in Heb. 4:2. I challenge you to get off any seeds of despair that rise against you. You can defeat it with hope in Jesus Christ because the victory to overcome anything you're going through is through Jesus.

What is the difference between hope and optimism? Optimism is "hope for the best" without a guarantee. Christian hope is faith. Faith looks at the promises of God and knows with absolute assurance that God has written in His book concerning what He is willing to do. We see it demonstrated by what He has done in the past and what He can and will make for you if you simply believe and apply it.

Death is common to every man. Heb 9:27 says, *"it is appointed for men to die once but after this the judgment."* Then what?" Those who are "optimistic" have a wish without a guarantee. "Well, I've lived a good honest life..." That means nothing; eternity with Jesus is about relationship, not behaviour. Certainty only comes with hope in Jesus Christ based on God's Word. Jesus arrives at the time of death only if you believe in Him and have accepted Him. (John 11:25,14:19) Your last second here on Earth is followed by your first second in eternity (either in the "H" place or the other "h" place). Jesus said, *"because I live, you shall live also."* (John 14:19)

*Life is a test...*

## Hope (Part 3 of 4)

Christians are the only group of people on earth that can see the future and know that the best is to come. John 14:2-3 says that Jesus has gone to prepare a place for us (with mansions). The resurrection of Jesus Christ guarantees this because Jesus is our "blessed hope."

Atheists mock the idea of Christian hope because they think we are delusional. That's calling the kettle black. Atheism has never dreamed a dream, lifted a burden, solved an internal problem, or brought joy to a wounded soul. The atheist will say that time heals all wounds, which is simply not true; only Jesus can heal. In short, the atheist has no good news, no future and no hope. Atheists spend their life fighting against a God that they believe does not exist (like fighting the wind). Go figure...

An atheist has no hope. They consider themselves brilliant because they have overcome religion and don't need a crutch. They say, "I am in charge of my destiny." Well, here is the intellectual profile of an atheist written by God himself. Psalm 14:1 *"The fool has said in his heart, 'There is no God.'"* To be successful now and in the future, all you need to know is, "Jesus is Lord." He is the source of all life, the universe, our happiness, joy and health - everything - and it can all be found in 1 Cor. 1: 18-31 (I like the Message Translation of this scripture.)

People are eager to find the answer to life and its problems, but they cannot accept God's Word. That is called humanism. Prov. 1:7 says, *"The fear of the Lord is the beginning of knowledge, but fools despise wisdom and instruction."*

Where did we go wrong? God and Bible teaching were kicked out of our schools in the 1960s and look where we are today. We have very much reaped what we have sown (Gal. 6:7). We have embraced evolution and atheism. We may know many things about our technological advancements, but we have missed it all.

*"For what will it profit a man if he gains the whole world, and loses his own soul? "* (Mark 8:36)

## Hope (Part 4 of 4)

What does it profit a man if he is a great architect and does not know the chief cornerstone, Jesus Christ? A baker who makes bread but doesn't know the bread of life; a scholar may know many things, but if he doesn't know Jesus Christ, he knows nothing. Many scientists turn to God as they continue their research; they realize that the world could not be created by anything or anyone other than God!

Our hope is in Jesus Christ. Hope looks at the coming storm and shouts hallelujah! The King is coming! Hope sees what the natural eye cannot. Hope believes in the impossible. Why? Because nothing is mpossible with God. Remember hope when you are surrounded by suffering. No one escapes suffering. Hope is seeing the desired outcome and finding a scripture to support it. Why? Because that is what faith is and how it works! God's provision is in His promises. Hold onto these promises by faith until the storm is gone. Keep in faith until peace comes and joy floods your soul.

**The bottom line:**
*"Jesus said to him, "If you can believe, all things are possible to him who believes." (Mark 9:23 23)*
*"Why are you cast down, O my soul? And why are you disquieted within me? Hope in God; For I shall yet praise Him, The help of my countenance and my God." (Ps. 42:5)*
*"But You, O Lord, are a shield for me, My glory and the One who lifts up my head." (Ps. 3:3)*
*"Then the Lord answered me and said: 'Write the vision And make it plain on tablets, That he may run who reads it. For the vision is yet for an appointed time, But at the end it will speak, and it will not lie. Though it tarries, wait for it; Because it will surely come, It will not tarry.'"* (Hab. 2:2-3)

Use a journal, write your problem, find the scripture to match and keep it taped to your bathroom mirror.

*ife* is a test...   Are you a hope filled person?

## Three Key Elements of God's Nature.

We understand these three key elements of God's nature:

**1.** His thoughts toward us are good (Ps. 139:16-17). He saw us before we were formed and fashioned us into being. His thoughts toward us are beautiful and beyond our understanding.

**2.** His plans for us are good (Jer. 29:11). Even when our plans feel like they are falling apart, His plans are not. For example, despite the Israelites' exile, God had plans to see them walk in His goodness and rebuild the Temple.

**3.** He is good to us (Ps. 145:9). Goodness is God's nature; He is good to one and all. His every action is soaked in His grace, enabling all things He has promised to pass.

The Holy Spirit alerts us to the enemy's tactics to move against the dreams God has planted in our hearts. It is a time to stand upon the nature of God and speak out, in faith, what you know God has placed in your heart. Don't let the enemy steal your dreams. Sing out over what you know God has promised you and keep moving forward in faith. He is the God who fulfills His Word, and as you speak this truth over your circumstances, you will see the enemy flee before you.

Know that His plans for you are good, and you will build that which He has given you to do. Keep surrendering your fears and expectations to Him and let Him work it all for good. (Rom. 8:28). You will find that this time is just a bump in the road of a beautiful journey that you are on with God.

*Life* is a test... Do you know God as a good father?

## I will Leave You with this...

I think a great concluding (pun intended) scripture is this one:

*"Let us hear the conclusion of the whole matter: Fear God, and keep his commandments: for this is the whole duty of man. For God shall bring every work into judgment, with every secret thing, whether it be good, or whether it be evil."* (Ecc. 12:13-14 KJV)

And remember, it is all about love, the definition of which can be found in 1 Cor. 13.

*"A new command I give you: Love one another. As I have loved you, so you must love one another."* (John 13:34)

*"The second is this: 'Love your neighbour as yourself.' There is no commandment greater than these."* (Mark 12:31)

In fact, this is love for God: to keep his commands. And His commands are not burdensome, (1 John 5:3)

*"Dear friends, let us love one another, for love comes from God. Everyone who loves has been born of God and knows God. Whoever does not love does not know God, because God is love. This is how God showed his love among us: He sent his one and only Son into the world that we might live through him. This is love: not that we loved God, but that he loved us and sent his Son as an atoning sacrifice for our sins. Dear friends, since God so loved us, we also ought to love one another..."* (1 John 4:7-11)

*"My son, do not forget my teaching, but keep my commands in your heart,"* (Prov. 3:1)

*Life* is a test... There is no test today, Happy New Year!

# Epilogue

Assuming that you started reading this book last January, we have been together for 365 days. Or perhaps you picked up this devotional sometime during the year. In any event, we are now at the end of the Gregorian calendar year. As I have mentioned, I follow God's calendar, but there's also an unavoidable reality of living in this man-made world. Hotel reservations, flight departures and appointments in our daily life are based on the Gregorian calendar. Consequently, I use both calendars in conjunction with each other.

Regardless, this book starts with January 1 and continues to today, and 365 "sermonettes" later, I am finished. Thanks for being with me on this journey. An answered prayer for me is that you will have had many new encounters with Jesus along the way. I know I have. I can't begin to tell you how much I have learned from writing this book because Holy Spirit wrote about 80% of it.

God bless you, and thanks for sharing a part of your day with Holy Spirit and me.

If you have enjoyed this devotional, I would very much appreciate it if you could go to Amazon, Chapters/Indigo, or Barnes & Noble and write a review. I have learned some hard lessons about book publishing, and one of them is that despite getting five-star reviews, you need to get a lot of them; otherwise, the books don't sell. If you desire, an endorsement emailed to me would be greatly appreciated. A mention in "Goodreads" would be fantastic too. Thank-you. As a Christian writer, the goal is never to sell books, nor is it fame and fortune. It's simply about getting the Word out! Can you help with that?

Blessings and Happy Trails,


**"Doc"**

# Shopping and Seminars!

## Posters:

Available from New Start Ministries for download.

## Books:

Available from Amazon, Indigo/Chapters, Barnes & Noble, or order from your favourite bookstore via Ingram Sparks.

**1.** *"Biblical Economics 101; Living Under God's Financial Blessing."*
**2.** *"Life is a Test: Hope in a Confusing World. Volume One"*
**3.** *"Life is a Test: Hope in a Confusing World. Volume Two"*

## Teaching, Seminars and Consulting:

**Invite Dr. Watkins to your church, conference or business event!**

Pastor, would you and your church like to sponsor a seminar and have Dr. Watkins teach? Consult with you and your board? Then book a Biblical Economics 101 weekend. This seminar is perfect for those who wish to:

• Get out of unnecessary debt.
• Build kingdom wealth.
• Break free from a scarcity and poverty mentality?
• Break the mindset that to be a good Christian, you must be broke and poor.
• Destroy the lie that if we love God, we must commit to a life of poverty.
• Learn how wealth and a heart for Jesus go hand-in-hand and are not mutually exclusive.
• Understand finances through the laws of seedtime and harvest and how - tithing can change your finances.

# Learn about:
- False Ideas about Money
- The Purpose of Money
- Does God want you to be Blest? (yes, and out of debt too!)
- God's Economy
- A Study of Wealth and Success
- The Way to Prosperity

The schedule for a Biblical Economics 101 weekend is usually 3 hours Friday night, all day Saturday (12 hours' worth of teaching!) and then he can give a message at your Sunday service if you desire. Dr. Watkins can come a few days early or stay a few days after the seminar for individual financial consulting, free of charge.

Dr. Watkins does not charge for teaching his courses, but requests two love offerings be taken for his ministry. As a church, you can charge for the seminar or host it for free.

# Additional Teaching Courses:

- Spiritual Gifts (including an individual survey for participants)
- Operating in the Courts of Heaven
- Healing
- Deliverance
- Spiritual Mapping and Cleansing of the Land

For a complete updated list, go to www.newstartministries.ca

*Life* is a test...

# BIBLICAL ECONOMICS 101

## LIVING UNDER GOD'S FINANCIAL BLESSING

# S. R. WATKINS, PhD

www.newstartministries.ca

Hope in a Confusing World

# A Daily Devotional
## Volume 1

from the author of
*"Biblical Economics 101: Living Under God's Financial Blessing"*

## S. R. Watkins, Ph.D

www.newstartministries.ca

# Jesus was beyond WEALTH.

Without the obligations of managing/owning a vineyard, Jesus turned water into wine, and it wasn't even His water! Not just wine, but "the best wine," without even paying for it! (John 2:10)

As an inside trader in the fishing industry, He had prior knowledge in respect to the location and volume of catch that would make any futures trader on the New York Stock Exchange a millionaire in 30 days. (John 21:6)

Of the twelve businessmen He dined with on one occasion, Jesus could predict which one could not be trusted, right down to the time that the betrayal took place (Matthew 26:21), as well as which of the twelve would deny Him, even after publicly confirming a vote of confidence in favour of Jesus' leadership. (Matthew 26:34) Any executive demonstrating such insight into people's character as Jesus possessed could easily demand a "mega salary" to chair the board meetings of any multinational conglomerate corporation and they would be to willingly pay.

When it came to paying taxes, He was able to extinguish His liability simply by having a fish pay the tax for Him! (Matthew 17:27)

He could heal the incurable diseases of His day with just a touch and no medical costs. (Luke 5:13)

When He wanted to travel into town, without so much as a phone call, He had a donkey waiting that He had never bred, never fed, never stabled, or ever trained, and He never had to worry about parking when He arrived at His destination! He received a voluntary "red carpet" reception. (Matthew 21:7)

If "knowledge is wealth," Jesus tops the list again, as the intellectuals of His day marveled at His knowledge. (Luke 20:26; John 7: 14-15)

His Father owns the largest cattle ranch on the planet (Psalm 50:10), the whole Earth itself, and everything in it. (Psalm 24:1)

Jesus' house contains many mansions, and the road on the main street in His neighborhood is constructed with gold. (Rev. 21:21)

He was able to multiply assets exponentially! In the case of the feeding of the 5,000 men, if we conclude that one person would have eaten half a loaf of bread and one fish, then Jesus' "food fund" showed a capital growth rate of 50,000% per day (bread) and over 250,000% per day (fish)!

Jesus was a unique dresser, so much so that after His death, rather than cut up His coat and divide it four ways as a souvenir, the soldiers decided to draw straws for this trophy and keep this quality seamless garment as one piece. (John 19: 23-24)

His burial was that reserved for the very, very rich. In this case, the mega rich merchant Joseph, from the town of Arimathea, donated the tomb that Jesus was buried in. Jesus didn't even have to pay a dime for the tomb! (Matthew 27:60)

Jesus was beyond wealth, because you clearly can't give what you haven't got, and you can't lead from behind, so when Jesus' Father promised to give wealth, He could only do so if He first possessed wealth (Ecclesiatis 5:19). You would, therefore, not be surprised to discover that this same Jesus was able to teach His wealth techniques to the "apprentices" that followed Him and do the things that He did with His power, which He said we could also do – and even greater things! (Deuteronomy 8:18; John 14:12)

## Jesus was clearly beyond wealth!

### (and He is willing to teach it to us. Are you willing to learn it?)

The "Wealth" Poster is part of the The Christian Life Manifesto Series. Produced in Calgary, Alberta, Canada by New Start Ministries Ltd. Written by Dr. Peter J. Daniels and re-printed with permission. www.newstartministries.ca COPYRIGHT 2022

**www.newstartministries.ca**

# THE BLESSING

In the **NAME** of **JESUS**, I bless you with the **PROMISES** of **GOD**, which are **YES** and **AMEN.** I pray the **HOLY SPIRIT** will make you **HEALTHY** and **STRONG** in **BODY, MIND** and **SPIRIT** and move you in **FAITH** and **EXPECTANCY.**

May **GOD'S ANGELS** be with you to **PROTECT** and **KEEP YOU.**

**GOD BLESS YOU WITH:**

- **ABILITY, ABUNDANCE**, and an assurance of **HIS LOVE** and **GRACE**
- **CLEAR DIRECTION** and a **CONTROLLED** and **DISCIPLINED LIFE**
- **COURAGE** and **CREATIVITY**
- **SPIRITUAL PERCEPTION** of **HIS TRUTH**
- **GREAT FAITH, HIS FAVOUR** and **MAN'S**
- **GOOD HEALTH** and a **GOOD (AND GODLY) SPOUSE**
- **HANDS** to **BLESS OTHERS**
- **HAPPINESS, FULFILLMENT, CONTENTMENT, HOPE**, and a **GOOD OUTLOOK ON LIFE**
- **A LISTENING EAR, LONG LIFE** and an **OBEDIENT HEART TO THE SPIRIT OF GOD**
- **HIS PEACE, PLEASANT SPEECH**, and a **PLEASANT PERSONALITY**
- **PROMOTION, PROTECTION, PROVISION, SAFETY** and **STRENGTH**
- **FINANCIAL SUCCESS**
- **TRUST AND WISDOM**

**AND MAY GOD BLESS YOU WITH:**

Goodness and mercy following you all the days of your life, that you might dwell in the house of the Lord forever.

The Lord bless you and keep you.
The Lord makes His face shine upon you and be gracious to you.
The Lord turns His face towards you and gives you peace.

I bless you in the Name of the Father, the Son, and the Holy Spirit. **AMEN.**

www.newstartministries.ca

*Life is a test...*

# The Christian Life
# COMMANDMENTS

1. Be humble. (I Peter 5: 6-7)
1. Be humble. (I Peter 5: 6-7)
2. Live by faith. (Romans 1:17)
3. Give to the poor. (Proverbs 19:17)
4. Listen more, and talk less. (James 1:19)
5. Be kind to unkind people. (Ephesians 4:32)
6. Know when to keep quiet. (Proverbs 15: 1-2)
7. Confess your mistakes and sins. (I John 1:19)
8. Life is not fair; get used to it. (Ephesians 9:11)
9. Strive for excellence, not perfection. (Titus 3:8)
10. Be on time. Don't make excuses. (Philippians 2:4)
11. Don't worry about anything. Trust God. (Matthew 6:25-27)
12. Stop blaming others for your circumstances. (Romans 2:1)
13. Bless someone when they cut you off in line. (Luke 16:27)
14. Cultivate good manners, including table manners. (Titus 3:2)
15. Love God and your neighbours as yourself. (Mark 12:30-31)
16. Tithe 10% of your gross income to your church. (Malachi 3:10)
17. Change your circumstances with positive confessions. (Matthew 12:37)
18. Exercise and take care of your temple of the Holy Spirit every day. (3 John 1:2)
19. Return what you borrow in better shape than when you borrowed it. (2 Kings 6:5)
20. Take time daily to be alone with God, and learn to hear His voice. (John 10:27-28)
21. Learn from the past. Plan for the future, and live in the present. (Deuteronomy 4:9)
22. Do something nice anonymously. God knows about it; no one else has to. (Matthew 6:4)
23. When you travel, learn everything about the country you are going to. (2 Timothy 2:15)
24. The entire world can change if people would humble, pray, seek and turn to God. (II Chronicles 7:14)
25. Meditate on the Word daily. "This Book of the Law shall not depart from your mouth, but you shall meditate on it day and night, so that you may be careful to do according to all that is written in it. For then you will make your way prosperous, and then you will have good success." (Joshua 1:8 ESV)

www.newstartministries.ca

## GOD By Design

### By Design:

- You were created before the earth was. (Eph. 1:4, Jer.1:5)
- You were created in His image. (Gen. 1:27)
- You were created to worship. (Is. 43:21) If it's not God you are worshiping, then it will be some other thing or narcissistic endeavour; it is God's nature for you to worship.
- You were created to do good works. (Eph. 2:10)
- You were created to connect with Him; depend on Him moment by moment. (Acts 17:28)
- You were created to live in an "earth suit" here on this planet for a limited time to bring heaven into the earth (Matt. 6:10), and in doing so, your job is to go out into the world and make disciples of all men. (Matt. 28:19)
- You are to continue this life as soul and spirit only, in eternal heaven (paradise) with God. However, God gives you freedom, and that freedom is the ability to "choose" as to whether you live for Him now and with Him later. (Deut. 30:19, Jos. 24:15)

### Starting Life and Living it to the Fullest.

Years ago, an article in our local newspaper about a community building under construction to help the "bored youth." I wrote the following letter to the editor:

To our "bored youth." Here are some suggestions to help you with your problem: rake the lawn, plant a garden, paint the fence, clean the garage, wash the car, make some repairs around the house, learn to cook, sew, paint, build, or any of dozens of other hobbies; shovel the snow for a senior, give help to a pastor or priest, tutor someone, read to the blind, visit the sick or the senior's centre, coach a minor-league, become a Brownie or Scout Leader, learn to play a musical instrument, go to church, work on volunteer organizations, help a disabled person, go buy the groceries for people who are "shut ins," help your parents and a teacher, do your homework, start a fund raiser for charity, register for a continuing education course, participate in any of dozens of recreational activities that are in abundance in our community, get involved in politics, get a job, start your own business, surf the net and learn something, babysit, and if all else fails go to the library and read a non-fiction book! (note: a man I know started mowing lawns when he was 14. Here it is years later, and he has 35 staff.)

Your parents do not owe you entertainment, your community does not owe you recreational facilities, and the world does not owe you anything. On the contrary, you owe the world something - your time, energy, gifts, talents, and money so that no one will be at war, in poverty, sick or lonely again. Life is about making the world a better place when you leave than when you arrived. Don't be a protester; grow up and be an agent of change...

Billions of people are, cold, poor, sick, hurt, hungry, or at war because you haven't helped them. Life is not about you. So, what are you bored about and what are you waiting for?

# What is

# FAITH?

**H**aving been saved by **FAITH**, *"If you declare with your mouth, "Jesus is Lord," and believe in your heart that God raised him from the dead, you will be saved."* (Rom. 10:9) It makes sense that we should continue to live by **FAITH**, *"The righteous shall live by faith."* (Rom. 1:17b) What does it mean to live by **FAITH**, though, and how do we do it? The Bible tells us, *"by the* **FAITH** *God has distributed to each of you"* (Rom. 12:3) so we all have **FAITH**. We increase our **FAITH** by hearing the Word of God. Consequently, *"***FAITH** *comes from hearing the message, and the message is heard through the word about Christ"* (Rom. 10:17), and we express **FAITH** by walking in love *"The only thing that counts is* **FAITH** *expressing itself through love."* (Gal. 5:6) Hebrews 11:6 tells us that if we are not living by **FAITH**, we are not pleasing God *"And without* **FAITH**, *it is impossible to please God,"* and Rom. 14:23 confirms this by saying that *"everything that does not come from* **FAITH** *is sin."*

Therefore, we are to grab hold of the promises of God, stand on them, confess them, believe them, and exercise our **FAITH**, which is to *"calls into being things that were not."* (Rom. 4:17) Hebrews 11:1 tells us, *"Now* **FAITH** *is confidence in what we hope for and assurance about what we do not see."* In Matthew, *"When he had gone indoors, the blind men came to him, and he asked them, 'Do you believe that I am able to do this?' 'Yes, Lord,' they replied. Then he touched their eyes and said, 'According to your* **FAITH**, *let it be done to you;' Their sight was restored."* (Matt. 9:28-29) Finally, we build our **FAITH** by praying in the Holy Spirit, *"by building yourselves up in your most holy* **FAITH** *and praying in the Holy Spirit."* (Jude 20)

Scripture quotations identified NIV are from the Holy Bible, New International Version®. NIV®.

Copyright© 1973, 1978, 1984, 2011 by Biblical, Inc.TM Used by permission of Zondervan. All rights reserved worldwide. www.zondervan.com.

**www.newstartministries.ca**

# The Fruit of the SPIRIT

There is a difference between Spiritual Gifts and Spiritual Fruit. Gifts are precisely that; a gift that God gives believers, and they are exactly that, Gifts, not loans with conditions for they are irrevocable (Rom. 11:29). Even if we don't use them or misuse them, we still have them. (The "Gifts of the Spirit" Poster is available as part of this poster series.)

There are 9 Spiritual Fruits that are more like characters of behaviour. Love is listed first, which is then part of the other eight, which are different ways in which love manifests itself.

- Joy is love rejoicing.
- Peace is love resting.
- Long-suffering is love forbearing.
- Kindness is love serving others.
- Goodness is love seeking the best for others.
- Faithfulness is love keeping its promises.
- Gentleness is love ministering to the hurt and pain of others.
- Self-control is love in control.

www.newstartministries.ca

The one that God gave you. Find out what He has called you to do, and do it (hint, it will be something you like and that you are good at. If in doubt, ask Him.) If you don't like something in the world, then...

# Be an agent of change.

If you don't have enough time, shut off your phone, computer, and TV and plant your money into His Kingdom to help preach the Gospel (it isn't your money anyway). If you are looking for the love of your life, stop. You will find them when you start doing what God has called you to do. Jesus loves you, and that is all that matters. Meditate on His Word, do His Word and live His Word. Yes...

# It really is that simple.

Emotions are great, but keep them under His control. Look after your body - it is the temple of the Holy Spirit. Open your heart, life and money to people and let your light shine by doing good works. Live by God's faith. Help others to build their dream, and in doing so, you will build your own. Then you can...

# Travel & help.

It really is the best education in the world, and you will find your life if you lose it by doing the works of God. Life is not about finding yourself but rather about creating yourself in the image of Jesus and making the world a better place when you leave than when you arrived. The world does not owe you anything. You owe the world everything. Don't talk about your rights. Fulfill your duties and responsibilities. Don't protest, pray. Because...

# Life is short.

Billions of people are hungry, cold, poor, sick, hurt, at war, and going to hell because you haven't helped them and told them about Jesus. After all, your real calling in life is to go out and make disciples of all men. It is not about you. So...

## What are you waiting for?

**www.newstartministries.ca**

# What is your **Mission** Impossible? *(1)

A mission is a vision given and powered by God through impartation.

The spiritual replication of Jesus into you is the goal of your life.*(2) Any other goal is secondary at best and harmful at worst. God built you to be His Spiritual being and for you to live out your life from His Spirit in you, rather than from within your soul.*(3)

Your mission (should you be willing to accept it) is the biggest gift that God can give you. It will be all life-consuming and give you the clarity to know what your life is all about. When God gives you your mission (ask Him; He will tell you)*(4), then preparation will be next:

- What will you have to do to fill the mission?
- What character, knowledge and discipline will you have to do to develop the mission?

Problems are not from a lack of discipline but rather a lack of vision.*(5) If discipline is an issue, you have not received God's full impartation. Using your faith,*(6) God will give you the plans,*(7) resources*(8) and energy(9) to accomplish His mission for you.

Be guaranteed that you will be hit with obstacles*(10). God's barbells build spiritual muscle. Sin in you, others and satan creates the barriers you must go through to transform you into being Christ-like. Human soulish will won't work, as it leaves you tired, angry, hurt and bitter.

## God → Vision → Mission → Obstacles → Transformation → Goal Achieved

Question: Are you willing to give up your life to another being (God) and lose it so that you can find it*(11) by Him working through you to accomplish the mission you're trying to find?*(12)

| | | | |
|---|---|---|---|
| *1. Mathew 19:26 | *4. John 10:27 | *7. Proverbs 8:12 | *10. 2 Corinthians 4:8-9 |
| *2. John 3:13 | *5. Proverbs 29:18 | *8. Deuteronomy 8:18 | *11. Mathew 10:39 |
| *3 .Romans 8 | *6. Hebrews 11:1,6 | *9. Galatians 6:9 | *12. Luke 19:17; 1 Corinthians 9:24 |

www.newstartministries.ca

# What God says about MONEY.

There are over 2480 scriptures that refer to money or stewardship. The words "rich" or "riches" are in the Bible 186 times. "Money" is in the Bible 114 times. Jesus spoke more about money and stewardship than any other subject. The purpose of money is to build up the Kingdom of God (Deuteronomy 8:18) so that the great commission can be fulfilled. (The gospel is free – it just takes money to preach it.)

Jesus was born rich into royalty and said we were to be like Him. The Magi's gifts were worth $400 million in today's dollars.* Jesus owned a house (John 1:38-39), paid taxes (Matthew 17:24), was on the lecture circuit at age 12 (Luke 2:47), ran a business with his dad, had a treasurer, had a staff of 12 and later 72 (Luke 10:17), had people giving financial support to His ministry (Luke 8:2-3), wore designer clothes (John 19:23-24), and became poor once in His life for us on the cross (2 Corinthians 8:9). His first miracle was one of luxury in a setting of wealth (John 2: 1-8) and He had the skills to supply lunch for 5,000 men and their families (John 6:7).

## Success is the ability to endure pain; wealth is the ability to obtain what is immediately required,* and prosperity is having enough provision to complete God's instructions.

Money may not bring happiness, but it brings more joy than poverty ever did! Tithing is not a method of getting money from you but a method of getting money to you.

## Money is the answer to everything. (Ecclesiastes 10:19b)

Poverty is not a financial problem. It is a spiritual one – a curse (Deuteronomy 28: 1). Worldly wealth is all about financial accumulation for self. True prosperity is all about economic expansion for God, who wants you to use it for distribution to others.

## Meditate on the Word, and you will be prosperous (Joshua 1:8).

The greatest tragedy of human existence is not knowing what you don't know. Now you know...

## So what are you going to do about it?

# How to be RICH God's way

Tithe 10% of your gross income to your local church. It is not yours or yours to keep. Plant financial seeds into His Kingdom through alms to the poor (like missions) and firstfruits to your church and other ministries. Use cash (not credit or debit cards) as much as possible (when you see money slipping out of your fingers, you will think twice about spending it.) Pay credit card balances immediately when they are due.

Reduce your consumer spending. Learn how to be thrifty and economical in your shopping. Buy used as much as possible.

Pay down the mortgage on your house, which should have a basement suite or some rental income to it. Payments should be weekly, starting on Monday.

Get a retirement plan started when you are 18. Invest wisely in solid "blue-chip, dividend-paying stocks."

Establish an education fund for your children. When they reach college age, they buy a house with the education fund in their name. They get rent-paying roommates to pay the mortgage and pay their own tuition.

Buy term life insurance to care for your loved ones.

Save 10% of your gross income for emergencies. If there is something that you want to buy, learn to save for it by putting 20% of your money away to save for significant expenditures.

Get all the education that you can to get a good, well-paying job with excellent benefits and be a good employee.

Establish a trust fund for your grandchildren.

Start this plan when you are 18, and by retirement, you will be a millionaire.

**www.newstartministries.ca**

*Life is a test...*

# What **Spiritual Gifts** has God given you?

1. **Administration** - The Gift of Administration is the exceptional power that God gives to Christians to clearly understand the immediate and long-range goals of a particular unit of the Body of Christ and devise and execute effective plans to accomplish those goals. (Luke 14:28-30 • Acts 6:1-7 • Acts 27:11 • 1 Corinthians 12:28 • Titus 1:5)

2. **Apostle** - The Gift of Apostle is the exceptional power that God gives to Christians to assume and exercise divinely imparted authority to establish the foundational government of an assigned sphere of ministry within the Church by setting things in order. (Luke 6:12-13 • 1 Corinthians 12:28 • Ephesians 2:20 • Ephesians 4:11-13)

3. **Celibacy** - The Gift of Celibacy is the exceptional power that God gives to Christians to remain single and enjoy it, to be unmarried and not suffer undue sexual temptations. (Matthew 19:10-12 • 1 Corinthians 7:7-8)

4. **Craftsman** - The Gift of Craftsman is the exceptional power that God gives to Christians to design and craft items based on an inherent skill given by God to create objects to glorify God. (Exodus 28:3 • Exodus 28:26 • Exodus 35:10 • Exodus 35:35 • Exodus 36:4)

5. **Deliverance** - The Gift of Deliverance is the exceptional power that God gives to Christians to cast out demons and evil spirits. (Acts 8:5-8; 16:16-18 • Matthew 12:22-32 • Luke 10:12-20)

6. **Discerning of Spirits** - The Gift of Discerning of spirits is the exceptional power that God gives to Christians to know whether certain behaviour purported to be of God is in reality divine, human or satanic. (Matthew 16:21-23 • Acts 5:1-11 • Acts 16:16-18 • 1 Corinthians 12:10 • 1 John 4:1-6)

7. **Evangelist** - The Gift of Evangelist is the exceptional power that God gives to Christians to share the gospel with non-believers in such a way that they become Jesus' disciples and responsible members of the Body of Christ. (Acts 8:5-6 • Acts 8:26-40 • Acts 14:21 • Ephesians 4:11-13 • 2 Timothy 4:5)

8. **Exhortation** - The Gift of Exhortation is the exceptional power that God gives to Christians to minister words of comfort, consolation, encouragement and counsel to other members of the Body in such a way that they feel helped and healed. (Acts 14:22 • Romans 12:8 • 1 Timothy 4:13 • Hebrews 10:25)

9. **Faith** - The Gift of Faith is the exceptional power that God gives to Christians to discern with extraordinary confidence the will and purposes of God for His work. (Acts 11:22-24 • Acts 27:21-25 • Romans 4:18-21 • 1 Corinthians 12:9 • Hebrews 11)

10. **Giving** - The Gift of Giving is the exceptional power that God gives to Christians to contribute their material resources to the work of the Lord liberally and cheerfully, above and beyond the tithes and offerings expected of all believers. (Mark 12:41-44 • Romans12:8 • 2 Corinthians 8:1-7 • 2 Corinthians 9:2-8)

11. **Healing** - The Gift of Healing is the exceptional power that God gives to Christians to serve as human intermediaries through whom it pleases God to cure illness and restore health apart from the use of natural means. (Acts 3:1-10 • Acts 5:12-16 • Acts 9:32-35 • Acts 28:7-10 • 1 Corinthians 12:9, 28)

12. **Helps** - The Gift of Helps is the exceptional power that God gives to Christians to invest the talents they have in the life and ministry of other members of the Body thus enabling those others to increase the effectiveness of their own spiritual gifts. (Mark 15:40-41 • Luke 8:2-3 • Acts 9:36 • Romans 16:1-2 • 1 Corinthians 12:28)

13. **Hospitality** - The Gift of Hospitality is the exceptional power that God gives to Christians to provide an open house and a warm welcome to those in need of food and lodging. (Acts 16:14-15 • Romans 12:9-13 • Romans 16:23 • Hebrews 13:1-2 • 1 Peter 4:9)

14. **Intercession** - The Gift of Intercession is the exceptional power that God gives to Christians to pray for extended periods and see frequent and specific answers to their prayers, to a degree much greater than that which is expected of the average Christian. (Colossians 1:9-12 • Colossians 4:12-13 • Acts 12:12 • James 5:14-16 • Luke 22:41-44 • 1 Timothy 2:1-2)

15. **Interpretation** - The Gift of Interpretation is the exceptional power that God gives Christians to make known the message of another person who speaks in tongues. (1 Corinthians 12:10, 30 • 1 Corinthians 14:13 • 1 Corinthians 14:26-28)

16. **Knowledge** - The Gift of Knowledge is the exceptional power that God gives to Christians to discover, accumulate, analyze, and clarify information and ideas pertinent to the Body's well-being. (Acts 5:1-11 • 1 Corinthians 2:14 • 1 Corinthians 12:8 • 2 Corinthians 11:6 • Colossians 2:2-3)

17. **Leadership** - The Gift of Leadership is the exceptional power that God gives to Christians to set goals for the future and communicate these goals to others so that they voluntarily and harmoniously work together to accomplish those goals for the glory of God. (Luke 9:51 • Acts 7:10 • Acts 15:7-11 • Romans 12:8 • 1 Timothy 5:17 • Hebrews 13:17)

18. **Mercy** - The Gift of Mercy is the exceptional power that God gives to Christians to feel genuine empathy and compassion for individuals, both Christian and non-Christian, who suffer distressing physical, mental or emotional problems and to translate that compassion into cheerfully done deeds which reflect Christ's love and alleviate the suffering. (Matthew 20:29-34 • Romans 12:8 • Mark 9:41 • Luke 10:33-35 • Acts 11:28-30 • Acts 16:33-34)

19. **Miracles** - The Gift of Miracles is the exceptional power that God gives to Christians to serve as human intermediaries through whom it pleases God to perform powerful acts that observers perceive to have altered the ordinary course of nature. (Acts 9:36-42 • Acts 19:11-20 • Romans 15:18-19 • Acts 20:7-12 • 1 Corinthians 12:10, 28 • 2 Corinthians 12:12)

20. **Missionary** - The Gift of Missionary is the exceptional power that God gives to Christians to minister whatever other spiritual gifts they have in a second culture. (Acts 8:4 • Acts 13:2-3 • Acts 22:21 • Romans 10:15 • 1 Corinthians 9:19-23 • Ephesians 3:6-8)

21. **Musician** - The Gift of Musician is the exceptional power that God gives to Christians to play an instrument and/or sing or create musical compositions and/or communicate by song, music that inspires others and offers praise and worship to God. (1 Chronicles 16:16-27 • 1 Chronicles 16:42 • Deuteronomy 31:19 • Deuteronomy 32:34)

22. **Pastor** - The Gift of Pastor is the exceptional power that God gives to Christians to assume long-term personal responsibility for the spiritual welfare of a group of believers. (John 10:1-18 • Ephesians 4:11-13 • 1 Timothy 3:1-7 • 1 Peter 5:1-3)

23. **Poverty** - The Gift of Voluntary Poverty is the exceptional power that God gives to Christians to renounce material comfort and luxury and adopt a personal lifestyle equivalent to those living at the poverty level in a given society to serve God more effectively. (1 Corinthians 13:1-3 • 2 Corinthians 6:10 • 2 Corinthians 8:9 • Acts 2:44-45)

24. **Preaching/speaking** - The Gift of Preaching/Speaking is the exceptional power that God gives to Christians to minister by speaking publically (or through writing) the Word of God to indicate teaching, revelation, evangelism, and knowledge. (1 Peter 4:11)

25. **Prophecy** - The Gift of Prophecy is the exceptional power that God gives to Christians to receive and communicate an immediate message of God to His people through a divinely anointed utterance. (Luke 7:26 • Acts 15:32 • Acts 21:9-11 • Romans 12:6 • 1 Corinthians 12:10, 28 • Ephesians 4:11-13)

26. **Service** - The Gift of Service is the exceptional power that God gives to Christians to identify the unmet needs involved in a task related to God's work and make use of available resources to meet those needs and help accomplish the desired results. (Acts 6:1-7 • Romans 12:7 • Galatians 6:2, 10 • 2 Timothy 1:16-18 • Titus 3:14)

27. **Teaching** - The Gift of Teaching is the exceptional power that God gives to Christians to communicate information relevant to the health and ministry of the Body and its members in such a way that others will learn and learn well. (Acts 18:24-28 • Acts 20:20-21 • 1 Corinthians 12:28 • Ephesians 4:11-13)

28. **Tongues** - The Gift of Tongues is the exceptional power that God gives to Christians to speak in a language they have never learned and/or to receive and communicate an immediate message of God to His people through a divinely anointed utterance in a language they never learned. (Mark 16:17 • Acts 2:1-13 • Acts 10:44-46 • Acts 19:1-7 • 1 Corinthians 12:10, 28 • 1 Corinthians 14:13-19)

29. **Wisdom** - The Gift of Wisdom is the exceptional power that God gives to Christians to know the mind of the Holy Spirit in such a way as to receive insight into how given knowledge may best be applied to specific needs arising in the Body of Christ. (Acts 6:3, 10 • 1 Corinthians 2:1-13 • 1 Corinthians 12:8 • James 1:5-6 • 2 Peter 3:15-16)

30. **Worship Leader** - The Gift of Leading worship is the exceptional power that God gives to Christians to accurately discern the heart of God for a particular public worship service, to draw others into an intimate experience with God during the worship time and to allow the Holy Spirit to change directions. (1 Samuel16:23 • 1 Chronicles 9:33 • 2 Chronicles 5:12-14)

## Spiritual Gift Classifcations within the Five-Fold Ministry

| Apostle | Prophet | Evangelist | Teacher | Pastor |
|---|---|---|---|---|
| Apostle | Prophecy | Evangelist | Teacher | Pastor |
| Leadership | Discernment | Faith | Wisdom | Administration |
| Giving | Exhortation | Miracles | Knowledge | Hospitality |
| Celibacy | Intercessor | Healing | Mercy | Service & Help |
| | Tongues & Interpretations | Missionary | Preaching | Worship Leader |
| | Musician | Deliverance | | Poverty (voluntary) |
| | | | | Craftsman |

www.newstartministries.ca

# The Ten Stages in the Life of a Christian
# ENTREPRENEUR

1. **I THOUGHT IT** – God gives you the vision, and you have a flash of euphoric inspiration. (Prov. 8:12)

2. **I CAUGHT IT** – You start to get excited about the vision but make the mistake of telling your family and friends, and they tell you that you are crazy and that your idea will never work. (Proverbs 29:18)

3. **I BOUGHT IT** – You consider the cost of the vision, pay the price and get nothing but discouragement, but you decide to live by faith. (Romans 1:17; Galatians 3:17)

4. **I SOUGHT IT** – Nobody can talk you out of it, but despite that, you lose money and begin to second guess yourself. Then you remember that God is bigger. (Philippians 4:13)

5. **I FOUGHT IT** – To keep from "losing it" while others are mocking you. You want to quit. (Psalm 27:14)

6. **I WAS FRAUGHT WITH FEAR** – but I persevered. (Isaiah 41:10)

7. **I GOT IT** – YOU MEET WITH SUCCESS! You actually possess the dream and are glad you paid the price. (I Samuel 18:14)

8. **I HAD AN ONSLAUGHT** – Suddenly, everyone wants to be your "best friend," and your family completely supports you. (Ezekiel 16:14) So,

9. **I TAUGHT IT** – You pass it on to the next generation. (Matthew 5:19)

10. **I HAVE AN AFTERTHOUGHT** – and realize that God was with me all the time. (Deuteronomy 31:6b)

# Notes:

_____

_____

_____

_____

_____

_____

_____

_____

_____

_____

_____

_____

_____

_____

_____

_____

_____

_____

_____

_____

_____

_____

_____

_____

_____

_____

_____

_____

_____

_____

_____

_____

_____

CPSIA information can be obtained
at www.ICGtesting.com
Printed in the USA
BVHW031150271122
652861BV00001B/1